Necropolitics, Racialization, and Global Capitalism

Necropolitics, Racialization, and Global Capitalism

Historicization of Biopolitics and Forensics of Politics, Art, and Life

Marina Gržinić and Šefik Tatlić

LEXINGTON BOOKS
Lanham • Boulder • New York • London

Published by Lexington Books
An imprint of Rowman & Littlefield
4501 Forbes Boulevard, Suite 200, Lanham, Maryland 20706
www.rowman.com

10 Thornbury Road, Plymouth PL6 7PP, United Kingdom

British Library Cataloguing in Publication Information Available

Library of Congress Cataloging-in-Publication Data

Gržinić, Marina, 1958-
Necropolitics, racialization, and global capitalism : historicization of biopolitics and forensics in politics, art, and life / Gržinić & Šefik Tatlić.
pages cm
Includes bibliographical references and index.
ISBN 978-0-7391-9196-5 (cloth : alk. paper) -- ISBN 978-0-7391-9197-2 (electronic)
1. Biopolitics. 2. Racism. 3. Capitalism. 4. Neoliberalism. 5. Globalization. I. Tatlić, Šefik, 1976- II. Title.
JA80.G79 2014
320.01--dc23
                                                                                2014008426
ISBN 978-0-7391-9585-7 (pbk : alk. paper)

∞™ The paper used in this publication meets the minimum requirements of American National Standard for Information Sciences Permanence of Paper for Printed Library Materials, ANSI/NISO Z39.48-1992.

Printed in the United States of America

Contents

Acknowledgments

We would like to extend our sincere gratitude and thanks to numerous friends, collaborators, and editors that, in the last few years, have supported our writings by commenting, suggesting, and finally publishing our works in books and journals.

Particularly we want to thank the editors from Lexington Books, Justin Race and Brian Hill, for their support and guidance. We want to thank Professor Dr. Oto Luthar, director of the Scientific and Research Centre of the Slovenian Academy of Science and Arts in Ljubljana, Slovenia, for his continuous support of Marina Gržinić's work and publishing projects, and the Academy of Fine Arts in Vienna for the concerned management of Gržinić's more than a decade-long teaching work at this institution. And last, but not least, our families and life partners, Borut Mauhler and Iva Šaronja.

We wish to extend our sincere gratitude to:

Reartikulacija, journal from Ljubljana (Slovenia) for allowing use of references that were published in this journal from 2007 to 2010, before the journal, due to increased neoliberal policies against the critical press in the fallout of capitalist crisis of 2008, was terminated.

The University of California Press for allowing to quote from Achille Mbembe's book *On the Postcolony*.

The Global South, published by Indiana University Press (Indiana: Bloomington) for allowing to republish the article by Marina Gržinić, "Southeastern Europe and the Question of Knowledge, Capital, and Power." *The Global South*, vol. 5, no. 1, 2011.

E-flux for allowing to republish the article by Marina Gržinić, "A Refugee Protest Camp in Vienna and the European Union's Processes of Racialization, Seclusion, and Discrimination." *e-flux journal*, #43, 03/2013.

Identities for allowing to republish the article by Marina Gržinić, "Entanglement." *Identities*, vol. 10, no. 1/2, 2013.

Introduction

This book presents an analysis and/or an articulation of the principles on which global, contemporary capitalism organizes its own reproduction in economic, political, ideological, and institutional aspects. It consists of two parts through which the authors—by utilizing the theoretical apparatuses found in the fields of political philosophy, cultural critique, contemporary radical art theory, and decolonial theory—structure an analysis of currently dominant forms of capitalism and neoliberalism within a wider context in which contemporary forms of racism, coloniality, democracy, and contemporary art/culture are seen as inherently connected to the processes of reproduction of capitalism.

While it could be said that the radicalization of the discrepancies in the distribution of global wealth applies to the whole planet, these discrepancies are, in this book, primarily approached and analyzed as discrepancies between the First World of capital and the rest of the world; specifically, the overexploited Third World and the erased Second World. In this sense, this book dismisses the universalized notion of a *common* predicament which the globalized society is experiencing.

Although the existence of the gap in global distribution of wealth is far from being a *new* situation of the radicalization of that gap in the first decade of the twenty-first century, it is surely marked by increased levels of intensity and explicitness. This radicalization by far transcends the question of possibility of having a *good life* and ventures toward the question of the possibility of having a *life at all*.

In this context, necropolitics, as an obscene form of politics that resides in the organized imposition of death as a tool for the maximization of profit, and racialization, as contemporary form of racism (or racialism) on the basis of which social differentiations are being produced, are not just neologisms constructed in order to describe the effect of capital. In a sense what the authors present in the book is a radically theoretical *historicization* and at the same time *de-universalization* of all the main notions with which contemporary philosophy and theory deal with. The outcome is a decolonial matrix of epistemology on the basis of which globalization of capitalism and sustainment of capitalist hierarchies of exploitation are being questioned. The principles on which reproduction of contemporary capitalism resides, entails contemporary reorganization of colonialism, politics and dominant ideological discourses that form the framework in which society is being produced. In this book these processes are made visible and entangled, hence the title: Necropolitics, Racialization, and Global Capitalism. Although a gap between those who are destitute and those are prosperous by far precedes the twenty-first century, it is certain that the radical widening of the same gap marks the first decade of this century.

In regard to these points both parts of the book are conceived to function in an interrelation.

The first part of the book written by Marina Gržinić focuses on an articulation of the genealogy and nature of the relation between biopolitics and necropolitics in contemporary capitalism; on the analysis of different forms of State and on the effects that contemporary forms of racism and modalities of racialization have in neoliberal global capitalism; and last (but not least) it exposes the role of *precarization, financialization,* and the function of depoliticization within these processes.

More specifically, the first part of the book begins with an analysis of the historical genealogy of the modern history of the First World from a decolonial perspective which specifically (and by relating to the work of Kwame Nimako, Étienne Balibar, Araba Evelyn Johnston-Arthur, Aimé Césaire, and others) entails an analysis of the meaning of perpetuation of the ideological dictum between the East and the West in the period after the fall of the Berlin Wall.

The second chapter (on the basis of upgrading of the work of Santiago López Petit, Giorgio Agamben, Achille Mbembe, Michel Foucault, and Žarana Papić) progresses toward the analysis of a genealogy of necropolitics in a context in which it is seen as a successive stage of biopolitics — where biopolitics as a paradigmatical principle of rule based as it was on differentiation between forms of living has now been deposed in favor of necropolitics — as a paradigmatical principle of rule that differentiates among, and capitalizes on, the imposition of various forms of death.

On this basis, this chapter ventures toward the construction of a structural connection which a shift from biopolitics to necropolitics, financialization of capital and the rise of fascism (and consequent racial-State) produces. Privatization and deregulation (as principle neoliberal capitalist strategies) are therefore not being strictly interpreted as exclusively economic categories, but are treated as ideological, representational, and discursive marks of the utter unrestrainment of capitalism.

The third chapter of the book focuses on Eastern Europe; that is, on the principles of which post-socialist transformation (integration) of Eastern Europe into the (periphery) of the First World was organized. Questions of knowledge, power, and capitalism (relating to the work of Goldie Osuri, Biljana Kašić, Suvendrini Perera, and Pierre Hazan) are addressed in a context in which major political, social, cultural, and representational discourses — that were produced by the transition to capitalism — are being treated in a context of progression of normalization of necropolitical and racialized social discourses. However, this third chapter does not confine itself into a specific regional niche, but ventures toward a global analysis of the ramifications of the dissolution of the nation-State into a (post)modern war–State and consequentially a racial–State.

Setting itself into a global context, the analysis in chapter 4 (through implementation of Jacques Lacan's insights into decolonial theory) progresses toward the interpretation of colonialism, postcolonialism, and imperialism as constitutive of the project of modernity in general. This chapter (based on the work of Arturo Escobar, Giorgio Agamben, Aníbal Quijano, Nelson Maldonado-Torres, Gabriele Dietze, Araba Evelyn Johnston-Arthur, Achille Mbembe, Hortense J. Spillers, and Brian Carr) produces a division; it de-univerzalizes a perception of modernity as a neutral, human progressivist narrative and deems it as a particular narrative whose function is to perpetuate the centrality of the First World and its epistemologies in the processes of the globalization of capitalism.

Successively, chapter 5 focuses on the paradigmatic and most notable victims of globalization of capitalism—im/migrant refugees—and treats the predicaments these people are going through as a reflection of the failure of capitalist promises on universal freedom (that have saturated dominant public discourses in the fallout of the binary ideological division of the world). Additionally this chapter deals with these predicaments as a reflection and a symptom of the wider depoliticization of society under way in the European Union and/or in the First World of capitalism in general.

Chapter 6 (based on the work of Marissa Lôbo, Beatriz Preciado, Marie-Hélène Bourcier, Luzenir Caixeta, bell hooks, etc., with a decolonial emphasis) deals with the (meaning of) depoliticization of the gender-based struggle and the depoliticization of art, which is now being turned into an apolitical niche that functions as a token of aestheticization of performativity itself on the expanse of political and ideological content. Both these vectors of depoliticization are additionally compared with the emptying of politics in favor of aestheticization of pure ideology—that now exchanges, or more precisely *represses*, the possibilities of production of political ideologies.

In this sense, chapter 7 (by referring to Lacanian theory, by the upgrading of Giorgio Agamben's work, and by combining Louis Althusser's work with the work of Agon Hamza, Santiago López Petit, Peter Gratton, and Sara Ahmed) bases its analytical focus on critique of the depoliticization of politics and emptying of ideology of any politically substantial content. The political meaning of (or a lack of political dimension in) the relation between the content and the form is therefore treated in the context in which post-ideological and post-political narratives (in which paradigmatic capitalist political imaginaries tend to base themselves) are being tackled as concepts constitutive to a wider process of de-historicization and the erasure of capitalism (and its most prominent beneficiaries) from history. This does not only mean that historical revision-

ism and rejecting of responsibility (for colonialism, sustainment of colonial difference etc.) is being organized under the post-ideological, univer-
zalizing aureole, but also (as this chapter postulates), that the social and
political imaginary that deems political antagonization of capitalism viable and/or possible is being made abnormal, while the social reality
devastated by capitalism is increasingly being normalized and/or disconnected from its structural connection to capitalism and/or its effect. In this
chapter Marina Gržinić specifically tackle the questions of a radicalized
analysis of contemporary art and culture, referring directly to the subtitle
of the book.

The subtitle of this book is "Historicization of Biopolitics and Forensics of Politics, Art, and Life." The forensics applies to art, culture, and
politics being examined through judicial apparatuses of neoliberal global
capitalism, civil law, and the state of exception. To this later point Gržinić
in chapter 3 dedicates an ample investigation. Art, culture, and politics
are conceptualized not only inside the shift from biopolitics to necropolitics, but Gržinić elaborates how the originary biopolitical characteristics
of contemporary art (seen as ideological and power Institution) transforms into a necropolitical dispositive that effects essentially a new articulation between form and content.

The second part of the book written by Šefik Tatlić ventures more
toward an articulation of the relations between State and society, democracy and capitalism, and the oppressed and the oppressors. The second
part of the book relating to the work of Walter Mignolo, Santiago Castro-
Gómez, Marina Gržinić, Aníbal Quijano, and Étienne Balibar (in chapter
8) lays out a brief historical genealogy in (re)structuring the First World's
capitalism, which in this sense serves as a wider historical context in
which capitalism's ideological and power discourses were scrutinized on
the basis of the establishment of a structural connection between capitalism and its liberal narratives. The basic premise here is that the liberalization of political power led to destruction of those prerogatives of political
power potent enough to tackle the utilization of non-political logic in
production of society. Racialization and Eurocentric colonial epistemological logics are here seen as means that depoliticize social conflicts and
political antagonism—deprive ideology of its political dimension and deprive politics of its ideological foundations.

The next chapter, chapter 9, (by referring to the work of Carl Schmitt
and Giorgio Agamben) analyzes the effects of this gap between politics
and ideology, which includes an articulation of the function of political
power, as well as articulating the coordinates of the succumbing of politics and political antagonisms to the logic of liberal capitalism and its
humanist narratives, such is democracy. Consequentially, the text (by
relating to the work of Carl Schmitt and Santiago López Petit) progresses
in chapter 10 toward an analysis of the function of democracy in the
process of the normalization of contemporary capitalist hegemony.

After it is postulated that democracy sustains, but not completely destroys, the gap between politics and ideology, the text (by referring to the work of Subhabrata Bobby Banerjee, Achille Mbembe, Walter Mignolo, Alain Badiou, and Marina Gržinić) ventures in chapter 11 into an analysis of the kind of ideology global capitalism does operate with. Epistemological and ideological formalization of necropolitics, as the principle kind of politics contemporary racial-States operate with, is articulated here as an instrument that (by the instituting of racialization into a main matrix of production of social differentiation) leads to the revival of ideological firmness with which capitalist States and their power structures used to sustain a colonial divide of the world. The rules invested in sustainment of this divide are (following Achille Mbembe's and Walter Mignolo's work) analyzed in chapter 12 on a template found in the relationship Southeast Europe has, in its post-socialist period, with the First World.

Furthermore, since the depoliticization of the distance between the oppressors and the oppressed (in a global context) was seen as the result of racialization under necropolitical rule, it did not mean that social antagonisms were pacified. On the contrary, chapter 13 (that refers to certain aspects of Achille Mbembe's and Aimé Césaire's work) postulates, they were intensified, but also conformed into a framework in which the results of such antagonisms could lead only toward the acquisition of another position on a racially prefixed field of social interaction. The political functions of the flexibility of racial hierarchies were therefore found in both intensification of (models) of social differentiation and pacification of politically ideological class struggles.

The final chapter (14) therefore (in relation to Marina Gržinić's and Santiago López Petit's work) synthesizes an apparently paradoxical interplay between the intensification of capitalism and its dis-intensifying rigidness. The meaning of unrestrainment of capital and its repetitions is here articulated through a process of substantialization of depoliticized ideology which results in pure, "post-liberal" ideology that sustains its liberal mantle in that measure in which it is becoming explicitly hegemonic.

Both parts of the book are made to function as two entangled approaches in determination of *depoliticized politics* and anti-social (racially, biologically based) production of society as dominant models in First World's interpretation (and implementation) of politics and production of society. While the first part of the book relies more on the articulation of genealogies in emergence, sustainment and normalization of the concepts, the second part focuses more on the (function) of liberal and humanist super-narratives under which that sustainment and normalization takes place.

In other words, those aspects of the analysis which are not intensively tackled in the first part are tackled in the second part of the book, and vice versa.

This most heavily relates to the extensive analysis of necropolitics as a successor of biopolitics; to the state of contemporary art and the role of performativity; gender policies; visual regimes of representation and the analysis of the epistemological distortion of the notions of content and form in critique of depoliticization of the social reality, which are all objects of interest of the first part of the book.

On the other hand, the second part of the book elaborates on what depoliticization means for the function of politics; how does democracy, as a grand liberal narrative, function as a grand pacifier of political antagonisms; what is the ideological function of internal logic of racialization and how does substantialization of politically empty ideology support the reorganization of capitalism.

Since the scope of analysis this book envelopes does entail a number of complexities, having it in two distinctive parts surely contributes to the clarity of the articulation it entails.

On the other hand, it could be said that this book only *provisionally* has two parts.

So, the main motive for such a disposition of this book can be found in the authors' desire not to exclude those aspects of (sociopolitical) complexities of globalized world that are usually either rigidly particularized within the limits of a specific academic discipline, either neglected in their interrelational capacity. Hence, the effort this book represents does not aim at the reduction of complexities; it aims to provide an articulation that would put all those predicaments, which these authors find to have a similar point of origin, in a coherent, analytical relation.

Marina Gržinić and Šefik Tatlić

Part I

ONE

The Darkest Sides of Europe and Global Capitalism

Kwame Nimako: "We are here (in the EU) because you were there (in Africa!)"
Marina Gržinić: "We are here (in the EU) because you want to go there (in Eastern Europe!)"[1]

This first chapter has a dual role, it is an introduction to the first part of this book and an elaboration of what is at stake when we approach critically the subjects of *neoliberal global capitalism* and *Europe.*

The darkest[2] sides of the Europe/European Union (EU) and of neoliberal global capitalism consist of four entangled levels of violent events and processes:

- two modes of life biopolitics and necropolitics, colonialism and coloniality, former Eastern Europe, "former" Western Europe, Black European citizens, migrants, refugees, and asylum seekers
- the question of global capitalism and its processes of financialization, dispossession, repetition, and the never-ending process of capitalist humanization (becoming human) with dehumanization as its darkest side
- capital's racialization as a process of socialized/normalized system of discrimination, of sorting bodies, labor, life under the policy of violent exclusion, seclusion, surveillance and last, but not least, death and enduring war
- the question of race, gender, class, citizenship, and non-citizenship.

We have two discontinuities in Europe that marked it significantly in the last decades: Europe after the fall of the Berlin Wall and after the destruction of the Twin Towers in New York. The outcome of the fall of the Berlin Wall in 1989 followed by the September 11, 2001 attacks (a series of

3

coordinated attacks launched by the Islamic terrorist group al-Qaeda upon the United States in New York City and Washington, D.C.) has been that Europe/EU has been "reborn" in a necropolitical global capitalist mode of reproduction of life and subjectivities. It is possible to state that what happened is a "colonizing turn in Western thought," as described by Nelson Maldonado-Torres, by which he means "the paradigm of discovery and newness that also included the gradual propagation of capitalism, racism, the modern/gender system, and the naturalization of the death ethics of war" (Maldonado-Torres 2011, 1).

After the fall of the Berlin Wall in 1989, post-Cold War Eastern Europe was re-launched as the former Eastern Europe in the 1990s to be again made obsolete in 2004 when the largest enlargement to date of the economic and political union of the West European States known as European Union (EU) occurred. In 2004, ten former Eastern European countries happily joined the EU and soon, a few years later, some others followed in greater or lesser numbers.

The EU project started after WWII when a core of West European countries (among them quite a number of former colonial, fascist, and Nazi States) decided to strengthen their capitalist economic trade ideals by forming the EU (at its origin are the creation of two associations: the European Coal and Steel Community [ECSC] and the European Economic Community [EEC], both formed by Six Western European countries in 1951 and 1958, respectively).

Then in 2008 and, of course, through arts and culture (as arts and culture are used these days mostly for different unsavory jobs of cleansing/formalizing/hiding the capitalist social, political and economic contradictions, exploitations, dispossessions, etc.), a project for contemporary art research, education, publishing and exhibition called "Former West"[3] (the project is due to last until 2014) was launched. "Former West" is supported by the European Cultural Foundation[4] and represents, from my perspective, a final performative-repetitive rhetoric emptying of history, politics, economy, and society of the former Eastern Europe and consequently of the EU (more about this in the next chapters).

At this point it is important to state that in the case of Eastern Europe, *the former* means that the historical processes of evacuation, abstraction, and expropriation are actually "over" (as it was proclaimed by Germany in 2009, celebrating its twentieth anniversary of the fall of the Berlin Wall, "Come, come to the country without borders," and I would say without history as well); but in the case of *former* Western Europe, it implies a purely performative, empty, speculative gesture. While the East is excluded more and more from history, knowledge, memory, etc., the West is just *performing* its obsolescence.

The West plays with a speculative form of itself, it wants us to think that it is all about fiction[alization]; that it is somehow imaginative or fictional. The word "former" presents a speculative setting that gives the West the possibility to perform repetitively its own supposedly outdated or (to put it better) *obsolete* condition of historical existence; being former means to be passé and therefore for Western Europe is not necessary to be any more conscientious of its own historical (colonialism, slavery, invigorate anti-Semitism, exploitation) and contemporary hegemonic regimes of power (that is based precisely on these ultra-violent processes of past capitalist accumulation)—and therefore not responsible for it.

In accordance with these claims, I use the word *former* in "former" Western Europe in quotation marks; the quotation marks point to a performative trope, while in the case of former Eastern Europe, *the former* denotes its conditions of im/possibility.

Making obsolete the West/East divide after the fall of the Berlin Wall in the EU allows for a repetition and subsequently a multiplication of another division in the EU: the Occident/Orient division. This presents firstly a new normativization of the re/construction of the European Union (EU) as a unified entity (the One), and, secondly, it works by individuating a new Other in this newly homogenized EU space. The question is why? The answer is, according to Gabriele Dietze, that this allows for the dispensing with a substantial contingent of im/migrants, refugees, sanspapier (paperless), asylum seekers composed of former colonized peoples from North Africa to Pakistan, Indonesia, etc., coming to Europe (Dietze 2010). They are today represented as the new Other through the internalizing of the global external division produced after 2001 as the clash between on the one hand the occidental, capitalist, western, civilized modes of life, culture, the social, and the political and, on the other, the oriental, barbaric, noncivilized life of the Other(s).

On the back of this genealogy stays Germany that, throughout the 1990s, was fiercely supporting (selecting and awarding in collaboration with many other EU agencies and West European branches and NGOs) numerous projects with which, at that time, already the nonexistent former communist East Germany (that was integrated after the 1989 inside the powerful capitalist and democratic West Germany) had to be constantly reflected in relation and through other former Eastern European realities. Finally, all of them together as "a package" were speedily washed from their communist (or better to say totalitarian) past. The differences between the nonexistent East Germany and the much present and active West Germany (that was reborn after 1989 as Germany) were big and Germany carried out a process of deconstruction and reconstruction of East Germany (culturally, artistically, socially and architecturally). In the next paragraph, I write about East German economic de/re/construction that was conceived "just" (!) before 1989 and realized from 1990 onward.

For the twentieth anniversary of the fall of the Berlin Wall in 2009, Berlin showed itself renovated and rebuilt to such a magnitude that it

was said that the unification of the country resembled more an occupation than unification. On the eve of the twentieth anniversary, the unified
Germany launched the aforementioned slogan "Come, come to the country without borders" with which it celebrated the anniversary and concluded, at the same time, the chapter named former East Germany, (thus
ending the story of former Eastern Europe). Parallel to the celebration of
the twentieth anniversary of the fall of the Berlin Wall, the project "Former West" was launched in order to constitute one single and at the same
time historically "purified" Europe or more accurately stated: the EU.

In a documentary film with the title *Catastroika* (2012, 87 min) by two
Greek journalists Aris Chatzistefanou and Katerina Kitidi, (a film that is
the sequel of *Debtocracy* [2011, Greece, 74 min] another of their documen-
taries), Chatzistefanou and Kitidi analyze the shifting of State assets into
private hands. They travel around the world gathering data on privatization and search for clues about the Greece's massive and extreme privatization program in the recent past. The film exposes the creation, on June
17, 1990 of a specific "Trust Agency" named in the German language as
Treuhandanstalt. It was created by the West German State for privatizing
East German enterprises owned until then as public property. Treuhandanstalt supervised the restructuring and selling of about 8,000 firms
with initially around 4.5 million employees. At that time Treuhandanstalt
was the world's largest industrial enterprise, controlling everything from
steel works to the Babelsberg Studios.

I here relate to some of the most interesting statements in the film to
illustrate how Treuhandanstalt undertook the sell-off of East Germany's
public assets. It transformed the tenth largest industrial power in former
East Germany into a shopping catalogue of 510 pages. It started working
before the dissolution of East Germany, but it was basically influenced by
western politicians, managers, and economic sharks. In order for the bureaucratic monster to function, it used equipment and networks of the
East German armed forces. When the people of East Germany realized
that reunification was in fact an acquisition by West Germany, Treuhandanstalt was already a "State" within a German State in Berlin. Even on
weekends they privatized up to ten to fifteen businesses. This of course
created a situation which brought about chaos and fraud. A lot of companies went bankrupt. At the end of the process, out of 4.5 million industrial economy workers only 1.5 million jobs remained. The privatization
criteria were not always financial; many decisions were taken in political
offices, while several businesses closed so as not to threaten their compet-
itors in West Germany.

When the crisis hit Greece after 2008, the Treuhandanstalt model was
brought to Athens to save the EU economy and EU investments (Germany is one of the principal investors) in Greece. Though it is reported by
Chatzistefanou and Kitidi, that Treuhandanstalt was a disastrous experi-
ment for former East Germany, that resulted in millions of unemployed

workers and crushed the industrial base in the area, it was implemented in Greece without hesitation.

Some of the processes involved in the "vanishing Eastern Europe" parallel the Latin American situation. Instead of recognizing larger social, self-organizational, and communal possibilities for new politics, Latin America was "sold"; sacrificed to the infrastructure of the US neoliberal capitalist mode of production. With such a move, critical power was taken from communities and a brutal passage of transfer of power from public to private took place; a perverse process of capitalist moderniza-tion that expropriated the social space and nullified indigenous revolu-tions and other systems of knowledge.

The "former" western European States (that are the first capitalist States, and are also all direct or indirect colonial States and anti-Semitic States), which pushed the vision of the welfare-State after WWII, are increasingly putting pressure on their own citizens, pushing them into debt, misery, and precarity through the normalization of control. The welfare nation-State's public funds have been cut or are unavailable for the public good as a result of more or less hidden processes of privatiza-tion in all possible forms (depending of course on the place from which we speak, that is, in which nation-State we live in, in the European Un-ion). Those who are citizens of the EU and are yet being pushed toward the limits still "enjoy" benefits, for example that of going to the polls, and not (yet!) being deported, etc. This is one side of global capitalism, the other is about the violent deterioration of life, work and less and less possibilities of free mobility for those "not-yet-integrated" migrants, sec-ond-grade citizens, refugees, the non-citizens who have no papers to re-side in respective EU nation-States or in the first capitalist world's "oasis of good life and opportunities."

At this point we can even schematically, in an almost *unplugged* way, indicate two trajectories:

A) FROM 9/11 2001 TO SNOWDEN: THE WHISTLEBLOWER

The first trajectory starts with September 11, 2001 and I would argue closes with the whistleblower case of Edward Snowden. After 2001 we entered the space of neoliberal global capitalism with its multifaceted capitalist-dictatorial State systems that ask for continuing wars and cru-sades. As it is stated in the aforementioned documentary by Chatzistefa-nou and Kitidi, the core of neoliberal policy is privatization, deregulation, and cuts to social spending accompanied by increases in military spend-ing; the kind of policies that were first imposed under dictatorships.

This decade witnessed abundantly available Internet and mobile tele-phone technology. The social media has become for millions the only social space where intimacy and big brother collude. At the end of the decade comes Edward Snowden's whistleblowing. American computer specialist and a former CIA and NSA employee, Snowden, leaked details of several top-secret United States and British government mass-surveillance programs to the press. On June 14, 2013, U.S. federal prosecutors charged Snowden with espionage and theft of government property. He now resides in Russia, where he has received temporary asylum.

B) FROM *OPERATION SPRING* IN VIENNA IN 1999 TO THE *REFUGEE PROTEST CAMP IN VIENNA* IN 2012

The other starts with what is known as *Operation Spring* in 1999 in Vienna. Operation Spring is one of the most brutal sequences of arrest, persecution, and criminalization of the black community in Austria since 1945. Early in the morning on May 27, 1999, 850 police officers stormed apartments and refugee dormitories throughout Austria. The code name for the police raid was "Operation Spring." One hundred Africans were arrested and convicted in questionable trials on the basis of weak evidence.

Linking her experiences with Charles Ofoedu's thoughts, Araba Evelyn Johnston-Arthur says, "the way Operation Spring worked, the arrests, the video images that were used in the process, the anonymous witnesses, the media have all created a deep distrust in the community" (Johnston-Arthur and Görg 2005). This shameless event that was never fully clarified by the politicians and the media in Austria has also its historical end and marked a new escalation of struggles. These resurfaced in November 24, 2012 with the formation of the Refugee Protest Camp in Vienna, a protest by refuges for the right to stay and to live a decent life and work. I write about it in a separate chapter in this book.

In 2010, I provoked Kwame Nimako, lecturer of international relations at the Graduate School of Social Sciences (GSSS), University of Amsterdam, and organizer of the Summer School on Black Europe in the Netherlands (that is taking place from 2008) to reflect on the relation between Africa, colonialism, and post-Cold War Eastern Europe. We were both taking part in the workshop "Education, Development, Freedom" at Duke University, Durham, North Carolina in the United States (February, 25–27, 2010). Nimako presented a harsh critique on contemporary Europe, stating that it is strongly preventing any serious rethinking of colonialism. This has a consequence for the status of Black European citizens, as Nimako argued that their citizenship and status, (or their citizenship genealogy) has to be seen as the following: "We are here because you were there!" With this Nimako provided a topological structure (or even a decolonial matheme,[5] an axiomatic connection between power, discourse, and inscription) on the relation between Africa, Europe, colonialism, and citizenship. I elaborated further on that point at the workshop and argued that the topological relation concerning former

Eastern Europe, West Europe, and coloniality has to be seen as the following: "We are here because you want to go there!"

I insist that these two topological structures of Europe/EU are not two faces of the same coin of global capitalism but are positions on a Mobius strip of global capitalism that is a surface with only one side and only one boundary component (that is also the explanation of the Mobius strip).

Kwame Nimako: "We are here (in the EU) because you were there (in Africa!)"

Marina Gržinić: "We are here (in the EU) because you want to go there (in Eastern Europe!)"

Kwame Nimako advanced further in the workshop, commenting on what I said:

> I mean [that] the issue of "We are here because you want to go there" is very correct. Because when the Berlin Wall fell, Africa would be a trouble for Europe. I said why? Because "former" Western Europe had claimed Africa within the context of the ACP (African-Caribbean-Pacific) group of nations, as its—backyard. South-East of Asia was seen by the G7 as the sphere of influence of Japan, and Latin America as the sphere of influence of the United States. This was the "gentlemen agreement" within the G7. Within Europe itself Africa was seen as the future supplier of agriculture products. As the "former" Western European agricultural productivity had reached 94 percent, Western Europe could not grow more. Asia has reached productivity of 60 percent and Africa has reached productivity of 25 percent. Therefore this meant more room for Africa to grow from the point of view of agriculture. This is how in the time of the Cold War things were constructed. Now that the Berlin Wall had fallen they had Eastern Europe to go and they could do away with Africa. Africa was no more relevant. Africans started to be migration controlled; this is the major preoccupation of Europe today. It is about how to prevent Africans from coming to Europe. Now Eastern Europe has become the source of full agricultural production. In that sense you are correct by saying "we are here because you want to go there." Another factor is the civilization mission of the "former" Western Europe in Eastern Europe. They are going to civilize the Eastern Europeans to teach them democracy, to teach them how to treat the Roma citizens, to teach them about race relations and human rights. They are bringing that to Eastern Europe. That also means that you cannot discard the issue of race in "former" Western Europe. As Western Europe "solved" all these problems, the problem of education, the problem of development, the problem of freedom and it is the rest that has to be taught. From the point of view of race relations, it also marginalizes the Black community; because once Europe becomes larger the Black community becomes small.[6]

On one side the white Europe is becoming bigger and the Black Europe smaller, even more non-whites are seen as exclusively migrants, though many are European citizens and not solely the second and third generations of post colonized people. All this heavily opens the question of racialization in relation to issues of citizenship, labor and mode of life. I argue that citizenship and non-citizenship are extreme historical categories and notions that have to be constantly contested by political struggle. My intention is to expose the way in which gender, class and race were and are overdetermined (without falling into a simplification that they are simply "contradictory").

Present EU hyperbolic regained whiteness and reiterated ideology of Occidentalism is brutally reproducing regimes of racial and class-coding that govern economic, social and political inequality in Europe. Europe has therefore to critically review its colonial and racial history as well as present actions. Grada Kilomba describes the process clearly:

> Once confronted with the collective secrets of racist oppression and the pieces of that very dirty history, the white subject commonly argues "not to know," "not to understand," "not to remember," or "not to believe." These are expressions of this process of repression by which the subject resists making the unconscious information conscious; that is, one wants to make the known unknown [EntErwähnung]. Repression [EntErwähnung] is, in this sense, the defense by which the ego controls and exercises censorship of what is instigated as an "unpleasant" truth. They say they do not know! But if I know, they too have to know as we co-exist in the same scenario. They say they have never heard of it! But how come, if we have been speaking it for 500 years? Five hundred years is such a long time. What do they want to know? And what do they want to hear? (Kilomba 2008, quoted after Lockward 2010)

The notion of race, as Kwame Nimako explains, is used in the Anglo-Saxon context as a question represented within colonialism and postcolonial studies, included in the process of teaching, while race and racialization are feverishly excluded from any talk in continental Europe because of the history of Nazism (Nimako 2013). Nimako retold the story of when the English football team was visiting Ukraine and Poland, the British Foreign Ministry informed Black people in Britain that they should not go there because there would be a lot of neo-Nazi's and skinheads, who could attack them. Nimako stated: "They didn't say that all British people should not go; they said Black people shouldn't go. So the whole idea of Europe is racialised, which shows that Europeans have to be of a certain skin color and a certain outlook to be granted full citizenship. This difference affects social mobility, it affects recruitment for job, if you write an application, they see your name, it rings a bell, it has impact on networking, it has impact on intermarriage, and all those things" (Nimako 2013).

In Slovenia, migrant workers coming from the former republics of the common state known as Yugoslavia are today working in conditions of enslavement; excluded from the law, they become "nonexistent," lacking the most basic humans rights. What occurs at the Schengen border (that is, the frontier between the European Union and the rest of Europe) can be placed in parallel with another border, the Tijuana border (thirty-two kilometers from downtown San Diego, the busiest point of entrance into the United States from Mexico). At the frontier, according to Angela Mitropoulos, "a violent space of exploration, cultivation and extraction of wealth—in the scarcities that are obliged as precondition and condition of a market in labor, in the criminalization and recapture of fugitive and wayward (re)production . . . there would be a periodic recourse to the naturalizing magic of genealogy to settle matters of orderly progression and authenticity" (Mitropoulos 2009) .

Today the EU as the fortress Europe is a regime that produces an accelerated legally sanctioned system of restrictions, discriminations and economic dispossessions; a space of intensified racialization that has at its core *racism*. Racialization refers to a process by which certain groups of people are singled out for unique treatment on the basis of real or imagined physical characteristics. Mostly it targets activities of those termed as (ethnic) minorities. It transforms societies into racialized societies. This process is today going so far that we have a process of racialization being imputed, without any "race" prerogatives but serving as a measure of class discrimination, subjugation, and finally dispossession.

We have today "different types of racisms" that are "more vicious and more deadly" than ever. The EU is providing the grounds for not only a state of exception but for a racial-State, giving a free hand to detention, segregation and discrimination under the veil of the protection of nation-State citizens and even the protection of refugees from "themselves," from their "drive" to try to illegally enter fortress Europe and therefore probably being in a situation to die.[7]

These processes of invigorated control of borders, expulsion of refugees, etc., are judicially, economically and, last but not least, discursively and representationally (as different semio-technological regimes), ratified, legislated, and normativized. Today it is central to draw a genealogy of racism that parallels capitalism's historical transformation and historicization.

Racism passed from *institutionalized* to *structural* to be today identified as *social racism*. To talk about social racism means, (as argued by Nasim Lomani, Afghan refugee that works in the immigrant social center run by volunteers in Athens, Steki Metanaston[8]), "to talk about an all-pervasive racism; its violence legitimized by the State itself."

In the proposed genealogy of racism we identify processes of racialization that pass from institutional mechanisms of ordering individuals within a given community toward structures that expand the institutionalization of racism to structural mechanisms of racialization. And yet, institutionalized racism that is not simply *institutional* racism subsumes in this precise difference (institutional vs. institutionalized) not only its historical format but also the structural violence necessary for its maintenance and reproduction. Kwame Nimako exposes a similar difference between slaves and enslaved, "while slave is a neutral description, enslaved incorporates a violent mechanism as somebody had to make somebody other a slave." Contemporary social racism is an all-pervasive racism that impregnates fully the neoliberal social body and is approved by the government. It is socially (approved) and internalized to such a micro level that the structures of violence produced by social racism are said to be a type of (micro) fascism. Making reference to Étienne Balibar's repeated interventions on racism already in 1988 before the fall of the Berlin Wall in 1989, it is possible to claim that social racism constitutes the essential form of "European apartheid" (Balibar 1988).

Kwame Nimako describes in the aforementioned interview that the history of Nazism and Fascism in Europe so much presses on the analysis of race that this category is today squeezed solely within Ethnic studies. He explains:

> In the 1980s we had the Centre for Race and Ethnic Studies; it was closed down in 1991. A year later they opened it and called it the Institute for Migration and Ethnic Studies, because they prefer to talk about black people as immigrants, where we talk about black people as citizens of Europe. If you change immigration for citizenship then you have a different way of approaching the thing, because the marker of citizenship is that you are European, but the point is, if you are a European citizen speaking the same language, and having almost the same religion or whatever the case is, then what is the issue which people use to distinguish you as different? It is only your facial features, or your name, or such markers for identification of difference. (Nimako 2013)

Michael Omi and Howard Winant have argued in their book *Racial Formation in the United States: From the 1960s to the 1990s* that the substitution of a *rights-based* conception of race in the 1960s with *ethnicity theory* in the 1970s and 1980s has meant that the issue of systemic racism has been replaced by issues of adaptation and assimilation. Omi and Winant's arguments make clear that the historical development of race has to connect to racism, race-class-gender interrelationships and everyday life while they insist that an effort must be made to understand race as an unstable and "decentered" complex of social meanings constantly being transformed by political struggle.

I am elaborating racialization as a process of capital's differentiation between citizens (first and second grade citizens), non-citizens (refuges, asylum seekers), and migrants; they are all violently, but differently discriminated, as the labor market under global capitalism imposes violent processes of racial, class and gender selection of im/migration in Europe. Europe is renewed today through a genealogy that excludes all those who are seen from its Western perspective as unimportant (that are constructed as *subhuman* through a process of dehumanization). This process stays unreflected also due to the new rhetoric developed in contemporary philosophy and theory of the *posthuman*. As stated by Maldonado-Torres

> these dehumanizing forces, logics, and discourses hardly seem to find an end in the current neoconservative and neoliberal moment, or in the liberal and Eurocentric radical responses that it sometimes generate. Continued Manichean polarities between sectors considered more human than others, the accelerated rhythm of capitalist exploitation of land and human labor—sometimes facilitated, as Fanon well put it, by neocolonial elites among the groups of the oppressed themselves—as well as anxieties created by migration and rights claims by populations considered pathological, undesirable, or abnormal—to name only a few of the most common issues found today—make clear that decolonization will remain unfinished for some time. (Maldonado-Torres 2011, 2-3)

In all these processes the human (as outcome of a capital's regime of humanization and as contemporary human capital subsumed in the unfinished project of Western modernization) stays largely untouched. The Occident doesn't want to deal with it, and therefore engages in all imaginable post-human modes while the present and historical modes of Occidental colonial *de*-humanization remain largely undiscussed.

This leads to a process of internal division that could be named in relation to Franz Fanon's "Zone of Being and Zone of Non-Being." Kwame Nimako, making a reference to Ramón Grosfoguel elaborates further on Fanon's division, stating that

> if you take a white American worker in a Boeing factory in America, who earns 1,560 dollars an hour, and you take at the Mexican border maquiladoras women who are working in a factory there for 2 dollars a day, you can look at both as working class. In the first case, the person has the right to form a trade union, on the other side the woman has no right to form a trade union, if she tries, she would be killed or kidnapped. So it is for the whites that there is freedom, but this is an incomplete history. In this way you have two types of history: one in what we call the zone of being, and the other one the zone of non-being. So you have the human line here, and then you have the zone of being above it, that is people who are considered human, and the enslaved and colonized people who are considered subhuman. (Nimako 2013)

This makes a sharp contrast not only between the former Eastern Europe and "former Western Europe," but also in relation the Black diaspora citizens, refugees and asylum seekers in Europe. Nimako emphasizes that "the people in the zone of being, that is Europeans, whether they are middle class, upper class, working class, are different from the zone of non-being, because the worker can go to the zone of non-being as a soldier or as a seaman to oppress the people in the zone of non-being, so we consider European history as one-sided" (Nimako 2013).

This relation opens new perspectives on the whole process of becoming human or civilized in Europe. Araba Evelyn Johnston-Arthur describes the situation in Austria as twofold. On the one side, we have migrants who were invited into the country by the government in the 1960s to help post-war reconstruction of the country, and on the other, we have a new, vast group of refugees, fugitives, asylum seekers, and deported persons (as in from August 2010, when France—supposedly "legally," as it was based on EU laws—deported hundreds of Roma back to Romania and Bulgaria) who find themselves victims of ever-changing immigration laws established and reinforced daily by the EU and implemented and improved nationally (Johnston-Arthur and Kazeem 2007).

I am interested in this new Europe that (in the same way as global capitalism) can be described, as Angela Mitropoulos has labeled it: the "confluence of foreigners, slaves, women and children" (Mitropoulos 2009). And, I hasten to add, migrants, queer, and all those who disrupt "a question of genealogy, of the authentication of power through origin-stories and their transmission, as fact and naturalized foundation" of Europe and of the global world. I argue (referring to Mitropoulos) that Europe today is—in its most basic sense—constituted by "the problem of the legal form of value, of its imposition and perseverance," and by "origin and lineage" (Mitropoulos 2009). Europe's migration/labor, capital, sexual reproduction and race are nowhere more disputed and uneasy than at the frontier between the spectral former East and "former" Western Europe—at the meeting point of "natural" citizens and migrants, colonizers and descendants of the colonized, in the European Union and non-EU states.

This brings us close to a more specific point: the Cold War. Nikhil Pal Singh argues that Cold War discourses and particularly the theory of totalitarianism (as the Cold War's primary ideology), born immediately after World War II, displaced the imperial and colonial genealogies of the Nazi Holocaust, as a form of industrialized killing, outside the context of Western history and theory (Singh 2009). So the period of decolonization or, to be more precise, the anti-colonial struggles of the 1960s, were filtered through the Cold War discourses on totalitarianism, allowing for a disavowal of colonial violence and its undisturbed continuity. This allowed a shift toward an opposition between democracy and fascism that was soon replaced by totalitarianism. Singh cites William Peitz's essay "The Post-Colonialism of Cold War Discourse" (Peitz 1988, quoted after Singh 2009, 68), which states that "what happened in the debate on the Cold War and totalitarianism helped to frame a profoundly dishonest historical conversation" (Singh 2009, 67). Singh writes that the theory of totalitarianism "enacted a displacement of fascism outside the main historical currents of Western moral, political, and intellectual life" (Singh 2009, 67). The result was that Nazism, first identified as being part of "the family of Western imperialisms and as the exemplary modern instance of rationalized, technology-driven state terror" (Singh 2009, 67), was transferred elsewhere.

Actually, the anti-colonial movements after WWII in Africa, Asia, and elsewhere, were harshly opposed by the West's "democratic" former colonial and fascist-States (Fanon 2005). This was going on under the shield of Cold War discourse with the rhetoric of fighting anti-colonial movements being derivative of Marxism and Communism. We have numerous unfinished decolonization struggles that were, at the time of the Cold War, brutally suppressed, suspended, etc., in the name of fighting communism by the First Capitalist World. Today it is clear that due to the coexistence of two divisions at the same time in Europe, the presently made obsolete West/East divide and the newly reactivated Occident/Orient division, we witness a shift in the process of subjugating by re-westernized global capitalism, a shift from communism toward Islamic extremism.

Aimé Césaire, in his book *Discourse on Colonialism* (Césaire 2000, originally published in 1955), elaborated clearly "that Hitler applied to Europe colonialist procedures, which until then had been reserved exclusively for the Arabs of Algeria, the coolies of India and the Blacks of Africa" (Césaire 2000, quoted after Singh 2009, 67). As Singh states, "the theory of totalitarianism (as the major ideological point of the Cold War), not only linked fascist destruction to the Soviet regime, it also suggested an extended chain of reasoning about existential dangers posed by 'terrorist uses' of technology, by those lacking proper philosophical conditioning and historical preparation for exercising state power" (Singh 2009, 67).

This resulted in shifting the debate regarding the systematic procedures of death exercised in the colonies away from the systematic procedures of death in the concentration camps in Europe during WWII.

At this point we have to pose the question regarding a radical theoretical turn that will allow a delinking from such a context of exploitation, hegemony, and racism.

I propose the *decolonial turn* (Maldonado-Torres 2011) that opposes the above explained colonizing turn and effectuates first a move from modernization toward decoloniality (Maldonado-Torres 2011, 3) followed by a demand for decolonization of Occidental knowledge (as the key ideological hegemonic regime of global capitalism), capital, power, politics and economy. I elaborate on the decolonial turn in future chapters. The decolonial turn has to remain (according to Nelson Maldonado-Torres 2011, 2) an unfinished project to present a political intervention; a *frontier* in the *infinite* (to borrow a term used so much by the new philosophers) of coloniality (Gržinić 2013c).

Decoloniality is instrumental in understanding the First World's capitalist colonial regimes, the larger geopolitical body of knowledge in the
modern/colonial world, and the reproduction of racial and class matrices
within the Euro-Atlantic colonial axis. It is instrumental in understanding
the current situation of former Eastern Europe vis-à-vis Western Europe
and/or the European Union: as the European Union appears to be the
modernizing savior of the whole region. It is said that Eastern Europe no
longer exists and it is therefore now called *former Eastern Europe*. However, paradoxically, its very non-existence as former Eastern Europe is over-
present and over-existent when we consider the allocation of Western
European capital. This move allows me to interpret, read, and understand Eastern Europe as the non-existing frontier of (as/in/at) the new
Europe, (more precisely of the European Union), which sets its hegemony against the rest of Europe. To formulate this differently, former Eastern Europe is a frontier, but it is a spectral one; it does not divide, as a
frontier normally does, but rather allows for a repetition and reproduction within itself of modes of life (biopolitics), modes of death (necropolitics), structures of governmentality, institutional control, systems of
knowledge and regimes of aesthetics, and contemporary art and theory
from "former" Western Europe.

What is to be done? Aigul Hakimova, an activist from the Social Center Rog in Ljubljana is clear, when she elaborates on this question. She
states:

> We have to re-open the issue of migration, to mobilize, to start working
> on alternative economies, such as co-operatives. In fact we have to
> make alliances; we have to travel a lot, to learn, to somehow be part of
> a larger movement, not of a political party, or a syndicalist union, but
> part of simple social movements from below, grassroots movement.
> Some countries have a very strong tradition in this regard. It is also
> necessary to experiment, to go a little over the border that lies ahead, to
> cross the limit. The future of the EU in the light of what is currently
> happening is open for battles. Over uprisings, struggles, people will
> come up with better rights. Otherwise, we will be a Babylon, in terms
> many love to use it, as some people will always remain at the margins,
> and we will witness the constant cyclical reproduction of the capitalist
> elite,.but without this interface. (Hakimova 2013)

As Jonathan Crary argues in his book *24/7: Late Capitalism and the Ends of
Sleep* (alluding not to 9/11 but to the 24/7; which is a term which refers to
a service which is available 24 hours a day and 7 days a week regardless
of the time or the day), 24/7 is provided by screen time, by the magical
windows of phones, computers, iPad's, etc., (of course for those who
have one). The 24/7 is as well, I contend, provided by a 24/7 convenience
store, or by an elderly-care service in the shape of cheap migrant labor
and/or undocumented servant work. Crary states that all these ITC gad-
gets put us in a state of constant alert, a state of "a disabled and derelict

diachrony" that prevents us from engaging in anything important (Crary 2013). He suggests a way to escape this condition (that I could refer to as *a prison*) of an artificial time that only produces itself, and advises us to "take a time for yourself." But I will argue differently: "do not take time for yourself, make time *for* and *with* others!" That means, (referencing Beatriz Preciado), insisting on a critical awakening, or a coming together of the "'proletariat of feminism' whose monstrous subjects are whores, lesbians, the raped, butch, male and transgender women who are not white . . . in short, almost all of us" (Preciado 2013, 251).

Essential is to emphasize, following Maldonado-Torres, that the discourse of decolonization in order to perform a pertinent political turn goes "beyond the dialectics of identity and liberation, recognition, and distribution" (Maldonado-Torres 2011, 4), and effectuates instead "epistemic decolonization and a consistent decolonization of human reality" (Maldonado-Torres 2011, 4).

In the last instance a pertinent decolonial turn constitutively deploys the linkages between colonialism, coloniality, capital, power, biopolitics and necropolitics, racism and other forms of racist dehumanization including exploitation, extractions, and dispossessions on one side and positions of subjectivities, agencies, and empowerment on the other. These open the possibilities for different inter-linking of decolonial transmigrant and transfeminist conceptualizations of history, life, and agency in order to delink from what could be called deep contradictions and antagonisms between the economic, social, cultural, and political norms and forms of global necrocapitalism.

Last but not least it is important to claim that all that has been discussed up until now is clearly visible or better to say *entangled* with art and culture, practices and theories, institutions and education-critical discourses.

Modernity in former Eastern Europe has been, and still is, passing through similar capitalist visions of modernity that are recognized only as historical repetitions of Western modernism in the local Eastern European framework. What they (the West) have "managed to bring to the present" is the old and dead conceptualism from the 1960s/1970s, now rediscovered in the former Eastern European context, but not as a political demand to change the ossified institutions of art, but as an individual "existential ethos." Therefore, the political art of (post)socialism is nullified through Western individualism; Rambo politics is repeated in the former Eastern Europe by the figure of the existentialist conceptual artist fighting for freedom in the totalitarian society.

We have to disassemble the processes of depoliticization of the whole space of global capitalism that goes hand in hand with the hyper branding of art and culture, theory and critical discourses. We currently live in an art and cultural context of spectacular branding. Artists are entrenched in the Western gallery system that consists of commercial galleries whose efforts are guided toward feeding the appetites of a small but powerful group of contemporary art collectors. Super-rich groups of collectors and art dealers, located in the Middle East, Asia, Latin America, and Russia, define generations of elite curators that are servicing them through a system of art fairs and biennales. A further characteristic of the art scene is the fusion of fine arts and show business, a fusion of "social" entertainment, which turns gallery and museum spaces into multi-purpose entertaining environments. Art is popular and branded but it is not where change occurs. Change is produced by activists; plebian curators in off-spaces.

Today, art institutions, too, rely more and more on private or semi-private funding, which is also the reality of the public art education system. Art is, more or less, a system of production of goods, but also (or primarily) the production of encounters, performances and installations for the enjoyment of the so-called mobs with good lives in the First, oops . . . global, capitalist world. It is also important to mention that art and culture are subjugated to science, biotechnology, and to all kinds of life sciences.

Branding is the new reality, with popular events and spectacles impregnated with marketing and media advertising. We are witnessing the process of the co-branding of art, while elite squadrons of curators are invigorating art tourism through art fairs and biennials. In simple terms, all is blurred, or better to say entangled, every space is implicated in something else; what we get is the image of a communal bordello with depoliticized politics and show-business art.

To conclude, a way to activate the decolonial turn is to engage in the analysis of the complicity between capital, racism, Eurocentrism and us, in order to put forward a decolonization not only of the heavily re-westernized Occidental view (see the hyper hegemonic pleonasm I put forward of western and Occidental of power, capital and knowledge that is central for the supposedly "borderless" global capitalism) and its theories, discourses and sciences but to effectuate the decolonization of imperial modes of life in global capitalism that are based on violent colonizing modes of capital reproduction.

Therefore a proposal that this book carries is that along decolonial movements of racialized populations in Africa, Asia, and Latin America we embrace the insurgent policies by the Black Diaspora citizens in Europe as well as the movements of heavily racialized non-citizens (refugees and paperless people) in West Europe and sectors of insurgent decolonization movements from the former Eastern Europe.

NOTES

1. Exchange at the conference *Education, Development, Freedom* at Duke University, Durham, USA (February, 25-27, 2010).

2. The title of this chapter "The Darkest Sides of Europe" exposes the extreme forms of dispossession, coloniality, and racialization that are in the background of contemporary Europe; they are logics that regulate, manage and govern Europe and EU policy. I make also a direct connection to theoreticians of the decolonial turn who state that on the back of modernity functions a *colonial matrix of power*; this matrix is modernity's darker side. As neoliberal global capitalism is an absolute historical form of capitalism, that means that is "pure" in terms of being raw and non-mediated in the way it disposes and makes surplus value from death, racialization and subjugation, I propose that when speaking of coloniality, racialization and dispossession in the back of Europe and neoliberal global capitalism we use absolute comparisons. Therefore, I propose to talk not only about "just" the darker side of Europe but about the darkest sides of it.

3. See http://www.formerwest.org/Front

4. As it is stated online "ECF supports art and culture for the contribution it makes to Europe. Through art and culture, people are engaged and empowered to make change happen and to help shape the future of the continent." See http://www.culturalfoundation.eu/about-us

5. I refer here on Jacques Lacan matheme.

6. See the video film *Naked Freedom* by Marina Gržinić, Aina Šmid, 2010. This whole conversation between Nimako and Gržinić is documented in this video film. http://grzinic-smid.si/?p=41

7. EU established a special agency *Frontex* that for years effectuated border surveillance in the Schengen border zones. The Schengen Area operates very much like a single state for international travel purposes with external border controls for travelers entering and exiting the area, with common visas and no internal border controls. In 2013 the EU established *Eurosur* that it is the new Frontex's European Union's borders protection agency that uses high technology to coordinate activities on the EU's external borders. Supposedly Eurosur was established to prevent incidents on the Schengen border and to stop refugees even before they try to smuggle themselves into the EU. One of the reasons for establishing Eurosur was because the EU was facing harsh critique due to the extreme number of dead refugees found in its charge. In one case, in Italian Lampedusa, 350 refugees from Africa drowned in a single day on October 12, 2013.

8. Steki Metanaston was opened in 1997 under the auspices of Diktio, the Network for Social Support to Immigrants and Refugees. Its main aim is to fight institutionalized racism by providing legal assistance and educating migrants to advocate for themselves.

TWO

Biopolitics, Necropolitics, Unrestrained Financialization, and Fascisms

Neoliberalism is the technology of optimization, from economics to politics, from nature to the environment, and is used, as argued by Aihwa Ong, by management and administrations to run our social lives through a system of calculations (Ong 2006). Exception in such a context functions as a mechanism of differential inclusion and can be implemented by any political regime whatsoever, be it China or the United States (where no changes of the system whatsoever are any longer necessary when it comes to "improving" the conditions of life of the nation-State's citizens), in order to effectuate only one single calculation: the calculation for the capital's surplus value. I would like to point out that neoliberal global capitalism's most internal logic is precisely the deregulation that tends toward a complete reversal and shattering of every relation (that was once seen as logical) into the normalization and rationalization of the most illogical processes. Saying this is to understand that surplus value and private property are at the core of capitalism, and these two axioms of capital are not illogical at all, but only historical.

The logic goes even further, as Santiago López Petit (López Petit 2009) argues, as today there is almost nobody who talks about a waged laborforce being exploited by capitalism, but rather, the story more or less goes around about the beneficiary "capital" that belongs indissolubly to anyone who is merely ready to put it into play (read: business). According to this new narrative, the wage is no more than the "profit" of determined human capital. Though profit, that is extracted from financial capital, is not made only and solely through dis-investments in the stock markets, but is supported by a series of interventions and logics of exploitation

that are produced through a process of continuous massive impoverishment and massive digitalized ideological subdivisions and subjugations
that change the "Western" concept of governance over lives in the First
World (known as biopolitics (bio [*life*] politics). This concept changed into
necropolitics (necro [*death*] politics) in the once named Second and Third
Worlds. This means making surplus value from a double form of death:
death from *real* massive impoverishment, and a *symbolical* death from
capital interventions in the social, political, and imaginary.

The contemporary theory of *human capital* perceives *humanity* as a
constant product (as a form) of investments (biopolitics is all based on
calculation, counting and regulations of life) in the First Capitalist World,
and dis-investments (necropolitics is all based on calculation, counting
and regulations of death) in order to make profits in the Third and other
(Second, "underdeveloped," "emerging," etc.) worlds. The theory of human capital presents human action as a maximized way of acting and
envisions one's behavior with the final objective of achieving more utility
or greater welfare. The consequences of such a view are, among other
things, complete financialization; a speculative dysfunctional logic that
sees and interprets every expense for education, health, social, or leisure
activities of the individual not as consumption but as investment.

BIOPOLITICS, NECROPOLITICS

In the past we had at least two regimes: socialism and capitalism, and a
myriad of constellations in between; today, we have a neoliberal global
capitalism that produces steady fragmentations inside (from within) each
and every condition, mode and notion that were historically brought to
light in capitalism. If, in the past, we talked about life and death, today
we have a differentiation within the category of life itself. The major
break happened when Giorgio Agamben explained in the 1990s a theoretical change that was consequent with the post-Cold War "disappearing" of borders; a conceptual division from within the category of life
itself. Agamben articulated a new process of distinction inside biopolitics
(the management of life) proposing to conceptualize life as a form-of-life
(mode-of-life), distinguishing between life *with* a form from a *bare* or
naked life, that is a life *without* a mode or a form. It is important to say that
this fragmentation of life has only been possible to elaborate due to the
post-Cold War "disappearing" of borders that brought very soon (globally visibly) fierce racial, class, and gender differences in the life of the
individuals of global capitalism.

Giorgio Agamben in the 1990s (Agamben 1998) elaborated the findings by Michel Foucault from the 1970. In Nuce, Agamben argued that
biopolitics is not only about how life is administered (Michel Foucault's
biopolitics), but is about life's differentiation, about its fragmentation

from within. This is as well an outcome of the ideology of neoliberal multiculturalism in the 1990s after the fall of the Berlin Wall. Agamben conceptualized that contemporary biopolitics differentiates between life with *forms-of-life* (life as style) and life without a form or style, that is, *bare* or *naked* life. It presents a new division, life is now divided within itself; life that was in the past seen as the antagonism of death has been divided now into two. Or to say it differently, this process of differentiation is, in fact, the procedure by which life is administered and managed, how it is controlled on the supposition of its improvement. It is a process that only allows life as a form-of-life, life as style (allowing only for new forms, new styles of life). It is a process of a pure formalization of life. The result is that the only thing that matters in the First Capitalist World (global capitalism) are forms-of-life or life-as-style.

In order to rationalize the differences, while eschewing the class, race and gender "content" in between different systems and social, political and economic structures, a shift toward a process of formalization of life as a mode-of-life occurred. In that precise moment politics has been exchanged for anthropology in critical discourses.

It is our thesis that Foucault's biopolitics, (a term coined in the 1970s, in the time of the Cold War), is a specific conceptualization of capitalist liberal governmentality exclusively reserved for the First Capitalist World. Biopolitics denotes a horizon of articulating society from the so-called politics of life, where life is seen as the zero degree of intervention of each and every politics into contemporary societies. It presented 1970s liberal capitalism as "taking care" but only of the citizens of the First Capitalist World nation-States. What was going on in the Second (the Eastern European space) and Third World was not at the center of the management of life in the First Capitalist World. It is important to note as well that Foucault warned us in his *Society Must Be Defended* (Foucault 1991, 2004) that with the predominance of biopolitics, death would be gradually banned. Foucault warned that death is "something to be hidden away." Foucault asserted in the mid-1970s that "power no longer recognizes death." What Foucault meant was that the First World Capitalism's biopolitical power was not prepared to recognize death, as death was exported outside the West and let to "live" there, also on the other side of the Iron Curtain. One of the 007/James Bond films from the 1970s is an accurate description of biopolitics: "Live and Let Die" (1973).

Thirty-five years later death has been brought back. In 2003 Achille Mbembe brought it back with his necropolitics (*necro* meaning *death* in Latin). In his seminal text "Necropolitics" Mbembe (2003) discusses a new capital's logic and its processes of geopolitical demarcation of world zones that are based on the mobilization of the war machine. Necropolitics is connected to the concept of necrocapitalism, that is, contemporary capitalism, which organizes its forms of capital accumulation around dispossession and the subjugation of life to the power of death (Banerjee

2006). The necrocapitalist capturing of the social space implies new modes of governmentality that are informed by the norms of corporate rationality and deployed in managing violence, social conflicts, fear, and the Multitude. No conflict is tolerable that challenges the supreme requirements of capitalist rationalization—economic growth, profit maximization, productivity, efficiency, and the like. Mbembe claims that the concept of biopolitics, due to the war machine and the state of exception being one of the major logics of contemporary capitalist societies, should be replaced with necropolitics.

Let's use the decolonial matheme (proposed in the previous chapter) and its topology to understand even better the seminal differences between biopolitics and necropolitics.

Therefore I state that Foucault's *biopolitics*, a term in-between bio (LIFE) and politics can be designated in an axiomatic way as *"make live and let die."* With necropolitics we can on the other hand define the transformation of regulation of life within extreme conditions produced by capital. Necropolitics is a term in-between necro (DEATH) and politics. Necropolitics regulates life through the perspective of death, therefore transforming life into a mere existence below every life minimum. I designate *necropolitics* as *"let live and make die."*

These two modes of life present brutal differences in the managing of life and death. In biopolitics, life is controlled but for the citizens of the sovereign First World capitalist countries it is about providing a good life, but today what is at hand is the pure abandonment of this structure (let live) and at the same time death is managed, used and capitalized by the war machine. If biopower, according to Foucault, is the exercise of the power that I present in a short form as "to make live and let die," then necropower is the exercise of the power that I presented in a short form as "to let live and make die." To make live (to provide conditions for a better life) and/or to let live (being abandoned to a life without means) presents two different biopolitics; the latter is, in fact, pure necropolitics.

With *necropolitics* Mbembe gave us the possibility by which to repoliticize biopolitics. With necropolitics, I argue, we get a "necropolitical" intensification of biopolitics, and at the same time we provide for the historicization of biopolitics in the time of neoliberal global capitalism.

Already in his book on Africa as the postcolony, *On the Postcolony: On Private Indirect Government*, Mbembe (2001) conceptualizes Africa's social, political and economic condition in the new millennium in relation to the capital surplus value that is explicitly based on the capitalization of death (Latin, *necro*) worlds. During a discussion on Africa as the postcolony, Mbembe overcharges Africa with an extreme contemporaneity, as he does not talk about the continent as an agenda of post-colonialism, but as a postcolony; as something present here and now.

In *On the Postcolony: On Private Indirect Government* Mbembe stated, that though taking into account specific conditions of environmental exploitation and warfare in Africa and while war tactics in Africa are quite rudimentary, they still result in human catastrophes. This is because military pressure sometimes targets the straightforward destruction of, if not of the civilian population, at least the very means of its survival, such as food reserves, cattle, and agricultural implements. In some cases, these wars have enabled warlords to exercise more or less continuous control over territory. Such control gives them access not only to those living in the territories, but also to the natural resources and the goods produced there—for instance, the extraction of precious stones, exploitation of timber or rubber, or ivory poaching. The financing of these wars is very complex. In addition to the financial contribution provided by diasporas and the assignment of men and women into forced labor, there is the resorting to loans, appeals to private financiers and special forms of taxation.

Mbembe argues that these new forms of more or less total control not only blur the supposed relationship between citizenship and democracy they, in fact, incapacitate whole sections of the population politically (Höller 2002) and I will add socially and economically. Therefore, it is possible to state that what is becoming globally evident (with a reference to Mbembe) and in relation to Africa is the emergence of a new form of relation between capital and power named "private indirect government," which presents a new configuration of power: the privatization of violence (the myriad of militias and private armies) that work hand in hand with the neoliberal global economy. Private indirect governments push through the process of total privatization that results in the emergence of an informal system and relations of power (through lobbies, associations, family ties, etc.).

In agreement with Höller and stated on the occasion of the publication of his aforementioned book *On the Postcolony*, Mbembe firmly believes that democracy as a form of government and as a culture of public life does not have a future in Africa—or, for that matter, elsewhere in the world—unless it is rethought precisely from the condition of "necropower." By "necropower," Mbembe refers to a sovereign power that is set up for the maximum destruction of persons and the creation of deathscapes, unique forms of social existence in which vast populations are subjected to conditions of life which confer upon them the status of the living dead.

It is possible to think in these terms also about the war in the Balkans in the 1990s. Let's take Srebrenica, Bosnia and Herzegovina, in the mid-1990s where around 8,000 Muslim men and boys were killed while the international military forces (the United Nations Protection Force [UN-PROFOR]), represented on the ground by a 400-strong contingent of Dutch peacekeepers, *Dutchbat*, did not prevent the town's capture by units of the Army of Republika Srpska ("Serbian Republic") under the command of General Ratko Mladić and the subsequent genocide. They were standing next to them saying: "We cannot intervene, it is not our fault; we can just be here monitoring, but we can't do anything." This can be described as the most direct necropolitical mode of the logic of international sovereign power. To make thousands die and let the others live, claiming that international law is prohibiting the international peace force from to intervening—this is pure necropolitics.

Maybe one can choose to imagine that this is something that is only going on "over there" in Africa, or "over here" in the Balkans. On the contrary, necropolitics is a reality both in the EU and globally. Necropolitics is not "a peculiar African reality," but something that is becoming more and more of a normal "landscape," first in all of the territories outside of the First Capitalist World (Palestine, Chechnya, etc.), and after 2001 more and more in the First Capitalist World itself. In relation to this, we have to point to Hurricane Katrina's devastation of the U.S. city of New Orleans and thousands that were left to live (if they could) or made to die, as the system of public help and evacuation failed, was absent, and/or denied to the poor, ill etc. This is one of the most obvious recent necropolitical acts in the First Capitalist World.

So necropolitics is not only reserved only for the Second and Third Worlds (though it was elaborated by Mbembe in the African context), but is operated in First World Capitalism, as well. Today, in the European Union, the United States, and Japan, etc., the logic of the organization of life and the division of labor is not (and never was) to achieve maximum life, but in reality is a pledge only to provide the bare minimum for living and sometimes (today, too often) not even this. A necropolitical logic organizes the contemporary neoliberal global capitalist social body. The minimum that is being imposed can be clearly seen through an analysis of all the battles that are going on around Europe at the moment to preserve the once social-State, the once guaranteed (and achieved only through workers class struggles) social and health security, etc. An excellent example is the complete dissolution of the social, medical and pension rights that were once part of the former socialist European countries. Wild neoliberal global capitalization has transformed these countries into hubs of misery, nationalism, racism, etc. The necropolitical can also be clearly seen in the measures of control (seclusion, deportation and the ferocious anti-immigrant EU law policy) within and without the borders of the Schengen zone of Europe.

Private indirect government functions by way of organizing exhibitions or constituting histories or managing institutions of art and culture, too. Therefore the way capital, power and institutions are working today is not only present on the level of "securing" money and distributing jobs but in culture and arts as well.

The outcome of these processes is that in the First Capitalist World, with its biopolitical procedures and forms-of-life are seen in their smallest angle of torsion. These (infinite) torsions are just processes of individualization where the only subject is an individual; a more or less successful brand. The situation is a complete interiorization and this is what capitalism does: it changes every social or political dimension, or every common interest, so to speak, into an individual matter through a process of individualization. Therefore, it's not surprising, the claim that there is no "outside" to the biopolitical of the First Capitalist World. Everything that has its source on the "outside" (misery, death, illegality, etc.) has to disappear.

Biopolitics is reserved only for the fictitious battle of forms-of life, although death is all around it.

The consequence is that there are practically no longer any political subjects in the First Capitalist World. Or better, we need to start thinking how to define political subjectivity differently. It is not that it has vanished; it just needs to be reframed and posited differently.

It is necessary to expose other agencies that are acting in the social and political space (communities, activists, etc.) and that are not political brands competing for more or less stylish forms-of-life. In the First Capitalist World, death is produced and reproduced constantly, but it is constantly hidden as well. According to Rubia Salgado of *maiz. Autonomous Center of and for Migrant Women* in Linz, Austria,[1] today, the interest in the lives of migrants may well be a hot topic, but in reality it is nothing but an instrumentalized topic. The biopolitical in the First Capitalist World includes life as a political concern, but only through its *exclusion* from the political sphere.

It is not possible to understand biopolitics without a process of its repoliticization through necropolitics and necropower. That means to frame biopolitics from the perspective of all those who do not count for biopower, but who are fiercely over-exploited (migrants, paperless peoples, third world populations, etc.). European Union states are today necropolitical regimes that defend the biopolitical and hide the necropolitical extremely well, the latter is exported in the immiserated territory of the EU, as for example in Greece or Spain, and there it is also applied on the proper nation-State bodies through a system of internal racializations.

Therefore, we are at the point where we should acknowledge that Europe's "different types of racisms" (already announced in the past by Étienne Balibar) are being effective today to the extent that they acquire a "pure meaning" (that means that presently detected, all pervasive *social racism* is possible to be named in Lacanese as the *minimal difference* between the presence and absence of the meaning of racism itself). These racisms are more multiple, "more vicious and more deadly" than ever.

Moreover, it is possible to argue that, in global capitalism, the institutions—primarily—of the ideological State apparatuses function as biopower; therefore art and culture, along with theory and criticism, and education as well, are today pure biopolitical machines (only taking care of themselves and their hegemonic Euro-Atlantic interests), while the social and the political (with its, as it is claimed, "autonomous" judicial system), not to mention economy, are pure instruments of and conductors for the necropolitical global capitalism. Why has this happened? Capitalism is a system that lives from exploitation, dispossession, and discrimination and is not at all cultural (though it affects culture) but is an economic and therefore social and political system. This has the consequence that presently art and its institutions are only biopolitical machines, while the social is necropolitical.

PRIVATIZATION, DEREGULATION

We should also add to necropolitics two other major processes fundamental to the way neoliberalism functions today: the privatization and deregulation of each and every stratum of society, its institutions and its social, political, economic, cultural, and artistic practices. The most important point is to understand that neoliberal necrocapitalism thrives on the intensification of its two primal conditions of reproduction: deregulation and privatization. To refer to these two conditions means to refer to a state of psychosis, or rather, to a state of (at first) exceptionality that is soon seen as completely normalized and accepted. Privatization means that the state withdraws step by step from social, cultural and public life, and leaves all public sectors to struggle for private money. But privatization also implies a form of private property or of a private instrumentalization of public institutions by those who run them.

What we see is that these artistic, cultural, social, health, public, etc. sectors, which before were primarily used for the ideological reproduction of the capitalist mode of re/production and its labor force, are today vital for the direct capitalization (acquiring surplus value) of capital. Therefore, when we speak about the neoliberal necrocapitalist radical deregulation of each and every institution in society, be it the institution of art, culture, politics, health, social security, law, religion, etc., it means that this affects not only global capitalism (dis)investment policy, but its histories, strategies of intervention, ideologies, rituals and modes of life.

In neoliberalism, as the *AREA Chicago* team formulates (Tucker 2008) four processes apply: financialization of capital, speculative movements of financial capital, interspatial competition, and place-marketing. Financialization of capital means that surplus value, as the central drive of capital, is produced with a bubble mechanism of "virtual" money movements, dis-investments, etc. This is not rooted in classical industrial production anymore, as was the case in the *direct* expropriation of people, regions, and territories in the not-so-distant past of capitalist colonialism. Even though such processes are still active (if we think about extractions of oil, precious metals, quality real estate, farm dis-investments, etc.), financialization makes money from money (virtually) without the so-called background of classical capspitalist industrial production. It does not come as a surprise that in the last week of September 2008, in the week of Wall Street's darkest scenario of collapse (since the 1929 Great Depression), billions of Euros simply disappeared (so to speak) overnight. What we witness here is a performative aspect of the speculative power of the capitalization of money that has no base in anything but itself. The outcome of such a situation is at once auto-cannibalistic; a "pure" circular capitalist auto-dispossession as well as a neoliberal *global capitalist vampirism*, a hyper blood-thirsty condition that produces always new and infinite number of *deathscapes*.

What more does this tell us? If the *financialization of capital* reflects the domination of financial markets (foreign exchange trading, futures, debt trading, U.S. government securities trading, and other forms of speculative investment) over industrial economies in contemporary capitalism, as stated by the *AREA Chicago* team, I therefore put forward additionally that the process of *financialization of institutions* is in parallel to the financialization of capital, leading to the over-empowerment of institutions, but only and solely through performative speculative processes that have no base in anything other than the institutions themselves. These speculative processes are becoming more important than any art, cultural, social, critical, discursive or theoretical productions, more important that any art work, more important that any artist or artistic group position, etc.

It is fundamental to expose the role of *debt servitude* being imposed on mass populations in the interest of transnational capital. When the "democratic" era began in the 1980s, it is stated in the documentary film *Catastroika* by Chatzistefanou and Kitidi, that there was the need for another mechanism to keep countries in line, and this mechanism was debt; which works hand in hand with harsh privatization and the sell-off of whole States. In the film it is precisely elaborated that the "institutions such as the International Monetary Fund (IMF) and the World Trade Organization played a leading role in the sell-off of whole countries. The European Union followed suit. The emergency packages with the IMF have enabled the EU for the first time to actually advocate privatizations. Technically, under the EU treaty, it shouldn't do this, but of course as part of the TROIKA (a group of three ["troika"], European Commission, International Monetary Fund, and European Central Bank, who formed a group of international lenders) it has imposed stringent austerity measures on Iceland, Greece, Portugal, etc., that has allowed unconditional privitization.

My proposal is not only to name the processes that are going on in the field of economics financialization but to reframe them as being terminally fundamental for the functioning of art and culture in the time of neoliberal global capitalism. Financialization is overtly restructured and deregulated in art, culture, theory, and critical thinking to the extent that is possible to say that we should investigate financialization not only as a radical *necro* process in the sphere of economics, but as a process that works through the whole of social and political, artistic, and cultural life. Today we have to speak not only of financialization of capital, but also of the financialization of (cultural) institutions as such, with highly visible characteristics of speculation, interspatial competition and place-marketing. In neoliberal necrocapitalism, a process of over-determination (that is definitively financialization) affects not only every level of the economy, but it is also highly operative in contemporary art and culture, theory, and critical discourses.

As it was formulated by the *AREA Chicago* group, speculation "could be understood as buying, holding and selling something (anything from real estate to fine art) in order to profit from the fluctuations in the market (something like 'buy low, sell high')." What is bought and sold here is information itself, as it were, devoid of any content. Moreover, a process of "a cleansing of the terrain" is to be added, as was learned from the Balkan Wars. Practices and theories that disturb the flow of incessant production of information should be erased, they have to vanish. Very similar processes were and still are—not only in relation to the brutality in the Balkan Wars in the 1990s and in Chechnya, etc.— implemented in relation to the *Erased People* in Slovenia (more about this case in the next chapter).

Therefore, to summarize, what is taking place is a two-fold process: on the one hand, speculations are the outcome of a hyper-activity, not of production, but of a hyper-production of information itself; institutions are activated as incubators for the constant production of information— about themselves. The result is, to put it simply, a daily bombardment of an unbelievable quantity of information about projects and activities that nobody can follow anymore. A boom is fabricated in the infinite speculative sending and distributing of whatever. We are witnessing a completely psychotic process of total evacuation of history, counter knowledges and alternative modes of life.

I want to emphasize that the time of the particularization of levels of society (let's think about culture and art, being "outside," so to speak, of the processes that are going on in the wider economic, social and political contexts) are over. There has always been a firm relationship of interdependency between the superstructure (art, culture, the social field, etc.) and the economic base. The difference is that, in the past, this logic was hidden, but in neoliberalism, these connections are clearly visible. In neoliberal necrocapitalism, the whole of society has been transformed into merely one *big invesment* sector that provides new opportunities for the incessant capitalization of capital in order to make surplus value.

Within this whole process, other maybe less visible procedures are additionally taking place in order that institutions can maintain their power at any cost. For example, one can think of cases such as when the institution declares a "war," provoking a state of exception in order to hide its own irresponsibility. What does it mean to provoke a state of exception as a strategy for obfuscating its own position in order to pre-serve power? In order to survive and reproduce its power in the national realm, the institutions need a total war. This is produced through a process that delegates its incitement through somebody else and in a format that hides the institution's responsibility. Here, to delegate means to find completely unscrupulous individuals on one side, or NGOs or international institutions on the other, that are willing to "help" in the dirty business or to accept to financially support the whole war "art (dirty) business" on the presupposition that it takes part in another cultural (national) space. Though in a proper national context, such an international institution is far from "implementing" the same "measures," as those are being implemented only in countries that are seen from the international "supporting" institution as not being civilized enough. In reality, the international supporting institution turns the provoked state of disorder and power games, which are known as *balkanization*, to its advantage. It presents itself as being "subversive" and completely "autonomous" in the international context, while being completely submissive to the governmental structures at home.

For contemporary deregulated and speculative state institutions, it is difficult to grasp the social and political space as a possible space of alliances. Through their optics, marginalized groups and practices are presented as those with the most power, which mean (of course in a distorted way) that the marginalized alternative spaces and positions are presented on the same level as State institutional power positions. It is a process of obfuscation that has as a result a situation where everybody is engaged, so to speak, in mutually destructive place-marketing strategies against each other. At the same time, the official institutions of art, culture, etc., are cleared of any actual responsibility for the system, and present themselves as only being victims of it.

Neoliberal necrocapitalism is continually being produced and repro-duced, not only economically and politically, but obviously institutionally, socially, and culturally as well. All these processes have an effect of being totally and straightforwardly completely "dysfunctional"; they generate consequences that are very difficult to be fully understood. Nowadays it is necessary to de-link ourselves from this war of everybody against everybody, ex/changing everything with everything, everybody with everybody; it is necessary to be capable of drawing a line of diffe-rentiation, while building local and international (strategic) alliances. These are the only possible ways for changing the presently deregulated and privatized economic, social, and institutional spheres of our life and work.

It is important to add that the present situation gives a free hand to capital's most urgent task, which is the intensification of collapse and/or of a complete de/re/structuring of the working class within the described line of the intensified precarization of life that covers the way of a shift from the biopolitical to the necropolitical. This has been conducted through an intensification that can be named, according to Ignacio Ramonet (2008), as *four great rationalization principles*: reducing the number of employees and wages, introducing more and more work obligations, restructuring companies, and redistributing goods and resources.

This intensification of brutal exploitation and the intensified management of the whole of society (only and solely to extract more and more surplus value) can be connected with what was argued by Walter Mignolo in 2010: that in between the sixteenth and twenty-first centuries, capitalism went through many mutations—one being that, in the sixteenth century, the economy was part of society, whereas in the twenty-first century, society is part of the economy.[2]

These processes are performed by capital in many different situations: in executing control over life, in pushing the war on terrorism and in civilizing those that are not yet "civilized" enough!

THE UNRESTRAINMENT OF CAPITAL

I want to continue with an in-depth analysis of global capitalism. In order to do this, I will make specific reference to Santiago López Petit's book *La movilización global. Breve tratado para atacar la realidad*, published in Spanish in 2009 (which I translated as *Global Mobilization: A Brief Treatise for Attacking Reality*). López Petit's book is a militant demand for further politicization of life.

But contrary to numerous analyses of globalization seen solely as a process, López Petit claims an eventual structure of capitalism. López Petit states that if we think of globalization as the result of just a process, we imply a development and a progression (also, temporarily, a regression, a crisis), and therefore, we are not capable of understanding the way capitalism functions. If we think about neoliberal globalization, global capitalism, just as a process, we therefore even imply capital emancipation (as it had been stated throughout the previous decade in numerous exhibitions, symposia, books, throughout Europe and the United States, that capital is social, etc.). In such a situation, we are ready to accept, almost naturally, I would say, fake discourses of morality with which neoliberal global capitalism tries to cover up the outcome of the crisis these days (financialization of capital) by stating that it was all just some sort of a mistake, as capital is noble and that financialization (making money from money without investing into production), is just a single perversion, a mistake. No!

Capitalism, as elaborated by López Petit, is not an irreversible process but a reversible, circular and conflictual event. The core of this reversibility is presented by López Petit in the following way: He states that in the world today all is brought back to one single event, and I will add that this is not *the crisis,* nor even Obama, but what he calls the unrestrainment of capital (in Spanish *des[z]boc[k]amiento*), that can be more colloquially grasped as "unrestraining" or "unleashing" (or a runaway) of capital. Neoliberal globalization, as stated by López Petit, is nothing more than the *repetition* of this single event, that is, the unrestrainment of capital (López Petit 2009, 24).

Marxism, says López Petit, has traditionally connected the critique of capitalism with the defense of the idea of a limit that is accessed by capitalist development and proper to it. To access the limit means to reach the point of its imminent collapse. The hypothesis of the imminent collapse takes its point of departure from the crisis, on one hand that is a crisis, of over-supply and, on the other, of under-consumption. However, as López Petit argues, the over-production of the means of production and over-abundance of market commodities that prevent the realization of profit are nothing more than an excess of the means of production that are, in a particular present and already-historical moment, not suitable to function as capital. There is nothing new to add! For what is happening today is the logic that stands at the core of capital: production solely for the benefit of capital in order to generate surplus value, and not at all for the benefit of social life. Such a situation, that is an antinomy at the core of capital, does produce a living contradiction, but it is not bringing capitalism to an end.

On the contrary, as stated by Marx and quoted by López Petit: "The true limit of the capitalist production is capital itself" (López Petit 2009, 24). Please keep this in mind, I will return to this point later.

The unrestrainment of capital creates a paradoxical spatialization that requires two repetitions: on the one hand, according to López Petit, a *founding repetition* with which a system of hierarchy is reestablished, leading to the constant reconstruction of a center and a periphery; and, on the other hand, a so-called *de-foundational repetition* that presents itself as the erosion of hierarchies, producing dispersion, multiplicity, and multi-reality. The unrestrainment of capital, as argued by López Petit, implicates both repetitions at once. Thus, not only does repetition produce the "jouissance" of minimal difference, but *repetition* is also a mechanism of control, subjugation and repression. Repetition of the unrestrainment of capital repeated vertically and horizontally, rearticulates a global space-time that repeatedly effectuates the co-propriety of capital and power. The unrestrainment of capital is, as argued by López Petit, the only event that—being repeated at any moment and in any place—unifies the world and connects everything that is going on within it. Repetition is also de-foundational to the degree with which, according to López Petit, capital repeats indifference for equality.

I can propose, therefore, three major fields with which López Petit tackles global capitalism. These are: reality, capital/power, and democracy.

These segments are linked together through two almost old-fashioned mechanisms that are evidently still operative today: *circularity* in the way of self-referentiality on one side and *empty formalism* (pure formalization) as tautology that produces obviousness, on the other. *Tautology* is *obviousness*, and, as argued by López Petit, presents itself today as the complete and total coincidence of capitalism and reality. To say that capitalism and reality totally coincide means that today *reality is reality*. The date of the event that made that reality and capitalism coincide totally is, as argued by López Petit, September 11, 2001. López Petit states that the outcome of September 11, 2001 was the excess of reality; it was the moment when reality exploded (López Petit 2009, 80).

López Petit warns us that in the global era, the debate between modernity and postmodernity has become obsolete. The global era is a break with modernity and with the postmodern radicalizations of modernity that were developed by Giddens, Beck and Lash. López Petit states that the classical concept of modernity is about modernization (López Petit 2009, 18). It is presented as an *endogenous process* that is caused by factors within the system. Modernity is presented as the work of reason itself. Likewise, modernity constructs a rationalist image of the world that implicates the duality subject/object, and the distance is, says López Petit, that of man and the world. Postmodernism abolishes the distance and situates man inside the world that is made of signs and ahistorical languages. The global era oscillates this distance between zero and infinity. That is why there is the feeling of the absence of the world and at the same time we witness its over-abundance. So it comes as no surprise that most of the theoretical findings that have been published recently deal with this oscillation between zero and infinity. The limit of the postmodern discourse resides, therefore, in the contemplation of reality as neutral that turned into political neutrality. But what it is necessary to do today is to call for the repoliticization of reality, and to de-link ourselves from its political neutrality.

We are in the middle of a voracious, unrestrained capitalism (that is again called "late capitalism," as it was in 1984 when Fredric Jameson started his discussion about postmodernism and multinational capitalism)—a financial capitalism that is more than just a cultural condition, it is our reality. To state that in neoliberal global capitalism *reality* and capitalism coincide means in the final analysis to say that the World is a Closed World. The impossibility of having another world makes difficult the radical criticism of this world, and this does not mean that critical thought is obliged to offer "alternatives," but, as argued by Santiago López Petit, a statement about a world that is a closed one makes it impossible to *perform politics*.

The identification of a distinction between contemporary capitalism and reality indicates on the one hand that there exists a series of historical forms of capitalism, and on the other hand, the coincidence of capitalism

and reality proves that capitalism has entered its "last" historical formation—the global age. This transformation that has happened to the working class, that is, its precarization and being forced into "mobility" (that is
a postmodern word with which to hide past colonialism and present
formats of seclusion, deportation and discrimination with which the First
Capitalist World handle/control/govern migration) has also had an impact on how we understand modernity, postmodernity, and today's global capitalism.

Therefore, if we take into consideration this trait, we can say that
neoliberal global capitalism is primarily about governance or governmentality, a control and redirection of actions; fundamentally it is conceived as a social plot, as argued by López Petit, whose units are businesses. Therefore, it is too simplistic, if not altogether misleading, to reduce neoliberal capitalist societies only and solely to a "homo economi-
cus" equation; it is necessary to take into consideration governance or
governmentality.

To come to a further point, López Petit states that it is necessary to
refresh our memory and bring to the forefront Ludwig von Mises (that
with Friedrich August von Hayek are the two most prominent economists and ideologists of liberalism). In his book *Human Action*, which he
wrote in 1949, Mises introduced *praxeology* as a framework for modeling
human action. From praxeology, Mises derived the idea that every conscious action is intended to improve a person's satisfaction. These utilitarian and behaviorist views would be generalized by Mises into an economic doctrine and from there it would be extended to the whole of
society. Mises prepared, in fact, the terrain by which to translate the
coinage known as "the life of the market" (developed by "pre-liberal"
economists) into "the life as market." From here it was only a step away
from today's usage and conceptualization of humanity—in Santiago
López Petit's words—as human capital. It is necessary to connect this
book with another. In 1948, Lawrence Wiener wrote *Cybernetics, or Control and Communication in the Animal and Machine*. Wiener's cybernetics
was coined to denote the study of the structure (as formulated on Wikipedia) of regulatory systems and is closely related to control theory and
systems theory: in a simple parlance, it is about control, governance, and
governmentality.

It is no surprise that presently on the Internet a debate is taking place
over a possibly more "emancipative" view on the so-called second order/
generation of cybernetics. It is possible to connect this debate on the
Internet with what Christian Marazzi defines as the "the crisis of the
governance of the U.S. as a monetary authority in the World" which is
the cause of the present financial bankruptcy (read: the biggest bank
robbery ever, performed by the bankers and managers themselves) in the
First Capitalist World, and with it, everywhere in the global world.
Nevertheless, the debate on second order cybernetics is another cry in the

desert, I would say, as it is an attempt to get rid of the historically "bad" cybernetics logic (that through recording, analyzing, and simulating has been designated to the "environment"). This bad logic is the so-called U.S. military hubris that has been made visible today, for example, through new analysis of reports on the Vietnam War. The question remains as to whether we can think of second order cybernetics as something less dangerous, that is an ideological claim that wants to connect second order cybernetics with some kind of purifying, new therapeutic ideas.

In order to grasp the logic of present capitalism—López Petit insists—it is important to include capitalist exploitation inside what he names "global mobilization," that is to say, inside the mobilization of our lives that (re)produces this obvious reality which crushes us and which is confused with our existence. Global mobilization coincides with total production. It is that which (re)produces this obvious reality in which we live. We alone inscribe ourselves within the global mobilization only as individuals. The individual is the unit of mobilization. López Petit emphasizes that in order to be able to advance in the study of the politicization of the social uneasiness; we have to formulate it more precisely: the unit of mobilization is the individual perceived as "conscience." The theory of private property that is at the core of capitalism becomes inseparable from the affirmation of the individual and his or her rights to property. One of the consequences is that in neoliberal capitalism; fundamentally the individual is an owner of himself, or more precisely of his or her own conscience.

López Petit reworks this point steadily. My conscience is constituted as a brand, and the brands—that are not so much material as immaterial and subjective—compete among themselves. The conscience as a commercial brand produces a universe of meanings and is obliged to signify and to reaffirm its existence; otherwise it disappears. Therefore, the conscience as a brand has to be externalized. López Petit states that *I* is not in relation to itself, because there exists no interiority. The interiority is exteriority: it is my brand. Global mobilization presents competitiveness without any piety among brands, mediated by money. This process of externalization (that says that individuals and their consciences are only able to act as part of the global mobilization) is actually accurately capturing another process of externalization that is the core feature of the process of financialization of capital.

In financial capitalism, profit can only be produced if the production process is externalized and turned toward other areas. Though the difference is crucial, this does not present an extension of production toward consumption, but consumption as the place of production as well. The financial capitalist mode of production implies an extension of production toward the reproductive spheres: toward education, health, arts, culture, and leisure. Therefore, of course, as stated by López Petit, all is bought and all is sold today, but global mobilization represents a further step beyond. Global mobilization is a war, the war for its brands, that is to say, to signify something for the other, and to be able to accumulate meaning in the shape of money. López Petit therefore makes a detailed analysis of the way in which biopolitics capitalizes and governs the conscience in the First Capitalist World.

Each brand mobilizes its resources (credibility, legitimacy, etc.) in order to obtain its own public. Therefore, the border between the private and public space is erased, intimacy is aired and becomes a pure Big Brother show, with the only private matter tolerated, states López Petit, being the religious one. The externalization of the conscience extends its transparency to all of reality. The reality is obvious because it is transparent. The brand is the only value, and to increase it is the objective. But López Petit is precise; here it is not about a commodification, as this would be too simple and the analysis would be a sociologist's preoccupation with consumerist culture. A possible solution in such a situation would be, according to López Petit, to oppose the brand(s) of the global mobilization against each other. But this would also be too cozy; what we would get in the end is a situation of polarity, active brands against the dead one, or the so-called *third way*; "a living zombie." But conscience that is externalized is not at all a dead person, on the contrary, it functions perfectly as part of the global mobilization. Brands are true semiotic motors, states López Petit, whose fuels are colors, sensations, feelings, etc. In short (and maybe coming to a point prematurely) all of López Petit's brilliant points can be summarized as: today life itself is the field of battle!

Marina Garcés, in her book *In the Prisons of the Possible*, states that contemporary capitalism is not circumscribed within the articulation of a determined economic system and its production, but subsumes all spheres of life, thus coinciding with reality itself in the final analysis. The outcome is a political consensus, called *democracy*, whose institutions no longer carry any political status, but are seen as an "environment" that can only be adjusted and improved but not subverted nor ousted. Garcés talks about the democracy-market in which anything can pass, or be taken for granted, and where the world is presented in its naked truth (Garcés 2002). Meaning: this is what it is! It is a terminal obviousness that presents a world not as open, but as closed and without a future, despite seeing such an intensified theoretical reworking of infinity. In the background of the unrestrainment of capital, it is nevertheless necessary to think about the limits of capital. But to say that the unrestrainment of capital means going over the limit is, as López Petit has stated, not at all what this event is about. Because the only limit of capital is capital itself, so the unrestrainment of capital is not about something outside of it (as is said about the crisis, being something "abnormal," and also something that will bring capitalism to its end); the unrestrainment of capital just means something more than capital.

López Petit links capital and power in the following ways: (1) Capital is more (than) capital and (2) Capital that is more than capital is power. Such a relation presents a new situation between capital and power, which is named by López Petit as the *co-propriety capital/power* (López Petit 2009, 30). Before we could talk about the *unity capital/power*. To this I will return later.

NATION-STATE, WAR-STATE

The co-propriety capital/power has according to López Petit three fundamental territories where capital and power own each other: innovation, public space, and war (López Petit 2009, 38).

Innovation: new information and communication technologies, biotechnologies, the pharmaceutical industry and science are proposed as fields of innovation with which we will supposedly overcome the present crisis. According to Marx, capital has historically increased the production of surplus value by further developing the technological processes in the working production and society—making it as technologically possible and thus exploiting it endlessly (Gržinić and Leban 2008). Thus it is not surprising that the solution for the current crisis by those in power is supposedly in massive investments in technological development. By the end the 1970s, as stated by Adolfo Gilly and Rhina Roux, Christopher Lasch had already argued that the notion of technological determinism is at the base of all popular comprehensions of industrial and technological revolutions (Gilly and Roux 2008). Lasch stated that it is taken for granted that changes in technology have been the main cause of industrialization, and that technological development is therefore seen as a pure revolution. Nevertheless, he argued, we have to be aware that new inventions, new processes and new applications of scientific discoveries do not put forward these same changes in order to ameliorate production. Therefore, according to Lasch, far from revolutionizing society, technological inventions primarily reinforce the existing privileges and the appropriation of surplus value by capitalism only.

Public space is increasingly privatized and depoliticized; instead of politics, we talk about catastrophes (ecological, educational).

War allows for the management of life through the capitalization of death (Iraq, Pakistan, and Afghanistan). It allows for a passage from biopolitics to necropolitics, and also a passage from nation-State to war-State. The nation-State is not a victim of globalization, as is constantly argued; rather the nation-State successfully adapts itself to globalization. We see this in the intensified measures that are implemented by nation-States in terms of the privatization of all public sectors, from education to health and culture, and also in the way that class division and racism are managed in our capitalist contemporaneity. Intensified racism, if we just think about EU legislative policy, presents processes of class racializations that are supported by new, constantly reinvented neo-colonial structures. For the unrestrainment of capital to handle conflicts, it needs a formal frame, and this is neoliberal capitalist democracy.

Democracy articulates two modes of power. As argued by López Petit, one is the war-State (governance and violence with brutal exploitation, expropriation, discrimination, repression), and the other is postmodern fascism (López Petit 2009, 84). The war-State is a pure necropolitical mode of life. War-State and postmodern fascism work as a grid of vertical and horizontal forces, and in order to escape Frederic Jameson's old cognitive mapping, we can think, I propose, of their working together as in the case of computed tomography (CT). CT creates an image by using an array of small individual X-ray sensors and a computer. By spinning the X-ray source, data is collected from multiple angles. A computer then processes information to create an image on the screen. This also means (as I have stated numerous times in the past) that it is not possible to understand global capitalism if we do not include new media technology, the digitalized mode of programming in its logic of functioning. Computed tomography (CT) is a specialized X-ray imaging technique. It may be performed, as it is stated in medical technical language, as "plain" or with the injection of a "contrast agent." Both are perfect mathemes for analysis.

It is used as "plain" in Africa, Kosovo, Chechnya, as well on the workers (without any rights and over-exploited) from the former Yugoslav republics now working in Slovenia, or when "just fixing" the situation with refugees, asylum seekers, illegalized migrants (hunting them in order to prevent them to enter the Fortress EU, secluding them in refugees centers, and/or deporting them to the other side of the European Union Schengen Area). Plain means with raw force.

Or as "contrast agent," in Iraq or Afghanistan or Pakistan. In these regions, major economic interests are at stake, such as petrol and heroin, vital for the United States, EU, etc., and therefore, to cover this up, it is necessary to have agents for a disguise and provoking misperception.

The other face of neoliberal global capitalism is postmodern fascism. It serves as the dissolution of the democratic state in a multi-reality of social technologies. Postmodern fascism, as stated by López Petit, is constructed on the autonomy of each individual and as such, is a self-governmentality that is based on the self-management of a proper autonomy. The war-State produces coherency. It homogenizes: its action is propaganda. Think of the mobilization of the masses against terrorism, for example. Postmodern fascism, on the other hand, is informal, non-coherent, as it is based on the autonomy of differences. It produces differences.

Its action is communication. All these differences are brilliantly described in the already mentioned book by López Petit (López Petit 2009, 87–88) .

I claim that the war-State, in its verticality—functioning by way of force, violence and fear—is but a pure fascist state. However, it would be too simple if we were to use historical fascism to name it, because we would fail to emphasize what is the major logic of dominance in the world today and this is the logic of war. The war-State definitely has elements of classical fascism: a sovereign leader, people, death as the management of life. While, on the other hand, there is also the neoliberal context of the autonomy of individuals, which is the neoliberal freedom of having rights to just be an individual brand. It is rightly so, as proposed by López Petit, to name it postmodern fascism. As López Petit says, postmodern fascism sterilizes the "Other," evacuates the conflict from public space and neutralizes the political. It is not strange that we continuously repeat that global capitalism is about depoliticization. Postmodern fascism works through a constant self-mobilization, just think about all these mobilizations after blockbuster music bands on world tours, or mourning the death of show business brands (Michael Jackson's death, etc.).

FROM POSTMODERN FASCISM TO NEOLIBERAL TURBO FASCISM AND BACK

Making reference to the aforementioned founding repetition of global capitalism (with which López Petit's says a system of hierarchy is reestablished that leads to a constant repetition of the center and the periphery) it is necessary to emphasize that former Eastern European States, notably former Yugoslavia—as almost a model deriving from a turbo neoliberal capitalist laboratory that exemplifies and expands upon intensified processes of deregulation, racialization and necropolitics in global capitalism—especially Serbia, have to pass (at the moment it is still there) through what Žarana Papić called Turbo-Fascism, before they will be ready to "embrace" postmodern fascism.

Turbo-Fascism was a term proposed by Žarana Papić (2002) in order to conceptualize in the 1990s in the Balkans, specifically in Serbia, hegemonic nationalisms, that is, national separatisms, chauvinist and racist exclusion or marginalization of (old and new) minority groups; all processes that were, and are, closely connected with patriarchal, discriminatory and violent politics against women and their civil and social rights.

I make reference to the coinage by the late Serbian theoretician and feminist scholar Žarana Papić that described the process at the end of the 1990s in Serbia, saying, "I am freely labeling this as Turbo-Fascism" (Papić 2002). She continues,

It is, of course, known that Fascism is a historical term; that the history of Nazi Germany is not the same as that of Milošević's Serbia. However, in post-modernist and feminist theory we speak of "shifting concepts," when a new epoch inherits with some additions concepts belonging to an earlier one, like, for instance the feminist notion of shifting patriarchy. In my view, we should not fear the use of "big terms" if they accurately describe certain political realities. (Papić 2002)

I think that what is conceived as the main characteristics of turbo-fascist elements of post-socialist transitional States which are heading toward fully developed neoliberal global capitalism (that has its own postmodern fascism) can be excellently implied in the present moment of many former Eastern European States, such as Armenia, Russia, Slovenia, Bulgaria, and as well Greece.

Therefore I quote Žarana Papić designation of turbo-fascism in present tense. She stated:

> Serbian Turbo-Fascism [she refers specifically to Serbia but we can extend this to the post-socialist former Eastern European countries and some old Western European countries as well] has its own concentration camps, its own systematic representation of violence against Others, its own cult of the family and cult of the leader, an explicitly patriarchal structure, a culture of indifference towards the exclusion of the Other, a closure of society upon itself. Upon its own past; it has a taboo on empathy and a taboo on multiculturalism; it has a powerful media acting as proponents of genocide; it has a nationalist ideology; it has an epic mentality of listening to the word and obeying authority. The prefix "turbo" refers to the specific mixture of politics, culture, "mental powers," and the pauperization of life: the mixture of rural and urban, pre-modern and post-modern, pop culture and heroines, real and virtual, mystical and "normal," etc. In this term, despite its naive or innocent appearances, fascism exists in its proper sense. Like all fascisms, Turbo-Fascism includes and celebrates a pejorative renaming, alienation, and finally removal, of the Other(s). Turbo-Fascism in fact demands and basically relies on this culture of the normality of fascism that had been structurally constituted well before all the killings in the wars started. (modified by Gržinić, based on Papić 2002)

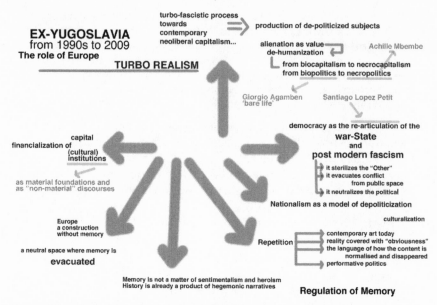

Figure 2.1. Diagram elaborated by M. Gržinić, realized by G. Cilla and V. Kostayola, 2011.

The above diagram bears as its central title: ex-Yugoslavia in the last twenty years with a focus on the regulation of memory. After the fall of the Berlin Wall in 1989 the role of "former" Western Europe (my quotation marks, as West Europe likes to call itself) has been centered in the re/composition of the former Eastern Europe, transforming it expediently into a defunct, concluded, obsolete and buried story. This process takes the shape of *turbo realism*. It presents a turbo trajectory from 1990 until today that goes from a transitional space of post socialism toward a space of/for a neoliberal global capitalism.

The turbo-fascist reality of the former space of Yugoslavia is to be connected with another, again more general, process that occurred after the 2001 that López Petit refers to as a change from nation-State to war-State. In fact this change means that the former Imperial capitalist colonial states (the so called Capitalist First World, West European States, and the United States) were transformed into war-States. At the same time the post-socialist countries (or neoliberal turbo fascist countries) remained just nation-States without an international sovereignty but with enough domestic power to control and systematically push homophobic terror and the systematic erasure of the socialist history; which includes the suppression of all counter or alternative and emancipatory leftist though modernist projects, practices, and interventions. Nationalism plays an important role as an atavistic format of ideology.

This process of turbo neoliberal fascism coincides with the general situation in neoliberal global capitalism as well and its production of an evacuated, privatized space that resulted in a process of depoliticization. The implications are at least twofold: for the modes of life and for the form of capital/power relation.

As developed earlier, we have two modes of life; Foucault's biopolitics ("make live and let die") and Mbembe's necropolitics that regulates life through the perspective of death ("let live and make die"). These two modes of life present a brutal difference in managing life and death. In biopolitics, life was under control but it was still about providing a "good" life (if only for the citizens of the sovereign first world capitalist countries), today this is more and more abandoned and what is at the hand is "let live" under harsh systems of surveillance; at the same time death is managed, used and capitalized by the war machine. Today in global neoliberal capitalism biopolitical and necropolitical modes of life reproduce themselves near one another; transforming many of the former biopolitical sovereign States into necropolitical ones. Finally the diagram refers to the regulation of memory as well as history. Memory is a question of biopolitics and history is the main terrain of necropolitics: it is constantly under attack, being erased, rewritten, and evacuated.

UNITY CAPITAL/POWER, CO-PROPRIETY CAPITAL/POWER

At end of the 1960s and in the beginning of the 1970s, (which is the beginning of what is theoretically called the *Great Transformation*, signifying the beginning of the transformation of the working class by way of its total decomposition, as stated by Sandro Mezzadra and Agostino Petrillo), capital had to free itself from the antagonistic force that had historically constituted it and correspondingly limited and conditioned it (López Petit 2009, 26). This defines precisely the change from Fordism to post-Fordism as the change of the mode of labor in capitalism that allowed for the new accumulation of capital. This change was induced in order to start a new cycle of capitalist accumulation. The Great Transformation brought a decomposition of society, politics and economy through a series of events which López Petit lists as: free circulation of capital, the fall of the Berlin Wall (and with it the collapse of communism), and the advancement of new media and digital technologies.

The downfall of the Berlin Wall in 1989 was not driven by humanist sensibility that "smart" political leaders in the West of Europe, in collaboration with "not so smart" (but more at the verge of being defunct) former communist political leaders, offered to the people of former Eastern Europe as an act of liberation from communist's totalitarianism. This was the outcome of the logic of repetition of the unrestrainment of capital. The creation in 1990 by West Germany of the Trust Agency named *Treuhandanstalt* that turbo privatized (in a turbo expedient period after the fall of the Berlin Wall) all publicly owned enterprises in former East Germany, (as explained in the first chapter), speaks clear in favor of this thesis. Similarly the war in Iraq was presented as freeing the Iraqi people; a similar scenario was put into motion in Afghanistan (i.e., to help the liberation of Afghan women from the burka). In the first case (Iraq) it was oil that was at stake and in the second (Afghanistan) heroin, both vital for the imperial contemporary war-States.

The effect of this transformation is the present decomposition of society, the changed status of the nation-State (as we have presented, not a disappearance but) an explosion of inequalities; for example with migrants in Europe today seen as an underclass and Roma being ferociously attacked.

Therefore, nationalisms, chauvinisms, racisms, homophobic madness and anti-Semitism are all processes that were and are used precisely to canalize the intensified effects of the Great Transformation. It is no surprise that they are most visible in the former Eastern European context, where they function as a genuine buffer to hide the "truth" that the fall of the Berlin Wall was necessary not to bring freedom, etc., but to adjust the limit (and not just to go beyond the limit) in order to provide new possibilities for capital accumulation.

Carlo Galli reported in his book *Political Spaces: The Modern Age and the Global Age* [Espacios políticos. La edad moderna y la edad global] (quoted after López Petit 2009, 28) that the modern space was a space that was constituted by a plurality of interests and ideologies, but I emphasize that neoliberal globalization is something else. It presents an inextricable complexity, which means it is not a pluralistic space but a space in which complexity does not permit *extrication*. It is therefore a space that is not at all plural, but one that cannot be disentangled or untied. Achille Mbembe, in his analysis of Africa as the "postcolony," envisioned precisely such a process, which he calls *"entanglement."*

If we try to delineate a genealogy of a short but a dramatic restructuring of the composition of capital and its consequences for the historicization of capitalism, then we have to take into account its transformation that started in the 1970s and that today, as stated by López Petit, has come to its end. This is why we talk about global capitalism and its logic of financialization.

The transformation that is named the *Great Transformation* presents the dis-articulation of politics, of the economy, and of the social life of the working class (the main protagonist of capitalism and its cycle of struggles in the 1970s). This period is best illustrated by Margaret Thatcher and the class struggle at the time of Thatcher against the miners in Great Britain, or in Poland by Solidarnost. The outcome was a rearticulation, or, a mode of re-exploitation of the working class through its dis-articulation that transformed it into a new motor for capital. The working class, through processes of precarization, was transformed "from an obstacle to capital into its new motor." It is also necessary to take into consideration new media technology and scientific developments ("the banal" event of MTV, or the Internet) that started to be of enormous importance already at that time.

In contrast to the society of discipline, the society of control extends its control outside the structured sites of social institutions through "flexible and fluctuating networks." One such example, the case of Google's intervention into mobile phones market by offering an open-source operating system for VoIP phones that includes a GPS function alerting friends or signaling contacts that are in the immediate vicinity of the user, is a mode of such "playful" control. In the United States, Google has already managed to internalize entire cityscapes by photographing them systematically and pasting the results into three-dimensionally rendered and geo-coordinated representations used for environmental analysis and simulation, allowing business profit to radically change (read: to fully privatize) the urban environment. It is claimed that digital technologies are allowing for processes of networking and exchange that are being performed in the "immaterial" space of information and are virtually "free." But if we think of Information Communication Technology (ITC) and their owners as monopolizing "the free world" of communication and making profits as owners of these protocols and networks, then we see that private property and profit are their major regulators.

Therefore, globalization cannot be explained in terms of one single displacement of the limit because it stays within the limit of capital; which is its very motor of unrestrainment and functions with the logic of repetition. As stated by López Petit, it is about thinking of the event of the unrestrainment of capital as its new way of accumulation. The consequences of the Great Transformation that brought the complete decomposition of society in the sole interest of capital were extracted from the terrain of politics and shifted into the space of culture. It was also the beginning of the advancement of theories about the cultural turn (with Fredric Jameson) that allowed for the unbelievable expansion of cultural studies in the realm of theory; a process of "culturalization" of politics and the economy instead of the "re-politicization" of political economy.

The Great Transformation presents a shift in the relation between capital and power. Before the disarticulation of the working class we could talk, via López Petit, about the *unity capital/power*; in the course of the Great Transformation we see the dismantlement of this unity and its transformation into the *co-propriety capital/power*. Therefore, this relation can be historicized, and it changes with the historical/present mode of capitalism. The changes are not a question of a nice established narrative, but they do show a process of intensification of the processes of expropriation and exploitation carried out in accordance with each specific historical moment of capitalism. The discussion pushed forward by Paolo Virno regarding the important shift from Fordist to post-Fordist mode of labor in capitalism can also be reworked, as proposed by López Petit, as a shift from unity to co-propriety of capital/power (López Petit 2009, 35–36).

This unity capital/power presented a social pact between workers and capitalists (i.e., the bourgeoisie) and the outcome was capitalist social democracy that brought—not as a generous gift but as a process of a struggle—social, health, and pension benefits for the workers (the welfare-State was the most advanced form of this unity). The syndicates/ unions had an extremely important role in this process. López Petit argues that the class struggle was functioning so to speak within the plan of capital. Capitalism needed a pact in order to make surplus value; moreover, the way labor functioned within the composition of capital production presented the only way for capital to survive.

The socialist planning State that was/is rarely part of the discussion in the West (and if it is, then only as a totalitarian restriction of working rights) was the best example of this unity. Therefore, it is possible to say that the imposed vision of socialism as only and solely totalitarian was necessary in order to hide the best example (of the already realized nightmarish form) of the West's Fordism, which was the socialist planning State. Former Yugoslavia was almost a role model at the time, but was hidden; while today, being a true historical model, it is being presented in numerous panels in the East and West as a brand (I will argue) for a defunct future. The Socialist planned economy was the perfect display of what was in Fordist capitalism, so to speak, hidden.

When the unity capital/power was threatened, the response (better to say, the punishment) by capitalists, as explained by López Petit, was exemplary. López Petit talks of true social engineering methods of punishment (and not of the "control" that is connected with post-Fordism) that were presented in a vertiginous form of inflation, and open-ended crisis, etc. This is why the penalization of the miners by Margaret Thatcher in Great Britain in the 1980s, when post-Fordism was already in the house so to speak, was so exemplarily tough (what we witnessed was "class struggle" in the West at its purest).

In Socialism, the State responded to this threat not only with inflation (which was used as a repressive apparatus in capitalism anyway), but also with true food shortages (that proliferated, in the last decades of the 1970s and 1980s, in humorous narratives of how to get a cup of coffee). It is clear that such narratives are today needed (especially for former East Germany) in order to prevent the study of the period and especially to prevent the study of what it is that we can conceptualize regarding these relations today.

In the background of the unrestrainment of capital is the absence of the limit of capital, but beware, it is not about going beyond the limit. Therefore, the crash of the neocons and neoliberals is not to be the end of globalization, but its continuation—though maybe (I repeat, maybe) without a neoliberal ideology (or, to put it differently, with a neoliberal ideology that is modified), because, as stated by López Petit, neoliberal globalization, or global capitalism, is a historical form of capitalism.

Therefore, to recapitulate what we have so far, it is possible to say that there exists two modes of the relation between capital and power. One is the unity capital/power and the other is co-propriety capital/power. The co-propriety capital/power signifies a mutual drive, force, push of capital, and power. Capital is going further over its limit thanks to power, and, as stated by López Petit, at the same time, power expands thanks to capital. We saw this with the proposal not only to rescue Wall Street and U.S. banks from collapsing in November 2008 by the U.S. Senate, but also a shift of capital's voracity onto the level of morality. When capital pushes power beyond it (further away from it), and, inversely, when power pushes capital, then we effectively start to explicate the unrestrainment of capital. Co-propriety means that there exists interchangeability in between them, allowing for mutual substitution, but under a condition, with a proviso, emphasized by López Petit, that they have to maintain their specific identity; or, to them is given a status of equivalence, but under the condition, with a proviso, of maintaining their difference.

NOTES

1. See http://maiz.at
2. See Walter Mignolo's presentation in the framework of the project "Estéticas Decoloniales" (Decolonial Aesthetics) organized by Walter Mignolo (Argentina, USA), Pedro Pablo Gómez (ASAB, Bogota) and others in Bogota, Colombia, November 7–12, 2010.

THREE

Southeastern Europe and the Question of Knowledge, Capital, and Power

I want to rethink further some of the processes implemented in Southeastern Europe in order to explore the logic of global capitalism, the changes it brought to the territory, the understanding of hegemony, democracy, zoning, ideology, and "underdevelopment." Southeastern Europe (which, for the purpose of clarification, consists of Albania, Bosnia-Herzegovina, Bulgaria, Croatia, Greece, Kosovo, Macedonia, Montenegro, Romania, Serbia, and Slovenia) has come to be synonymous with animosity between the above States.

If one looks at the political agenda of the States classified by the European Union (EU) as part of the Southeastern European region, becoming a Member State of the European Union is a common feature of their process of dis-affiliation with the Southeastern European region. With the exception of Greece, which has been a member of the European Union since 1981, and Slovenia, which became a member on May 1, 2004, and followed by Bulgaria and Romania in the second wave of enlargement of EU (January 1, 2007), the "rest" of the region within Southeastern Europe has been currently renamed—the "West Balkans."

This occurred when the term Southeastern Europe was used as part of the 2008 EU conference held in Ljubljana, Slovenia. Therefore the process of *zoning* (as we call this shifting of names), is one that changes the territory from one paradigmatic space of economic interest to another paradigmatic space of economic interest and that coincidentally requires transformations in judicial, political, and cultural prerogatives to conform to EU needs. The most important condition that the "Southeastern/ West Balkans rest" must satisfy to be eligible to enter the future EU membership is the establishment of a functioning *democracy*, with its coincident rule of embracing fully the (neoliberal capitalist) law. Kosovo offers a paradigmatic example of this shift.

NATIONALISM

Nationalism has surfaced as the prevalent mode in which social and political life is organized in countries of the former Eastern Europe. Since the fall of the Berlin Wall, the countries comprising Southeastern Europe have been considered *transitional*. It is said that the appearance of nationalism only presents what has been already there for decades, but had been successfully suppressed during the past socialist and communist periods, and came overtly out with the "liberation" of these countries from under the totalitarian communist system. Our thesis is that nationalism is, contrary to such a claim, the mode in which the present transitional elites (from the East of Europe, helped by those from the West of Europe) buffer or hide their direct submission to neoliberal global capitalism—in short, nationalism is the way they hide their readiness to open their countries to the worse possible exploitation and expropriation by capital.

This nationalism is also supported by the EU, even more so by the old (West Europe) EU core, as they need the disorder and pathology of nationalist social and political spaces in order for them to execute the allocation of capital. What does the implementation of neoliberal global capitalism mean? In the former Eastern European context (where some parts are renamed as present Southeastern Europe and/or West Balkans) it means an intensifying process of expropriation and exploitation that is connected with losing historically gained social rights (rights to health insurance, to social benefits, to work, etc.). The paradox, of course, is that losing social rights is presented as gaining neoliberal "capitalist freedom and democracy" (this shift in reality means being forced into a condition of wild precariousness and instability, marked by a loss of jobs and rights). To be socially de-privileged, without social, health, and labor rights, today means being "emancipated" within neoliberal global capitalism. This is presented through a system of intensified rationalizations (read: real shortages, etc.) that are imposed with radicalized management control as well as with extreme privatization of the social, political, and economic space.

In the Western European context, this means the total embracing of the biopolitical machine as a force regulating every level of the capitalist system. The past capitalist "social" State, the so-called 1970s capitalist *welfare-State* (a product of capitalist social democratic vision) is dismantled today as well, though the reasons behind this are presented differently (different histories are constructed and different vocabularies are implemented). In Eastern and Western Europe, the vision of public interest does not exist anymore. Public health insurance, public social insurance, public education, and other public interests are being slowly and steadily privatized. In both contexts what is at stake is depoliticization, eschewing the social contradiction (class antagonism) from the social and political space.

Depoliticization in the East and West of Europe is the core logic of functioning, but it is presented differently. To "smoothly" handle these over-intensified privatizations, two different processes are implemented. In the "former" West, a process of radical individualization, as biopolitical subjectivity, is pushed forward, where the individual is presented as a manager of her/himself; seen as the most effective element of neoliberal global capitalism. Conversely, due to the incomplete process of capitalization, which prevents the smooth implementation of the complete fragmentation of the social and political space through radical individualization, to the former East (presently seen as Southeastern Europe and/or West Balkans) has been imposed a process of national "unification." The result is nationalism, a pathological model that provokes social disorder and allows capital allocation to bring order.

Accordingly, nationalism is in fact a model of depoliticization that is simultaneously embraced differently by both the Right and Left political elites. While the Right political parties in the transitional countries rely on nationalism and feed themselves with it (and also use it in such a way as to capitalize upon their own position), the Left political forces have to make a double turn. On the one hand, they have to de-link themselves, at least on the surface, from right-wing nationalistic forces. On the other hand, they have to de-link themselves from what was left from the working class from the past that still pushes forward political demands. The latter de-linking is necessary to prove their proper position as *apolitical* neoliberal managerial depoliticized capitalist forces. In order to enter the big family of the depoliticized EU (which is, on the other side, harshly organized, framed and made into a *Fortress Europe* through measures of intensified administrative, bureaucratic acts, and acts of law), the left transitional political forces have to prove their capability to de-link themselves from past communism which is today placed on the same level as Nazism. On January 27, 2006, The Council of Europe Parliamentary Assembly (PACE), which brings together parliamentarians from forty-six European countries, passed a resolution that for the first time strongly condemned the crimes committed by totalitarian communist regimes. The resolution urges former Eastern European communist countries to modify their textbooks and to build monuments for victims of the totalitarian communist regimes, therefore, prompting a paradoxical form of an obscene "de-Nazification." As it has been argued by many writers it would be "easier" to take the condemnation of communist State crimes seriously if the EU denounced the far bloodier record of European colonialism, which was a system of racist despotism that dominated the World in Stalin's time and before.

One consequence of these superficially claimed paradoxical demands (that is consistent with the process of total depoliticization) is the use of gender as the marker with which to testify and to "check" the process of emancipation of a certain territory. Instead of talking about politics or changes brought about by neoliberal global capitalism, we are forced to talk about a certain situation, for example, of "emancipation" through gender zoning of a certain territory. This act is then presented as a new way of politics.

I have already stated that the Left transitional political elite have to prove clearly that they are capable of performing and embracing depoliticization in a proper State in order to be embraced by their Western comrades. In the 1990s, after the fall of the Berlin Wall, we witnessed the development of capitalist society, with its tendency to instill brutal exploitation (coming near to enslavement) and bureaucratic violent formalization (of responsibilities, etc.) into every level of society. The former Left (now transitional neoliberal managers) despises workers and their demands for political answers. From the leftist perspective, the working class should be a political force aiming for change, but this class is so demeaned as to make the leftist intellectuals ashamed of being connected to it. On the Right side, a whole strata of society (sexual minorities, migrant minorities, etc.) are identified as disrupting national unity (Greif 2008), which is associated increasingly with the "decent" people of the nation through a mechanism of clearly chauvinistic and racist processes. In Serbia, Slovenia, Slovakia, and Romania, it is the Roma people who are targeted. In France, it is the second and third generations of French citizens from the colonies; in Austria, refugees and migrants. Intellectuals, artists, cultural workers, and theoreticians are also distancing themselves from what is being increasingly publicly identified as "lower class elements."

Therefore, in parallel to what was defined as the unique cultural postmodernism of former Yugoslavia (in the 1980s), another process has to be envisioned and elaborated, a process that would permeate the culture, social fabric, politics, and economy of former Yugoslavia and all its respective republics that are today new states in Europe. It was a process of the construction of second-rate citizens in Serbia, Croatia, Slovenia and throughout former Yugoslavia, based on the myth of lost ancient territories disseminated by communist party nomenclature and the military apparatus of former Yugoslavia that started the "Balkan war" there in the 1990s.

The war resulted in a massive annihilation of people, an *ethnic cleansing*, and the destruction of cities; all hastened to emblematic cases of contemporary genocides after World War II in the heart of Europe. The Srebrenica massacre, also known as the Srebrenica genocide, refers to killings in July 1995 during the "Balkan war" in Bosnia and Herzegovina when more than 8,000 Bosnians (Bosnian Muslims), mainly men and boys, were slaughtered in and around the town of Srebrenica (Bosnia and Herzegovina) by units of the Army of Republika Srpska (in BiH) under the command of General Ratko Mladić, supported by Slobodan Milošević and by the mass media and public opinion in Serbia.

After the war the ethnic cleansing continued through a myriad of processes of racialization, dispossession, exploitation and deregulation. Žarana Papić (2002) described this process in Serbia with the notion of neoliberal *Turbo-Fascism*. It has at its core a racialization that refers to the assigning of racial connotations to those termed as (ethnic) minorities. These processes are judicially, economically, discursively and, last but not least, representationally conceived and normativized, and they have started to metastasize more and more.

Alternately, the only possible unity that is proposed and tolerated is the organic national body that is actually based on the old ideology of blood and soil that therefore has to expel from the nation (seen as "natural") body all who threaten it (from im/migrants to ethnic Roma to non-heterosexual groups). The results of such nationalistic operations in Slovenia are the *Erased People*. Slovenia (not Slovakia) was seen for a long as a case of successful transformation from a totalitarian socialist republic in a miniature capitalist nation-State. However in 2013 it then presented itself as a flop, a ruin, increasingly disintegrating with unemployment, misery, bribery, merciless privatization of social and health facilities, and with a political nomenclature that is ready to be driven to the court at any moment, if such an instrument to do this were to exist! Many of the features that are concentrated in Slovenia specifically due to its small size and lack of critical mass are interesting for us as it has as part of its history and present a case of what is called the *Erased People*. This is possible to be seen as a clear necropolitical measure in the heart of contemporary Europe, (even before the term *necropolitics* was coined by Achille Mbembe).

WHO ARE THE ERASED PEOPLE?

The *Erased People* are 30,000 people from ex-Yugoslavia that had their residency rights taken away in Slovenia in 1991 and 1992 because they were "of other ethnicity." They lost the right to work, social care, everything. They simply stopped existing in the eyes of Slovenia.

How did this happen? In February 1992, at the time when Slovenia was still in its infancy, the Slovenian government, which was headed by then-Prime Minister Lojze Peterle (offically Alojz Peterle, a member of the European Parliament since 2004) and the Minister for Internal Affairs, Igor Bavčar (with the support of the State Secretary of the Ministry for

Internal Affairs, Slavko Debelak), adopted a macabre necropolitical measure of erasure, transforming 30,000 people into people without residency permits and depriving them of any rights. These 30,000 people were mostly workers and internal migrants that were working and living in Slovenia; they were of non-Slovenian ethnic roots, Bosniaks, Croats, Serbs, Roma people, Kosovars, Macedonians, etc.

What happened on February 26, 1992 was the total confiscation of their status of permanent residence, and this confiscation was triggered by a simple bureaucratic telegram sent by Slavko Debelak on that same date, February 26, 1992. The number of the telegram is 0016/4-14968. Slavko Debelak was at the time subordinate to Igor Bavčar. Janez Drnovšek was elected president of the Slovenian government in April 1992. Matevž Krivic refers to the recorded transcription of the first meeting of Drnovšek's cabinet in June 1992, when Bavčar, being the Minister of Internal Affairs in Drnovšek's government as well, informed him about the "problem regarding the violation of human rights in Slovenia."

In the 2000s Igor Bavčar, due to his political connections, was one of the most influential capitalists in Slovenia and in charge of the multinational corporation Istrabenz which he "succeeded" through privatization processes to completely ruin (Istrabenz was one of the most prosperous corporations of Slovenia). Bavčar transformed the corporation into a "death world," and left workers without jobs or futures. Though this is all known he did not face (yet?) any legal charges. To put an even clearer light on the 1992 event through the darkness of the present reality, lets read carefully how the 1992 case is explained by the *Erased People* themselves:

> It is important to state that the status of permanent residence, at least in a state of law, that respects human rights, can be obtained or confiscated only on the basis of law, administrative acts, or court decisions. The status of permanent residence is provided by birth or through other legal means. This status provides duties and rights. Slovenia was in 1992 the legal successor of the former common federative state of Yugoslavia, together with permanent residents appurtenant to it, regardless of the nationality, sex, race, or religion of respective individuals. The basic existential status of the Erased has been taken from them without any law, legal act, or notification, only by a simple telegram!
> (*Journal for Critique of Science, Imagination and New Anthropology* 2008)

On June 26, 2012 the Grand Chamber of The European Court of Human Rights (ECtHR), a supra-national or an international court established by the European Convention on Human Rights, based in Strasbourg, France, found that Slovenia failed to provide effective domestic remedies which would enable *Erased People* to regularize their legal status. Slovenia also interfered with the *Erased People*'s rights to protection of private and family life. The dealine for setting up the compensation scheme for *Erased People* by the Slovenian State expired on June 26, 2013.

After twenty years Slovenia did not repair the necropolitical measures with which it victimized thousands of people simply because of their ethnicity; they were pushed into a complete social, political and economic death, many suffered extreme isolation and many died or disappeared after being deported out of Slovenia in the 1990s at the time of the Balkan war.

The European Union continuously speaks of how everything is becoming increasingly democratic as well as liberal and open to democratic possibilities and potentialities. However, in reality we witness fascist tendencies, racist public speeches and a torrent of attitudes of hate. These tendencies have become normalized and cohabit easily with the neoliberal capitalist machine, which is disgustingly tolerant of the social and political processes of discrimination. In order to further understand the situation, we must both consider historical factors and analyze contemporary forms of racism within Europe and the rest of the world that are hidden behind different rhetoric. The Italian contemporary philosopher Domenico Losurdo (2005) stated that in order to understand historical and contemporary imperialism, it is necessary to endorse the analysis of liberalism (at present, neoliberalism is the major ideology of global capitalism) and the analysis of colonialism, which forms the foundation of Western imperial wealth.

GENDER AND ZONING

The changes brought about by neoliberal global capitalism force the space of Southeastern Europe to address "emancipation" through gender zoning. I refer here to a massive exhibition project that took place in Vienna on the twentieth anniversary of the fall of the Berlin Wall in Europe in 2009. The exhibition *Gender Check— Femininity and Masculinity in the Art of Eastern Europe* was presented in the Museum of Modern Art (MUMOK) in Vienna and was curated by Bojana Pejić, an art historian who has lived in Berlin for the two last decades and who was an important figure in the Student Cultural Center in Belgrade, Serbia in the 1970s and 1980s.[1]

My reasons for inclusion of the exhibition in this specific chapter are three-fold. The exhibition provides us with, first, with a platform for developing new ways of thinking about the relation between capital and power. Secondly, it was produced and financially underwritten by the ERSTE Foundation: a foundation that manages the ERSTE Bank. Finally, theoretical analysis of the exhibition's numerous ERSTE Foundation-funded projects has tended to understand them to be "art and cultural interventions" — that is, made by the Vienna-based multinational bank corporation ERSTE, to save the face for their invasive allocation of capital mostly throughout the former Eastern European territory.

First Thesis

This "new situation" only reconfirms what was stated by Santiago López Petit in his book *Global Mobilization: A Brief Treatise for Attacking Reality*—namely—that global capitalism today has two major characteristics. One feature of global capitalism is its reversibility—it is not an irreversible process but rather a reversible and conflictual event that is nothing more than the repetition of the unrestrainment of capital. The second feature is the co-propriety of capital/power. This second feature was unconsciously presented by the ERSTE Foundation's temporary ownership of cultural, artistic, and educational institutions like MUMOK, "freely" endowing the project in order to get money in return.[2]

The invitation to the exhibition did not mention any of the included artists' names. This is something that would not be possible if Western artists were taking part in the show. One of the reasons for this "omission" by ERSTE, MUMOK, and the curator (that were passing the "problem" to each other) was that more than 200 artists were invited. What is described here is not a joke; it is banal evidence of the status of Eastern European artists, though this banality has its theoretical framework.

One of the most challenging presentations at the symposium, organized immediately after the opening of the *Gender Check— Femininity and Masculinity in the Art of Eastern Europe* exhibition, was the lecture by Vjollca Krasniqi (a theoretician from Prishtina, Kosovo). In her talk entitled "Returning the Gaze: Gender and Power in Kosovo," she presented a reading of the neocolonial capture of Kosovo by the European Union. Her analysis showed that the processes of discrimination and racialization that are presently implemented by the EU in Kosovo are all presented as needed for the "emancipation" of Kosovars. Krasniqi made clear that the discrimination imposed on Kosovo/Kosovars by the EU is necessary (in the view of the EU) in order for Kosovars to become, as she stated, "mature political subjects" ready for future entrance into the EU. She clearly indicated that "becoming mature" is only possible through changing Kosovo into a neoliberal capitalist protectorate, where maturity is practiced as an infantilization of the citizens of Kosovo and their constant discrimination. Similarly, I can state that the few Eastern European artists who were after all listed as participating in the "Gender Check" exhibition were chosen on the presupposition that they were "mature" enough to be listed as part of the various CVs of different institutions (ERSTE, MUMOK, the curator).

I can also state, quoting Goldie Osuri who refers to Arjun Appadurai's "*Number in the Colonial Imagination*" (Appadurai 1993, 314–339), that the "Gender Check" exhibition can be conceptualized as a juncture of a certain *colonial epistemology* committed to constructing a certain space of visibility and *necropolitical governmentality* for the unnamed artists in the show. Appadurai talks of a specific way of constituting the colony (in contemporary times, such logic can be applied to Iraq, etc., which is the case in Osuri's brilliant analysis of Iraq necropolitics) with what he calls the concept of *"enumerative community."* As was repeatedly stated in the exhibit's opening speeches, "Gender Check" is not about Eastern and Western Europe (and therefore the word "East" is actually a mistake in the title of the exhibition), but rather, I would say, about establishing a colonial logic of producing "the former Eastern Europe" as an enumerative community of some 200 artists presenting more than 400 works. The division between East and West is not at stake here. Rather, what is at stake is the making of the neoliberal capitalist logic of governmentality workable. Necropolitics is always established in the post-colony through a counting that allows for an infinity of statistics, which collectively clears the social, political, and conceptual space of meaning.

In "Gender Check," some bodies or more precisely, some *nameless* bodies, (as the invitation that was sent to "everybody," so to speak, did not list a single artist's name, except the name of the artist from the invitation's cover image) were taken to stand for other bodies, because of the "enumerative principle of metonymy." Additionally, metaphor and metonymy were used to produce meaning throughout the exhibition, bypassing the social and political. It would not be possible to invite speakers from Austria or "Former Western Europe" (as they like to call it these days) and not have them listed! The enumerative logic implemented in the construction of the exhibition also comes close to a logic of constituting protectorates and zones of control through "genderization." A neo-liberal capitalist procedure of governmentality is applied, through gender, onto the whole territory of the East of Europe, after having been successfully used on the much more mature terrain of the West of Europe.

The term "genderization" (Perera 2006) in this paradigm, presents not a gentle "gendering" process, but a brutal colonial logic of forced subjugation of the whole territory of former Eastern Europe to Western practices of gender that are transformed into a mechanism of control and normalization. "Gender Check" is a repetition of the gender mainstreaming from Western Europe onto a territory that requires less subtle mechanisms of checking.

Second Thesis

It was repeatedly stated that the exhibition is not about Eastern and Western Europe, as they do not exist anymore. This was a paradoxical statement coming from the curator, donors, and panelists, as the title of the show was *Gender Check— Femininity and Masculinity in the Art of East-*

ern Europe. This paradox encourages us to ask: What is the logic that organizes a possibility to declare that the borders are gone?

The so-called imbalance between Eastern and Western Europe today is no longer a question of opposition, but rather of repetition. It is the same repetition I suggested when speaking of global capitalism—a repetition of one event alone (according to López Petit): capital's lack of restraint.

However, this repetition does not involve a process of mirroring, if this was the case we would then talk about repetition bringing the enjoyment of minimal difference. The repetition that is repeated presents a repetition of one part within the other. Today, there is a lot of talk about the disturbance between the nationalistic East of Europe and the neoliberal West of Europe. But as we can see, we are witnesses to a repetition of the neoliberal capitalist West amidst the nationalistic East, but they do not disturb, so to speak, each other, but reinforce each other.

Based on Ugo Vlaisavljević's insights in "From Berlin to Sarajevo," I can claim that the fall of the Berlin Wall, and consequent disappearance of the border dividing the East and West, while enthusiastically celebrated, results from the wrong conceptualization of the border itself (Vlaisavljević 2009, 23–25). Maybe it is necessary to rethink the concept of the border and to ask: What does this present celebration of the fall of the Berlin Wall really mean? Ugo Vlaisavljević, referring to Étienne Balibar, points to a process in Europe that states that the way we perceive borders changes, and with this change, we can conceptualize Europe differently as well.

Vlaisavljević states that the best way to understand the position within the EU is to actually look toward the borders that have been established by it within those states that are not integrated into it. Balibar, reactualized by Vlaisavljević in his text, is presented as the theoretician who had already begun to identify a process of change in the definition of borders in his major works about Europe in the 1990s. Balibar envisioned a process of simultaneous fragmentation and multiplication of borders on the one hand, and a disappearance of certain borders on the other. In 1997, he posited that the borders are flexing, though he warned that this does not mean that they are disappearing. On the contrary, borders are becoming multiplied and diminished in their localization and in their function, stretched or doubled, becoming zones, regions, border-*territories*. Precisely what is at stake here is a reversed relation between "borders" and "territories": borders, after the fall of the Berlin Wall, started to be transformed into zones (Balibar 1997, 386–387).

One consequence of establishing zones or territories instead of fixed borders is that the question of borders disappears so that the physiognomy of the border can change radically. We do not talk about Eastern and Western Europe anymore, but about the transformation of an entire territory into a zone which functions in such a way that it becomes a (new) border. Vlaisavljević clearly points out that this is the function of a new territory called the "Western Balkans," which has the function of just such a border-zone.

If we take this point, which was almost prematurely developed in the 1990s, and only coming into full maturity now, then it is not only "insulting" to talk about Eastern and Western Europe (especially about former Eastern Europe, as it has been distorted through its repetition in the format of the "former Western Europe"), but it is also necessary to implicate "Gender Check" in a process of genderization as border-zoning. It constitutes former Eastern Europe as a border-zone, transforming it into a field for testing the level of genderization of the whole territory. In the last few years gender was appropriated by Western neoliberal global capitalism, and gender mainstreaming subsequently saw a dramatic uptake throughout all of "former Western Europe." Therefore, the twentieth anniversary commemoration of the fall of the Wall is the commemoration of the fall of a paper wall, as other walls are in the meantime still built of concrete and present the border as a zone. This border-zone is not at all at the border, but it is inside the territory, or rather it could be said that the whole territory itself is the border now.

When the "Reading Gender: Art, Power, and Politics of Representation in Eastern Europe" panel of the "Gender Check" symposium rhetorically asked, "Can Gender Speak East?" those who responded affirmatively were those who did not understand the changes that had affected former Eastern Europe or Europe as such. As the shifting of the border into a zone implies, the border is not a line or even a wall (which is why the fall of the Berlin Wall can be cherished so enthusiastically). The border, rather, presents a whole zone, and, as "Gender Check" illustrates, *gender* is such a bordered zone!

For this reason the other symposium panel (organized by the Western participants) was entitled "Fuck Your Gender," clearly suggesting that gender mainstreaming means the complicity of gender with neoliberal global capitalist governmentality. But for the former Eastern Europe, it seemed as though *gender* was still good enough, as *queer* was reserved for the West. The Western participants took *queer* and left *gender* for the East. Queer is to be seen in a certain dialectical genealogy that starts with feminism, passes through gender, and is today realized as a radically queered feminism. Because of gender mainstreaming (*male*streaming), we can see gender's failed, negative side.

Biljana Kašić suggests that it is necessary to emphasize "three ordering systems that are at play in feminism and Europe today: gender mainstreaming, the capitalist order, and the market-consumer dictate that includes control over representation" (Kašić 2008, 457). We can see that the "Gender Check" exhibition utilizes and blurs these systems, making none of them possible to be identified. "Gender Check" is therefore a mainstreaming of gender, in which the capitalist order shifts from borders to

60   *Chapter 3*

zones, and control over representation occurs through an enumerative logic; which is the new juncture between colonial epistemology and ne-cropolitical governmentality. To paraphrase Angela Mitropoulos, "Gen-der Check" normalizes an economy of sex, gender and sexuality, blurring the line that binds the zone to the border, as well as connecting sex and desire to race and (re-)production in a hegemonic way.

The reversal of borders into territories or zones suggests that borders are disappearing, and we can then cheerfully greet the fall of the Berlin Wall (as it is a paper wall) as a transformation into a zone that will be repeated as a border elsewhere. Vlaisavljević stated that the Berlin Wall is gone, but has been replaced by a bureaucratic process of visas, and that the border police are not at the borders anymore, but in the hearts of those cities that are not yet part of the EU. Within fortified embassy offices, policemen, rather than embassy and consular bureaucrats, keep the walls firmly standing. Today, as Vlaisavljević notes, the "former Western European" states' embassy personnel are more and more profes-sionalized bureaucratic police. Vlaisavljević stated that the integration into the EU starts before the future EU Member State is integrated. In short, Europe does not need the Berlin Wall anymore, as it has estab-lished invisible internal judicial police and managerial borders that func-tion as just as well.

The slogan of the unified Germany proclaimed in 2009: "Come, come to the country without borders"—the only problem being if you (we) happen to be, by "chance," in any of the many detention camps or deten-tion prisons in Germany or in similar facilities elsewhere in the EU, or if you (we) are waiting in line somewhere in "the land without borders," to get a visa or asylum papers.

FROM NATION-STATE TO WAR-STATE AND GLOBAL JUSTICE

In this third section I want to enlarge the analysis of Southeastern Europe even more. Actually, Southeastern Europe consists of seven mostly new states (Bosnia-Herzegovina, Croatia, Kosovo, Macedonia, Montenegro, Serbia, and Slovenia) that were created as a result of the war during the 1990s in the ex-Yugoslav "Balkan" space. In addition to these new South-eastern European states, other regions demanded autonomy, and in what follows I analyze this process in connection to global capitalism.[3]

Third Thesis

My major thesis is that the *proliferation* of new states after the fall of the Berlin Wall (in the so called post-Cold War era), notably in the South-eastern Europe, was only possible because of the simultaneous *disintegra-tion* of the Westphalian principle of the sovereignty of nation-States.

What the 1648 Peace of Westphalia established was a way of working and managing the World which remained in place almost until the fall of the Berlin Wall. The Westphalian model is recognized by international relations scholars as the modern, Western-originated power principle that established an international system of States, multinational corporations, and organizations as sovereign subjects. The *"proliferation-disintegration"* mechanism that took place with the fall of the Berlin Wall is based on two processes (working simultaneously but not necessarily visibly linked). Though entangled, these two processes are perceived as disconnected, and it is this logic that enabled great international powers to succeed in maintaining *order* in the mass of new states "reborn" with the fall of the Berlin Wall.

Therefore I can state that the "proliferation-disintegration" mechanism sustains the thesis developed by Santiago López Petit that global capitalism is nothing less than the repetition of one single event, which is the *unrestrainment of capital*. And what is more, unlike previous historical forms of capitalism, the repetition of the capital's lack of restraint requires two repetitions working at once. These two repetitions are the founding repetition and the de-foundational repetition, providing alibis for each other and hiding their constitutive entanglement.

The uneasiness provoked by the proliferation of new states therefore was not solved as in the past with world powers' direct and brutal force of control. Rather, it was resolved through an intensified process of disintegration of the Westphalian principle of nation-States' sovereignty and the transformation of imperial nation-States into war-States.

It is at this point that global justice enters the equation. What does global justice have to do with these changes? It facilitated, initiated, and implemented the transition of imperial nation-States to war-States and allowed for the proliferation of numerous new states without the old nation-State sovereignty. In the trajectory of capitalism's development we can grasp the notion of a transition of sovereignty from nation-State sovereignty to transnational institutions of power and war-State politics. This transition has curbed the sovereign nation-State since the 1990s. Until that moment the old nation-State prevailed, but today nation-States can no longer (Hazan 2010, 152) give amnesty, at least theoretically, to those who have committed war crimes, crimes against humanity, and genocide. In fact, we can clearly see the development of a new sovereign entity—the war-State.

Transitional justice and the demand for "universal" respect of human rights played a key role in this process. *Global justice* was the framework in which these processes were conceptualized and naturalized. This is why within such a context the question posed by Hazan—whether the 1999 NATO bombing of Yugoslavia, with the subsequent *de facto* partitioning of Kosovo, and the 2003 Iraq War reflect higher principles, or are simply the United States' and the West's promotion of their political and economic interests—is of primal importance. Those without economic and military power have to accept the universal, global capitalism protocol of international justice. This does not apply, however, when the interests of major power forces/war-States (the United States, Russia, and China) are at stake. In the case of Srebrenica for example it is therefore accepted by the International community that the Dutch soldiers/UN have no need to show repentance.[4]

Hazan points out the genealogical shift in the principle of universal justice from the 1990s to the present day, resulted from the second major reshuffling in the international community brought about by September 11, 2001. The major difference between post-1989 (the Fall of the Berlin Wall) and post 2001 (the Attacks on the World Trade Center Towers in New York) is that the majority of cases listed in the 2000s—unlike the 1990s "ethnical wars" (as they were called)—remain in open conflict or prosecuted on the basis of acts of terrorism. The cases from the 1990s involve societies themselves in transition: ex-dictatorships of South America, ex-Communist regimes of Central and Eastern Europe, the post-apartheid regime of South Africa (the Truth and Reconciliation Commission [TRC]) and the Rwandan genocide. In 1995, the victims of gross human rights violations were invited to go before the South African TRC and give testimony about their experience. This transition, as Hazan says, was less about "criminalization" than about a certain social reconstruction. In the 2000s, Belgian, British, New Zealand, and Spanish national courts (which acted under the principle of universal jurisdiction) developed tribunals and commissions of inquiry for international crimes (war crimes, crimes against humanity, and acts of terrorism).

According to Hazan, the history of transitional justice has three principal stages that frame a world we have been witnessing over the last twenty years. In these two decades we talk about the post-Cold War period that has changed the world radically. After the fall of the Berlin Wall, globalization shaped a new global world in order to allocate capital and privatize public goods as well as to make profit.

The first period described by Hazan focuses on the steps that satisfy the post-Fordist model of labor mobility and connects to waning dictatorship(s). It began with the Argentinian truth commission's establishment and ended with the 1995 South African TRC. If the first stage had a clear division, with perpetrators on the one side and the victims on the other, the second stage was marked by a transition and multiplication of ethnic identities. Occurring in the 1990s, the second stage overlaps with the first, but differs radically from it. It covers the former Yugoslavia and the construction of ICTY International Criminal Tribunal for the former Yugoslavia in 1993 that failed to stop the 1995 Srebrenica genocide.

The second period stretches from 1992 to 2001. It is characterized by the governmentalization and judicialization of international relations, putting the post-Cold War into administrative, legal forms. This period is described as *multiculturalist,* but it hides its judicialization of the entire global capitalist society, and even of culture, as the lawsuits against U.S. artists from Andreas Serrano to Critical Art Ensemble illustrate. The second period ends in 2001, when global capitalism is enthroned with a new format of the nation-State—the war-State (the United States, Britain, etc.) that demands and shapes justice. If the first and second stages deal with the fall of the Berlin Wall, now it is time to get rid of the curtain and open up the full setting of a newly elaborated capitalism that needs markets, cheap labor, and administrative frameworks.

After 2001, criminalization replaces the reconciliation and restoration that characterized the 1990s. The war-States represent great powers while the new nation-States are transitional in their restricted sovereignty or lack of any sovereignty; artificially constructed through a biotechnological process of military intervention and capital allocation. The State of Kosovo was born in vitro, without any self-determination, but by a decree by international power(s), namely the United States.

Fourth Thesis

What Hazan describes with these stages, is in fact, I would insist, the change of the biopolitical into the necropolitical, where acts of genocide and human rights violations are managed by "administrative sciences." As Hazan notes, separating transitional justice into different periods also emphasizes its successive reorientation. It reveals a purely instrumental vision—that of the "toolbox"—that tends to hide: the ideological changes, the intervention of new actors, the role of Great Powers—in one word, transitional justice's relation to *politics.*

If we look closer to South Africa, it presented the promise of restorative justice in the 1990s—the new social engineering of transitional justice. In the context of South Africa, the contradictory demands for justice and amnesty—namely—resulted in a compromise, and "it was a process with which the incapacity of rendering justice was transformed into the affirmation of a higher truth and justice" (Hazan 2010, 152). In the South African case, complete confession was necessary to get amnesty, and so suddenly amnesty was equivalent to a certain accepted "amnesia." Victims' families obtained the information that would not have been available in a normal trial, and they did so without spending as much money. The result was national healing occurring through the remembering of crimes as part of elaborating a new social contract (Hazan 2010, 36). Another result was the association of Christian forgiveness with African *ubuntu* (the very essence of being human). Unlike during the Cold War, amnesty was considered the catalyst for reunification par excellence (Hazan 2010, 38). As South Africa illustrated, the truth commission was no longer appearing as a default solution but, on the contrary, as a positive choice, as much in moral terms as in political and strategic ones (Hazan

2010, 33). Practically, the confessions were concluded with the obligatory point of a certain social reconstruction. Truth, as emphasized by Hazan, is already part of the political and ideological mechanism, presupposing the adjustment of memory. This is why in 1996, Margalit and Morzkin, as reported in Hazan, suggested that through the process " of how people are made to vanish has become a distinctive feature of the postwar conceptions of what memory is."

But in the post-Cold War era, sacredness is transferred from the State to the victims. This shift very much follows the functioning of a global capitalism, grounded in hegemony on one side and fragmentation, multireality, and multi-dispersity on the other. Following the 1970 shift from Fordism to post-Fordist capitalism, this shift articulates a different relation between capital and power. If there was a unity between capital and power in Fordism, today they stay in a co-propriety relation. *Unity* used to mean silence instead of justice, that is now changed into truth instead of justice, where truth is the proliferation of victims' stories, measured by a co-propriety of capital and power. This transition from silence to speech, from forgetting to recounting, is translated into the resurgence of international relations' morality, which seeks to expel violence from history.

The political is fragmented, while geopolitical influences grow unchecked, as we can see by considering the 2001 Durban Conference conceptualized transitional justice. A world conference "Against Racism, Racial Discrimination, Xenophobia, and Related Intolerance," the Durban Conference held on August 31, 2001, was largely overshadowed by September 11, 2001—a premonitory sign of the move from restorative justice toward its criminalization that began to occur around 2000.

In short, if the South African process of reconciliation offered the last hope of judicialization as a restorative mechanism for a new social contract, then the Durban conference was a flop and represents the accelerating logic of criminalization. It signals a radically changing perception of the whole judicialization of international relations from reconciliation toward punishment. Hazan terms this process "ameriglobalization," which indicates "the political weight of the American superpower and the attractiveness of the cultural model of the 'benevolent hegemon'" (Hazan 2010, 44). The result is the Agambenian state of exception in which international justice becomes an act of perverted benevolence, an exception of the law, yet guaranteed by the law.

Fifth Thesis

Therefore I can propose a final thesis (based on Hazan and López Petit) that if education and religion were exported during colonialism, the time of (neo)coloniality evinces another process. The West exports concepts of justice and the universal order to smoothly safeguard its economic interests with a system of legally framed procedures. Culture and religion can be, as is the case with reform in present-day universities (the Bologna agreement to create European Higher Education), formalized and borderless at the same time. What we have today is the "international community's neo-Kantian vision of universal values defended by supranational legal institutions" (Hazan 2010, 48).

It is important to recall that this process impacts the role of NGOs in global capitalism. Judicializing international relations were spearheaded by the "new entrepreneurs of norms" — the NGOs — these missionaries of humane globalization have become moral guardian referees and mediators to the States and have developed a niche market in international relations, such is the case in Switzerland, Sweden, Norway, and Canada. Their exemption from WWII and lack of a colonial past privileges them as players on the field of international relations and human rights.

It is obvious that transitional justice with its judicial framework has served the purpose of protecting the interests of global capitalism. International justice has dual, integrated aims: reconciliation between two violently opposed groups (between the civil society and the State) and reconciliation between capitalism and its persistent exploitation. Hopelessly entangled with economy and culture, the future within the logic of the war-State and its established global judicial framework is far from promising.

THE "MISSING" LINK: THE RACIAL-STATE

I have tried to rearticulate in this genealogy of the State of neoliberal global capitalism its major shift as being from nation-State to war-State. This is connected to the new role that the nation-State plays in the current global system of capital accumulation. Global capital presses on the nation-State in order that it removes the legal-political barriers that prevent unconditional mobility of trans-multinational capital. This is one of the major functions of European Union legislation that is made operative onto the whole space of the EU. The civilization mission of the old bourgeois of Western Colonial European States indicates that at the core of the EU is not a benevolent mission to help the Former Eastern European States to "progress," it is a way to make new regulation more effective. The EU worked in the past through "gentlemen agreements" that kept concealed outlawed transactions and violent processes of colonizations, and this is what is to be understood and implemented as well today. Capital within global neoliberal capitalism specifically presses onto the legal-political State barriers. The fact we live in this so-called neoliberal global world, means not that we are exempted from borders, but that they are "removed" in order that the mobility of transnational capital flourishes, while at the same time other borders are reinforced.

The process started already in the transition from Fordism to post-Fordism. During the time of Fordism (whether we talk about capitalist Fordism of a Keynes type or about Fordism in the socialist countries) the State was protecting national capital. In doing this it had to establish a sort of class compromise with the trade unions (the syndicates). This was seen in Fordism as a unity between capital and power that established a jurisdiction and a system of general employment, free public education, public health systems, social security, and old-age care. In capitalism this was the case of the welfare-State in the Western European space. It is possible to also identify, with Foucault, a nation-State biopolitics that was meant only for the population seen as "natural" citizens of the nation-State; the *others* both inside and outside the nation-State simply meant nothing. Racism was a specific inclusion with exclusion; it was a situation of apartheid within and without the nation-State. Rastko Močnik has argued that the function of the nation-State and its State apparatuses was to "coordinate" the interests of national capital (with state coercion, of course) and to provide life benefits to those being recognized (in blood and soil) as fellow nationals of the respective nation-State (Močnik 2011).

But what do we have today? As I have elaborated we have not only a transformation of the nation-State but a development of a new form of State that is the *war-State*. Now it is the opposite (but not a binary) that we have in front of us. The task of the war-State is how to maintain the illusion of society despite the more and more brutal logic of capital exploitation and expropriation (which was also brutal in the 1970s, but in a different way). Using the machinery of war for profit suits just 1 percent of the global world while 99 percent of the population is increasingly being pushed into poverty—although it must be made clear that this 99 percent is still very much differentiated in its poverty and misery. This is why the unity of capital and power is no longer viable and instead we have to expose the co-propriety of capital and power. Attacks on the banks are not enough. It is necessary to also change the political structures that are caught in the relation of co-propriety with the centers of financial capital. So if we see a radical difference between the 1970s and today, we can reformulate it as having to do with two different biopolitics, the classical one of the 1970s and the other that has changed into a necropolitics.

In the war-State the State apparatuses exist only to maintain the illusion of social harmony and not to take care of the life of a proper population. This measure means that from its biopolitical perspective (the politics of taking care of the population while systematically controlling it) the contemporary State changes into a necropolitical regime (into a politics of the State, which is only taking part in the war of transnational capital—abandoning the citizens to find a way of their own how to survive). Therefore, as summarized by Rastko Močnik, if the State of the past took care of the socio-economic level of the society, today it is only concerned with the socio-political one (Močnik 2011). The *political* in such a case is but the management of keeping order in society and presents therefore a total depoliticization of politics. In reality, the agents of capital monopolize the political apparatus: a modern State policy, therefore, has the appearance of "general management" and uses, as stated by Močnik, strategies of show-business and mass media advertising, in order to manage the status quo (Močnik 2011).

The relation between capital and the State is therefore central to an understanding of the developments from the relations between the superpowers in the aftermath of the Cold War toward what is currently going on in the European Union and its relation with Russia and the United States, not to mention the new players in the world: China, India, and Brazil. The missing link is not missing at all, in fact, but it is not pronounced or named clearly! I owe most of what follows to the brilliant analysis on this topic by Ann Laura Stoler (2011).

What is the racial-State? We can take the formation of the Slovenian state as an example. The best example is the *Erased People*, in details described above. Put briefly, they are the internal immigrants from other republics of the former common State of Yugoslavia. They were removed from the register of permanent residence in 1992 when Slovenia had already declared its independence and was not under threat. What happened to them under the auspices of the new state can be termed as a "particularly brutal" policy of dispossession and "regroupment" (Stoler 2011, 134, note 39). The Slovenian State also has an absence of a history of internal-immigration from and to former Yugoslavia. It is necessary to acknowledge the existence not only in Slovenia but also in the EU (in the passage of the EU from a biopolitical to a necropolitical regime) of these "invisible" workers of the world. They are migrants, again from the former ex-Yugoslav republics, put under harsh procedures of exploitation, discrimination and segregation and completely abandoned by the Slovenian State, though all the time threatened by deportation. Benjamin Stora calls this "ethnoracial regulation" (Stora quoted after Stoler 2011, 125).

Already in 1987, as reported by Stoler, when she sought with Frederick Cooper to consider the "tensions of the French empire" they stated that the tensions reside in a network that "joined liberalism, racism, and social reform" (Stoler 2011, 125). Similarly we can say for Slovenia that it acquired the quasi-bourgeois EU identity as a malfunctioned copy of the European colonial-State, where Slovenia in a turbo way (in just two decades) joined neo/liberalism and racism, and moreover forgot about any social reforms.

What is necessary is to put racism as a central category within the parameters of the abstract-State. This is not about making denunciations of racism and then saying that the repressive apparatuses of the state exacerbated the regulations against migrants and youth of the second and third generations (though the consequences of the war against terror launched in 2001 imposed a radicalized discrimination procedure against those identified as Muslims). It is to acknowledge that in Europe we have a fully constructed entity of a racial-State and global capitalism. Our task is therefore to raise the question of what kind of political, economic, social and cultural (as well discursive) dispositions have made the racial coordinates of the nation-State and the racial epistemic coordinates of contemporary neoliberal global capitalist governance so legible. What has changed, perhaps, is not only what is known about racist politics, but how normalized they have become in Slovenia and Europe today. The unrecognized, but palpably visible, though denied, racist history is then normalized within other topics of security and protection policy of the EU, which in the final reckoning becomes nothing else than the fortress of Europe with its racist epistemic context.

Therefore the nation-State resides today on an infrastructural racism and it is a racial-State that has to be put at the center of the analysis. So any kind of a performative symbolic edifice that conceptualizes the contemporary State has to deal with these implications. Also we have to be alert to the fact, as stated by Stoler, that, "the racial states can be innovative and agile beasts, their categories flexible, and their classifications protean and subject to change. They thrive on ambiguities and falter on rigidities. . . . Racial formations have long marked differences by other names" (Stoler 2011, 130).

It is necessary to take a distance from the nation-State and its bourgeois sensibilities that are not capable of making proper reference to their racist histories. When these histories are looked at in relation to the imperial colonial pasts of Western European states in the EU, they have to include at their center, analysis of colonialism and contemporary forms of coloniality.

I presented the shift or transformation from nation-State to war-State to warn, similarly as Ramón Grosfoguel pointed out, that focusing on the conquering power over the juridical-political boundaries of a State, also over its cultural and artistic premises, is not sufficient when we talk only about a nation-State. This became obsolete after 9/11. This means that it is necessary to open the whole analysis to different parameters, even when it is about art projects that tackle the boundaries of such a nation-State. As Grosfoguel states: "projects that focus on policy-changes at the level of the nation-State are obsolete in today's world-economy and lead to developmentalist illusions" (Grosfoguel 2008).

In such a situation it is necessary to incorporate in every art and cultural project an analysis that deals with the conceptualisation of the three formations: nation-State, war-State and racial-State. As I have tried to show in the case of Slovenia, although the State is only twenty and some years old, racism is at the core of its organization. It is employed in exclusions, violations of basic human rights and discrimination together with exploitations—think of the violated rights of the *Erased People*, the invisible workers of the world, and the exploitation of migrants and other precarious workers. Racism is also central to the way Slovenia acquired its national history; by silencing histories of art and culture made by migrant intellectuals, by gay and lesbian groups and by alternative movements.

CONTEMPORARY ART AS A BIOPOLITICAL/NECROPOLITICAL MACHINE

At this point it is necessary to ask: In which way, what I have been elaborating until now, has to do with contemporary art and culture? How are we to connect the political and social, life in the last instance, global capitalism and turbo neoliberalism with the autonomy (i.e., "freedom") of conceiving a contemporary art project? What I want to emphasize is that contemporary art normalizes the state of exception. The same is true with the law. It is said and quoted by Agamben in relation to Savigny that "Law is nothing but life considered from a particular point of view" (Agamben 2005).

We can speak today of an originary biopolitical character of the paradigm of contemporary art; and when I say contemporary art, I mean not only contemporary art projects/practices from theater to performances or visual art, but also theory, criticism, etc. The consequences are terrifying—as art, similarly to law, has been co-opted within the machinery of the state of exception. Saying this, I want to emphasize that art is both reinforcing the state of exception and functioning in such a way so as not to disclose the state of exception, but to blur and conceal it.

Further, while contemporary art is becoming more and more a genuine biopolitical (regulative, governmental) machine, the social, political, and economic nature of contemporary global capitalism is more and more necropolitical. The originary biopolitical characteristics of contemporary art (seen as an Institution) are being effectuated in ways the arts projects deal with life, formally, aesthetically, and contextually. In such a situation art can become itself a necropolitical dispositive.

A good example for such a statement (and for its further re-articulation) again comes from Slovenia. In 2007/2008 three visual-performative and media artists from Ljubljana, Slovenia (Davide Grassi, Emil Hrvatin, and Žiga Kariž) changed their names to "Janez Janša"—not only symbolically, but also judicially-administratively (by changing all of their identity documents, from identity cards to passports, to say "Janez Janša"). *Janša, Janša, Janša* (JJJ) is not just a work centered on a live person—as the material for the work—it *is* the work!

In order to understand what JJJ is "doing," it is necessary to connect it with another event in 2008 in Slovenia, with the publishing of the thematic issue of the *Journal for Critique of Science, Imagination and New Anthropol-*

ogy (Časopis za kritiko znanosti, domišljijo in novo antropologijo—ČKZ, Ljubljana) entitled *The Story of an Erasure,* which presents an extensive chronology of the Erased Citizens/*Erased People* of Slovenia. I propose a thesis that these two art/cultural and performative/theoretical/critical projects—the *Janšas Performative Body* (JJJ) and *The Story of an Erasure*— represent diametrically opposed performative-theoretical and politico-aesthetical interventions within the art and cultural space of Slovenia and today European Union. *The Story of an Erasure* intervenes politically directly, while the art project of the ventriloquist three-headed "Janez Janša" simulates not only the dominant political position, but also obfuscates it by cloning the right-wing politician/fascist politics of/in Slovenia and aestheticizing the right-wing ideological and administrative State apparatus.

To understand my thesis, it is necessary to answer two questions: who is Janez Janša?, and who are the *Erased People?* I described in length in the first part of this chapter the violent production of the *Erased People* (the way how the Slovenian State produced them) and therefore I will just state that *the Erased Citizens* represent the macabre necropolitical measure by which the Slovenian State transformed around 30,000 people into *People* without residency permits (that were confiscated and destroyed by the Slovenian State), depriving them of any rights.

Therefore I will now proceed with the explanation of who Janez Janša is.

Janez Janša is a right-wing Slovenian politician who was running the Slovenian government from 2004 to 2008; he and his party lost the elections in 2008. The genealogy of his political position in Slovenia is two-fold and not historically fully evaluated. In the 1980s, he was the political figure that provoked (through a discovery of secret military documents) the declaration of Slovenian independence in 1991; today, he is the clearest representative of a new turbo neoliberal entanglement with clerical power (the Catholic church) in Slovenia that precisely synthesizes the genealogy of the Slovenian reality from socialist into turbo neoliberal capitalist. Janez Janša—*nomen est omen* ("the name is a sign")—the Prime Minister of Slovenia in the period from 2004 to 2008, was also one of the most ferocious political forces preventing the possible process of putting an end to the necro reality of the *Erased People*. In essence, Janez Janša's political methods can be described as necrocapitalist and dysfunctional. On one hand, he is implementing the past Communist methods of absolute power (total party discipline and control of the mass media), and on the other, he is exposing the clerical-fascist connection with the present turbo-capitalist Slovenian reality. For example, he pushes forward a European policy of privatization of education, whilst demanding "equality" for Partisans (members of armed resistance groups against WWII Nazi Germany) and Slovenian Nazi collaborators (the Domobrans).

Therefore, if we make a relation between the "ventriloquist three-headed 'Janez Janša' monster figure" and the real Janez Janša, the politician, it is necessary to emphasize that what is at *prima vista* seen as two different "projects," (one being art and the other being politics) must be seen together. We should not de-link the ventriloquist three-headed "Janez Janša" and the real Janša, as they do not remain on opposing sides: the "performance JanšaJanšaJanša" is not merely symbolical, while the other is simply "real." Both of them are real, having their documents fully registered by the (Slovenian) State.

LAIBACH

Further, it is necessary to expose on which possible historical-art reference the constitution of the "ventriloquist three-headed 'Janez Janša' monster figure" is based. Or to formulate this question differently, on what concept does this total identification with the right-wing populist political leader by the three-headed "Janez Janša" body rely?

The idea of the three-headed "Janša" can be conceptually defined as a re-enactment of what was strategically invented by the music group Laibach in the 1980s; Laibach, a music group from Ljubljana (still active), re-appropriated the German name of Ljubljana (the name became especially controversial when used during the time of the German occupation of Slovenia in WWII when the Nazis exercised aggressive Germanization of Slovenes); the group performed in a style that was a mixture between a party rally and a Mussolini speech, without offering any further explanation of their action. Laibach's gesture, which is also known as "over-identification" in psychoanalytical terms, (a total, complete identification with a body [Mussolini], name [Ljubljana], etc.), also succeeded to subvert the exhausted strategies of parody and irony performed by the Western contemporary art in the 1980s. Therefore, the over-identification (as a total simulation strategy) on which Laibach insisted presented a complete over-shadowing of their individual positions. Laibach's "real" member's names were totally disclosed in the 1980s; their public appearances, be it in music concerts or in interviews, did not produce relief, or catharsis.

Almost three decades later, in 2007/2008, the three-headed "Janša" inaugurated their name-changing in a spectacular fashion; they sent hundreds of e-mails with each "newborn baby Janša" being introduced through e-mails and other form of communicating to the general public. Every time they proudly announced a new art product, it was a spectacular power demonstration—having the pleasure, time and money to change their names. Ultimately, they sent the emails just to make sure that we, the public, wouldn't miss who had actually changed their names. Therefore, I will name this act as one of pure *parody exhibitionism*. I will call this an attempt to secure a terrain for future branding and money; and it worked, the three-headed "Janša" artifact was abundantly supported by the government in power! The Ministry of Culture abundantly supported almost all the projects in which at least one of, if not all three, "Janez Janšas" took part, while many other artists applying for co-financing from the Ministry of Culture in 2007/2008 were rejected and pushed into the grip of the fatal process of neoliberal pauperization.

It is important to understand that Laibach could only develop their over-identification as a genuinely new strategy in art under socialism. Why? Socialism functioned as a totalization of everyday politics imposed on every level of society that was paradoxically completely depoliticized. Therefore Laibach's over-identification functioned as genuine political art in the socialist postmodernism of 1980s former Yugoslavia, and presented a political totalization that stood in opposition to the overtly politicized communist party public discourse. This was paradoxical clash between totalitarian communist public discourse that found in front a monster of the same kind, a political art that did not throw off its mask after the art project was realized. Laibach art was as psychotic as the public discourse of the communist party. In contrast the postmodernism of the West was always a partial-identification, that produced its subversion as a parody. This was due to the process of intensified invidualization and fragmentation of any discourse in Capitalism. In global capitalism, politics is depoliticized, as is every other level of art, culture and social life. The characterization of this situation according to López Petit is (not without reason) named *postmodern fascism* (López Petit 2009) .

So what does postmodern fascism or (micro) fascism do? It transforms depoliticized units into totalitarian, psychotic and completely self-narcissistic entities that are only hyper-repetitions of themselves; hyper-financialized psychotic repeated selves. If we look again the diagram reproduced in this chapter of the book we will see that postmodern fascism is characterized by three main features: it sterilizes the Other, evacuates the conflict from the public space and neutralizes the political. Turbo global capitalism (as a historicization of capitalism) presents not a neurotic social bond, but a psychotic one (as it was once the social bond in socialism) though the difference matters. Turbo global capitalism presents an *infinite* generated space of multiple psychotic, narcissistic, and castrated selves or depoliticized units. Therefore over-determination cannot function as a strategy of *de-realization* as was the case with Laibach in socialism in the 1980s; parody, as a partial identification, is as well impotent in such a castrated hyper financialized, now, capitalist psychotic social bond, where Adorno famous *alienation* is just a mode or a form of capitalist subjectivity.

JJJ AND THE *ERASED PEOPLE*

The *Erased People* are the only possible context in which to read the act of performing of the three-headed "Janša," as the *Erased People* are an outcome of the necropolitical act by the Slovenian State through confiscating and destroying their residency papers and documents. The *Erased People* were deprived of the economic, social and political status that is granted to individuals through such papers and documents; in the final analysis, they were deprived of life.

The three-headed "Janša" on the other side developed their project precisely on the same "act," (but on the reverse) with judicially, administratively, changing all their documents and acquiring, spectacularly,—as was described—their new identities. Therefore it is possible to state that the truth (in Alain Badiou's term) of JJJ performance, of their art act, can be conceptualized and therefore politicized only in relation to the *Erased People*. The truth of the three "Janšas" is to be found in their over-cynical gesture *par excellence* through an "esthetical-artistic" level of "fun" that allowed them to change all their documents, while not taking into consideration what this meant in 2007/2008 in Slovenia that had "still" 18,000 *Erased Citizens*, without papers, whose status has not been solved at all, even after all these years!

The "Janšas," in turn, when they were asked in 2008 to write some kind of circular letters to each other, which were then published in the weekly supplement of the daily Ljubljana newspaper *Dnevnik*, used this very important public space for weeks to amuse the readers. The "Janšas" did not give any criticism of the cultural politics of the right-wing government, they just wrote speculations on their traveling and sentimental reminiscences about their different places of birth and origins. Not a word of "criticism" of Janša's politics.

I called the act of the Janšas' "three-headed body" an exhibitionist parody that did not provide a critique, but additionally reinforced the blurring of the political/artistic situation. The right-wing political space on the other hand needed and still needs such multiplication, such a spectacular cloning and branding of *nothing*, of the same *nothing* produced by the government and parties in power—*nothing* as an act of the total nullification of 30,000 people. However, this *nothing* had and has social and political effects, for it does reproduce *something*. That is, firstly, it aestheticizes a necro social and necro political space of misery and control, and secondly, it transforms administrative/judicial, and outlaw (erasure) by Slovenian State procedures into a playful game. The project is not reevaluating the work of Janez Janša, the politician, as in the old times; it is not about the name, it is only the name! It is not about the two bodies and practices, the real and the symbolical, working through each other, but they are One, the distinction is blurred.

Since Janez Janša lost the elections in September 2008, the whole project of the Janšas' "three-headed body" started suddenly to expose that all
that was actually taking place was a playful act of renaming, saying that
it does not matter what the name is, as it is just about to change it! Instead
of developing a criticism, the "Janšas" obfuscated the real Janša even
more, duplicating him ad nauseam and providing an artistic flavor to
necropolitics.

We have to overcome the fascination with new meanings (the fun,
indeed, for example, produced through the triplication of the name, etc.,
used by the mass media abundantly), it is not so much about testing our
capacity of producing all sorts of supplementary meanings; rather, we
have to rearticulate the relationship of meanings to hegemony! We have
to analyze the role such administrative renaming plays within the biopolitical and necropolitical logic of the contemporary (Slovenian) neoliberal
capitalist space.

In order to connect the two projects (the special issue entitled *The
Story of an Erasure* and the "Janšas") it is necessary to make direct and
precise relation to the past, as both of these cultural events are relating to
the past. *The Story of an Erasure* relates to the necropolitical event of erasure of 30,000 people in 1992 in Slovenia, the "Janšas" are relating to
Laibach and its almost thirty-year-old art strategy.

In a talk with Alexander Skidan and Dmitry Vilensky in the newspaper *What is to be Done?*, published in St. Petersburg, Artiom Magun
presents a very simple but crucially important difference in understanding the past in relation to two remarkable theoretical cases. One case is
Walter Benjamin and the other is Alain Badiou. Following Artiom Magun, this difference can be presented in the following way: "Badiou proposes that we find our support in something necessary and important
that happened in the past and move on from there. Benjamin, on the
contrary, searches for something that was suppressed in the past, something that did not happen, that perished and is reawakening only now.
The event that, for Badiou, happens in the past, is taking place right now
for Benjamin. That is, they both look back to the past, but from opposite
points of view. This is important as we try to understand potentiality:
either potential is the impulse generated by a positive past or present
event, or it is something that has not happened yet, that was interrupted
in mid-sentence" (Magun 2007).

The "Janšas" obfuscate and foreclose the cultural and political space
of Slovenia because of their incapacity to make a connection to past
events; notably to Laibach, to which they conceptually refer, not to mention the *Erased People*! If the "Janšas" have based their concept on fidelity
to Laibach, or to the *Erased People*, they could then connect and re-per-
form differently the art, social and political space, while opening a space
for criticism and emancipatory politics. They could have transformed
"the three-head monster Janša" into a real political subject able to subvert

the real Janša and the right-wing necropolitics. They could also have made reference to events of the 1980s and the 1990s: (a) to the underground (subcultural movement) of the 1980s, and (b) to the powerful awakening of the independent cultural and social structures situated in a squatted empty military barracks complex in 1992 (in the center of Ljubljana known as Metelkova City). If they had made a connection in terms of understanding what the political implications of these events were, they could have produced a political subject capable of emancipating the social and political space of Slovenia today. But JJJ failed. In contrast, *The Story of an Erasure* presents a gesture of a radical fidelity to the case of the *Erased People*.

JJJ IN 2009

Presented above is the analysis of the three-headed "Janša" project (JJJ) and the relation to the politician Janez Janša when he was in power as the Slovenian prime minister. In September 2008, he and his party lost the election. The JJJ artists did not change their names back to their originals. Only one of them is now using his real name: Žiga Kariž, being appointed professor at the Academy of Fine Arts and Design in Ljubljana.

Insisting on the shared name after the politician lost his real political power can on one side be viewed as an act of indisputable fidelity to the critical potential of such a project, as well presenting a direct critique of all those who were "hostile" to the project "JJJ." The argument could go as follows: Now that Janša the politician is not in power anymore, the fidelity to the name is an exemplary fidelity. The artists insist on the name of the person even though the politician is not in power anymore and therefore this is also a clear sign that the projects by JJJ were based on non-utilitarian logic, that their aim was, in the final analysis, purely artistically and aesthetically motivated. It was really about the autonomy of artistic expression in times so imbued by politics.

I would like now to extend the critique of the Janšas project further and to show the opposite, that insisting on the name of Janša the fallen right wing politician (on its total appropriation), is a precise and true signifier of the complete postmodern fascist nature of this and similar projects.

I will base this part of the analysis on Agamben's book *State of Exception* (2005). Before I continue it is important to ask how the state of exception with its violent spatial structure of the camp and its necropolitical sovereign power fits the decolonial turn? A precise answer is provided by Nelson Maldonado-Torres who draws a following structure of the relation between Western philosophy and the decolonial turn. He states that we have a dominant tripartite division between Anglo-analytic, continental, and U.S. American philosophy today. To this tripartite division Maldonado-Torres opposes a post-continental philosophy!

For him,

> post-continentality . . . relies on specific notions of spatiality. Instead of seeking a dialectic between Europe and other continents, post-continental philosophy suggests that the possibilities for generating and grounding theory and philosophy are multiple and include a variety of spatial and bodily references: the boat of the middle passage and the plantation, the black and the Chicana body, the island and the archipelago, the reservation and the boarding school, the prison and the camp. Post-continental philosophy revolves around "shifting the geography of reason," which defines activities of projects such as the one by the Caribbean Philosophical Association. (Maldonado-Torres 2011, 5)

Finally he parallels post-continental philosophy alongside the decolonial turn, and states that both can be traced back "to efforts in defining the specific character of Africana and Caribbean philosophy—and similar efforts—and the project of shifting the geography of reason, on the one hand, and to explicit efforts to put in practice decolonial theorizing as well as Chicana/o, Latina/o and Latin American philosophy, on the other" (Maldonado-Torres 2011, 5).

Agamben refers in his *State of Exception* to that which he defines the modern confusion of *auctoritas* and *potestas*. These are two concepts that Agamben, quoting Pueyo, names as "two concepts that express the originary sense through which the Roman people conceived their communal life" (Agamben 2005, 75). The *auctoritas* is, according to Agamben, to be read differently within public and private law. In the field of private law, *auctoritas* (authority) is the *pater familias*, the father that confers legal validity on the act of the subject who cannot independently bring a legally valid act into being. This simply means, and in a less complicated parlance, that the *auctoritas* of the father (which is the *pater familias*) authorizes the marriage of the son who, in *potestas* has not the ability to do so. Therefore, *auctoritas* and *potestas,* in cases of both private and public law, are not in opposition so to speak, but one (*auctoritas*) authorizes the other that is *potestas*. Additionally, in the public, *auctoritas* denotes not the increase in something which already exists as such, but presents the act of producing, so to say, from one's own breast: a creative act. Authority is not sufficient in itself, whether it authorizes or ratifies, it always implies an extraneous activity that it validates, though without this validation the structural power of *potestas* is also not enough!

The question posed by Agamben is from where does the force of authority come? For us, and for the past and present analysis of the project "Janšas" this same question matters enormously. As we saw, that if by chance we were "wrongly," thinking that the Janšas art projects are bound to a certain "real political power" of the politician Janša, this proved not to be the case neither historically nor politically. In 2009, after Janša the politician lost the election, Janšas the artists insisted on fidelity to the name.

Even more, the convergence into one body (of the political and of the artistic bodies of "Janša") is in relation to the concept of sovereignty (as well of an art project), and is not just an academic "confusion" (between artistic "autonomy" and political complicity). As Agamben stated, the act of *auctoritas* did not present an increase in something which already existed as such, but presented the act of producing from one's own breast: a creative act. The JJJ project is today seen precisely as such; as a pure creative act, as a pure act of the autonomy of artistic freedom.

In Ljubljana, Slovenia many theoreticians, critics, journalists, and followers (some known internationally) stood (with their authority) in support and protection of JJJ who stated that the "artists have the right to be autonomous and not to think about what it is that is going on in the realm of the social and political." The most important point is that the *auctor* (authority), according to Agamben, is not founded upon some sort of legal power vested in him to act as a representative: it springs directly from his condition as *pater familias*, as father. It presents therefore an actualization of an impersonal power (*potestas*) in the very person of the *auctor*, authority. This is for us the point why JJJ (if it is possible to state "unconsciously") insists on being Janša the politician, after he lost the elections in 2008 and was forced into opposition in the Slovenian parliament. Therefore, Janez Janša, the politician, is not interesting for us as a politician and even less deserving to write about, as he is merely a template of similar positions throughout the present European Union and global capitalist world reality (a right wing fascist and nationalist politician). Our interest is in the artistic project JJJ (in its form!) that claims to be a critique of Janša the politician by literally repeating and (administratively, judicially) taking his name in global turbo neoliberal capitalism; even after the real politician (Janša) lost the prime ministerial political power in 2008 the JJJ insist perversely on fidelity to the name.

Agamben states that *auctoritas* and *potestas* are clearly distinct, and yet together they form a binary system. On what relies the overlapping that forms a binary? *Potestas* (power) are the magistrates, as it is explained by Agamben, who have power because of the place they occupy (that is, a structural place of power, without being rooted in any extra capability or aura of the magistrates), while *auctoritas*, (authority's power) is generated by a power that is not coming from a structural place but *emanates* from the person itself. Even more, as Agamben writes, under extreme conditions (as in a state of exception or war), *auctoritas* seems to act as a force that suspends *potestas* and reactivates it where it is no longer in force. *Auctoritas*, authority, is a power that suspends or reactivates law, but is not formally in force as law. This relationship is, as argued by Agamben, at once of exclusion and of supplementation between *auctoritas* and *potes-*

tas. It is also possible to find this relationship in the period of *interregnum*, meaning in the period of a change of power or when a parliament is not yet constituted and the senior member is to initiate its work (Agamben 2005, 79). It is in the interregnum that the *patres auctoritas* proposes an *interrex* (somebody to take the power in the in-between time). The formula used, as stated by Agamben, is that the republic returns to the fathers (*patres*).

Practically, what is important for us is that *auctoritas* (authority) shows its connection with the suspension of *potestas* and, at the same time, it shows its capacity to ensure the functioning of the republic under exceptional circumstances. Although Janša the politician lost the elections in 2008, his authority "emanates" and this is why JJJ keeps the name and insists upon it, presenting therefore a necro-fidelity that is the point through which we can make a precise analysis of the necropolitical social and necropolitical artistic conditions of Slovenia today.

The difference is possible to be defined as follows: whereas the magistrate, as a *potestas* in the Roman principate, is a pre-established form (something structural without a personal body) that the individual enters into and which constitutes the source of his power when "sitting" in such a place, the *auctoritas*, on the other hand, springs from the person as something that is constituted through him (Agamben 2005, 82). Agamben points out clearly that to understand modern phenomena such as the Fascist Duce and the Nazi Fuhrer, it is important not to forget their continuity with the principle of the *auctoritas principia* (Agamben 2005, 83). As Agamben points out, even though Mussolini held the office of Head of the Government and Hitler that of Chancellor of the Reich, neither represented a constitutionally defined public office or magistracy (Agamben 2005, 83). The qualities of the Duce or Fuhrer were immediately bound to the physical person and belonged to the necropolitical tradition of *auctoritas* and not to the biopolitical tradition of *potestas*.

JJJ (the three-headed monster Janša), in the past, claimed that its gesture was a gesture of criticism, which was indeed (maybe) possible at the time when Janša the politician was in power, as it could have been interpreted as an analysis of his *potestas*. However, after Janez Janša lost his election in 2008, it is obvious that it was not about this at all, but was about the total identification with the authority of Janša, the politician. If it was all about criticism of Janša, the politician, by JJJ, as it was stated, when Janša was the Slovenian prime minister (in the period 2004 – 2008), then why keep the name after the politician lost the election in the period 2008/2009? Why show fidelity to the name after Janša's political fall?

If we think about the differentiation between *auctoritas* (authority that emanates from the person as such) and *potestas* (power that is structurally given by being in a certain moment in a certain position, let's say by being a prime minister), there is no longer a reason for JJJ to keep the name after 2008. Or? Does JJJ in the final analysis trust/believe in Janša's emanating authority? Is their fidelity today a proof that they are relating to Janez Janša not as *potestas* (as a structural place for the analysis of power in the system of contemporary Slovenian society), but to Janez Janša as *auctoritas*? As presented by Agamben, the power of Duce and Hitler was lawless, it was beyond the structural position which they held, it was based in *auctoritas*, authority, and is today alive precisely because of this, after it has been clearly exposed that they were just merely criminals!

The three-headed artistic monster Janša(s) project is ultimately attached to the father figure, the authority of Janša; a fact which demonstrates how contemporary Slovenian society functions. JJJ repeats the patriarchal, chauvinistic, white, male, heterosexual matrix of the Slovenian State that is also at the core of the EU. Therefore, the stubborn insistence on the body of the fallen politician in order to prove that the JJJ art project was (is) not a mistake or a fashionable gesture today testifies to its even more of a reactionary horizon and to the neoliberal capitalist society in which it takes place.

As Agamben states, "Kantorowicz's theory of the king's two bodies should be re-read" (Agamben 2005, 83). Kantorowicz, as stated by Agamben, generally undervalues the importance of the Roman precedent to the theory that he seeks to reconstruct for the English and French monarchies, and he does not relate to the distinction between *auctoritas* and *potestas* when he talks about the king's two bodies and about the principle that dignities do not die with the death of the king (Agamben 2005, 83). And yet, as continued by Agamben, "it is precisely because the sovereign was first and foremost the embodiment of the *auctoritas* and not only of a *potestas*, that *auctoritas* was so closely bound to his physical person, thus requiring the complicated ritual of constructing a wax double of the sovereign in the *funus imaginarium*" (Agamben 2005, 83)— something that happened some years ago when one of the art projects by the three-headed artistic monster Janša presented a monumental sculpture (a self-monumentalization) of their projects.

Agamben therefore insists that, already by Roman times, precisely because of this lack of distinction between authority and power (where the private and public life have entered into a zone of *absolute indistinction*) it becomes necessary to *distinguish* between the two bodies. Or to put differently, it matters profoundly which body in what circumstances we will repeat, with which body we will become one and to which body we will express our utmost fidelity.

This was already our thesis before the political fall of Janez Janša; but paradoxically, after Janez Janša, the politician, lost his power, the aforementioned analysis is becoming even more urgent. Agamben argues that modern scholars, as our modern artists, have been only too ready to uphold the claim that *auctoritas* inheres immediately in the living person of the *pater familias*, so to speak, in the immanent power, outside its structural position. Agamben states that this was "clearly an ideology or a fiction intended to ground the preeminence or, in any case, it meant that the specific rank of *auctoritas* in relation to *potestas* became a figure of law's immanence to life."

It is not by chance, Agamben continues, "that this had happened precisely in the years when the authoritarian principle saw an unexpected rebirth in Europe through fascism and National Socialism." Our three-headed monster Janša is taking part as well in such a procedure, reinforcing it and making a profit from it, almost counting on a similar position in the future of their figure; that could make evident a figure of art's immanence parallel to the life of the State. That this is the case is also proved by a series of some other projects by the artist Janša; repeating as faithful reconstructions some theater performances that are seen as indisputably avant-garde from the not-so-distant modernist socialist Slovenian (or it would be better to say former-Yugoslav) past.

In this case, Janša(s), the artist(s), tries to acquire his legacy by linking himself directly to a past high modernist socialist theater director who is still alive today, but who was for a while (also due to the post-socialist transitional changes) without artistic power (although he still bears the informal power of a certain un-discussed *pater familias* of the Slovenian high modernist theater family). These reenactments also allow the eradication of the political, post-socialist-radical postmodernist times of the 1980s that brought to the surface the alternative (subcultural) movement in Ljubljana and the emergence of the homosexual scene in Slovenia and former Eastern Europe.

Slovenian socialist (high) modernism (bypassing the radical political times of the alternative movement of the 1980s) is now being continued (*tout court*, without a break) and reconnected with the independent (highly nationalist) Slovenian state. This also means to bypass any interpretational contemporary discourse that would question precisely the different timing of the execution (the repetition) of the same performance (socialism and capitalism) and, therefore, the three Janšas are cherished as those that connect the present time with the undisputed authority of the (nationalist) modernist (!) past.

The three-headed Janša seems, as in the case of those that are criticized by Agamben, "to take for granted that authoritarian-charismatic power springs almost magically from the very person of the Fuhrer." This, in the final analysis, comes near to the traditional juridical thought that saw law as ultimately identical with or immediately articulated to life. Therefore, we can speak of an eminent necropolitical character of the paradigm of *auctoritas*, authority. Such a norm can be applied to the normal situation and can be suspended without totally annulling the juridical order, because in the form of *auctoritas* or sovereign decision it seems to refer immediately to life: almost as it springs from life (Agamben 2005,

85), though as I tried to prove up until now, it is in fact connected directly with death.

As Agamben develops, the authority of the Duce or Fuhrer can never be derivative but is always originary and springs from his person; furthermore, in its essence, it is not coercive, but is rather *founded on consent and the free acknowledgment of a superiority of value*; as we also have attempted to present up to now. This consent is in the case of the three-headed Janša a rather broader one, including not only the artists but also a whole raft of writers, journalists and ministerial bodies, in a word, of an impressive list of "agents" that constitute the Slovenian Institution of Contemporary Art, Theory and Journalist-Critical Thinking.

With Janez Janša the politician, (similar to the old theater figure from modernist socialist time), this charisma (on which the Janšas count in order to use some of it for their present position) supposedly stays on even after the politician has lost the election; this coincides with what Agamben writes, that this charisma is in the final analysis a measure for the neutralization of law, even more than just reproducing, repeating, the originary figure of power. So, finally, the body of the politician and the artist as one (Janša), and the body of the past modernist theater director becoming one with the body of the JJJ, is not just about the repetition of these two bodies (Janša the politician, and the modernist theater director), but is about neutralizing the capability of the Institution of art, theory and critique to develop an analysis of the art institution as a biopolitical (moving directly into a necropolitical) machine. What we have is a situation of a state of exception, a necropolitical measure within contemporary art taken for granted in the broadest sense, from institutions to discourses, from ministerial bodies that give public funds to the "free" (as they are called themselves) mass media.

Behind the Janšas, big machinery is put to work that almost blindly supports the art autonomy's immanence to life. In the case of the project *Janša, Janša, Janša*, the theoreticians and critics write in superlatives about the project, and since by "chance" they also happen to be journalists of major daily newspapers, they can then report in the daily newspapers what they wrote in their published books, etc. What an incestuous situation! So then not only is the institution of contemporary art giving its blessing to this project, but the State is supporting it in financial abundance. The outcome is a pure state of exception that I can also name, in relation to Santiago López Petit, a postmodern fascism. *Postmodern fascism* (different from the classical fascism and not in any way connected with standard conspiracy theory) presents and displays these enthusiastic writers, theoreticians, journalist, critics, curators, directors, ministry administrators, professors, etc. as serving the "project" JJJ, *freely*, autonomously; they are convinced that these JJJ works are a gesture of a "pure art freedom."

The state of exception is a device, as formulated by Agamben, or something we call a *dispositive* (and not simply a process) with which is ultimately imposed an articulation that holds together three different aspects, in our case, art, life (the *Erased Citizens*), and the State judicial/ administrative and its repressive apparatus (acquiring artistic documents for fun on one side and violently being deprived of them and therefore being deprived of life on the other). This articulation is instituting a certain normative aspect that is possible to be defined as a state of *undecidability*. What is at the center of this relation is the state of exception, but, and I quote Agamben, "this is essentially an empty space in which human action with no relation to law stands before a norm with no relation to life" (Agamben 2005).

This does not mean that the machine, with its empty center, is not effective; on the contrary, it has been working since WWI up until the present day. It means that life is seen as the raw material of art, though it must be clear that *bare life* (the life that is *without a form*) is a product of this same machine and not something that is there as a preexist/ed/ing reality! It is not that we have bare life (the *Erased Citizens*) on one side and modal life (the art project JJJ) on the other, no; they are both an outcome of a process of the articulation of neoliberal global capitalism and life, art, law, and power.

Law and life, art and life result from the fracture of something to which we have no other access than through their articulation. The political task will be to separate them, art and life and law and life, but not as two pure entities, but to show (as I have tried) that they are both an outcome of a process of articulation. On the one hand the political stance will consist of showing this fiction of *art and life being one* not as a simple fiction but as the *real*, and on the other hand it will disclose this process of fictionalization as being the process of articulation of art, life, and law. Such is the case of the art work *Janša, Janša, Janša*.

What has been written up to now also demonstrates a shift away from Žarana Papić's turbo fascism (as part of the transitional spaces of the former Eastern Europe States) into what López Petit calls postmodern fascism, as the new characteristic of neoliberalism's complete blurring (entanglement) of the public and private, etc. To which we could add the feature (also recognized in the way of functioning of the Moderna Galerija/Museum of Modern Art, Ljubljana) named by Achille Mbembe as "private indirect power."

In the end we can state that although we departed from the thesis that the Institution of contemporary art today is a biopolitical machine, the JanšaJanšaJanša ventriloquists' monster body presents a clear necropolitical move, amidst the "normalized" neoliberal capitalist contemporary art biopolitical machine.

NOTES

1. See the exhibition *Gender Check— Femininity and Masculinity* in the Art of Eastern Europe, Museum of Modern Art (MUMOK), Vienna, Austria, 2009/2010. Available at http://www.erstestiftung.org/factory/gender-check-femininity-and-masculinity-in-the-art-of-eastern-europe/

2. Though the artists in the show were not paid, we, the panelists, were.

3. Two books are important for what is elaborated in this section. See Santiago López Petit, *Global Mobilization: A Brief Treatise for Attacking Reality*, and Pierre Hazan, *Judging War, Judging History: Behind Truth and Reconciliation*.

4. In the Bosnian silver-mining town of Srebrenica in July 1995, one of the most notorious modern acts of gendercide took place. While the international community and U.N. peacekeepers/Dutch soldiers looked on, Serb forces separated civilian men from women and killed thousands of Muslim men *en masse*, or hunted them down in the forests.

FOUR

Racialized Dehumanization, the Binary Occident/Orient in EU, and Decoloniality

Global capitalism functions not with division but with *entanglement*. It is a specific entanglement of power and capital that can be precisely described as a Christian white capitalist world reiterated through a constant of *humanization*. This functions in the European Union through the manufacturing of the former Eastern Europeans—so to say former "non-subjects"—into gendered, European, white, (petit-) bourgeois humans. It is about *us* acquiring our capitalistic, conservative, chauvinistic, patriarchal, mostly petit-bourgeois lineage in order to safeguard the heterosexual family and the racialized EU nation-State "substance." The European Union aims to transform former "barbarian Communist" Eastern Europeans into "humanized" and "civilized" Europeans. To understand this process I presented in the previous chapter the analysis of the project *Gender Check— Femininity and Masculinity in the Art of Eastern Europe*.

Of course, this process has its "ghastly underside: the story of the racialized subject's dehumanization" (Carr 1998). In 1998, Brian Carr elaborated on this relation of production of "humans" (that leaves the so-called "nonhumans" untouched) by asking: What is left at the threshold in the process of manufacturing humans? His answer is brief: Race!

The white (petit-) bourgeois subject is made through gender, race, and class, and is manufactured in a specific way, akin to Lacan's *extimité* by applying the prefix, *ex*, from *exterieur*, or exterior, to the Freudian term, *intimité*, or intimacy. *Extimité* defies the inside/outside, self/other boundaries and is thus both exterior and intimate at the same time. Brian Carr's proposed coinage of "sextimate" in order to register the gap in Nella Larsen's novel *Passing*, regarding sex and race (Carr 2004). In *Gen-*

der Check we could speak as well of "sextimate." While Feminity and Masculinity were manufactured through a gender regime, capital's allocations and discriminations were "unmade," "dispersed," "lost" (in translation) in the space of neoliberal global necrocapitalism.

There exists a limit in the Foucauldian understanding of the modern regime of power on which the contemporary biopolitical resides today. Actually when biopolitics was first elaborated in the 1970s, it was for the capitalist First World and its apparatuses, where the "Other" did not exist; it was only *insisting* in the space by working. Therefore in Europe we have two modern regimes of power working at once! One is the generalizable modern regime of power that goes from Foucault through Agamben and is radicalized in the time of crises throughout the global world; the other is the regime of colonial power. In distinction to the former regime that today functions by demanding integration and even more so by the "distribution" of debt, fear, and fantasies; the latter regime functions with exclusion, marginalization, desymbolization and disfiguration.[1] We have, therefore, two regimes of discrimination, racialization, and exploitation that are *almost* the same, but the latter is not white (Bhabha 1994, quoted after Carr 1998, 146).

The entanglement between them is visible in the myriad of class racializations.

"Race thus stands at the vanishing point where sexual difference and the human resolve," states Carr, "into the ungendered figure of dehumanized racial 'flesh'" (Carr 1998, 125). I will revisit here the notion of race that I originally developed in 2007 in relation to Lacanian psychoanalysis. I will do this, as it may be possible, as argued by Carr, "to ward off the threat of our own racialization" (Carr 1998, 131). The revision functions at least on three levels:

1. As vanishing mediator. What does this mean? Migrants, women of color, etc., those coming from other worlds outside the First capitalist World—which is presented as the only "properly" civilized world, and that stubbornly and bloodily exports its civilization everywhere else—are today in a position where they are not seen as human excess (as in the past!), but we get a paradoxical turn through which that which was perceived in the past as "animality" (just think about Fanon's analysis), is seen today as *the zero level of humanity*. It covers up the monstrosity of the "human" as such; *the zero level of humanity* presents today a perverse, almost "sublime" human essence that has to be upgraded and civilized. On the larger territory of Europe, according to Gail Lewis, it is the Black woman's body, or women's bodies of any other color that do not match the white color of the old and new Europeans, which are the bodies in constant processes of trafficking, exploitation, and subsumption within different stories of contemporary racism.

2. As real difference. Within such a horizon we can demand not to expand the struggle for different conditions of life into a series of equivalences, but to retake a single social antagonism, that of *race*, as the main force of change. An excellent example of such a political and structurally grounded struggle is the work by the *Research Group on Black Austrian History and Presence*, from Vienna. As it was precisely stated by Araba Evelyn Johnston-Arthur and Belinda Kazeem (who is also active within the Black Women Community in Vienna[2]), by

> founding a Black Research Group we are thereby recovering displaced knowledge about the Black Austrian history, building up a space for it and for us, Black people in this country (Austria). Crucial for this counter-history writing is the Black perspective, which [lets us] reconstruct hidden (his)stories: visionary history writings far beyond voyeuristic representations of the "exotic other," that is emancipated from usual racisms and sexisms. Even though Black history of this country stays fragmentary in the end, we—as Black researchers—are not afraid of asking for aspects that cannot be reconstructed and of creating possible counter historical concepts. The aim of the research group, to crack up invisibilities and open new grounds for history writings, is therefore inseparably connected with processes of self-definition, and of making visible and audible the Black Austrian experience and presence in a (self-)determined way. (The Research Group on Black Austrian History and Presence, 2007)

In the case of our (my) former Eastern European and now newly acquired white petit-bourgeois crippled genealogy, we have to critically conceptualize, as stated by Hortense Spillers, that "race" signals gender's sociosymbolic unmaking (Spillers quoted after Carr 1998, 125). Our change from communist uncivilized nonsubjects to capitalist, post-Cold War "not yet quite, not yet right," civilized and human subjects (from one propriety relation to another) testifies only to our potentiality for convertibility on the capitalist market. Though it is possible to state, as argued by Carr, that "white bodies are not imaginable as nonhuman *because of their race* as their whiteness does not have the linguistic gravity of animality, primitivity, or property," I will propose a correction, arguing: *capitalist, western, occidental* white bodies. Though it definitely remains true that, "whiteness is not enough to detect *us* as humans [italics added, in Carr's essay the "us" refers to the replicants from the film *Blade Runner*], as whiteness is not 'in and of itself' a differential mark" (Carr 1998, 139), whiteness is nevertheless a tediously-administratively and horrifyingly-monstrously re/produced, nurtured, and manufactured regime of power, subjugation, dispossession, and racialization.

3. As minimal difference. By contesting the exclusion of *race* from mainstream political and philosophical theory, African American critics expose the confusion between the normative and descriptive levels of liberal theory. bell hooks is skeptical about the universal principles of color-blind justice. She argues (as presented in Ewa Płonowska Ziarek's *An Ethics of Dissensus. Postmodernity, Feminism, and the Politics of Radical Democracy*), that such abstractions obliterate the acute historical contradiction between the histories of Euro-American and New World African modernities (hooks 1990, quoted after Płonowska Ziarek 2001). Kelly Oliver analyzes the rhetoric of color-blind society, and argues that this rhetoric denies the social fact of race and its effects as well as the "white" provenance of supposedly neutral categories such as "human" or "American" (Oliver 2001).

Quoting Orlando Patterson, Brian Carr provides us with an illuminating difference. Already in 1982, Patterson, referring to African Americans, argued that, "exclusion from the scene of subjecthood is not always on the order of death proper." Carr continues: "Symbolic designification has more regularly, in its more historical and colonial dimensions, installed a condition of what Orlando Patterson, referring to African American slaves in the United States, calls 'social death'" (Patterson 1982, quoted after Carr 1998, 126). Patterson envisioned these two types of exclusions—these two types of life, and also two types of death—as something that would become the main logic of global capitalism after 2001, and would be named by Achille Mbembe in 2003 as necropolitics.

Carr therefore argues,

> Patterson's paradoxical framing of the "socially dead" allows us to think . . . about how "death" operates within the social and how excluded bodies are rendered dead at the level of sociosymbolic significa-tion. Here, evacuation from a symbolic of bourgeois subjecthood (and its attendant logic of sexual difference) marks a "condition" not analo-gous to an always nostalgic story about the imaginary "stuff" of a presymbolic subject or a body prior to the enjoining governance of phallic differentiation. That is, bodies excluded from subjecthood in the context of colonial rule should not be conflated with the psychoanalytic notion of the sexually undifferentiated pre-subject, ones whose (pre)history can never be rescued. (Carr 1998, 126)

These two types—one of *inclusion* and the other of *exclusion*—mark different temporal/historical logics that work today side-by-side.

It is possible to state that racism is divided from within and exists on at least two different lines of racism—or of technologies, discourses, judicial, economic, political, theoretical, artistic, cultural, semiotic, psychoanalytic implementations of racialization—in the space of Europe and in the global capitalist neoliberal world. Carr maintains that the line of division is the colonial difference (Carr 1998, 141).

THE DECOLONIAL TURN

In 2004, Arturo Escobar (2004), a Colombian theoretician living in the United States, summarized the theoretical points of the group known as the Latin American Modernity/Coloniality Research Group, established in 2000 of which he is a member. The points of summarization are:

1. The origins of modernity are located in the fifteenth century—with the conquest of America and the control of the Atlantic. If it is too complicated, we can just think of NATO/An alliance of countries from North America and West Europe committed to fulfilling the goals of the North Atlantic Treaty signed in 1949 and of course enlarged due to the events produced by NATO itself.
2. Colonialism, postcolonialism, and imperialism are constitutive of modernity.
3. The domination of non-Europeans is a central and necessary feature of modernity.
4. The link between modernity and coloniality (that is exemplified in the notion of Eurocentrism) is a mode of knowing and a hegemonic representation that derives from Europe's position as the center; claiming universality for itself (These four points are elaborated in relation to Escobar 2004, 217).

Therefore, to establish a decolonial turn, or a decolonial thinking that delinks itself from Modernity/Coloniality, it is necessary to intervene on at least three main levels:

1. To effectuate an internal critique of modernity. However, it is important to state that a critique of post-modernism and post-structuralism is not enough, as we have to elaborate on the concept of colonial difference that is a racial difference.
2. To elaborate the significance of the geopolitical location of knowledge in a global capitalism and its "spaceless space." What does this oxymoron delineate? That in global neoliberal capitalism, time is the major parameter, a parameter that includes modernization, progress and civilization and that works with the evacuation of spaces. "Spaceless space" is not a hyperbolic description but indicates that *time*, as *the space* and *the subject*, are not neutral notions. In global capitalism time has to be conceptualized as colonial time. It is important to state that in global capitalism no theoretical notion can assume its neutral mode of elaboration. In the moment that Giorgio Agamben (in the mid-1990s) proposed the concept of

forms-of-life that presented the division of life within itself, into form-of-life and life-without-form (or naked life) it became urgent that every notion or concept had to be re-signified.

In regard to this point that goes into details in what is the time-space matrix of the decolonial turn, Nelson Maldonado-Torres is precise, he states that

> decolonial thinking has existed since the very inception of modern forms of colonization—that is, since at least the late fifteenth and early sixteenth centuries—, and, to that extent, a certain decolonial turn has existed as well, but the more massive and possibly more profound shift away from modernization towards decoloniality as an unfinished project took place in the twentieth century and is still unfolding now. This more substantial decolonial turn was announced by W. E. B. Du Bois in the early twentieth century and made explicit in a line of figures that goes from Aimée Césaire and Frantz Fanon in the mid-twentieth century, to Sylvia Wynter, Enrique Dussel, Gloria Anzaldúa, Lewis Gordon, Chela Sandoval, and Linda Tuhiwai Smith, among others, throughout the second half of the twentieth to the beginning of the twenty-first century. The events that led to its solidification include the collapse of the European Age in the two World Wars, and the second wave of decolonization in Africa, Asia, the Caribbean, and other territories across the globe, including the Bandung Conference [Afro–Asian Conference—also known as the Bandung Conference—was a meeting of Asian and African states, most of which were newly independent, which took place on April 18–24, 1955 in Bandung, Indonesia]. Moments and movements that played a role in it and that are constitutive of it include the heightened perception of the linkages between colonialism, racism, and other forms of dehumanization in the twentieth-century, the formation of ethnic movements of empowerment and feminisms of color, and the appearance of queer decolonial theorizing. (Maldonado-Torres 2011, 2)

3. If we do not take into account the colonial/racial difference or fracture, or colonial rift (as Achille Mbembe expands it, connecting it with the geopolitical location of knowledge), then we are in the situation to constantly reproduce the matrix of coloniality. In 1997 the Peruvian theoretician Aníbal Quijano (1997) conceived a matrix of power, which he named the *colonial matrix of power*. Quijano conceptualized the neoliberal world of capitalism as an entanglement of different hierarchies that works at the axis of sexual, political, epistemic, economic, linguistic, and racial forms of domination and exploitation. This matrix affects all dimensions of social existence, such as sexuality, authority, subjectivity, and labor. At the center of the matrix is the viewpoint of how race (and racism)

becomes the organizing principle of all social, political, and economic structures of different capitalist's regimes.

Coloniality is therefore conceptualized as a global hegemonic model of power in place since the conquest of the Americas, that articulates race and labor, space and people according to the needs of capital and to the benefit of white European people (Escobar 2004, 218). In the e-mail exchange between Walter Mignolo and Arturo Escobar, they theorize that if modernity is conceptualized as the project of the Christian and secular West, then coloniality is precisely what the project of modernity needs to rule out and roll over, in order to implant itself as modernity. It is the site of enunciation where the blindness of the modern project is revealed and therefore it is the site where new projects, possibilities, contingencies begin to unfold as well (Escobar 2004, 218). Quijano's colonial matrix of power functions as the overall dimension of modernity (its "darker side"); coloniality is constitutive of modernity, rather than something derivative from it (Escobar 2004, 210). In this sense, colonialism is conceptualized as a Western process of expansion and a mode of production with which the West had accumulated its wealth. The West and European colonial States, through exploitation and expropriation of natural resources and the annihilation of millions enslaved persons, accumulated wealth and then started to present themselves as, the most progressive, claiming Universality for themselves. Santiago Slabodsky talks about racializations during Iberian imperialism in the sixteenth century that allow us to understand modernity as a world of economic exploitation and what he straightforwardly denotes as State terrorism (Slabodsky 2009).

THE OCCIDENTAL UNIVERSALIST THINKING AND RACIALIZATION

At this point, is also important to be particularly precise regarding the relation of Occidental Universalist Thinking and Racialization. Occidental Universalist Thinking is just not any kind of universal philosophy but a specific one. The German researcher Gabriele Dietze in her brilliant analysis with the title "Occidentalism, European Identity, and Sexual Politics" (2010) is very precise when claiming that since the fall of the Berlin Wall in 1989 but particularly since September 11, 2001, after the attack on the twin towers in New York's Manhattan "'occidentality' has developed into a new 'leading marker of difference' of European societies" (Dietze 2010, 90).

In order to connect an invigorated logic of Occidentalism to the center of global capitalism, Dietze proposes to analyze the definition of Occidentalism in the Oxford English Dictionary. Occidentalism is "the part of the world situated to the west of some recognized region; specifically it is the countries, civilization, or culture of the West. Originally with reference to Western Christendom or the Western Roman Empire, or to Europe as opposed to Asia and the Orient; now usually with reference to Europe and America as opposed to Asia and the Orient, or occasionally to America or the Western hemisphere as opposed to the Old World." (*Oxford English Dictionary*, quoted after Dietze 2010, 92.)

This definition elaborates Occidentalism as argued by Dietze into a political term. Of course, the analysis has to make a relation to Orientalism, which was coined by the founding father of post-colonialism, Edward Said. Edward Said, as formulated by Dietze, has analyzed the "oriental other" as an invention and knowledge formation of the European colonial enterprise based on the "ontological and epistemological construction between the 'Orient' and the 'Occident'" (Dietze 2010, 92).

Fernando Coronil (1996) elaborates that Occidentalism is not the reverse of Orientalism but the condition of its possibility, "[it is] an ensemble of representational practices that participates in the production of the construction of the world, which (1) separates the world's components into bounded units; (2) disaggregates their relational histories; (3) turns difference into hierarchy; (4) naturalizes these representations; and thus (5) intervenes, however unwittingly, in the reproduction of existing asymmetrical power relations" (Dietze 2010, 93).

What Dietze is explaining here is the shift (or substitution, repetition, multiplication) of the West/East post-Cold War divide into an Occident/Orient divide in the European Union (she particularly analyses the situation in Germany). This repetition or, better to say, *multiplication* (as now we have two divisions which are placed side by side and/or one on top of the other) has two exact functions. Firstly, it presents a new normativization of the reconstructed European Union (EU) now as a unified entity (the One). The EU although stitched together (as the EU is a bundle of sequences of erasures and performative repetitions: post Cold Europe, former Eastern Europe and "former" West), acts as One (Fortress). Secondly, it works by individuating new Others in this new EU space. Who they are? They are a substantial contingent of former colonized peoples, refugees, migrants, sans-papier (paperless), asylum seekers, etc., from North Africa, Pakistan, Indonesia, etc., coming to Europe.

It is important to state that the Occident/Orient divide brings "home" to the EU an old divide (upon which was founded classical Colonialism), now loyal to the "War on Terror" launched after 2001 by the USA (and supported by Great Britain and NATO) in the Middle East as a response to the September 11, 2001 attacks on the Twin Towers in New York. "War on Terror" is promoted as the war for the protection of "our," Occidental civilization and "our" Christian-Capitalist way of life.

Therefore the years 1989 and 2001 (and let's not overlook that September 11, 2001 presents the entrance of global capitalism onto center-stage) are two intervals more akin to the suspensions of suspension, as Giorgio Agamben would say, to a certain contraction of space (maybe is even more accurate to say akin to the oxymoron *spaceless space*) promulgated by the Occident in the time of neoliberal global capitalism.

What we see with these suspensions of suspension is the construction of a new inside/outside binary. But this is not just a division as it was in the past, on the contrary, it is about the multiplication of these binaries that collapse/clash into each other. Dietze states that the binary Occident/Orient runs along the sliding line of division, and this is "Occidentalism." If once again we tell the story narrated by Kwame Nimako that when the British football team was visiting Ukraine and Poland, the British Foreign Ministry informed the Black people in Britain that they should not go there because there would be a lot of neo-Nazi's and skinheads, who could attack the Black people, then it is clear that we have a multiplication of binaries (and not a binary) that run along the line of division, and this is the Occidental West.

With the processes of reconstruction (enlargement) of the European Union after the fall of the Berlin Wall (1989), the external division of Europe, the Cold War Europe of the 1950s-1970s, was changed into an internal division to be soon offered as completely obsolete with the project "former West" launched in 2008 in the Netherlands. After 2001 the EU started to re/produce another divide, namely the Occident/Orient, transforming it from an external (the War on Terror in the Middle East) into an internal division.

The question is why? The answer is that this allows dispensing with a substantial contingent of im/migrants composed of former colonized peoples, from North Africa, Pakistan, Indonesia. They are today produced as the new Other. Dietze states that these former colonized peoples (from North Africa, Pakistan, Indonesia coming to Europe) are now "subjected to varying regimes of migration: to secular laicism in France, separatist multiculturalism in the Netherlands (Michalowski 2005), and diversity politics in England (Modood 2002). The respective peculiarities engendered different theorizations of late-modern racisms such as Étienne Balibar's 'neo-racism' for France (Balibar 1991), Philomena Essed's 'everyday-Racism' in the Netherlands (Essed 1995), and Stuart Hall's 'cultural racism' for England," etc. (Dietze 2010, 94–95).

Germany declined any relation between national immigration politics and its colonial past and executed the same restrictive citizenship model as Austria until 2005, which left all im/migrants (and their children and grandchildren) in the position of (legal) aliens or foreigners (Ausländer). As a consequence, in Germany, racism against immigrants is called Ausländerfeindlichkeit (hostility toward foreigners) (Dietze 2010, 95).

Regulated from the point of Occidentalism, the binary Occident/Orient allows, according to Dietze, for a systematic usage of covert neo-racism that works through the rhetoric of "emancipation and enlightenment." In her in-depth analysis, she gives a vivid description of the space

of Europe, where contemporary Occidentalism develops different racialization procedures that work at the junction of race, class, and gender.

The Occident/Orient division masks the European Union's special
drive for apartheid, as the new Europe no longer wants to deal with post-
WWII Muslim migrants and the growth of the Muslim population.
Though, as argued by Mbembe, this is a paradoxical situation, since the
migrant population after 1974 (in the wake of the oil crisis) has drastically
diminished or, more accurately stated, has been controlled and racialized.

Although Western Europe has been considered a leading example for
protecting human rights, today it has developed an invigorated system of
control, exclusion and deportations. This is how then we can understand
unmistakably Achille Mbembe when he clarifies that

> as Frantz Fanon explains so clearly in *Black Skin, White Masks*, racializa-
> tion was the driving force . . . and race was the Beast at the heart of
> European colonial humanism. . . . It shows that there is in European
> colonial humanism something that has to be called unconscious self-
> hatred. Indeed racism in general and colonial racism in particular, rep-
> resents the transference of this self-hatred to the Other. . . . The totem
> that colonized peoples discovered behind the mask of European hu-
> manism and universalism was not only deaf and blind most of the
> time. It was also, above all, characterized by the desire for self-destruc-
> tion. But insofar as this form of death was necessarily conveyed
> through that of others, it was a "delegated death." Once again, it is
> Fanon who has analyzed, better than anyone else, this kind of necropo-
> litical side of life itself, or else which, in an act of reversion, takes
> "giving death" for "giving life." That is why the colonial relationship
> fluctuated constantly between the desire to extract resources and ex-
> ploit the natives, and the temptation to exterminate them. (Mbembe
> 2006)

FROM POSTCOLONIALISM TO DECOLONIALITY OR THE
QUESTION OF DIS/CONTINUITY

I shall now proceed with the implications of Black Critique in relation to
Europe, emphasizing the colonial/racial line that cuts and multiplies
within Europe and the global world. I will also be positioning Black
Critique in relation to former Eastern Europe while rethinking the dan-
gers of different appropriations of anti-racist struggles by the regime of
Whiteness.

Achille Mbembe argued that postcolonial thought with its critique of
European humanism and imperial forms of universalism, is not an end in
itself. It is carried out with the aim of paving the way for an enquiry into
the possibility of a politics of the future, of mutuality and of the common.
So for Mbembe the answer to the question of "what constitutes the politi-

cal strength of postcolonial thought?" lies in its enrolment in the historical social struggles of colonized societies and especially in its re-reading
of the theoretical praxis of what he calls *liberation movements*. He continues that, "if postcolonial thought today is the preserve of British and
American academia and of English-speaking scholars, it should not be
forgotten that this current was largely inspired by French and Afro-
French thinking" (Mbembe 2006). Therefore this is why to the influence
of Fanon, Césaire and Senghor, Mbembe adds the influence of French
thinkers like Merleau-Ponty, Sartre, Foucault, Derrida, and even Lacan.
He concludes that the postcolonial is "therefore a mode of thinking that
in several respects is very close to a peculiarly French approach to reasoning. So it is rather paradoxical that, because of its cultural insularity and
the narcissism of its elites, France has cut itself off from these new ventures in world thought" (Mbembe 2006).

And where then stands decoloniality? As Ramón Grosfoguel, (one of
the key figures of the Latin American Modernity/Coloniality Research
Group, that was established in 2000), asks: "Which are the concepts of
decolonial theory and how are they different from those of postcolonial
theory? How is migration related to a decolonization of the West?" (Grosfoguel 2011a). Ramón Grosfoguel answers by stating that the postcolonial
as a concept enters critical discourse in its current meaning in the late
1970s and early 1980s, but both the practice and the theory of postcolonial
resistance go back much further (indeed to the origins of colonialism
itself). He continues making reference to Fanon stating that the postcolonial means to suggest both resistance to the "colonial" and that the "colonial" and its discourses continue to shape cultures whose revolutions
have overthrown formal ties to their former colonial rulers. This ambiguity owes a good deal "to post-structuralist linguistic theory as it has influenced and been transformed by the three most influential postcolonial
critics Edward Said, Gayatri Spivak and Homi Bhabha" (Grosfoguel
2011a).

Hortense Spillers is very clear when she comments on Homi Bhabha's
"escalator" that he introduces in his *The Location of Culture* (Bhabha 1994).
She argues:

> The notion of hybridity and ambiguity is a very powerful notion, it has
> a certain glamour and sex appeal, but I don't *live* on an escalator. I
> mean at some point, I *land*. . . . The post-colonial and the post-modern
> have a way of always moving the discussion somewhere else. But you
> take the "local" with you, whatever your "local" is, into these various
> cultural and theoretical zones. A lot of this comes back to what you
> actually do on the ground, in the everyday. What I'm suggesting is that
> it is one thing to make pronouncements in public spaces about frater-
> nity, brotherhood, liberty, and justice. But it's another thing to come
> back where you live and to make that a part of your practice. The
> disparity between those two things is what we call hypocrisy, and

observing it makes me realize that I don't like my own lapses, I don't like other people's lapses, even though we know we have to live with them. It's a way of making people responsible beyond the pressures of their own rhetorical commitments, and the realization that commitments have to be something other than *rhetorical*; they have to be practical or praxial, in the sense of a practice. (Spillers 1998)

Both the term and various theoretical formulations of the "postcolonial" have been controversial, this is why, Grosfoguel concludes, scholars such as Emma Pérez and Linda Tuhiwai Smith, use the term *decolonial* to emphasize that we are not past (post) colonial, and that only the active agency of the colonized will complete the process of eradicating the most pernicious legacies of the colonial and neo-colonial eras.

But on a similar point that opens with asking on a possible future after 2001 in neoliberal global capitalism, Achille Mbembe argues that,

the postcolonial thought stresses the fact that identity arises from multiplicity and dispersion. . . . Seen from this perspective, colonization no longer appears as mechanical and unilateral domination forcing the subjugated into silence and inaction. Quite the reverse: the colonized person is a living, talking, conscious, active individual whose identity arises from violation, erasure and self-rewriting. Moreover, the universalization of imperialism cannot be explained by the violence of coercion alone. It was a consequence too of the fact that many colonized people were complicit in a fable that they found attractive in a number of respects. (Mbembe 2006)

Still the most pertinent question remains: what is the political core of decoloniality? The answer is, according to Grosfoguel, that decoloniality retraces the matrix of racialization as the main capitalist matrix from colonial times to today. He states,

The decolonial analysis insists on two points; first is to build a genealogy of racialization(s) that includes at least two systems of annihilation, one is colonialism and the other is Holocaust with its contemporary formats of anti-Semitism. On the other decolonial discourse should be political discourse with an agenda to de-universalize particular truths and realities; it tries to question the formation of imperial figures in liberal democracy. In other words, universalized imperial figures appear as the barrier to the analysis that try to de-universalize particular agendas that sustain homogeneous system of control through heterogeneous approach to racist ideologies. The decolonial turn on the other side tries to renegotiate this situation and dismantle this position of imperial figures. Subsequently decolonial discourse (that is not at all post-colonialism!) makes particularly important the annihilations of millions of slaves in colonialism that is a point at the core of the historical colonialism that transforms and invigorates today to the point we can talk of the word after colonialism and the regime of the postcolonial. (Grosfoguel 2011)

LEARNING AND DE-LEARNING: THE REGIME OF WHITENESS

In the 1990s after the fall of the Berlin Wall we witnessed a blossoming of identity politics that in the form of multiculturalism was seen as a purely cultural phenomenon, but maybe we missed to call it as already a process of racialization connected to the racialization of capital? That means that a process of racialization is actually at the core of the organization of contemporary global capitalist society that supports the process of identity politics. This process is not simply a multicultural process, not simply a cultural differentiation in society, but a process of steady racializations within the racial scale of contemporary society. The identity politics that we were so much pushing into the culturalization of contemporary capitalist societies is in fact a process of racialization. This latter we did not see as such but it is the process that transformed from the past colonial processes of steady racism into a neoliberal global contemporary set of discriminations. Racialization functions as *classificatory matrix* that sustains a monopoly on classification, at the same time racialization is obfuscated with the processes of *rationalization* of capitalist expansion and exploitation.

To these processes we have to add, as elaborated by Šefik Tatlić (Gržinić and Tatlić 2012), the firmness of prohibition of "racism," or in wider sense, stereotypical "rigidness" in relation to representational stunts through which western power structures insist they were founded, as for example on anti-fascist foundations to which the EU refers. Supposedly the EU has nothing to do with racism or with the political articulation of processes of racialization of identity. This is as well hidden by the demand in global capitalism not to talk about racism, under the saying that there is no racism in contemporary global societies. Or, it is prohibited as a normative demand to talk about it, while racialization still remains the main logic of the differentiation of the social and political and economic space of global capitalism. Though it is becoming clear that it has a lot to do with the construction of the institutional and economic basis on which utter fascism and racism could be conducted under the performative aegis of the defense of anti-fascism, and for that matter, anti-racist values. These two processes opened up clearly at the inaugural and closing manifestations of the last Olympics game in London 2012.

In relation to this conceptualization about racism and racializations it is also necessary to pose the question *about a proper position of enunciation*.

I have to ask why a snow-white European scholar, as I am, enters the topic of Black studies? This is not a polite question for a politically correct written theoretical essay, but an important question for a *former* Eastern European (which I also presently am). Being *former* is not an excuse nor an identity marker but a social, political and epistemological condition of my work. I pose this question as being somebody who was born in hard core socialism, went through the processes of transition from socialism to bloody neoliberal global capitalism and is as well-rooted in the Western epistemological edifice of contemporary theory and philosophy that daily reestablishes the processes of racializations through a Western, or (maybe it is more accurate to say) an intensified Occidental epistemological hegemony. But as being somebody coming from the former Eastern Europe now in the European Union without borders, we the *former* "taste" the conditions of racialization "without a race," on a daily basis.

In the processes described above of an unspoken, but reiterated reproduction and repetition of differences between the East and the West of Europe, racism, hegemony and discrimination reverberate constantly. This condition along with an intensified dissymmetry in the global world regarding allocation of capital, discrimination, dispossession, and coloniality made me aware that to understand and analyze such situations of racism and racialization, it is necessary to enter deeply into the findings of Black studies/Black thinking; as these studies provide historically and presently the most important tools, strategies and tactics for the future.

What we can learn from the established relations of differences and similarities in the writings by Black scholars and (former Eastern) Europeans thinkers, (both trained in and dissociated from the Western Occidental epistemology edifice, while occupying different places in relation to the most important line of division in neoliberal global capitalism that is the colonial/racial divide), is the way how to discard the present necroracist corpse of Europe (more precisely the EU).

Two important points are to be taken into account for the future.

The first was developed by Hortense Spillers in 2006. She maintains in *The Idea of Black Culture* that the return "to the idea of black culture must be considered today in a critical climate that is not hospitable to the topic, even though hospitality and accommodation have never been attributes of the context in which the idea was either engendered or understood" (Spillers 2006). Therefore she suggested in 2006 that "Perhaps it would be more accurate to say that a powerful repertory of refusals that make the topic a virtual impossibility now blocks one's view: (1) the recession of the subject, historical and otherwise; (2) a dimensionless present, on an analogy with television; and so, (3) the impoverishment of history; (4) the decline of the concept and practices of the nation-State, except that current U.S. foreign policy, the dramatic rise of post-Soviet states, and China's sensational emergence on the contemporary world stage would all urge a serious rethinking of such claims; (5) the 'exhaustion of difference'; (6) the new impulses of a globalization so complete, we are led to believe, that locality, or the 'local' itself, apparently vanishes as a discrete moment of perception; and paradoxically, (7) an Afrocentric conceptual space that so collapses the distance between a putative African Diaspora and the cultures of the African Continent that little differentiation is interposed between them" (Spillers 2006).

The second was elaborated in 2004 by Araba Evelyn Johnston-Arthur regarding whiteness as an oppressive system of hegemony (Johnston-Arthur 2004). She argues that the "very way of defining and naming of the white ethnicity (Weißheit in German, M. Gržinić note)" in her Austrian context that is still predominantly white and "colored" by "the white 'antiracist' practice . . . often remains unthematized, and thus its power and violence keep continuously being established as a normality, that is also how they (power and violence) get realized, and how whiteness hegemony doubles due to the attributed neutrality" (Johnston-Arthur 2004). She continues "that in order to call whiteness as whiteness for her being a Black subject in a white Austria [context] where predominately 'white anti-racist' practice reigns" she needs "a radicalism and enormous effort" (Johnston-Arthur 2004). As Johnston-Arthur exposes: "Whiteness, as a realized concept of racism, has been, apart from the global dimension of white superiority, marked by its own specific, historically-established national reality. In the Austrian context the concept of whiteness is usually shrouded in a veil of silence and is constantly realized in very obvious dimensions in the so-called anti-racist working practice" (Johnston-Arthur 2004).

Therefore she argues that,

> Black criticism, living daily in this context and being explicitly formulated, has been adapted to this national reality. If fragments of a "well-established" Black critical discourse, such as in the U.S. context, for instance, are simply imported into Austria and presented there as outstanding theoretical progressive pieces of self-criticism, then it all results in something such as "pseudo-thematisation." In that way "Austrian whiteness" pulls away rather eloquently from the practical and action-orientated local Black criticism and from the conflicts with specifically Austrian whiteness. (Johnston-Arthur 2004)

Because of this pseudo-thematization Johnston-Arthur says that we have to be aware of the danger of this topic of anti-racism becoming a new segment on the critical intellectual market. Therefore she states that,

> the very dynamics of the deconstruction of whiteness as a continuous political process within the anti-racist struggle, lies in the relationship between theory and practice. This must not turn out to be the building a kind of white "anti-racist" critical elite that "pseudo thematizes" its whiteness and produces from their camp discourses that allow it to refall in love with its own white progressivity. In this way, Black criticism in this exclusive, powerful white "critical" discourse seems suitable for self-representation of anti-racist whiteness. Whiteness is in such a way not decentralized, but just presents itself as a kind of a critical package, and the violence that underlies it remains therefore intact and normalized. (Johnston-Arthur 2004)

Achille Mbembe elaborates as Araba Evelyn Johnston-Arthur on this same point in an interview for *Esprit*. For him

> it is the time both of the end and of reinvention, starting with the reinvention of what has suffered the most damage—in the case of Afro-modern history, the "commodity body." As is clearly shown by the example of South Africa on its emergence from apartheid, nothing can be reinvented unless one is capable both of glancing backward and of looking forward. . . . It requires that we keep documenting the apartheid archive: the gaping scars, demolished homes, broken lives; the skeletons, the debris and the rubble; the ruins and the fading memories of that there once was. . . . But it also demands that we pay attention to Black people's capacity for self-making, self-reference and self-expression and to alternative versions of whiteness that are not primarily constituted around property and privilege, but around an ethics of mutuality and human solidarity. Looking forward—the politics of possibility, a future-oriented politics—implies a meditation about how to illuminate anew the experience of being human, of human life. (Mbembe 2006)

In short, it is obvious that my interest lies in politically, theoretically and critically shaped reflections and activations developed by Black scholars in order to dismantle colonialism, coloniality and the normalizing processes of the regime of whiteness with its procedures of dispossession, racialization, erasure and genocides. At the same time we have to be clear about the expanding violence reiterated with and through pseudo-thematization of antiracism by the regime of Whiteness that has been re/constituted lately around capital, property and privilege. The question of *agency*, (it does not matter how it will be named in the future), implies a struggle against and delinking from colonial dispossessions and brutal racial, class, and gender discriminations.

Let's reformulate this with Hortense Spillers's words in her "Mama's Baby, Papa's Maybe: An American Grammar Book" (Spillers 1987), when she states that while witnessing violence against a Black person, in that violent and traumatic way she also envisioned processes of a constitution of a "body of history." This body of different, counter, insurgent histories is also something that we want to constitute with this book in order to think about a different future.

NOTES

1. All terms are used by Brian Carr in relation to numerous other scholars, among others Hortense J. Spillers.

2. Schwarze Frauen Community (Black Women community), http://www.wuk.at/WUK/GESELLSCHAFT_POLITIK/Initiativen_Gruppen/Schwarze_Frauen_Community

FIVE

A Refugee Protest Camp in Vienna and the European Union's Processes of Racialization, Seclusion, and Discrimination

"We ourselves, the refugees, make the demonstration, and we are the ones who want it. It is our fight. We thank everybody for their help, but we don't allow anybody to use us. This is a self-organized struggle of and by refugees, one that needs your support, your presence on the street on Saturday."
—From a speech by refugee Salaheddine Najah during a protest song contest at the Rabenhof Theatre, Vienna, February 12, 2013

Since November 2012, refugees have been protesting in Austria.[1] At the center of this protest lies the formation of the Refugee Protest Camp in Vienna, which started with a ten-hour march of approximately a hundred refugees and their supporters. The march, which took place on November 24, 2012, started at the refugee reception center in Traiskirchen and ended at the Vienna city center—a distance of around twenty kilometers. The march resulted in the erection of the Refugee Protest Camp, which included tents, a kitchen, and activities in Sigmund Freud Park, in front of the Votive Church in the center of Vienna. This camp was cleared by police on December 28, 2012. After negotiating with personnel from the Votive Church, the refugees entered the church itself. They decided to "camp" in the freezing cold church building (while at the same time being monitored and controlled by Caritas, a Catholic Church charity relief organization). As nothing was offered to them by that point—no answer from the authorities regarding their demands—a group of refugees went on a hunger strike.

The Refugee Protest Camp in Vienna was supported by multiple NGOs and many activists and students, including a number from the Academy of Fine Arts in Vienna. The hunger strike ended after a month (in January 2013) and the archbishop himself promised the refugees that they could remain in the church and would not be expelled by police.

On February 1, 2013, after a break of ten days, the refugees in the Votive Church announced the resumption of their hunger strike, since the government had made no effort to meet their demands to find a solution regarding their legal status. On February 5, one of the hunger strikers was deported to Hungary. Presumably, he will be expelled from the European Union, or worse, deported back to Pakistan. On February 16, around 2,500 people in Vienna and other EU cities marched in solidarity with the refugees, a day after the refugees decided to stop their hunger strike for a second time in order to consider their next move. At the beginning of March 2013, the protesting refugees agreed to move the Refugee Protest Camp Vienna into a former monastery that was offered to them by the Austrian cardinal Schönborn. In the monastery they are offered legal counsel and legal representation—a "safe space" for continuing their struggle to change the asylum system.

At the press conference held on March 4, 2013, the refugees declared that their new home would not be a small "Traiskirchen" (a refugee camp with a function to isolate refugees from society), but another step towards the solution of their problems. By August 2013, eight activists of the Vienna refugee protest movement had been deported to Pakistan, and twelve other persons are being threatened to be deported very soon. The Austrian Ministry of Interior Johanna Mikl-Leitner justified the deportations by stating that regions in Pakistan are not all dangerous and that especially those regions, where the deported refugees are from, were secure. Some journalists have been taking a closer look and report that at least some of the regions into which the refugees were deported are considered to be the most dangerous in Pakistan. This life-threatening situation for the refugees demands concrete action against the repressive politics and for solidarity with the self-organized movement in this city, in the State, in the EU, and in the world.

Gin/i Müller, performer, dramaturge, and activist of the Refugee Protest Camp Movement in Vienna stated in an interview reflecting on the yearlong Refugee Protest Camp Movement that "never before in Austria there was a church that was squatted by the refugees, and I think in a Catholic country like Austria, from the confrontational level, this was a big step. Because also through the church, through that step, from camp to church, this brought a bigger political discussion because Austria is also a very Catholic country and also very influenced by the Catholic church; also by the Catholic party, the ÖVP party (Österreichische Volkspartei [ÖVP, "Austrian People's Party"] is a Christian democratic and conservative political party in Austria); this made a confrontational level much more explicit, to go inside of the church and question the refugee movement on a level of society. I think that the movement by itself so far didn't reach a lot, of course you can see it from different perspectives that it did, it opened a lot of different discourses, so that people also started to discuss about different issues, like for example on EU Schengen's border system and the Dublin II asylum applications; but on the other hand I totally understand the depression of the refugees right now, that say actually we didn't achieve anything, or maybe it was even more danger-ous to participate in a process like this in a Refugee Protest Movement, and maybe they could achieve more for themselves if they wouldn't be part of the Refugee Protest Movement" (Müller 2013).

Khan Adalat, a refuge, and first line activist of the Refugee Protest Camp Movement in Austria upholds this "I'm a refugee for ten years, I can do this everywhere, my political responsibility and my political posi-tion increased also, but my political position and of my family is not possible in this region because we cannot talk about the real situation in the region; it means also that we cannot do our political activity and just start a normal life, and start some business, or something . . . so my example is just one example, there are thousands of people living in Europe, the African communities, Arab communities and Asian commu-nities, and yes the system is—the system is old, the bloody system is thirty years old and they need to change something" (Adalat 2013). On December 9, 2013, several people were deported from Austria to Lahore, Pakistan. According to informations from fellow refugees there were at least eight persons from Vorarlberg, Vienna, Salzburg, Innsbruck, and Linz refugee centers. According to refugee reports, the police arrested people by surprise, without informing them beforehand that they were facing deportation.

At the present moment, this historic self-organized movement of refu-gees in Vienna and throughout Europe is constantly changing, as the refugees are hostages of the European "sovereign" states and the Fortress of EU policies. What is becoming clear is, to use Achille Mbembe words, that Europe's "good conscience . . . has wanted to be responsible for nothing, guilty of nothing" (Mbembe 2010, 171). The international Hu-man Rights regime that was developed in Western Europe after World War II and that has spread globally has reached a dead end. It must be rethought and radically changed—politically, economically, and ideolog-ically—to keep refugees from being left at the mercy of a regime of im-prisonment, exclusion, marginalization, and death.

The intention of this chapter is to open up a discussion about solutions and to rethink the frame within which the self-organized movement of refugees takes place. The fact is that the movement and the demands put forward by the refugees are of historic importance. For the first time, refugees have self-organized themselves and have started a public dis-cussion on the subject of asylum and human rights. This has resulted in the formation of a political platform with demands to change the situation of refugees in Austria and in the EU as a whole.

In March 2012, in Würzburg, Germany, refugees started a struggle to obtain the most elementary human rights.[2] Since May 2012, refugee strikes have occurred in Denmark, Turkey, Bulgaria, Greece, France, the Netherlands, and Austria. The protests in Germany, the Netherlands, and Austria formed, in effect, a platform of united forces. The Refugee Struggle Congress took place in March 2013 in Munich, Germany, where participants discussed future actions, organizational bodies, and a list of political demands aiming to change the awful conditions for refugees and asylum seekers in the EU and Europe.

The demands of the refugees of the Refugee Protest Camp in Vienna are twofold. One part demands better living conditions, from adequate food to a decent social life. (The refugees are completely isolated in refugee centers that prevent them from having a social life, from participating in the wider social and political life of Austria.) They want the chance to learn German and to have professional translators who will accurately translate their demands when they are caught in the limbo of State bureaucracy and are interrogated by the repressive State apparatus. The other part of their demands is the most important: the right to stay and the right to work. They want to exercise self-sufficiency and not be the object of charity captured by the State or any NGO.

For at least a decade, refugees have been caught in a situation of systematic abandonment. Their living conditions in the EU have gradually deteriorated; a process which has been neglected by the nation-States in the "former" Western European countries. For a long time refugees have been systematically forced into a situation of impoverishment, deprivation, and seclusion. They have been the victims of a process of racial discrimination that has diminished and depoliticized the concept and the status of human rights.

The refugees decided themselves to break out of such a situation. They started not only by making demands, but also by performing and acting out political equality in the space of the EU's pre-established political, social, and economic inequality. The EU survives on a constant reproduction of inequality, which is the axiom of neoliberal global capitalism. The refugees broke the predetermined space of politics in which only predetermined actors—let's say citizens—have visibility and are taken "seriously" when asking for democratic rights. But the struggles and demands of the refugees—who, in the parlance of Jacques Rancière, belong to the "part-of-no-part" in the present global capitalist political reality—imposed themselves in a way that forced the people of Europe to regard them as equal (Rancière 2004). In so doing, they re-politicized and rearticulated the space of Europe, imposing the axiom of equality in a space of political, social, and economic inequality.

The refugees did not ask for "some" rights that would only allow them to enter and maybe participate in the space of politics and the social, they were not captive to an old modernist idea of politics, waiting for their place in the political arena; a place reserved only for those already considered to belong to a determinate political space—for example, nation-State citizens with their form of good life (a "good" life that deteriorates for them too in times of crisis).

Instead, the refugees appropriated the space that was seen as inaccessible to them. They thereby changed the coordinates of the established and safeguarded notion of in/equality. They actually subverted the whole space of traditional politics. Their self-empowered action came as a surprise, and it opened up the possibility of demanding changes to the laws of EU nation-States. Moreover, their actions will force the NGOs and activists that support them to reorganize themselves and their struggles.

This political platform emerged forcefully when the refugees symbolically rejected the Ute Bock Prize for Moral Courage, which was given to them in January 2013 in Vienna. On the one hand, the refugees thanked the organizers of the Ute Bock Prize for awarding it to them, but on the other hand, they asserted that they did not need charity, but political and economic (human) rights—namely, to stay and to work!

Hence, the refugees repoliticized the space of the political not by simply asking to be included, but by appropriating the space. They showed that both politics and the "human" in "human rights" are outcomes of a process of reconfiguration and repoliticization, as described by Rancière. They opened up the possibility for equality in a situation of tightly controlled and of constantly reproduced inequality.

The actions of the refugees show that there are not two types of human beings, citizens and non-citizens. Either we are all citizens or we are all non-citizens! This conclusion came to the fore in a public talk by one of the refugees from the Refugee Protest Camp in Vienna. He implored the Austrian public: "You are citizens that support our demands. Therefore, why don't you demand that your political representatives—who you, as citizens, have elected—change this unbearable situation?!" The response was complete silence.

The refugees' demands pose a set of questions and problems that target not only the biopolitical regimes of the "former" Western European countries of the EU, but the whole Western concept of human rights as it was developed after WWII. Until the fall of the Berlin Wall in 1989, human rights and asylum politics were predominantly used to reproduce the division between Eastern and Western Europe. The East was presented as a totalitarian realm, while the West presented itself as a place of democracy and respect for human rights. Human rights policy has been one of the main shields used by democratic capitalist regimes in the West to deflect discussions regarding the fascist reality of Western Europe after WWII.

The question of human rights started to visibly disintegrate after the fall of the Berlin Wall. After 1989, the emergence of global capitalism caused refugee and asylum policy in Europe to deteriorate. It is said that the employment restrictions imposed in the EU today are meant to protect the citizens of the EU, especially in Western Europe, so their living standards do not decline. However, we are well-aware that wages have remained stagnant for a decade and that protests in the public spaces of European democracy are frequently suppressed by police and military forces (authorized by laws that originated in colonial times, as is the case in France). In her text "French Suburbia 2005: The Return of the Political Unrecognized," Rada Iveković writes: "When the [French] government reactivated the law about the state of emergency [in 2005], passed during the Algerian war in 1955, the French learned that colonial legislation had never been abrogated in the first place" (Iveković 2008).

In the biopolitics of the West, citizens are strongly differentiated in terms of class, gender, and race—differentiations, discriminations, and exploitations that multiply globally. This is not just a question of "diversity," as it is constantly presented to the public. On the contrary, the former proletariat has changed into a precariat, and increasingly sees itself as "the wretched of the earth" (Fanon 2005). The perspective of the world seen from the side of the colonized, as formulated in Frantz Fanon's famous work written during the Algerian anti-colonial struggle of the 1960s, shows that EU biopolitics is in fact constantly reproduced by and through necropolitics.

The second big change in the status of refugee rights happened after 9/11. The individual capitalist states asserted their own laws, and in so doing infringed upon international law and universal human rights. Anthony Burke wrote about this in a text published in 2002 in the first issue of the Australian journal e-borderlands. He stated that what had opened before us was "a world where terror is met with terror, where security is premised on insecurity, where the politics of fear and the inevitability of conflict—not freedom or justice—seem the only things enduring." The outcome was, as elaborated by Burke, that normalized patterns of violence and coercion—in the form of domestic security, surveillance, and the "deterring" of asylum seekers—took center stage in global capitalism (Burke 2002). Suvendrini Perera, in her text "What is a Camp . . . ?" published in the same issue, also questions the fluid and problematic categorizations that animated post-9/11 security politics (Perera 2002). She talks of the war on terror as a "category of confusions and bizarre doublings."

As Achille Mbembe has written in reference to the dispossession of life in Africa, "global capitalism cannot expand without what we should call massive racial subsidies or discounts." As Mbembe points out, "[capitalism] needs to work through and across different scales of race as it attempts to mark people either as disposable or as waste. It needs to produce, order, segment, and racialize surplus or superfluous populations to strategic effect" (Mbembe 2012).

Let's look into a genealogy of this process of producing massive racial subsidies, and the brutal racialization of the social, political, cultural, and economic space of the European Union after 1989 (Gržinić and Tatlić 2012). After the fall of the Berlin Wall, it was deemed obsolete to speak of any type of East/West division. Therefore gradually the "outside" binary was transformed into an internal process of division, fragmentation, classification, and discrimination based on race, class, and gender. If previously there was talk about life and death, today we have a differentiation within each category itself. The list of capitalism's victims is divided from within. Some victims have a higher status, while others are unimportant. Through this process, the capitalist Christian project of dispossession does not allow any "identity" to acquire a position from which to denote capitalism as such. These identities are pitted against each other, without understanding that they are a product of the processes of racialization, presented in the capitalist system as a kind of identity politics. The promise of liberation by capital is therefore a paradoxical and cynical measure in which liberation is presented as infinity of fragmentations. At work here is the process of capitalism's racialization, a control axis on which endlessly differential forms of capitalist expansion are being conceived.

Structural (and more and more social) racism is the core logic of global capitalism. Racialization is its internal administrative, judicial, and economic procedure, which regulates the space of financial capitalism as well as the system of representation, theory, and discursivity. Racism is not just an identity politics but something internal to the whole agenda of the transformation of the nation-State under global capitalism. It is possible to argue that in the transition from nation-State to war-State (which is the contemporary form of the old imperial and colonial nation-States of the past) we bump into a specific formation: the racial-State. All EU States are racial-States, as demonstrated by the way they have managed refugee and asylum politics.

This is to say that what supports the process of identity politics is not simply a multicultural project of differentiation in society, but a process of racialization that is actually at the core of contemporary global capitalist societies. The identity politics that we have defined as the product of a process of multiculturalization in contemporary capitalist societies is in fact a process of racialization.

At the same time, homogeneous control structures stay in the hands of those who have "defined" the purposes of capitalist public space, that is, First World capitalist centers of colonialism. They have created the pretense that the homogeneous center allows unprecedented liberty for heterogeneous difference, as long as these differentiations do not become political!

On the other hand, structural racism and other processes of racialization are pressing on us in global capitalism, and asks us not to talk about racism. Contemporary capitalism denies racism, claiming that it belongs to the era of colonialism, before the time of the the global world we live in today. Or more precisely, talking about racism is prohibited as a normative demand, while racialization still remains the main logic of differentiation in the social, political, and economic spaces of global capitalism.

Racialization is not just a process of producing tropes—it is not only about a process of capital's narrativization of its, so to speak, immanent levels of dispossessions; racialization is a process inherent to capital itself, or more precisely, to its white framework. The process of the internal racialization of capital functions as a "molding of the snake," which manifests itself as a transition from cognitive to financial capital, where molding is not cultural but racial. Maybe the next stage in molding will be—or already is—a transition to "human capital" that appropriates the spectrum of meanings associated with the word "humanity." This would allow capitalism to represent its antagonists as the ultimate *anti-humanists*.

As Achille Mbembe has noted,

> What distinguishes our age from previous ages, the breach over which there is apparently no going back, the absolute split of our times that breaks up the spirit and splits it into many, is again contingent, dispersed, and powerless existence: existence that is contingent, dispersed, and powerless but reveals itself in the guise of arbitrariness and the absolute power to give death anytime, anywhere, by any means, and for any reason. (Mbembe 2001, 13)

The notion of powerless existence in the context of racialization and representation, theory and discursitvity, should not be treated in binary terms that would imply the existence of a relation of dichotomy between the (powerless) subjugated and the (death bringing) subjugator. The "guise of arbitrariness" should be seen as the capacity for hegemonic power to give death at any time, while the powerless existence should not be seen as an a priori position, but as a property that has marked the closing of the distance between the subjugator and the subjugated, neutralizing antagonism between the paradigmatic protagonists in the cosmology of power. It is precisely this arbitrariness that is employed in the processes of (out)sourcing, deporting, and devising that are part of refugee centers' procedures when granting or rejecting papers to stay, work, or live. In a way, arbitrariness makes a coherent connection between racialization, rationalization, and the system that sustains them both.

It is also important to expose the fact that the process of racialization at work in the refugee and asylum centers, and in the whole system of refugee policy in Europe, allows for a brutally perverse structure of racialization. Racialization provides a kind of "internal clock" or a "set of guidelines" used by capitalist white racist ideology, that can be seen as well as the embodiment of a prohibition organized on the basis of "smashing of all prohibitions," but only when presented as the regime's ability to posit itself "antagonistically" toward its own racist ideology. For instance, political parties in power in the EU claim that they would like to do something about the situation, that is not at all "a case" of discriminatory policy, but simply an effect of laws and regulations that unfortunately take time to be changed.

This arbitrariness, as Achille Mbembe argues, "accomplishes its own work and validates itself through its own sovereignty, and thereby permits power to be exercised as a right to kill" (Mbembe 2001, 13).

Therefore, arbitrariness does not function as a mask for the absence of some profound "possibility." Nor is it a "new form" of capitalism based on mandatory transgression. Rather, arbitrariness is a symptom of an ideology based on utter emptiness—or more precisely, based on an emptiness that is being filled by transgression. The capitalist necropolitical turn (the one that produces a pure abandonment of life and at the same time the activation of the war machine) takes racism as "legitimizing" terrain for its processes of discrimination and dispossession, presenting racism and racialization as a sort of "benign" modernist (we could almost say atavistic) process of infinite narrations. These narrations are presented as a pure irregularity (and not a systematic process), hence, as an "erratic" framework that fosters struggles for the prominence of identity, culture, and race within the hierarchies of exploitation.

NOTES

1. See http://refugeecampvienna.noblogs.org/
2. This began when refugees pitched a small tent in Würzburg, Germany. It has since grown into a huge movement that has spread all over Europe. See http://refugee-congress.wordpress.com/english/

SIX

Elaborating on Transmigrant and Transfeminist Dissident Positions

I will make recourse to some contemporary performative practices and political spaces in Europe that dismantle the singular established contemporary history of art and performative practices in the European context. I will argue that Europe has to critically review its colonial and racist history and present.

IRON MASK, WHITE TORTURE

The point of departure for fastening these questions is the project *Iron Mask, White Torture*; a performance and installation, conceived by Marissa Lôbo in 2010 (Lôbo 2013). It was presented at the group exhibition "Where do we go from here?" at Secession (exhibition hall) in Vienna (also in 2010). Performers: Agnes Achola, Alessandra Klimpel, Belinda Kazeem, Flavia Inkiru, Grace Latigo, Steaze, Sheri Avraham, Njideka Stephanie Iroh, and Marissa Lôbo.

Why start with this project?

What is the most striking point that strikes us back but we refuse to go on strike? It is the absence of any word whatsoever in the mass media after the opening of the exhibition on this performance; a fact so strikingly obvious that it was impossible to miss. An article was published in the daily *Der Standard* (Vienna, Austria); the article that was published on the whole exhibition but not a single word was published concerning this performance. At a later stage, an interview with the author, Marissa Lôbo, was published online. Therefore the role of "empowerment," "agency" and "choice" had a double role in this performance. Shortly, I will state what the elements of the performance were, based on the "Re-

111

Figure 6.1.   Marissa Lôbo, *Iron Mask, White Torture*, performance, Secession, Vienna, 2010. Photo by Susi Krautgartner.

port by the Collective of Black Women Subjects in Art Space," written by Marissa Lôbo and Sheri Avraham, and published in *Reartikulacija*, a bilingual journal from Ljubljana (Lôbo 2010).

They said that they entered the museum space (the "Secession" that I mentioned above), "a space of production of an epistemological violence. Such a space presents an appropriation of the history of the 'other,' a constant reproduction of the white western desire of exposing and determining otherness—pure empire of voyeurisms" (Lôbo 2010). The performance consisted of nine black women and women of color, wearing black outfits and having bright blue eyes! The blue eyes represented a reference to Anastácia, a slave of the runaway slace communities know in Brazil as *quilombos*. Her struggle for freedom became the symbol of anti-colonial resistance.[1]

The curator chose the title "Where do we go from here?" for the group exhibition in Secession in 2010, at which Marisa Lôbo presented her performance and installation *Iron Mask, White Torture*.

"Where do we go from here, Vienna?" was suggested by Marissa Lôbo and Sheri Avraham as an ironic question to be asked when they argued "your history is imprinted in every corner, and at the same time we revile openly and legally a deep-rooted racist structure" (Lôbo 2013, 272). They commented that in one recent Austrian election campaign, one spoke of legislation that would enforce laws that are imposed on those who are defined as "aliens" that is the way of naming those coming from third states (States outside the European Union) (Lôbo 2013, 272). Lôbo refers to the parliamentary elections in Austria in 2008, and to the subsequent reinforcement after 2008 of the adopted major amendments to the Aliens Act and the Asylum Law in Austria in 2002.

A NEW INDECENT MATERIALISM

Now let us make a slight detour to contextualize the performance, the topic of racism and the silence. To get a wider perspective in which to situate the performance and to understand what is going on in the moment of its showing, it is necessary to make recourse at least briefly to what are the most propulsive positions in the West white queer context. I have two main positions in mind and they are: Marie-Hélène Bourcier (Bourcier 2011) and Beatriz Preciado (Preciado 2013). These two positions are developing an internal critique inside the western discourse within the following triadic format: feminism, gender, and queer. Especially important is Bourcier's statement when she predicated the death of feminism (Bourcier 2011).[2] She stated that it will not persist without taking into account the issues of "race, " class, sexuality, and gender.

For decades, the entanglement of these three elements has been pushed forwards by the Black, Chicana, and Asian feminists and the queer activists and theorists combining post-colonial and decolonial movements and studies. Today, the same entanglement is apparent in the European context too, especially in the Black Diaspora communities in "former" Western Europe, and in communities of migrants, queers, transsexuals, and sex workers.

Global capitalism functions not through a division but due to an *entanglement* that can be precisely described as the/a Christian white capitalist world reiterated through a constant—humanization. "Becoming human" is a specific process of racialization that works hand in hand with class racialization. Through stigmatization and labeling, based on the constructed category of race, racialization transforms societies into racially coded societies. This process is today going so far that we have a process of racialization being imputed without any "race" prerogatives while nevertheless serving as a measure of discrimination, subjugation and (finally) global capitalism's dispossession. It functions in Europe through the manufacturing of former Eastern European "non-subjects" into fully gendered European white middle class subjects. It is about *us* acquiring our capitalist conservative, chauvinistic, patriarchal, mostly petit-bourgeois lineage with which to safeguard the heterosexual family and the racialized nation's "substance." The European Union aims for the manufacturing of the former "barbarian communist" Eastern European into a "humanized" and "civilized" European.

The performance entitled *Iron Mask, White Torture* tackles precisely the entanglement formulated by Marissa Lôbo with regard to the context of her work. I quote: "all these processes affect us let's say as human beings inside of all complexities of ideological effects of racialized bodies in this historical and geographical moment, and force us to ask how the ideas of affect, sexuality, gender, class, modernity and citizenship co-articulate and racialize our bodies; this is what is to be elaborated and made conscious to us" (Lôbo 2010).

Therefore it is possible to argue that at the core of the demand is the politics of queer, gender and feminism through race. This is a thesis I started to develop in 2000 when I made an analysis regarding the triadic model of feminism, gender, and queer in the space of former Yugoslavia. An extremely relevant question, as after the fall of the Berlin Wall, in former Yugoslavia we started to be part of a *colonial narrative of rescue* under liberation in Western terms.

It reached its peak with the exhibition *Gender Check—Femininity and Masculinity in the Art of Eastern Europe*, displayed in the Museum of Modern Art, or MUMOK, in Vienna from November 2009 to February 2010, curated by Bojana Pejić.[3] The exhibition was initiated and what is even more important, enabled financially by ERSTE Foundation (a division of the Austrian ERSTE bank). It was a project through which the celebration of the twentieth anniversary of the fall of the Berlin Wall in 2009 gained its most perverse form.

In relation to such and similar projects I have asked how we pass from Sanja Iveković, a Croatian artist of international recognition, to the lesbian scene in Ljubljana in the 1980s, and to Tanja Ostojić and Šejla Kamerić in the 1990s in order to finally reach a discussion about a group in Ljubljana known as the "Uprising of the Lesborgs." As in the exhibition *Gender Check—Femininity and Masculinity in the Art of Eastern Europe* positions that come after the heterosexual feminist subject positions from the 1970s were missing. These positions are surely historically extremely important. However, we cannot understand anything after the 1970s if we do not subject to precise analysis the positions of lesbians and gays in the 1980s, in socialism, in former Yugoslavia.

Thinking about former Yugoslavia, or better, about different States that came out of its shadow, requires us to rethink at least three discontinuities of the last thirty years.

The first presents the space once known as Eastern Europe that was, in the 1990s, after the fall of the Berlin Wall (1989), transformed into former Eastern Europe partly in order to be integrated from 2004 onward into the European Union (EU) and partly left to wait at the EU's threshold.

The second happened after the period of transition in the 1990s and was elaborated in the new millennium through a genealogy of contemporary performative practices and political spaces in former Yugoslavia that dismantled the singular and established contemporary history of art and performative practices (conceptual, body, and performance) that had been imposed by Western Europe's historiography.

The third is connected with the EU's hyperbolic regained whiteness (as formulated by Kwame Nimako) with the reiterated ideology of Western Occidentalism that brutally reproduces the regimes of racial and class coding that governs economic, social and political inequality in Europe.

This constructed genealogy (genealogy always implies taking a political position) presents a trajectory that I propose to view as the passage from *sexually queer* to *politically queer*, where we have to recognize projects in the queer context that have no simple connotation of the sex/gender divide. We can recuperate the aforementioned genealogy by making the following point: we can trace a path beginning at a difference that matters and that establishes a relation between feminism and postmodernism; it develops in post-colonial theories of the embodied Other/s in the 1990s, and presents itself today as transmigrant and transfeminist positioning of affects and politics with a demand to re-take the question of race after 2001.

This genealogy I propose comes around the time when Bourcier, at the end of the 1990s started to think how to re-politicize and re-sexualize French Theory (Foucault, Derrida). It coincides with the first wave queer from the United States (today Bourcier talks of the second wave queer). Bourcier said that due to the simple fact that genders are constructed it was possible, as an outcome of the theoretical work produced by Judith Butler and others, to criticize the heteronormativity of the feminism of the 1970s and 1980s.

I will say that in this case it is important to differentiate between a "naive, benevolent" support of women's practices in Eastern Europe, on one side, and the feminist and theoretical imperialism that can be unmistakably recognized throughout recent decades. As was exposed by bell hooks, Gayatri Chakravorty Spivak, Chandra Talpade Mohanty, and Goldie Osuri, for example, at the center of such imperialism remains a colonial politics of representation, expressions of cultural tolerance and attempts to identify with the Other (wo/man). But this imperialism works hand in hand with the worship of capitalism as freedom, the celebration of a privatized selfhood, and a gender politics that becomes a measure of biopolitical governmentality. It is important to understand that after the fall of the Berlin Wall, this Other was celebrated precisely by privileging identity politics and culture as divided from the social and political, not to mention the colonial and neoliberal.

Bourcier emphasizes not only that queer feminism started to develop in its first wave by attacking heteronormativity, but that nowadays it is also important to engage in the questioning of homonormativity. Bourcier engages today with the critique of Butler and of the French materialist feminists and lesbians, notably Monique Wittig.

What is central with the translation of the U.S. queer movement in Europe were the questions posed by the Chicana, mestiza, and African American feminists and lesbian positions that were brought in with the first queer wave in Europe. Bourcier argues that in the American context the queer of color were always suppressed and subjugated by the white majority and therefore this recent call for intersectionality, when produced in the United States white context in between gender, class, race and sex, could be seen as a rather suspicious moment.

In the 1990s, Chicana and Asian feminists' positions asked for intersectionality. They also asked for their positions of empowerment to be recognized. Nonetheless, as pointed out by Bourcier concerning the European context: the political subject positions of identity politics were nullified by the structuralist and post-structuralist theories and their narratives concerning the death of the subject. Bourcier stated very precisely that the translation of the queer movement from the United States to Europe was asked the same questions by the queer of color and did not get a satisfactory answer. Moreover, it was made ridiculous through mocking "strategic essentialism" and subsumed immediately under the Republican Universalist (and I will emphasize colonial, as France is a colonial republic) context. Knowing that Bourcier is talking about the French Republic we know then that the ideals of the republic are the ideals of the colonial republic. The same can be applied to the Austrian republic, as we know this from the very precise work by migrant and diaspora groups, notably by the work of "The Research Group on Black Austrian History and Presence/Pamoja" from Vienna (Johnston-Arthur and Kazeem 2007).

What was the result of the incompetence—let us ask following Bourcier—by the irresponsible and tainted white theoreticians in the West of Europe? Racism and disregard for the positions of minorities resulted as the product of this process. Bourcier argued that the choice was to either get rid of identity politics or just to stop working in such a context due to an incapacity to recognize some important points within it. French intellectuals, followed by the official gay and lesbian movements have still not understood this argument and continue missing the political potential of cultural identities, Bourcier explained when criticizing the Republican Universalist claims. With such a gesture that continues missing the political potentials of cultural identities they include racism and misogyny in the very ideals of the colonial republic. Therefore, the point is, according to Bourcier, that today it is logical to emancipate ourselves from U.S. queer theory of the first wave: it is inappropriate to the French and European context as its limitations are numerous; a point also recognized by the transqueer of color and transstudies. Transstudies brought as a major contribution in the European context topics such as labor, job insecurity, sex, work, and I would say the very powerful questioning of the formation of the Western, occidental white epistemic matrix, which is the matrix of pure (colonial) violence.

This is what was elaborated in the performance *Iron Mask, White Torture* and as well what Bourcier calls a *new indecent materialism*.

When Grace Latigo, one of the performers, in the last minute of the performance *Iron Mask, White Torture*, asks why we applaud if they do not go anywhere from there, and they are here to stay, this new materialism is, frankly, indecent. So the questions that are reopened concern the possibility of the construction of a new migrant queer indecent political materialism.

To summarize, the possibility for a queer political materialism is to embrace the question of race that is according to Bourcier the *Achilles heel* of white feminism since the first queer wave movement. Taking into consideration the reaction after the performance in the "Secession" this is the most neuralgic point of the EU space as well. If in past studies, homology has been made between female oppression and slavery, this cannot be attainable anymore without the implication of postcolonial or decolonial studies on slavery. To understand that the second wave queer starts to bring forward this moment is very important. Moreover, queer theory of the first wave has constructed heterosexuality as the main enemy. Therefore these questions are at the core of the transfeminist epistemological matrix.

Here is also present a new demand for the critique of pseudo-naturality of the alignment of "the same sex/same gender" type. Indeed, this position has resulted in an enhancement of the gendered female subject who has been associated with a certain naturalization of women (against the male subject, and of course many others, including transsexuals). This presupposes, as pointed out by Bourcier, the existence of a woman and of domination that erases all differences among women. This then resulted into declaring that sexist domination is equal to slavery, but without questioning the colonial presuppositions of such a shift. It resulted in a deletion of the issue of racism in feminism, as a total absence of color in positions of feminist theory. Therefore, this is why the outsiders such as Audre Lorde or the mestiza consciousness of Chicana lesbians such as Cherríe Morraga that live at the borders, are important as they put into question this new purity. Donna Haraway's cyborg had initially the same aim. This aim was firmly pointed out by Bourcier to oppose any idea of female moral superiority, innocence or greater closeness to nature.

Still it is possible to formulate a critique about what Bourcier and Preciado have developed, and what they call *sexpolitics*, a term which refers to the current dominant configurations of the biopolitical (Bourcier 2005). Pedro Paulo Gomes Pereira in an interesting analysis on these two queer theoreticians develops a set of relations on which I will rely in the following (Gomes Pereira 2008). *Sexpolitics* focuses on forms of expression like pornographic cinema, sadomasochism, the construction of the figures of the transvestite, transgender and transsexual. The so-called *queer zones* constitute privileged intervention spaces. All this is part of a hot, punk capitalism as Beatriz Preciado stated in her text (Preciado 2013). Moreover, one arrives at *sexpolitics* after the persistent critique of the sex-gender distinction. Here is important to state that such a critique of the sex-gender distinction destabilizes both the category of biological sex and the category of gender identity. Pedro Paulo Gomes Pereira also issues a warning in relation to this form of critique. He refers to Toril Moi, who argued in 2001 that though this destabilization enabled to think of the plurality of identities and practices, it also increased their abstraction in relation to corporeity and, simultaneously, made the concept of gender become virtually useless in theorizing subjectivity and identity (Moi 2001, quoted after Gomes Pereira 2008). According to Toril Moi this is something that cannot be so easily overlooked.

Nevertheless, it is important to emphasize, as Pedro Paulo Gomes Pereira does, that Bourcier and Preciado both draw on Butler's theoretical legacy and both search for something more than a performativity theory that is supported by a language model based on speech acts; they are authors who act within the queer politics that bet on the subversive possibilities of the abnormal bodies (abject, strange, queer), and who search for the body's materiality. This is why their approach to the techniques that construct bodies (vibrators, pornography, cinema, surgeries), and the need to historicize the categories of sex, flesh, body, biology, and nature, make the concept of *sexpolitics* so important.

The question remains whether the queer politics can be seen without a more precise re-elaboration of the relation between queer—and the other two constructed categories of nationality and race? And if there does not exist a danger in leaving it out from the conceptualization of queer (in the relation to nation-State and its processes of racializations)—institutionalized, structural and social racism(s) would end up not naturalizing what we wish to denaturalize?

Simply put, if I connect what was said until now with the art project (the performance that was presented in the start of this text) we have to state that we would not be able to talk about it, if we were not able to question the relation between queer and the dilemmas of identity, sex politics that are constructed through the nation-State or through processes of racializations. Therefore we have to reflect on technologies that construct racialized bodies and to ask how they act. In short, I am asking about the place of race, nation-States and migrants in queer theory.

PUNK CAPITALISM AND NECROPOLITICAL CITIZENSHIP

I am interested in talking about politics and about color, even about gender, but definitely about another knowledge and politics that is transfeminist, migrant, politically subversive, and sexually transgressive.

I continue with the proposition given in the last few years by a transfeminist theoretician Beatriz Preciado. She talks about global capitalism that combines pharmaco-pornographic levels of biopolitical life, to what Beatriz Preciado refers as the hot, punk capitalism that is all centered under the belly and connects biogenetic, pharmaco-pornographic and drug substances (in an enormous quantity). Technology is taking a substantial place in producing a specific meaning that is mostly semiotically-tecnologically organized. This is the world of hot capitalism that is developing overwhelmingly in the "former" West and first capitalist world. On the other side, I propose to conceptualize global capitalism not as a coin, that has two sides, but as a Mobius strip, which is a surface with only one side and only one boundary component. In such a setting, I argue, exists a cold capitalism, a necropolitical one, one that extracts its surplus value from non-mediated dispossessions, exclusions, looting and death.

Biopolitics and necropolitics are working globally, though necropolitics' functions (mostly in the so-called periphery) making surplus value by death and social death of any kind (with the value of life equaling zero), where non-mediated violence is present. We see violence of unbelievable proportions against the LGBTQI people; beatings, killings, as well the negation of their basic human rights. This is the former east of Europe reality. We also see daily (literally) corpses floating in the sea, corpses of those who want to enter the "former" Western Europe: refugees, people without papers, from Africa and Asia, people that drowned along the coasts of Italy, Malta, etc.

Therefore on one side, we have the "former West," the once first capitalist world that is the Christian-capitalist patriarchal regime of power, with its processes of financialization and liberalism that go hand in hand with the inclusion inside its capitalist (global neoliberal) matrix of power of all those in the past perceived as "others": the non-heterosexual identities (although there is still a great discrimination of transsexuals and intersexuals). On the other, and at the same place and time, we have necropolitics, a brutal logic of violence, persecutions, discrimination and racializations in the former Eastern European space (former Yugoslavia, Russia, and other post-Soviet countries, etc.).

To be precise, this is not about a new "enlighten logic" of the "former West" being more civilized than the "former East," but a process of new racialized discrimination that takes into its borders the "others" that were discriminated against in the past (the white gays and lesbians, queer as Western nation-State citizens) to produce at the same moment new Others in the West: migrants, refugees, sans-papiers, people and women of color coming from other parts of the world and religious backgrounds.

While some are made "equal" the other Others are left to die and are brutally abandoned. An illustrative case is the disaster on October 2013 when the death toll of African migrants that drowned (measured in hundreds of bodies in one single day) near the Italian island of Lampedusa was an additional confirmation of the alarming scale of the refugee crisis in the EU. Though the most perverse situation happened afterwards when to these hundreds of dead bodies were given the Italian citizenship (but only in order that the Italian government and the EU could bury them in Italy—it was obviously cheaper than to send the dead bodies back to their countries of origin and to their respective families). The few who did survive the Italian government decided to prosecute as they tried to illegally enter Italy and the EU. This is the clearest sign of the perverse and violent new attitude that Western Europe has toward human rights (after the West had been for decades heavily capitalizing its democracy on it) and the occurrence of a new category of citizenship— the *necropolitical citizenship*.

The colonial/racial division is applied to citizenship and we have two categories of citizenship: one is the category of which I will name *biopolitical citizenship* (the EU "natural" nation-State citizens) and the other is *necropolitical citizenship* given to refugees and sans-papier (paperless) after they die on EU soil.

If in hot, punk capitalism we are an oppressed group of zombified positions, all medicated and doped-up, consuming sex as the *only* food in the time of austerity, in the cold former Eastern Europe under global capitalism we have only blood, death, being beaten, and killed. Therefore the *necropolitical turn* of dispossession and exploitation (part of the techno-sexual matrix of global capitalism today) teaches us fully that neither gender nor sex are natural conditions of our lives, less so misery, dispossession, enslavement, and killings.

In this context what is important is the construction of the transmigrant and transfeminist queer movement where the so called *not-right and not-quite* identities take advantage of the hot global capitalist pharmaco-pornography system of re/production and of sex and labor in order to point the finger toward these divisions and politically radicalize both their and our positions.

OVERKILL

The difference between biopolitics and necropolitics is very visible if we are to conceptualize a homophobic history in the post-Yugoslav space. This space is not on another continent, somewhere out there, but here and now, in the middle of Fortress EU (or just Europe). The processes that are to be captured from drawing this homophobic history are not possible to be called simply *biopolitical* measures by respective nation-States for the protection of nation-State heterosexual rights. We see all over bodies drenched in blood, LGBTQI members beaten and their lives threatened to the point that they are living under the constant threat of death, with basic human rights being denied them.

In 2001, Serbia's lesbian, gay, bisexual, transgender, and queer community (LGBTQ) attempted to hold the country's first Gay Pride in Belgrade. When the participants started to gather in one of Belgrade's principal squares, a huge crowd of opponents (right wing, fascist-orthodox organizations, and individuals) attacked the event, injuring several participants and stopping the march. The police were not prepared to suppress the riots or protect the Pride marchers. Non-governmental organizations and a number of public personalities criticized the assailants, the government and security officials. In 2009 a group of human rights activists announced their plans to organize a second Belgrade Pride. However, due to the heavy public threats of violence made by extreme right organizations, the Serbian Ministry of the Interior moved the location of the march out of the city center, thereby effectively banning the Pride. In October 2010 petrol bombs and rocks flew at the parade, after the authorities allowed it to go forward, announcing that they would protect the participants. A presence of some thousands of policemen guided the way for 1,000 marchers; several policemen were injured; a few dozen people were arrested in the wake of their anti-gay violence. In 2011 the interior ministry banned the Belgrade Pride Parade, allegedly because they saw the parade as an "obstruction of public transport, endangering health, public moral or safety of individuals and properties." Not a word from the Serbian Ministry of the Interior being preoccupied in this case with the obstruction of basic human rights. In 2013 it was the same.

Although the first LGBTQ event in Slovenia dates back almost thirty years, deep in the times of socialism, when in 1984 in Ljubljana the first coming-out public project called "Magnus" was organized (which was, in fact, the first *coming-out* in all of the former Eastern European States), the first pride parade in Slovenia was not organized until 2001, and it was the result of an immediate provocation by an incident in a Ljubljana cafe where a gay couple was asked to leave for being homosexual. Though vandalism and beatings targeting the LGBTQ population held sway in the new millennium and were repeated during the 2010s, the sign of Slovenian society becoming more and more openly homophobic and transphobic happened in 2012, when Slovenians voted against the new Family Code. The new Family Code expanded provisions protecting the rights of children, such as outlawing corporal punishment, and expanded existing same-sex registered partnerships to have all the rights of married couples, except adoption (excluding step-child adoption).

A conservative group called Civil Initiative for the Family and the Rights of Children, which proposed the referendum to ban the new Family Code, "opposed same-sex unions and demanded the referendum out of respect for motherhood and fatherhood," which allegedly was a statement that would function as a "counter" statement to the proposed definition of *family* in the new Family Code, described as a "union of a child or children with one or two parents or guardians." It was clearly presented in the debates (not exempted from an invigorated racist and homophobic rhetoric) that if accepted, the new Family Code would be the first comprehensive overhaul of family legislation in thirty-five years (the last one was approved in the 1970s). The Family Code was rejected in the referendum held on March 25, 2012.

In 2011 the Pride Parade in Split, Croatia, was met with a face of primitivism and violence that shocked many. The parade was surrounded by hundreds of very hostile citizens of Split who were shouting "Kill the fag," making the fascist salute with their right hands and continuing to throw stones and various objects. The situation was shameful for Croatia, who in 2011 signed the treaty of accession to become the twenty-eighth member of the European Union.

Therefore another task stands in front of us (and not just in front of queer necropolitics): to situate necropolitics into queer and to expose the "queer death" as a process that develops hand in hand with global capitalism. It is not going on somewhere else but rather, it is here and now, occupying and amplifying the turbo-fascist capitalist features in former Yugoslavia or the postmodern fascist disintegration of the social in the west European or U.S. context.

U.S. context? Eric Stanley in his text "Near Life, Queer Death: Overkill and Ontological Capture?" reported on thousands of cases of mutilation of transgender people in the last decade (Stanley 2011). He calls this *overkill* as the transgender individuals are so mutilated that it transcends violence; actually it is a fury of transphobic situation. The point is that this is not just a single situation somewhere in some rural space but a reality here and now in the developed urban spaces. Achille Mbembe has provocatively asked, "But what does it mean to do violence to what is nothing?" in order to explain how the queer approximates physical violence that marks the edges of subjectivity itself (Mbembe quoted after Stanley 2011).

RACE TROUBLE: TRANSFEMINISM AND DEHUMANIZATION

It is clear that what global capitalism brings in front of us is a necessity to revisit globally racist, homophobic, and discriminatory processes, not as simple identity differences but as processes that are entangled with capital, new media technology and with the change of the mode of life under capital's brutal modes of racialization and exploitation. Therefore I am interested to talk about politics and interventional politics, practices, and struggles that are transfeminist, transmigrant, and politically subversive.

If we depart from the most influential book in academic feminism and queer theory in the 1990, *Gender Trouble: Feminism and the Subversion of Identity* by Judith Butler (1990), taking into account the passage regarding feminism and biopolitics toward what I have tried to develop almost throughout the chapters: racialization and necropolitics on one side, and transfeminism and transmigration, on the other, can we then propose another book for the new decade of the twenty-first century? A book yet to be written, that will build on what Butler seminally produced: gender performativity, the fraught categories of "women" and "woman," but to be complicated further by class, race sexuality, and capital that take us elsewhere but not anywhere.

The title of this book will be *Race Trouble: Transfeminism and Dehumanization* (forthcoming). In summary this book will be asking about the place of race, nation-State, and migrants in queer theory and global necrocapitalism.

DISSIDENT FEMINISMS

I will discuss dissident feminisms that ask for disruption of the monolithic history of feminism that is heterosexual and white and is based on a defined subject of feminism that is supposedly a woman as a predefined biological reality (meaning based on a kind of a natural category of a woman). As such, dissident feminisms intervene in this history and present of monolithic feminism with positions that are marginalized causing antagonistic differentiations based on class, race and gender. These positions are marginalized in society in relation to a white majority in the Western world. Moreover, these positions, that are conceptualized as *minoritized* consists of people being migrants and refugees or paperless from Latin America, Africa, and former Eastern Europe, therefore coming from the perspective of European Union and Austria from minoritized geopolitical sectors. These people perform jobs which are seen as "minor" (that means that are seen simply to say as squalid within a hierarchy of a white middle class "decency") and as well these jobs are abusive and exploitative in terms of basic life conditions of reproduction and economic benefits.

Therefore based on such designated dissident feminism I want to elaborate on artistic intervention practices that in relation to sex, gender, race, and class develop agencies that are named transfeminist, transmigrant and transsexual positions. First I will give a contextualization of what dissident feminism means, how the notion developed and what are its critical theoretical points. I will continue with various dissident feminist artistic interventional positions.

Contextualization of Dissident Feminisms

My thesis is that today minoritized women (and here I am making reference to the title of the text "Minoritized Women Effect a Transformation in Feminism" written by Luzenir Caixeta in 2011 [reprinted 2013]), are those migrants, transgender, sex workers, lesbians, etc., who are producing a transformation in and of feminism. This implies dissident movements inside feminism that transform its white, heterosexual, essentialized contextualization of feminism (based on features that are seen as naturally appertaining to a category that is named "woman") into dissident feminisms (see that feminism is in plural!). Luzenir Caixeta, philosopher and theologian that works for *maiz. Autonomous Center of and for Migrant Women* in Linz, on health prevention, counseling and education of migrant sex workers, states that,

> [i]n recent years, a number of authors have become well known around the world who are of the opinion that the new feminism must go much further beyond the old demands of white, Western and heterosexual middle-class women for legal equality. Attention should be given to the women who have always been marginalized, and the causes leading to differentiation based on class, ethnicity and gender should be opposed. (Caixeta 2013, 146)

Reiterating the point further she subtitled a section in her aforementioned text straightforwardly with "Dissident Currents within Feminisms," pointing directly to the essay by the Spanish philosopher Beatriz Preciado, "Report after Feminism: Women on the Margins" (2007).

Luzenir Caixeta in reference to Preciado argues that in opposition to a past feminism that developed its political discourse based on the division "between men (as dominators) and women (as victims), modern feminism is developing new political concepts and strategies for action that call into question what has previously been regarded as generally true: namely that the political subject of feminism [was] women—meaning women in their predefined biological reality, but especially women according to a certain notion: white, heterosexual, submissive and from the middle class" (Caixeta 2013, 146).

Therefore the dissident demand in feminism asks for a process of radical differentiation. Beatriz Preciado asks for "feminisms for the excluded" (Preciado 2007, quoted after Caixeta 2013, 147). Or as Preciado argues in the text with the title "Pharmaco-Pornographic CapitalismPostporn Politics and the Decolonization of Sexual Representations," these new feminisms for the excluded are "dissident projects for the collective transformation of the twenty-first century" (Preciado 2013, 251). Dissident feminisms stand in opposition "to a gray, normed and puritanical feminism, which sees in cultural, sexual or political distinctions a threat to its heterosexual and Eurocentric image of women" (Caixeta 2013, 147).

Preciado lists names and delineates a genealogy of positions that challenge the naturalness and universality of the feminine condition. I quote from Preciado's text "Pharmaco-Pornographic Capitalism Postporn Politics and the Decolonization of Sexual Representations" in order to propose the genealogy of dissident feminisms:

> The first of these shifts is in the hands of theoretical gay and lesbian theorists like Guy Hocquenghem, Michel Foucault, Monique Wittig, Michael Warner and Adrienne Rich, who define heterosexuality as a political regime and a control device that makes the difference between men and women and transforms the resistance to gender standardization into pathology. Judith Butler and Judith Halberstam insist on the processes of cultural significance and stylization of the body through which the normalization of differences between the genders is effectuated, while Donna Haraway and Anne Fausto-Sterling bring into question the existence of two sexes as biological realities, regardless of the scientific-technical processes representation is constructed with. Moreover, along with the processes of emancipation of Blacks in the United States and the decolonization of the so-called "Third World," the voices of criticism are also raised against the racist assumptions of colonial and white feminism. We have become empowered with projects and thoughts by Angela Davis, bell hooks, Gloria Anzaldúa and Gayatri Spivak, and black feminist, postcolonial, postChristian, postJewish, postMuslim projects, or those from the Diaspora, that will require thinking gender in its constitutive relation to the geopolitical differences of race, class, sexuality, migration and human trafficking. (Preciado 2013, 251)

Dissident Feminist Artistic Positions

Until now I have addressed two questions in this sub-chapter: (1) What do we understand as dissident feminisms? and (2) How do dissident feminisms intervene in history in general and the histories of feminism in particular?

I will continue to present dissident feminist artistic positions whose main aims are to develop strategies to change the condition of artistic, social, political and economic reality in the historical moment in which the art practice takes place; intervening in order to exercise change and produce a demarcation within a certain space and on a public.

I can delineate, and this is my thesis, at least two lines that are sometimes parallel, or in other situations, cross each other.

The first line comes from dissident feminist artistic interventions whose positions "escape from the academia to flourish in audiovisual production, literary and performative action spaces" (Preciado 2013, 252).

As such, the purpose of these queer-feminist projects "would not be so much to liberate women or get legal equality, but the dismantling of the political devices producing differences of class, race, gender and sexuality, thereby creating transfeminism art and action networks for decolonization politics" (Preciado 2013, 252). The artists and their interventionists practices in the field of dissident feminisms seen in such a view are those connected with postporn strategies, as Preciado states:

> [We] have a history going from the feminist kitsch porn movies of Annie Sprinkle, the docu-fiction by Monika Treut, literary works by Virginie Despentes, Dorothy Allison, and Michelle Tea, Alison Bechdel's lesbian comics, photographs by Del LaGrace Volcano, dyke punk rock concerts by Tribe8, to the Gothic Revival sermons of Lydia Lunch, and the transgender porn science fiction of Shue-Lea Cheang, feminist postporn . . . aesthetics made of traffic signs and cultural artifacts with the critical redefinition of code standards that traditional feminism considered improper for femininity. Some of the references of this aesthetic and political discourse are queer-horror-porn movies of Bruce La Bruce and Christopher Lee, the distortion of sex shops of Maria Llopis, Post-Op or Orgy, queer-Gothic literature, dildos as instruments of tectonic redefinition of the sexed body, trans-sexual vampires and monsters, cyborgs living queer punk, performance in public space as a useful political intervention. . . . Sex was never so crude and gender has never been so cooked. (Preciado 2013, 252)

The second line of dissident feminist artistic interventions, I want to propose, is associated even more precisely with non-white feminists and activists who work directly with antiracism as well as post-colonial and decolonial positions. I make reference to names listed by Luzenir Caixeta that are critical positions by migrant women and Black women, such as Katharina Oguntoye,[4] May Ayim, FeMigra,[5] Lale Otyakmaz,[6] and Encarnación Gutiérrez Rodríguez.[7] An important framework of reference for this development is the critique from Women of Color in the United States in the 1980s—including Combahee River Collective,[8] Cherríe L. Moraga, Gloria Anzaldúa,[9] bell hooks[10] and Angela Davis.[11]

And I add to these names María Lugones, Gayatri Spivak,[12] and Chandra Talpade Mohanty. And last by not least, artists working in *maiz. Autonomous Center of and for Migrant Women* in Linz, principally Marissa Lôbo. I also expose in this context "The Research Group on Black Austrian History and Presence/Pamoja" from Vienna and their members: Araba Evelyn Johnston-Arthur, Belinda Kazeem, and Njideka Stephanie Iroh, among others.

Why are These Positions Important?

A very good case of the importance of such a work is the life and poetry of May Ayim (1960–1996) who was an Afro-German poet, educator, and activist. Margaret Catherine MacCarroll argues in her MA thesis "May Ayim: A Woman in the Margin of German Society" defended in 2005 at the Florida State University, College of Arts and Sciences that "although there is a long history of dark-skinned people living in Germany, this study focuses primarily on the period after World War II and examines concepts of culture, race and ethnicity in order to determine what role these concepts play in the experiences of Afro-Germans like Ayim" (MacCarroll 2005, 3).

MacCarroll exposes that Ayim's life was marked by a sense of displacement without belonging as she tried desperately to find her place in German and African society, and continues that in order "to better understand the atmosphere in which Ayim was raised there will be an ensuing discussion of Germany's history of racism with particular emphasis on the time period shortly after World War II, the time in which Ayim was born" (MacCarroll 2005, 3).

What is important for this and other dissident positions is that they cannot be contained only in an artistic field but in order to capture their importance and the way they radically intervene in art we have firstly to dismantle a standard division of art disciplines and secondly constantly take into consideration a wide social, political and economic context of art. Therefore Ayim's tragic life and powerful art cannot be understood outside the genealogy of racism in Germany as exposed by MacCarroll in *"Negerhuren* to *Mischlingskinder* to *Afro-Deutsche"* [N*whores to mongrel children to Afro-Germans] (MacCarroll 2005, 3); a form of racism that did not vanish but was "just" modified. The same processes can be detected in Austrian society.

If I continue in this line of reasoning then Cherríe L. Moraga is perhaps best known for co-editing, with Gloria Anzaldúa, the anthology of feminist thought *This Bridge Called My Back: Writings by Radical Women of Color* in 1981 (first edition). Her work is important for establishing a context of work for Chicana feminists and other feminists of color, and among scholars working in Chicano Studies and for the foundation of Third Wave Feminism or Third World Feminism in the United States.

María Lugones is an Argentinian scholar, philosopher, and feminist, who teaches at Binghamton University in New York. Lugones reworked the term "Colonial Matrix of Power," coined at the end of the 1990s by the Peruvian theorist Aníbal Quijano who used it to identify structures of power, control, and hegemony that emerged during colonialism and are reproduced in the present. Quijano talks about gender as biological but Lugones contends precisely that gender is a social construction. She coined the concept *Colonial/Modern Gender System* (Lugones 2007) to refer to the binary gender system as patriarchal and heterosexual organization of relations. She argues that gender itself is a violent colonial introduction, consistently and contemporarily used to destroy peoples, cosmologies, and communities as the building ground of the "civilized" West.

The Spanish colonizers introduced a gender formation system based on *heterosexualism*, a key term for Lugones (appearing in the title of her seminal text from 2007), and referring to a system that only accepts opposite-sex attraction, opposite-sex relationships, and excludes homosexuality.

The "oppressive colonial gender arrangements" or "oppressive organizations of life" which remained from colonialism have inherently naturalized a gender dichotomy. The same is true for what we have in Africa or in the Former Eastern Europe, that in opposition to the "civilized" West that today is emancipating itself with Queer, the East and the South are pushed to embrace a colonial/modern gender system that is a brutal system built on homophobic and transphobic violent attacks.

Chandra Talpade Mohanty, another prominent voice of dissident feminisms, proposes in her article "Under Western Eyes: Feminist Scholarship and Colonial Discourses" (Mohanty 1984), a shift not only from gender, but also from ethnicity, and thus proposes an anti-white-centrism. She develops the shift by making a reference to Teresa de Lauretis, who developed an anti-hetero-centrism. Mohanty develops a criticism of hegemonic Western scholarship on a big scale in general and of the colonialism in Western feminist scholarship in particular.

If I talk of very recent artistic practices then we have to name Marissa Lôbo, born in Brazil, who lives and works in Austria and is a Black activist and a member of *maíz. Autonomous Center of and for Migrant Women* in Linz. One of Lôbo's most impressive projects is *Iron Mask, White Torture*, performance and installation, conceived by Marissa Lôbo in 2010 (extensively described in the first part of this chapter). It was presented at the group exhibition "Where do we go from here?" at Secession, in Vienna in 2010. The installation and performance are important as they develop a relation to the role of "empowerment," "agency." and "choice" in terms of who speaks, and what is the role of de/colonial epistemology as well as about the role of art institutions such as galleries, museums, etc.

Another project by Marissa Lôbo is the video performance and lecture with the title "Safer sex? Fuck Europe, here I am to stay, Super puta Praderstern" (2013). This work exposes, as stated by Marissa Lôbo, colonial desire and violence, otherness, sexuality, racialized bodies, counter-aesthetics, migrant-precarious bodies, migrant identity, sex work, society's double morals, the regime of Western body politics, and white supremacy.

Another key project/position in the Austrian context is the "Research Group on Black Austrian History and Presence/Pamoja" with representatives as Araba Evelyn Johnston-Arthur, Belinda Kazeem, Njideka Stephanie Iroh, among others. The pan-African movement in Austria called "Pamoja" brought together young Africans in Austria to fight for their rights and against racism in Europe. The starting point of the group was the violent historical presences of (neo) colonial representations in Austria. The group works with gendered images that according to Araba

Evelyn Johnston-Arthur and in reference to Stuart Hall, completely re-press any existence of "homemade" neo-colonial imagery in Germany and Austria.[13]

The "Research Group on Black Austrian History and Presence" con-nects its work to Black, migrant, feminist, postcolonial theorists in Ger-man-speaking countries such as Fatima El-Tayeb, Maisha Maureen Eg-gers, May Ayim, Nicola Lauré Al-Samarai, Encarnación Gutiérrez Rodríguez, Grada Kilomba,[14] and Audre Lorde.[15] The group works to recover suppressed knowledge about Black Austrian history, creating new spaces and thereby situating Black people in Austria differently, namely from a Black perspective that situates itself beyond voyeuristic depictions of the "exotic other."

In short and in conclusion, I argue that the context provided for re-thinking feminism with elaboration on new movements focusing on mar-ginalized positions within feminism *dissident feminisms* opens a new dis-course of struggle in neoliberal global capitalism.

Dissident feminisms (in plural) dismantle the one sided history of feminism and put at its center the struggle against normative, discrimina-tive, patriarchal, and racist society of tomorrow that has at its core capi-talist neoliberal subjugations based on of exploitation, dispossession, ra-cialization, and privatization. Dissident feminisms insist on the destruc-tion of all political policies that codify distinctions between class, ethnic-ity, gender, and sexuality. Echoing Beatriz Preciado (2013), I can state that dissident feminisms strive for an artistic and political platform with a vision of the future for everyone. The list of artistic interventions and practices presented in this chapter radicalize the theoretical and critical thoughts forming dissident feminisms.

They do so in order to push forward a new configuration of categories such as epistemology, labor, history, im/migration, and consequently shape subjectivities at the crossroads of a world that has to deal seriously with transmigrant, transsexual and transgender positions.

Therefore, it comes as no surprise that positions I have mentioned as part of the dissident feminisms in Austria are active as well with the Refugee Protest Camp in Vienna, which started with a ten-hour march of approximately a hundred refugees and their supporters. This march on November 24, 2012 started at the refugee reception center in Traiskirchen (around twenty kilometers away from Vienna) and ended in the center of Vienna city. The demands of the refugees are better living conditions, from adequate food to a decent social life: the right to stay and the right to work. At this present moment the refugees are in deep isolation. Their demands were ignored by the Austrian authorities, and the refugees were first threatened by deportation to found themselves in a situation to be deported. On December 9, 2013, several refuges were deported from Austria to Lahore, Pakistan.

NOTES

1. Legend has it that Anastácia was a blue-eyed Bantu, enslaved and transported to Brazil and forced into silence by her owners with an iron gag. There are various reasons for this brutal form of punishment, depending on the perspective it is viewed from. One significant version places the iron mask as vengeance for resisting sexual exploitation by the so-called "master" of enslaved Africans; another portrays the mask as punishment for Anastácia's political disobedience as she joined the *quilombolos*, a resistance movement in Brazil of runaway enslaved Africans. Available at http://www.kronotop.org/ftexts/what-is-anastacia-keeping-silentor-what-does-anastacia-see.

2. This interview is a key reference for all the elaborations I made in relation to Marie-Hélène Bourcier (2011). See as well Bourcier (2013).

3. I made a detailed analysis of it in chapter 3.

4. Katharina Oguntoye is a historian and has influenced the Afro-German movement; she is a co-editor of the book *Showing Our Colors* (1986) and is the founding member of the "Initiative of Black People in Germany."

5. FeMigra (abbreviation for "Feminist Migrants") in Germany is an activist women's group mostly consisting of members with an academic background or who work in the social sector. They are also involved in strong networking activities with other ethnic, migrant, or Jewish women in Germany. FeMigra's theoretical reflection on how to act politically as feminist migrants is strongly influenced by the reception of post-structuralist, Black and post-colonial authors like Gayatri Spivak, Nira Yuval-Davis, Adrienne Rich, and Angela Davis.

6. Lale Otyakmaz works at the University Duisburg-Essen on and with questions of diversity management.

7. Encarnación Gutiérrez Rodríguez works at the Institute of Sociology at the Justus-Liebig University Gießen (Germany) and is known for the book *Decolonizing European Sociology*. The book challenges the androcentric, colonial, and ethnocentric perspectives eminent in mainstream European sociology. Cf. http://www.ashgate.com/isbn/9780754678724

8. The Combahee River Collective was a Black feminist Lesbian organization active in Boston from 1974 to 1980. They are perhaps best known for developing the Combahee River Collective Statement, a key document in the history of contemporary Black feminism and the development of the concepts of identity as used by political organizers and social theorists.

9. Gloria Anzaldúa (1942–2004) was a scholar of Chicana cultural, feminist, and queer theory. Her best-known book, *Borderlands/La Frontera: The New Mestiza* (1987) is based on her life growing up on the Mexican-Texas border and incorporated her lifelong feelings of social and cultural marginalization into her work.

10. Gloria Jean Watkins better known by her pen name bell hooks (written without capitals), is an American author, feminist, and social activist. Her writing focuses on the interconnectivity of race, capitalism, and gender and what she describes as their ability to produce and perpetuate systems of oppression and class domination. Primarily through a postmodern perspective, hooks has addressed race, class, and gender in education, art, history, sexuality, mass media, and feminism.

11. Angela Davis is an American political activist, scholar, Communist and author. She emerged as a nationally prominent counterculture activist and radical in the 1960s, as a leader of the Communist Party USA, and had close relations with the Black Panther Party through her involvement in the Civil Rights to abolish the prison-industrial complex. Her research interests are feminism, African-American studies, critical theory, Marxism, popular music, social consciousness, and the philosophy and history of punishment and prisons. Her membership in the Communist Party led to Ronald Reagan's request in 1969 to have her barred from teaching at any university in the State of California.

12. Gayatri Chakravorty Spivak is an Indian literary theorist, philosopher and professor at Columbia University, New York, where she is a founding member of the school's Institute for Comparative Literature and Society. Spivak is best known for her contemporary cultural and critical theories to challenge the "legacy of colonialism" and the way readers engage with literature and culture. She often focuses on the cultural texts of those who are marginalized by dominant western culture: the new im/migrant, the working class, women, and other positions of the subaltern. Her best-known essay was published in the 1980s with the title "Can the Subaltern Speak?"; it is considered a founding text of postcolonialism.

13. The references are coming from Araba Evelyn Johnston-Arthur who is a social justice activist based in Vienna, born to a Ghanaian family. Johnston-Arthur, as reported by Kali TV, managed to co-found a pan-African movement in Austria called "Pamoja," which brought together young Africans in Austria to fight for their rights and against racism in Europe. Published online March 26, 2013, at http://www.youtube.com/watch?v=sIiXyjOJj9U&feature=youtu.be (Accessed, December 5, 2013)

14. See Grada Kilomba's book *Plantation Memories. Episodes of Everyday Racist* (2008) that deconstructs the normality of racism, making visible what is often made invisible. The book is described as essential to anyone interested in Black studies, postcolonial studies, critical whiteness, gender studies, and psychoanalysis.

15. Audre Lorde (1934–1992) was a Caribbean-American writer and civil rights activist. She described herself as "Black, lesbian, mother, warrior, poet," that dedicated both her life and work to confronting and addressing the injustices of racism, sexism, and homophobia.

SEVEN

Content, Form, and Repetition

The question that remains for *art and theory, culture and political interven-tion*, and *the social and the political* concerns the social bond and our place within it. Are we capable of action, critical analysis, resistance, or better to say *insurgency*? If yes, how? What is the social bond that structures neoliberal global capitalism? How to talk about ideology, subjectivities, power and life, if it is said that we live today in a world of post-ideology, post–politics conditions?

The dominant discourse in the world today is no doubt the discourse of power. This was obvious in the four discourses Jacques Lacan devel-oped in the 1960s: The Discourse of the Master, The University Discourse, The Discourse of the Hysteric, and The Analyst Discourse. Lacanian psychoanalysis (which is the only one that interests me in relation to psychoanalysis) is not in itself a discourse of power. Psychoanalysis de-ploys the power of the cause of desire in order to bring about a reconfigu-ration of the analysand's desire. As such the analytic discourse is struc-tured differently from the discourse of power, but still in the discourses we can see how the social bond, the relation between agency, the other, the surplus, and/or the waste functions. Therefore we get a genealogy of a system of capitalism that is actually carrying the name of each of the discourses. Although a lot was written about The University Discourse being the one discourse that defines contemporary neoliberal global capi-talism (which means simply that to *knowledge* is given the position of agency, rationality, and objectivity), I will claim—that in the necropoliti-cal global capitalism—it is *more* and *more* becoming clear that the Analyst Discourse is the one that actually organizes global capitalism. It conveys a self-reflective or better to say a *perverse* situation of cynical reflectivity that allows for a situation not of emancipation but of a performative,

133

formalist, repetitive emptying that is a very powerful process of disintegration of any social bond.

Therefore saying this I will examine the political and ideological conditions of the re/production of life, art, and culture in the present moment of neoliberal global capitalism. This involves rethinking European cultural policies in the context of an analysis of the prevailing discourses on migration, integration, and the struggle against racism; as well as the re/production of capital.

My thesis is that the process of racialization develops a racist basis for practices, structures, and discourses in the field of culture and art, as well as being reproduced in the contemporary division of labor and in new forms of exploitation and expropriation. Racialization has, at its point of departure, *colonialism* that is today enabled through new forms of postcolonialism, that is, coloniality, in the specific field of our research culture and contemporary art made operative by three interrelated shifts.

The first tackles life and its management, and is conceptualized as the shift from biopolitics to necropolitics. What I want to say is that, in contemporary art and theory, not only is life being used at their core (as their *materia prima*, as their raw material) but that the originary biopolitical characteristics of contemporary art (seen as an Institution) are effectuated in the way these projects and discourses deal with life, formally, aesthetically and contextually. This has direct consequences regarding the articulation between form and content.

The second shift is on the level of ideology.

The third shift conceptualizes capitalism through rethinking how it formulates itself in the shape of the State. Through the racial-State, racism enters a new and perverted form, that now reigns in neoliberal global capitalism.

Within such a context, it is therefore necessary to ask how the political can be conceptualized in the light of neoliberal processes of governmentality within capitalism (that today constitutes a state of exception imposed on subjectivities) that regulate, subjugate and systematically control us? How are we to reconcile the overarching political and social structures of global capitalism and turbo-powered neo-liberalism with the autonomy (i.e., "freedom") of conceiving art projects, implied by our current configuration of the originary biopolitical character of the paradigm of contemporary art? The consequences of such a shift are terrifying. As artists are coopted within the machinery of the neo-liberal global state of exception, it becomes possible for the regime to spatially or temporally reintegrate its own transgressions as tokens of its functionality. This presents itself as the pacification of all contradictions and social antagonisms into a bizarre collusion based on a struggle for rights to become commodified (or less dispensable), on the one hand, or to get a license to kill, on the other, hence producing necropolitics as the politics par excellence of the First Capitalist World (Gržinić and Tatlić 2012).

THE ABNORMAL CONTENT AND THE EMPTY (NORMAL/IZING) FORM

That our lives have gone totally capitalist has numerous consequences for contemporary art, culture, theory, and for any radical political act, therefore I would like to summarize some of the consequences.

With regard to the relationship between globalization, capitalism and aesthetics, we should establish a critique of the formation of the so-called "universal culture and art" that takes place at three co-dependent and decisive levels (the economic, political, and institutional) and that establishes culture as a hegemonic and ideological apparatus. Today's frenetic global economy demands the production of more and more new commodities at increasingly larger profit rates and ascribes the essential role (position and function) to innovations and experimentation in the field of art.

The contemporary practices of art and culture are part of a very powerful Institution of art where a new generation of artists, curators, cultural workers, theoreticians, etc., depend terminally on old power structures. Be it through multinationals, banks, insurance companies, and/or powerful family business connections (or even only through friendships and business alliances based on sharing a "common" point of view) they decide who will be part of the core and, from time to time, who among the younger generation will be chosen to refresh the art and critical-theoretical scene. These decisions depend on money, power ("translated" into affectivity, sexuality) and, also, for those coming from other spaces that are not in the First Capitalist World, in their "emancipatory" capabilities (to be up to the level of the task, to refrain from radical criticality, to understand what the border of intervention is without being explicitly told, to be respectful and to allow patronizing, etc.; in summation to use the language properly and to have behavior, language and bodily manners that will fit within the institution which has already reached an "emancipated" way of working, behaving, and living). The reasons are very simple: the contemporary Institution of art depends on money, the market and collectors and will not jeopardize this power; what all of them, that is to say "us" (who want to enter the Institution of contemporary art), have in common, is the ideology of neoliberal capitalism, that protects with all means at its disposal "good life."

As Suely Rolnik stated, they are (or we all are) caught up in the vicious cycle of "luxury subjectivity production," part of the middle-class elite, traveling around to art festivals, eating and drinking well, and, of course, occasionally having sex and a lot of fun (Rolnik 2003). This is common to all of these structures, be they private, State, semi-private, or semi-State. All of them have only one agenda, power and more power based on a different channeling of the neoliberal ideology that translates this striving for the good life into the vocabulary of a fancy theory, using words such as: democratization, efficiency, development, and emancipation.

Up to now, I have presented the system of functioning of global capitalism and its reality, exposing a logic of repetition that has as its outcome circularity, obviousness, and formalization. These points are at the core of the Institution of Contemporary Art today. I name such a mechanism that simultaneously produces and eschews content and leaves us with an empty form—a performative repetitive mechanism. This mechanism will help us to understand what it is that makes more or less all large contemporary exhibitions and projects obsolete in terms of resistance and critique (though they are not obsolete from the perspective of those who organize, curate, and maybe take part in them, as it is possible they could make some money and get power out of them). To explain this differently: what we have today as part of exhibitions, especially big powerful exhibition projects (Biennials, Documentas, Manifestas, etc.) is a myriad of art works that present as content unbelievable features of contemporary capitalist exploitation; expropriations whose "features" are more and more visible. They show it all, so to speak, *tout court*, without any mediation. These art exhibitions are more and more intensified, they present art works that show capitalist corruption, police repression, massacres of people and animals, all is made visible with more and more drastically elaborated dimensions, reasons, connections of exploitation, expropriation, executions, etc., though all stay, so to speak, *impotent*.

The content is, at the same time of its presentation, made obsolete through a mechanism that I termed *performative repetition* and that functions as a process of voiding, emptying and extracting the meaning from these contents. What is left out of the discussion is precisely the ideological form with which the mentioned art works and projects are presented. I claim that this form presents, encapsulates so to speak, a process of emptying (not only of diminishing, but in many cases completely nullifying, etc.) what at the level of content was made visible. In the past, the social reality was presented as "normal"; that means on the level of content, it was displayed precisely differently from what was occurring in everyday life, therefore on the level of its reflection, on the level of the (art) form, it was necessary to produce something "abnormal"; something like a formal invention or as an excess, as an excessive surplus (in accordance with the social and political system in which they appeared, be it socialism or capitalism), in order to say that what was commonly accepted as *normality* was, in fact, a lie. But what we have today is precisely the obverse; on the level of "content," so to speak, in reality the world is captured as it is, in its full extension of abnormality, monstrosity, exploitation, expropriation, while on the level of "form," this abnormality is normalized, presented in such a way that the meaning of the powerful content becomes empty, obsolete.

Content is abnormal and the form is normal; and moreover, form misrecognition is today presented consciously, snobbishly stylized, so to speak, out of all proportion. In such a situation, the knowledge that is "captured" through a scientific or art work is transformed through the performative politics of repetition into pure ideological knowledge, but with a proviso saying that we should therefore not be preoccupied as its all just a process of pure performativity. Therefore, what we get is not just upside (turned) down, but ideology made "unconscious": presented in the form of a game or a joke which is given a life of its own.

Therefore, if we agree with what Althusser writes in the 1970s regarding the difference between art and science, saying that this difference lies in the specific form, as reported by Agon Hamza (2009) "in which the same object is given in quite a different way: art in the form of 'seeing' and 'perceiving' or 'feeling,' science in the form of knowledge (in the strict sense, by concepts)," then at that time all that was needed was to take a step on the other side in order to understand what was going on. But what in Althusser's time was presented as revolutionary is today a point of accepted knowledge and not any longer be a point of ideological dispute, and (this is an important difference) therefore, contemporary ideology no longer resides on the level of content but is already subsumed on the formal level of our knowledge.

What's additionally important is that today we witness the change between transparency and opacity. The "opacity" of the 1970s, which Althusser made clear by exposing the situation of ideological mystification between science and ideology, is today completely transparent. The specter of transparency is, in fact, as stated by Santiago López Petit, haunting us (López Petit 2009). The only abnormal field is social reality, which is excessive and opaque, while the mechanism of its presentation is totally transparent, framed within processes of total obviousness. This obviousness that presents itself as a performative repetitive mechanism makes ridiculous the abnormal social content.

If we follow Althusser's definition of ideology as an imaginary deformed representation of the imaginary relationship of individuals to their real conditions of existence (by which he meant the relations of production), we could say that what ideology misrepresents today is not reality, but itself. In a way, it behaves today as a cognizant post-Fordist mechanism that takes the presented mechanism of ideology's materiality (that was presented in the 1970s, in the Fordist era, so to speak, if we make reference to Paolo Virno, 2004) as its raw material, as its content. But what does this mean precisely? It makes imaginary today which was already identified as material. It transforms (again) through the repetitive performative ideological mechanism the materiality of ideology, and the materiality of its apparatuses, onto imaginary levels. The materiality of ideology is today made redundant, nullified and emptied through repetitive (ideological) performative mechanisms. To put it another way, what is clear on the level of *content*, so to speak, is on the level of *form* now made to be simply obsolete, ridiculous, not sexy or obvious enough, to the extent of not being attractive enough. What we have at work today is another misrecognition that is not a misrecognition at all, but a reflected cognition that takes as its basis the ideological misrecognition of the 1970s, and repeats it in such a way as to make it ridiculous, or perhaps more accurately, an old knowledge; the materiality of ideology is now taken as raw material to be integrated into performative representations where this materiality is consciously set back to the level of the imaginary.

A perfect example of what has been said up to now is the Eleventh International Istanbul Biennial in 2009 curated by What, How & for Whom (WHW), a non-profit organization/visual culture and curators' collective formed in 1999 and based in Zagreb, Croatia. The Eleventh International Istanbul Biennial had as its title "What Keeps Mankind Alive?," as proposed by WHW, which is the title of the song that closes the second act of the play The Threepenny Opera, written by Bertolt Brecht in collaboration with Elisabeth Hauptmann and Kurt Weill in 1928. As the online text of the Eleventh International Istanbul Biennial[1] (written by WHW) states, Brecht proposed with The Threepenny Opera the transformation of the "theatre apparatus" through an alteration of the existing notions of theatre "genres" and the play's relationship with the audience. This transformation was based on Brecht's assertion that "A criminal is a bourgeois and a bourgeois is a criminal." This assertion of Brecht's, obviously at the core of WHW's concept, is the main refrain that is also at the core of the biennial. WHW not only affirms that it is "working for the criminals" (their wording), as stated online, but is also constructing such a framework around the biennial that is taking away the very possibility of intervening critically—thereby transforming the critical discourse "working for the criminals" into a normalized fact, into a constative, making what we know obvious and, additionally, taking this obviousness as a side fact (a criminal is a bourgeois and a bourgeois is a criminal).

In short, we can say that today the level of dealing with ideology is at a level of transforming it into a commodity, into a source of normalization, through processes of performativity and repetition; the ruling ideology is not seen as preoccupying when being perceived as a process of misrecognition (as it was preoccupying for Althusser), but this misrecognition is today taken as the raw material for a stylish play. It is no longer a ghostly figure, but a terrain for experimentation, invention and infinite imagination.

Making reference to López Petit, we can state that the repetitive performative mechanism functions as indetermination, indecision, irresolution or what he calls *gelatinization* (López Petit 2009, 48). What was before solid ground, a materiality of intervention is today a process of multiplication that removes, empties the ground from its materiality. The repetitive performative mechanism functions as gelatinization, becoming opaque precisely through a process of transparency that is performed today as repetition. Gelatinization corresponds today, as argued by López Petit, to global capitalism as reification corresponded to modernity. If reification was in relation to the distinction between the living and the dead, gelatinization requires a triadic model, according to López Petit, *the living, the dead,* and *the inert* (López Petit 2009). Who is the possible example of the inert? Bartleby the Scrivener, of course.[2]

Gelatinization means giving an account of reality that presents itself as being occulted, abstract, and transparent. Reality is at the same time alive and dead and, therefore, as stated by Petit, it is multi-reality. Gelatinization is the solid surrounded by the liquid that is, I will claim, the repetitive performative mechanism. It is a double process, as stated by López Petit, of opening and closing. What is even more horrifying, according to López Petit, is that closing effectuates obviousness. Gelatinization means reality is covered with obviousness. Politically this presents a catastrophe. Multi-reality is open but has no outside! Gelatinization makes vague the political subject and multi-reality vaguely presents the enemy. It oscillates from maximum abstraction to absolute concreteness.

Therefore, in a departure from Marx's analysis of commodity fetishism, today we do not have something normal on the level of society from which the analysis of the form of its presentation in art, for example, or in theory, will show us that actually what is normal content is in reality the opposite; something strange and different from what is said, etc. Today, in a difference from Marx, (who was the point of reference for Althusser), we live in a time in which social reality is abnormal and the form of its articulation is here not only to normalize this abnormality but to intensify it through voiding this abnormality of any content, meaning, etc. This emptying is going on as obviousness. So, first the thing is being turned upside down, and then the form is just taking us somewhere else. This *somewhere else* is part of an obscene performative logic that is not even saying that what we are witnessing in reality is abnormal, but is simply emptying the content through indetermination, indecision and irresolution. Obfuscation is on the level of form practiced precisely with a double obfuscation. As Marx would say, this is also speculative, or as López Petit puts it, it is the former solid surrounded by the liquid that is the repetitive performative mechanism. The form is not hiding the content anymore, but the way in which it is presented through its formalization makes the content obsolete.

Šefik Tatlić, in his essay "Communication and Mass Intellect" (Tatlić 2010) states that one of the major problems of global capitalism today is precisely this process of not only *an upside-down*, but a complete distortion; a short-circuit between What, How and for Whom things are done and declared. For this distortion to be kept alive and undisturbed, what matters is not only the structure of events, the conditions of exhibitions that are privatized (this is so normalized today that a critique on this point is almost becoming obsolete), what is a problem is not that various places and infrastructures are monopolized (and that this monopolization is based on almost extreme intimate relations between money and affects, offering the possibility for unknown actors in the field of arts to be awarded with curating international exhibitions as payment for services done in the past), but what is at stake here and now is the very substance of the performative language used for the interaction, presentation and discursive rationalization of the project itself.

Culture that is being communicated within the necropolitical, is authentic and differential—authentic within the epistemic frame of references provided by the regime. Thus, the ideas, theories and discourses born under such circumstances are not any longer schematized cultural production, but consist exactly of "free" subjectivities that are critical of the system that produced them in the first place. As it was stated by López Petit , in order to function, a contemporary postmodern fascism needs a proliferation of unbelievable "freedom" of particularities.

Global capitalism colonizes life by appropriating language in itself, and not only its colloquial level, but its discursive formulations as well, upon which society and its different institutions stand. Through these appropriations, specifically the kidnapping of languages and discourses, structures and activations, we see a system of transformation of these machineries, as pointed out by Tatlić, into mechanisms of normalization of the system. Even more, such a truth is not hidden behind any global conspiracy or some "strange" ideology; this truth is brutal in its banal simplicity, as it was said: "A criminal is a bourgeois and a bourgeois is a criminal." So what? But with reference to Brecht, I can argue, the profit is less banal, and more divinized.

"FORMER" WEST

Another good example of this logic of repetition is the reusing of the word "former" from former Eastern Europe (that describes a precise geopolitical condition) for an empty performative—but fully ideological—move of de-re-framing what is functioning powerfully today as Western Europe. An excellent case of such a repetition is the project "Former West"[3] that was started in the Netherlands as an international research, publishing, and exhibition project that started in 2008 to last until 2014, curated by Charles Esche, Maria Hlavajova, and Kathrin Rhomberg. It was initially funded by the European Cultural Foundation (ECF) and organized and coordinated by BAK, *basis voor actuele kunst*, in Utrecht, The Netherlands. This project homogenizes the space of Europe, cruising from city to city, and, put plainly, implies a fictionalization of its Occidentalism, which means that not only does it fictionalize its position toward the East (making the East and West the same), but it evacuates its responsibility in history: western colonialism and capital's racialization are both fictionalized. This project has a precise task and this is the abolition of the effects of extraction of the colonial dimension from geopolitical analysis.

"Former" West is not at all a joke, although it could be seen as such, it is a perfectly logical repetition of the key logic of global capitalism of today. What does the project do? It claims a perverse demand of equal redistribution of "responsibility" and "positions" between the East and West of Europe today. That is, it responds specifically to the demand urgently imposed by Germany after the fall of the Berlin Wall when it was claimed that East Germany and West Germany were to become "equally" outdated. Therefore, it is possible today, as we are all in the same "merde," or simply to say *shit crisis* (though what is forgotten is that this was produced by the First Capitalist World), to talk about "former" Western Europe in the same way we talk about former Eastern Europe.

In the case of Eastern Europe, the *former* means that the processes of evacuation, abstraction and expropriation imposed by the West are actually "over"; as proclaimed by Germany in 2009, celebrating its twentieth anniversary of the fall of the Berlin Wall with the slogan, "Come, come to the country without borders" (and I will say without memory as well). But in the case of the "former" (as it should be at least written) West (Europe), it implies a purely performative, empty and speculative gesture. While the East is excluded more and more from the materiality of its history, knowledge, memory, etc., the West is just performing it. It plays with a speculative form of itself; it wants us to think that its roots of power and capital are fictional! But this is not a strange move today, as it comes at a time when we talk about financialization and the speculative turn in philosophy; the word *former* in front of *West* presents a speculative matrix that gives the West the possibility to not be conscious of its own historical and present hegemonic power—and therefore not responsible for it. This speculative character of the "former" Western Europe resembles with perfect accuracy the speculative character of financial capitalism at the present, and its crisis.

What should be included in the discussion between the former East and "former" West is precisely the ideological form of repetition. This form presents, or *encapsulates*, a process of emptying (not only of diminishing, but in many cases completely nullifying, etc.), what at the level of content was made visible. Alternatively, the former East and "former" West brilliantly describe the logic of the unrestrainment of capital that works by a paradoxical spatialization that requires two repetitions working at one at the same time. Santiago López Petit states that on the one hand, we have a founding repetition with which a system of hierarchy is reestablished, leading to the constant reconstruction of a center and a periphery (the exhibition *Gender Check!*); and on the other hand, a so-called de-foundational repetition (the project "Former West"!) that presents itself as the erosion of hierarchies—producing dispersion, multiplicity, and multi-reality—which makes *invisible* the always repeating production of the center and periphery. This de-foundational repetition is possible to name *postmodern fascism*, according to López Petit (2009).

Be sure that in the future we can expect projects, symposia and statements in which the imperial colonizing forces will try to prove how they were also colonized in the past, and that what is happening to them in the present is the result of some strange forces that have nothing to do with the internal logic of capitalism itself, logic driven by making profit at any cost and privatization.

I have argued in the past that it is just a matter of time before the West, the Occident, will start to claim that it was also colonized. This indeed happened in 2011, when as the result of repeated incidents between Argentina and Great Britain regarding the Falkland Islands, David Cameron, the prime minister of England appealed to the world saying that Argentina wants to invade the islands and that Britain faces colonization. What is at stake here is the imposition of the neoliberal global capitalism dogma that says we are all exploited by capital (the so-called homogeneity of exploitation).

The now reborn *"former" West*, the old colonial power, wants to convince us that it is capable of a process of decolonization, but, as stated by Achille Mbembe, without self-decolonizing itself. Similarly to financialization, this new decolonization is a "fictive decolonization." As Mbembe explains, "fictive" decolonization is decolonization without opposing racializations (Mbembe 2011). The structures of exploitation, inequality and racism stay in such a way untouched in the European Union—and even more accurately they are *reinforced*; the consequences are disastrous.

What we witness in global capitalism is a process of the evacuation of history that is constructed through two-fold epistemological violence: a) a brutal evacuation of history through its direct erasure, or b) a more sophisticated erasure through a process of history as over-fictionalized narratives.

THE CONTENT AND FORM OF "SOCIAL" CURATING

As stated, *content* is today seen as abnormal and the empty form is normalizing and depoliticizing it through performative and repetitive contemporary art, theory, critique, and curatorial modes.

In the few last years a demand has been proposed to critical thinking to envision the social potential of curating. This was for me a performative proposal to produce a paradigm with which we will have to deal with. I state that we have to address this demand for *social curating's* condition of appearance, by asking: how and why it emerges? And how it is to then be conceptualized at this specific conjuncture of our history?

Therefore to a social demand I answer with a political transformation. That I have such a point of departure is because of a diagnosis of curating within the larger Institution of contemporary art in global capitalism that is displaying elements of an over-privatization of itself (museums and other public institutions are more and more privatized and this is not a simple changing of owners but a changing of the source of money from where these once public institutions depart when envisioning their future lives). From this phenomenon follows the incommensurate commercialization of all the big curatorial projects, from Documentas to Biennales, that work hand-in-hand with the formation of monopolized curatorial groups and quasi-elite curatorial bodies of control and management of the practice and theory of curating.[4]

The most recent case in the history of monopolized curatorial groups and quasi-elite curatorial bodies was the open call for the second Curatorial Intensive (August 2013) developed by the organization Independent Curators International (ICI).[5] What they announced can be read similarly to many invitations that are often distributed over the last few years: blah, blah, blah, "to examine the developments of the curatorial field and the changing role of the curator, while exploring strategies and methodologies to develop programs and institutions, collection building, regional and international research, and the logistics of managing projects." The second Curatorial Intensive is to take place in Bogotá, Colombia and the curatorial task-force consists of only large institutions loaded with money and names loaded with power: the curatorial brands can be seen everywhere these days connected with money and power. The target of the school as announced is "toward self-motivated individuals—working independently or in institutions—who would benefit from a week of intensive conversations around the issues and questions that regularly arise for curators." Though the "truth" (again in Badiou's terms) of the event is to be found in the middle/end of the open call: "The program fee is 1,900 USD. Participants are also responsible for covering travel and accommodation expenses." Help is offered of course, another pile of institutions and etc., but selection, filtering, and the inclusion and exclusion is done through money, networking etc.

Let's leave this case and shift the focus that was at the core of my analysis in 2012: dOCUMENTA (13).[6] I am interested in curating as a discipline but one that can be politically transformed and transformative without submitting itself to disgusting "metaphysical extremes," or getting stuck in some normativity of curating or even in the morality (ethics?) of curating.

When I talk of "metaphysical extremes" I think of something that was announced to take place in August 2012 in the Banff Center, Alberta, Canada. It was a (post-)curatorial event being termed by the organizers

as a *Visual Arts Residency*, with the title "The Retreat: A Position of dOCU-
MENTA(13)." This "Retreat" termed as a *post*-dOCUMENTA (13) event
was characterized and criticized by a user on one of the usual lists where
such open calls are usually published (the *nettime* mailing list for net-
worked cultures, politics, and tactics), I quote:

> A kind of get-down of hobnobs of autonomist exiles at the Banff Cen-
> tre/Rocky Mountains/Canada and organized as a satellite of some sort
> of the art world's. I have to ask: who got to go to the Retreat? Who gets
> to meet Bifo in the elite setting of the Rocky Mountains? . . .This has led
> me to question the organization behind this Retreat. In particular, how
> such a Retreat can style itself as "open" to creating "new modes of
> becoming and belonging" when its application process is costly and
> anything but transparent. The guest list included autonomists and phi-
> losophers, many of whom I have been reading in some form or other (if
> not debating here on this list) for the past decade and some years:
> Franco Berardi (Bifo), Bruno Bosteels, Carolyn Christov-Bakargiev,
> Pierre Huyghe, Catherine Malabou, Gáspár Miklós Tamás.

This critique was offered by a person that applied and was rejected
(which can be seen as a reason for posting on the *nettime* list) nevertheless
the data reported was accurate and published on the website of the Banff
Centre.[7]

Here my analysis starts. Is it possible to say that the post-*documenta*
curatorial project "Retreat" spoke early enough to give us a chance to
make a dOCUMENTA (13) analysis of its curatorial goals? dOCUMEN-
TA (13) being a major curatorial-money-tourist-event in the world of visual arts was scheduled to open in June 2012, while the post-dOCUMEN-
TA (13) was announced to take part in August 2012.

Can we not say that the "Retreat" of the curatorial-theoretical gang
(that were all "white," but nevertheless "racialized" regarding which
place of influence they occupied in the contemporary Institution of art
and culture) was profoundly conditioned by capital-money entanglement of the institution of contemporary art in general and the discipline
of curating in particular, and that the concept of the "social" has a specific
common function in both of these contexts.

Therefore how to proceed with the reexamination of (social) curating?
Just to map different curatorial concepts binding them to their particular
social conditions is obviously not enough. We have to "grab" curating in
an almost Althusserian fashion and ask for the history of curating to be
seen as socially and politically antagonist and not agonistic.

At stake here is not a division (that was never the case) between on
one side the elite and on the other the plebs of curating (hundreds of
small important projects, curatorial struggles dispersed here and there on
the globe). In fact curating was already, from its very "beginning," not
divided into two poles but "overdetermined" (as Althusser would say) in
a double way.

On one side we have the *form of curating*, that traces transformations within the discipline of curating, exposing its logic (a kind of an epistemological endeavor), and on other side is the *content of curating* that is termed as *politics* or more accurately *the place of ideological struggle* within curating. I claim that we have ideology on both sides, which is why we talk of overdetermination. On one side it is the logic of the production of forms of curating and on the other the "bothering" politics of curating that is seen as being directly ideological. The latter could be seen precisely as the place where the social demand could be more or less conceptualized as something moral, or humanitarian.

The same mistake will happen if we think about the "Retreat" as an amoral flop by the curators of dOCUMENTA (13) that will nevertheless produce an important (can we be in any doubt about this?) "epistemological break." We have to get rid of these simple divisions, in order to be even more critical. Achille Mbembe, states that, while talking about postcolonial studies, if we will just see them as having to do with ideology, while the social sciences are to do with knowledge and are therefore supposedly neutral, this will be a position of "sublime ignorance." Mbembe is very precise when he states "there has always been, over a much longer history, a direct relationship between a certain form of nationalism and a theory of racial difference that is masked by the universalistic and republican paradigm" (Mbembe 2011). Indeed, he makes the point that it might well be that Occidental universalism is itself the product of *racial theory*. Therefore, we can suggest the existence of a persistent mode of coloniality in the center of Western capitalist power structures and its epistemological, historical, and philosophical edifice(s).

To maintain therefore that curating is ideological is not enough, it is necessary to understand these two parts of curating as *both* being ideological, and even more, to understand that what is perceived as its form also has a deep ideological foundation. We simply cannot afford to say that we have two histories, let us say on one side will be the sequence of the *documenta* powerful history of "epistemological breaks" and on the other the "more" ideological ("problematic") sequence of different elitist retreats (let's talk in plural as we do not know what else is programmed as the "special program" of post-dOCUMENTA (13)).

What is important is to understand that the ideological is fully present on both sides, on the side of the form and on the content. My thesis is that in global capitalism, ideological is not functioning more on the side of the "content" of curating, on the contrary, today the ideological is attached directly to the form, so that the process of forming "the knowledge" of curating is now presented as "social" (social curating) while the other side, the social ("the content") of curating, presents itself as completely empty. So while we are problematizing the social as ideological we have in fact no content at all or, better to say, we have a post-ideological setting that is empty; *the form* is on the other hand presented as an extra-ideological form of knowledge that is fully "social." Therefore the post-dOCU-MENTA (13) "Retreat" is simply (let's speculate) a deserved holiday after important "social curating" work that was performed at dOCUMENTA (13). In summary, (social) curating has to be seen as a *regime* of curating that appears precisely at the moment where there is no a trace of any social concern but, on the contrary, where the rhetorical of "social curating" hides the conditions and constraints of an invigorated global capitalist over-exploitative conjuncture.

To think of curating today as a pertinent political discipline and activity, we have to be precise in what it is that is at the core of the social and political conjuncture of our time. Making a reference to Achille Mbembe, Sara Ahmed, and many others, it is possible to state that at the core is: racism. Sara Ahmed argues that today it is possible to articulate political art only as an ongoing difficulty of speaking about racism as well as queer and color activism.

Mbembe contends that racism is exercised onto an ethical social body in Europe that is constituted of a myriad of ethnical groups and therefore, they are present, but not at the focus of discussion. Mbembe says that racial profiling has become commonplace, and deportation camps have been created for undesirables in the EU context. This is going on to such an extent that today one of the major characteristics of the nation-States in the EU is not them being *nation*-States but *racial*-States (Stoler 2011). Mbembe is talking about France although we will take this as a feature of the EU in general (or as they like to call themselves) "the former West" in particular. Mbembe argues that we have a paradoxical situation as the ideas of the European republic are those of the "colonial republic." This disgusting terminology in the end presents the demands of the republic ideals (equality, freedom, and fraternity) as "humanity" that is nothing more than a *colonial humanity*. This could easily become emblematic for "social curating" as well. Therefore, yes, let's talk about the social, but I will say at this point, again via Mbembe, that if we want to talk about the social question of curating then we have to talk about the racial, or (with Sara Ahmed), about racism.

Reflecting on social questions of curating is possible only within "the matrix of curating" that was coined by Efrat Shalem and Yanai Toister.[8] The matrix of curating allows us to connect curating with a "colonial power matrix" coined in the 1990s by the Peruvian sociologist Aníbal Quijano. He conceptualized the neoliberal world of capitalism as an entanglement of different hierarchies that work at the axes of sexual, political, epistemic, economic, linguistic, curatorial, and racial forms of domination and exploitation. This matrix said Quijano (2000) affects all dimensions of social existence such as sexuality, authority, subjectivity, and labor. At the center of the matrix is the viewpoint of how race and racism become the organizing principle of all the social, political, and economic structures of the capitalist regime.

Therefore what is necessary is a decolonial turn. Chandra Talpade Mohanty claims that it is necessary to challenge exploitation performed by colonial global capitalism with the elaboration of anti-racist and deco-lonial pedagogies.

Political transformation? I make a reference to the book by Adrian Johnston *Badiou, Žižek, and Political Transformations: The Cadence of Political Change* published in 2009 and to the review of the book by Peter Gratton in 2010 that is not at all fully sympathetic to it (judging from the title of his reviewing article: "A Change We Can't Believe In"). Gratton never-theless suggests departing from the rhetorical question of "is it happen-ing?" (the political transformation) and continues with Johnston's propo-sal that if "it is happening, I am with it in solidarity." But I will even more radicalize these boys' talks by Johnston and Gratton, as it is not enough to be in solidarity, we have to take the responsibility of its consequence. Secondly if there is a ghost, via Gratton, that Johnston wishes to exorcize, then this is the specter of a political quietism that regards political trans-formation as broadly therapeutic or remedial. And there is a good reason for this, as exposed by Gratton, since any theory of praxis (I will say of curating as well) that can have a certain political life in the contemporary "deadness of political inertia" must resist falling into micropolitics in light of the dominant order, or simply wait, as Gratton formulates these dangers, for "the transcendent moment to come."

The elements that are offered for political transformation are several but I will make use of two which here and now have particular relevance: materialism and the political act.

The question of materialism being connected with history is clearly being elaborated by Johnston. The question of the political act is a ques-tion of a political decision that has nothing to do with action. The materi-alist possibility of history that is at stake in Johnston's book is formulated as the third materialist position of history. The first is history as it is lived in and the second is the history as the heroic life of the engaged subject.

The latter could be depicted as a trajectory developed by Gilles De-leuze in his two historical books about theoretical philosophy of film written in the mid-1980s. In both books, as stated by Jonathan Beller,

> It is here that I find Deleuze's work limited and limiting. Not only because it confines itself to the analysis of the hundred or so geniuses of cinema, but because of its dual cathexis on films and on thought. My objection is not simply that this desire is aestheticizing or philosophi-cally motivated, but rather that in order to construct itself thusly, it misses the historical role of cinema in its entirety. No fetishist can know the true nature of his or her object. In other words, Deleuze's encounter confines itself to a rather narrow definition of cinema, in as much as it does not explore the global role of cinema as an emergent operating system for the coordination of the multiple variables of production. To do so, would of course historicize cinema in such a way that its formal

innovations were linked primarily to social conditions, and this move would impinge upon the centrality of aesthetics and philosophy, casting them as subroutines in the operation of a larger system. It would also raise questions about the social and historical significance of the industrialization of the visual and require a dialectical mode of analysis. Deleuze gets around this immanent pressure—pressure that he perceives precisely by the stemming of his own thought in the face of the image—by muttering something to the effect of what he is doing in the cinema books, is what philosophers do: produce concepts. But here, Marx's challenge to the role of the philosopher sounds as fresh as ever, "Up to now, philosophers have only interpreted the world, the point, however, is to change it. (Beller and Gržinić 2009b)

This leads us precisely to the 3rd position.

The third position is to be found in the materialist development of history. Which is what exactly? This is the *new indecent materialism* that would not merely diagnose the social pathology of the present but re-instantiate political subjectivities, or put another way, that would exemplify, elaborate, articulate, the working conditions of political subjectivities.

And the political act as developed by Johnston? Acting "essentially involves taking the risk of a gesture with no meta-level guarantee of being appropriate, correct, just, right, successful, and so on" (Johnston 2009, 149).

The Digital Mode of Production

There is a process of subjectivization (individualization) at work today in the field of contemporary artistic and cultural production, which does not take place through work, but through artistic creativity; the latter redefines precisely, or, if you wish, colonizes the very understanding of what work is today. The process of subjectivization does not mean only a production and reproduction of subjects, but, above all, the regulation and understanding of what the process of subjectivization means in itself. At the core here is the question of governance and governmentality. Therefore the whole dismantling and rearranging of the institution of contemporary higher education by the Bologna agreement (the changes of Higher Education) throughout Europe, is not about simple economization of the university or academy, making money through a system of equalization and nivelization of the university system around the world, it is in fact about governance!

The economy that is invested in the whole plot of reorganization is not the primal task of the Bologna agreement. Actually, such a reduction (as to say that the university is forced only to make more money) prevents an understanding that the change brought by the Bologna Higher Education agreement is about the neoliberal politics of violent governance (financialization and serialization) of education in contemporary capitalist societies.

Financial capital is working hand in hand with, as stated by Jonathan Beller (2009a), "computer-generated imagery that depends upon the mathematical computational power, if not cognition, of a machine. The attack by capital is launched in a space entirely shot through mathematicized vectors of not just computer graphics (as in the end of 1990s), but through an industry that supports silicon mathematics with its logics of genre, celebrity, distribution and the world market." So on the one hand we have, as argued by Beller, the "hypersensitivity" of the mind-body and, on the other, the off-screen universe of computerization, globalization and financialization scoring the action.

I would like to propose in relation to what I have just stated (developing further what Jonathan Beller developed in the 2000s as the *cinematic mode of production*), a mode of production that I call the *digital mode of production*. This digital mode codes, reproduces, and forms the grammar and logic of exploitation and expropriation of the present financial capitalism, and is not limited to the realms of art and culture. The digital mode of production is analogous to the cinematic mode of production, but also different from it, for it takes as its primal logic the calculation of the computer that is a form of social programming, a mode of constructing society and a mode of making profit that cannot be separated from the logic of financial capital. How does it function? As a new formation of the techno-capitalist-labor condition, it is performed through the overlapping of exploitation, digitalization, and financialization. Specifically it works through entanglement, that hides global post-Fordist division of labor, which can be best described as an international division of labor between the First, Second, and Third Worlds. This division is effective yet hidden under the veil of globalization. This is one side of this process that is in itself already divided. The other side of this process is going on at the local level, where labor is captured in a matrix of capitalized vectors; or to put it differently, affective and cognitive-linguistic activities are little by little converted into worksites for not only capitalist surplus value—i.e., profit—but also for what is termed simply as (according to Beller) capitalist *use value*.

The digital mode of production consists of the computerization or digitalization of representational and interventional forms in culture and arts working in relation to television, cinema, and computer screens, but also of forms in the imagination, the immaterial, the cognitive, the libidinal and the unconscious that are produced and reproduced by and through these form(at)s. The digital mode is not a symptom but is cosubstantive, which means that it works hand in hand with the process of calculation which also is at the base of financial capital. Therefore, the whole of the cultural industry today is not only about the creation of products, markets and consumers, but about "revolutionizing," as stated by Beller, the theater of capitalist production and reproduction (Beller 2009a). Science and technology are being implemented for figuration, representation, mediation and rationalization of the crisis, for new forms of coloniality, deep processes of racism, discrimination, and exploitation.

Beller argues: "A typical laptop computer running the calculations necessary to generate three minutes of industry standard CGI would have to run for nine hours. If one thinks not just of the immense number of calculations that inform such cinematic images (with/of exaggeration, human lifetimes worth of math), not to mention the entire history of mathematics and computing that lead up to our current abilities" (Beller 2009a)—we begin to get a real sense of what we are looking at in the digital mode of production. We can attest that these calculations are predominantly financial.

An exemplary case will make the present capitalist division (that presents, in fact, a multiplication) of labor and digitalization even clearer. Just think of the film *Slumdog Millionaire* by the British director Danny Boyle that received an Oscar in 2009; it is the story of a young man from the slums of Mumbai who appears in the Indian version of the show "Who Wants to be a Millionaire?" and exceeds all expectations. What draws our attention is precisely this double process of coloniality, exploitation, and digitalization. For what lies in the background? The film is a hallmark example of global fetishism in search of the spectacle of Third World poverty. Or rather it is a process of capitalization of the structure of desire (and disavowal) that is activated by First World capital for Third World labor. The coded images of the Third and Second Worlds by First World capital become an essential mechanism in the continued occupation and exploitation of the Third and Second Worlds; in addition to the creation of surplus value, there is the creation of surplus pleasure, or surplus desire. Again, in such products we see, as stated by Beller, that the ostensible extra-economic effects are subsumed and operative as ideological digital modes. This process is also effective in the First Capitalist World; just think of the erosion of the whole sector of critical thinking and the complete transformation of every critical discourse and resistance network into a brand. Or as it was posted on *nettime* by jaromil:

> Creativity must be rendered comprehensible, transparent and rational: there can be none of the destructive excesses evident in the lives of many of the greatest artists of European history. Creativity must circulate cleanly and quickly, and it should leave no dirty remainder. For what interests Hollywood and the market in general, is not creativity as a complex human process, but creativity as an abstraction, free of irrationality and pain, and light enough to hover like a great logo above the continents.[9]

In such a situation class division is not expired, it is actually intensified and, as stated by Beller (2009b), multiplicated in the meanders of new language inventions and modernized grammars—of digital exploitation, capital and surplus value relations. My thesis is that the digital as the dominant mode of representation of financial capital is not simply a mode of representation but is the dominant mode of reproduction of capital that is today its primary form of production. Digitalization has a double function: on one level, due to its hardware, it functions as a privileged place of biopolitics for open strategies of communication, predominately in the First World; and on the other, it exert necropolitics according to which digital exploitation becomes an essential mechanism for continual occupation and exploitation. New media technology is the condition for contemporary art to be an important part of the functioning of capitalist society.

Three strategies are at work here: the production of shock through the aid of cloning, the strategy of creating simulacra that work outside the human perspective (say, "paraspace"), and the strategy of mutation (theories of the "post-human"). These three strategies are a form of concealing, abstracting and evacuating from the economic, social, political and artistic space the conditions of social antagonism, the class war, transforming (almost unnoticed) biopolitics into necropolitics.

An Artist Who Cannot Speak English Well is No Artist!

In rearticulating a history of global capitalism and its borders, I can state that the so-called multicultural ideology of 1990s global neoliberal capitalism was a declaration of the existence of other worlds, but only and solely for the installment of a second step, which was the iron logic of the imperialism of circulation. In order to do this, an accelerated process of dispossession was put to work, which cleaned away and evacuated each and every difference through formalization. These two stages are excellently captured in the field of contemporary art by an art project I have already talked about many times and have undertaken an analysis of in the past. In the 1990s, Mladen Stilinović (Croatian conceptual artist) declared: "An artist who cannot speak English is NO artist."

This sentence, written on a piece of fabric, as his artwork, excellently depicted the initial multicultural logic of neoliberal global capitalism of the 1990s. It was an interest in a specificity that had to use the "common English language" translation regardless of (and at that time it seemed not to matter) how well it was used. A decade afterwards, in 2007, I proposed a correction to this artwork:

"An artist who cannot speak English WELL is NO artist."

Santiago López Petit states that the "difference" which was, in the not-so-distant past, known as *social antagonism* (class struggle), has been divided today within itself into *order and disorder*. In such a way the unity of levels are maintained and reality is made multiple (López Petit 2009, 38). The diagram of functioning that demonstrated the (unity of the) class struggle was *identity* is equal to *identity* plus *difference*. In the time of the unrestrainment of capital this changed into *difference* is equal to *difference* plus *identity* (López Petit 2009, 38). In such a way we can also read the primacy of difference but, as stated by Petit, this difference is now pushed forward, pointing to the sameness that is the appendix of the rearticulation of difference. This identity, or sameness, is today the established co-propriety of capital/power that takes on very different names, depending on the specific social and political space.

In art, the work of Mladen Stilinović is the best example to understand this shift from identity to difference (and back) that occurred in the period from the 1990s to the 2000s. In the world of capitalism, in the 1990s, immediately after the fall of the Berlin Wall, those coming from the former Eastern Europe, were seen as having an added value of "difference." This added value of difference was tolerated as it was only supplementary to the already established capitalist (neo)liberal identity. On the premise that the difference was still only an appendix, it was tolerated, but efforts were made to impose on us the use a common language that was (historically because of capital's exploitation, translation and colonialism) *English*.

At the height of global capitalism, following the new proposed equation by López Petit that states: difference is equal to difference plus identity, it is necessary to state, and I repeat: "An artist who cannot speak English WELL is NO artist!"

This is the new process of *dispossession* through *formalization*.

THE ULTRA-PERVERSE REASONING OF NEOLIBERAL GLOBAL CAPITALISM

To return to the repetitive performative mechanism which characterizes contemporary art, within its performative system we can now identify an even more subtle diversification. Sara Ahmed calls it "the non-performativity of the performative" when discussing the non-performativity of anti-racism (Ahmed 2006). Ahmed develops this non-performativity of the performative as another way of contemporary performative art disqualifying any content, meaning etc. When she examines different modes for declaring whiteness Ahmed is arguing that such declarations are non-performative: they do not do what they say.

As stated by Ahmed "The declarative mode involves a fantasy of transcendence in which 'what' is transcended is the very 'thing' admitted to in the declaration (for example, if we are say that we are racists, then we are not racists, as racists do not know they are racists)" (Ahmed 2006). In short, Ahmed states that it is precisely the non-performativity of anti-racism which allows racism to be articulated as a minority position (!), as an act of (majority whiteness) defiance of the multicultural (politically correct) stance that is today seen as "orthodoxy." This is a lethal attack on struggles against racism, and confirms once again that racism is the *lingua franca* through which the social and political spaces of Europe are articulated in today's global capitalism (Ahmed 2008).

Multiculturalism, the ideology of the 1990s, has been slowly installed as a norm of the new post-1990 society. In the last two decades it has been more and more concealed under a normative mainstream discourse of diversity. Sara Ahmed talks about a new form of hegemony, describing hegemony "as the dominant way of ordering things that reproduces things in a certain order" (Ahmed 2008). And she continues that "hegemony is not really reducible to facts as it involves semblance, fantasy and illusion, being a question of how things appear and the gap between appearance and the real" (Ahmed 2008).

With the injunction of liberal multiculturalism as the new hegemony and the prohibition of talking about racism and disqualification, Ahmed argues that: "[firstly] the speech act, 'we must support the other's difference' is read as hegemonic, and is taken literally as a sign not only that it is compulsory to support the other's difference, but we are not allowed to refuse this support, and, secondly, the speech act is read as doing what it says, but is not the case, as it is precisely blocking what it performatively declares, even more it is reproducing and reinforcing that what it should prohibited" (Ahmed 2008).

Ahmed argues: "We can see this at stake in the making of the multicultural nation: Britain is represented as being multicultural because of its national character: as being tolerant, open, loving, hospitable, and so on" (Ahmed 2008). She continues in her project on diversity in organizations:

> [w]hen Black staff spoke about racism, organizations often responded by pointing to their race equality and diversity policies, as if these policies were the point. Black staff spoke of how they deal with whiteness everyday and how diversity and equality as organizational ideals get in the way of reporting these experiences. . . . Diversity as an ego ideal conceals experiences of racism, which means that multiculturalism is a fantasy which supports the hegemony of whiteness. In such a fantasy, racism is "officially prohibited." (Ahmed 2008)

Ahmed argues, therefore, that the prohibition against racism

> is imaginary, and that it conceals everyday forms of racism, and involves a certain desire for racism. The prohibition of racist speech should not then be taken literally: rather it is a way of imagining "us" as beyond racism, as being good multicultural subjects who are not that. By saying racism is over there—"look, there it is! in the located body of the racist"—other forms of racism remain unnamed. (Ahmed 2008)

This "imagining of 'us' beyond racism" is imposed as a norm of multiculturality and diversity, as a majoritarian discourse which allows racism to
be, paradoxically and perversely, "articulated as a minority position, a
refusal of orthodoxy. In this perverse logic, racism can then be embraced
as a form of free speech. Racism then becomes a minority position which
has to be defended against the multicultural hegemony" (Ahmed 2008).
Moreover, she states: "Hegemonies are often presented as minority positions, as defences against what are perceived to be hegemonic, which is
how they can be presented as matter of life and death" (Ahmed 2008).

This perversity goes so far, Ahmed points out, that today *colonial* is
seen as a good sign of British character. As an example of such thinking,
she quotes Trevor Phillips: "And we can look at our own history to show
that the British people are not by nature bigots. We created something
called the empire where we mixed and mingled with people very different from those of these islands." [10] Ahmed formulated her critique,
"agreeing" precisely with Phillips:

> Empire here become[s] proof that British are "not bigots," but are able
> to "mix and mingle" with others. Indeed, empire itself becomes a sign
> of a British tendency towards happy diversity; towards mixing, loving
> and co-habiting with others. The violence of colonial occupation is re-
> imagined as a history of love (a story of mixing and mingling), whilst
> colonialism itself becomes a happy sign of a certain national disposi-
> tion. Here, diversity, mixing and multiculturalism become happy inso-
> far as they are "gifts" given by the British towards others. (Ahmed
> 2008)

The outcome of such thinking is that David Cameron, the current British
Prime Minister, can state, in Ahmed's paraphrase, that, "multiculturalism
went "too far": we gave the other "too much" respect, we celebrated
difference "too much," such that multiculturalism is read as the cause of
segregation, riots and even terrorism." The result is, as Ahmed points
out, monoculture instead of multiculture:

> [The] current monoculture political agenda functions as a kind of
> retrospective defence against multiculturalism. . . . So now migrants
> must be British; we must defend integration, as a defence against
> multiculturalism, which in turn is what threatens the well-being of the
> nation. We have a return to national pride as defence of Britishness, as
> if this is a minority position. So the speech act, "we must support the
> other's difference" is read as hegemonic, is taken literally as a sign not
> only that it is compulsory to support the other's difference, but that we
> are not allowed to refuse this support. (Ahmed 2008)

Moreover, in a recent speech on the end of multiculturalism, Cameron
noted that "[w]hen a white person holds objectionable views—racism, for
example—we rightly condemn them. But when equally unacceptable
views or practices have come from someone who isn't white, we've been

too cautious, frankly even fearful, to stand up to them."[11] Such an utterance by Cameron is deeply colonial as it presents, as stated by Šefik Tatlić, the typical rhetorical hijacking of the monopoly on judgment which implies that only a white man can condemn a white man; every other judgment is racist or "extremist" (Tatlić 2011).

In the perversities of neo-liberal global capitalism, "imagining . . . 'us' beyond racism" becomes an imposed norm of multiculturality and diversity, and therefore a kind of a majoritarian discourse which allows the bizarre utterance, that racism is "a proof of freedom of speech" in global capitalism. In this way racism is presented as an "instrument of struggle" against orthodoxy; not just any orthodoxy, but a capitalist orthodoxy that commands us to imagine ourselves "beyond racism." In the context of the reality of today's neo-liberal capitalist global society and its abnormality, the implication is thus that social reality is not abnormal *because* racism is represented and performed today as an allegedly political category, but because it is *not performed enough!*

The "heroic" story shaped by this thinking is that the acts of colonization perpetuated by the British Empire actually—allegedly—enabled the multicultural society we have today; or, even more perversely, that colonialism was a struggle for the equality of all of "us" and on our behalf. This ultra-perverse reasoning is the product of the way in which neo-liberal capitalism presents social reality as abnormal while the capitalist imaginary is presented as normal! This is a situation of pure disaster.

What To Do?

What is the phenomenon that can be seen if one looks closely at the different logics of functioning within the space of politics, and even more so, within the space of art and culture of today's new Europe? We see a disinterest in art and culture, etc. coming from the region of former Eastern Europe. This is not about being romantic or sad; this disinterest must clearly be connected with the escalation of all major exhibitions and biennials that show a special appetite for the positions of Third World artists, mostly Asian and Latin American. The past divisions and ideologies of difference within Europe are seen as obstacles to the process of capital circulation or, put more simply, obstacles to the circulation of money. Behaving as though this is already one space (Europe), it is not necessary to push any inclusion through exclusion; it is enough to behave as though differences no longer exist (something China also proved with the Olympic Games).

The process of the disappearance of borders is in fact connected to the processes of the new modes of accumulation of capital. One process is surely *accumulation by dispossession,* the other is what we are facing today: *the imperialism of circulation.* Michael Hudson in his 1972 book *Super Imperialism* says that instead of there being a crisis as regards gaps in distribution, today we are witnessing a process contrary to it, which is "the imperialism of circulation." But to come to the imperialism of circulation today, we had to be dispossessed. In 1972, Hudson already announced that the borders, which were preventing unrestrained distribution, and formed gaps in that distribution, would be removed by the imperialism of circulation.

David Harvey in *A Brief History of Neoliberalism* (2005) defines a new form of accumulation that is accumulation by dispossession; a process of a few dispossessing the "public" of their wealth and difference. When it is necessary, either a law is used to secure this accumulation (just think of the unbelievable legislative policy of the EU, which only specialists can understand) or a whole set of institutional, legislative, bureaucratic, infrastructural, theoretical and cultural processes are abruptly or "gently" installed. The process of "accumulation by dispossession" is perhaps no longer effective in Europe, as it is supposedly completed in the EU (with the German slogan for 2009 celebration of the twentieth anniversary of the fall of the Berlin Wall, "Come, come, to the country without borders!") but we can think of its violent and continuous repetition elsewhere, in the Third World, for example.

Both processes—the *accumulation by dispossession* and the *imperialism of circulation*—have to be seen not as a simple division between modes of the accumulation of capital (making accumulation by dispossession redundant), but as one having constituted the parameters (through dispossession) for the other in order to dominate at the present moment.

The borders are "gone," and the price to be paid is the total dispossession of all our ideas, stances, and specificities. Capital has only one agenda though—surplus value—and this is more than a television documentary or Hollywood film conspiracy claim. Capital is a drive; and a human desire that counteracts this madness does not seem to substantially challenge it. The imperialism of circulation without differences (as the primal logic of the condition of the production of global financial capitalism) implies that what is produced is money. The recent capitalist economic crisis, which can be described as a process of stagflation, that is, of differential inflation amid stagnation, is not only a sign, but also the realization of new processes of the capitalization of financial capital in connection with new modes of capital accumulation. The imperialism of circulation, in its frenetic processes, prevents subversion or attack from any master entity. Everything circulates, is exchanged, clearly dispossessed of any difference (precisely by the equalization of every and each difference under the spell of identity), and no obstacles are to be seen in the network that structures reality for us. Those once perceived as enemies, from individuals to institutions, behave as if we are all in the same "merde" (to use this juicy French word for "shit"), as if we were all together, and as if we all had to find the remedies to overcome our problems needs, obstacles, etc. (while those who generate expropriation and dispossession have to be forgotten about immediately).

It is almost impossible to say that something is impossible today.

In the past a subversive act was possible as it was subversion against clear foreclosure and division in the society. We had borders. The big Other, the virtual symbolic order, the network that structures/d reality for us, was the One giving "consistency," so to speak. It was almost a guarantee for our intervention against it.

The world today presents itself as an endless, repeated, circulation (imperialism is an excellent concept capturing this drive), a "friendly" and endless exchange, and therefore, in order to "solve" expropriation, enslavement, and colonial interventions by capital, only one measure is proposed, and this is called *coordination*. I recently found a completely serious political proposal that stated that the only thing to be done to solve our problems was effective "coordination." My question is, can we really be dumb enough to stick to such theories? Of course, they all have an ace hidden in their pocket or up their sleeve in order for things to circulate smoothly. It is necessary to successfully coordinate the process of getting rid of a small number of those who still bother us with social antagonism and class struggle. I am not saying, though, that there is not a need, as in the case of accumulation, for a new conceptualization and historicization of the class struggle!

To Act Politically

Therefore we have to draw a border. To show a border within the inconsistency of the big Other means to act: to act politically. The political act is a division, the setting of a border within a space. It reconfigures, closes, or stops the imperialism of the circulation by establishing new parameters within the space. It establishes a new structure to which to relate (decoloniality of knowledge, decoloniality of power, etc.). An act is always performed through enunciation and it not only sets the parameters that initiate the act itself, but the parameters in relation to the Other to whom it is also addressed. What is important is the establishment of the structure to which this line(s) of division will relate. In the case of the story of a non-existent past division in Europe, it is necessary to state that the biggest profit from the disappearance of borders in Europe is to be gained by financial capital. The point is that in order to push such logic, it was necessary to imply a ferocious process of equalization and leveling of all of the strata of the different European and World societies; from the social to the educational and cultural. It was necessary to install one of the most ferocious politics of repetition of the unrestrainment of capital (also through the politics of dispossession). Put another way, local specificities were changed into ethnic/ethnographical ones, and one general path of history and genealogy from art to culture and science was repeated and established as the only valid one: the First Capitalist World history that completely (de)regulates the history, the present and the future of the world.

The political act changes the very coordinates of this impossibility. It is only through a decolonial act that we set the border within the cynical situation where the only thing which is impossible is impossibility as such. Subsequently it is necessary to build the decolonial framework that would set the new parameters, giving new coordinates to the political work. Within such a context, I can claim that what is necessary, in fact, is a precise, new conceptual and paradigmatic political act, which implies the setting of a new framework.

The question that always stays indeed is to which histories do we attach our representational politics and how do we resituate our position within a certain social, economic and political territory that is connected with the act of building conditions for new possibilities?

NOTES

1. http://11b.iksv.org/anasayfa_en.asp

2. See *Bartleby, the Scrivener: A Story of Wall Street* was written by American novelist Herman Melville (1819–1891). The narrator, an elderly lawyer who has a very comfortable business helping wealthy men deal with mortgages, title deeds, and bonds, relates the story of the strangest man he has ever known. Bartleby arrives in answer to an ad for another scrivener in the office. Bartleby answers with what soon becomes his stock response: *I would prefer not to.* One weekend the narrator stops by the office unexpectedly and discovers that Bartleby has started living there. Bartleby remains willing to do his main work of scrivening, but eventually he "prefers not to" do this as well, so that finally he is doing nothing.

3. See *Former West* at http://www.formerwest.org

4. A good case in the matter is the project Janša, Janša, Janša /JJJ (the three-headed ventriloquist art project by three artists from Ljubljana, Slovenia who de facto changed their names to Janez Janša (the name of a key right-wing political figure of Slovenia in the last two decades). Janez Janša, the politician, is a controversial right-wing Slovenian politician with a fundamentally neo-fascist-nationalist policies. I analyzed in depth the artists JJJ in chapter 3.

5. http://curatorsintl.org/

6. dOCUMENTA(13) opened in June and closed in September 2012, in Kassel, Germany. The artistic director of dOCUMENTA(13) was Carolyn Christov-Bakargiev. Documenta is a cultural event with global reputation. The first edition of Documenta was established in 1955 in Kassel, at that time a city in the capitalist democracy of the Federal Republic of Germany (West Germany). Documenta had a dual mission: first, it started as an attempt to bring Germany up to speed with modern art, both banishing and repressing the cultural darkness of Nazism, and second, it was a sign of democratic openness (and a provocation, as Kassel bordered the German Democratic Republic [East Germany], which was seen as a totalitarian system and without contemporary art or culture). From 1955 Documenta was organized every four years and in the last decades every five years. Every Documenta lasted for only 100 days. The Documenta (100 days exhibition) has an appointed curator/curatorial team and is an event that is more and more connected with other big arts events in Europe and the world, forming a tourist summer caravan for contemporary art and investments. Documenta 14 will open to the public on June 10, 2017.

7. See http://www.banffcentre.ca/programs/program.aspx?id=1210).

8. See http://www.slashseconds.org/issues/001/003/articles/eshalem/index.php

9. jaromil.dyne.org

10. Phillips gave his speech on October 3, 2005, to the Conservative Party's Muslim Forum, www.blink.org.uk/docs/Trevor_Phillips_speech_Nov05.pdf , accessed 30 July, 2011. Quoted after Ahmed 2008.

11. David Cameron, "Speech on Radicalization and Muslim Extremism," Munich, February 5, 2011, transcript available at http://www.newstatesman.com/blogs/the-staggers/2011/02/terrorism-islam-ideology, accessed 30 July, 2011.

Part II

EIGHT

A Broad Overview of Basic Principles of Reorganization of Global Capitalism

An approach to the analysis of the basic characteristics of capital's entanglement with state, society, power and rule should not, in the interpretation of processes of globalization of capitalism, neglect the inextricability of these entanglements and the various humanist projects under which they are taking place.

The processes of liberalization that are taking place at the core of the reorganization and/or democratization of capital have therefore to be taken as the bases upon which global capitalism's search for hegemony and/ or post-liberal iteration of its ideological structures is taking place. Since the reorganization of the epistemological matrices that determine the nature of production of differentiations are included within these processes (the processes of fixation of prefixes of differentiations into biological, ethnical and cultural registers) they have not only brought to light the issue of racism and its iterations as essential in perpetuation of the globalization of capital, but have also marked the strategies of depoliticization as fundamental in the sustainment and analysis of global capitalism as reorganized colonial structure of power.

The wider geopolitical and historical framework to which this analysis refers might be seen as a contemporary phase of the process that was marked by the Westphalian principles (the principles of the Westphalian sovereignty as conceived in 1648) by which the relation between nation-States and the global spread of capitalism formed the foundations upon which the processes of liberalization and globalization were built.

LIBERALISM, MODERNISM, POWER—STRUCTURING OF AN EMPIRE

Aside from the wider treaties on the role the Westphalian principle played in the process of reorganization of the principles of sovereignty in the Euro-Atlantic theatre, the momentum that allowed a certain power sphere to combine the flexibilization of principles/double standards and to retain homogeneity of its sphere of power proved extremely important for analysis of the grounds on which this simultanousness was instituted into a paradigmatic core on the basis of which the globalization of capitalism was(is) being conducted.

As philosopher and theoretician Marina Gržinić has noted in the context of her analysis of the principles of reorganization of power in the post-Cold War era, "Global capitalism's *proliferation* of new states after the fall of the Berlin Wall (in the so called post-Cold War era in which we live today) was possible only with at the same time initiated *disintegration* of the Westphalian principle of the sovereignty of nation-States" (Gržinić 2010b, 20-21).

Since the adherence to the principles of non-intervention into internal affairs (as this principle entailed), was uphelded by, or reserved only for protagonists within the (Western and Central) European political theatre (which did not exclude conflicts among protagonists within this theatre of course), and since specific dimensions of nation-State's sovereignty (in relation to control over the processes of financialization of capital) had to be delegated to the supranational alliances in the post-Cold War era— whether under the terms of the Washington Consesus, Bretton Woods or under the terms laid out by political and economic alliances (such is European Union)—the principles of Westphalian sovereignty, and its iterations/interpretations, were obviously strictly tied to the processes of liberalization of capitalism that consequentlly produced the basic trademarks of institutional and ideological entanglements of power and rule; state and society; elites and the masses; democracy and capital and capital and society.

By avoiding the analysis of early historical phases in processes of liberalization of capitalism, this text deals with the contemporary phases of these processes in relation to neoliberalism and the search for a post-liberal prefix of global hegemonies. This text finds neoliberal modes of capitalism to be in a terminal, yet most prolific phase; interpreted on the basis of prominent analyst of neoliberal capitalism David Harvey, who saw it as: "A theory of political economic practices that proposes that human well being can best be advanced by liberating individual entrepreneurial freedoms and skills within an institutional framework characterized by strong private property rights, free markets and free trade" (Harvey 2005, 2).

Of course, the notion of liberalization of capitalism in the context of this text refers to a whole set of political and social processes that are able to organize the reorganizations of capitalism without having to rely exclusively on a specific mode of liberalization. The current dominance of a certain model of liberalization should therefore be seen as part of a wider agenda in the global institutionalization of capitalism that is able to transcend almost all of the rigid dimensions of the current mode of rule. As Harvey noticed: "The restructuring of state forms and of international relations after the Second World War was designed to prevent a return to the catastrophic conditions that had so threatened the capitalist order in the great slump of the 1930's. It was also supposed to prevent the reemergence of inter-state geopolitical rivalries that had led to the war" (Harvey 2005, 9-10). As Harvey continued,

> To ensure domestic peace and tranquility, some sort of class compromise between capital and labor had to be constructed. The thinking at the time is perhaps best represented by two eminent social scientists, Robert Dahl and Charles Lindblom, published in 1953. Both capitalism and communism in their raw forms had failed they argued. The only way ahead was to construct the right blend of state, market, and democratic institutions to guarantee peace, inclusion, well-being and stability. (Harvey 2005, 9-10)

While we could say that this blend has been found (or is being found) in a mixture of state, market and democratic institutions that have allowed the reorganization of the principles of the Westphalian sovereignty on the basis of both preservation and disintegration of the (specific) nation-State(s) into the global imposition of this blend as the ideal structure of global society, we could not say that these principles of blending were designed to produce a new form of politically explicit rigidness in response to the former. If something was (is being) rigidified in order to perpetuate the structuring of such a global order it is the continuous search for the right blend of state, market, and democratic institutions that would allow for constant narrowing of the distance between society and capital—not only as a trademark set of economic instructions, but as epistemological, ideological, institutional, and social relation.

So if contemporary momentum in the reorganization of capitalism was preceded by 1950s and 1960s *embedded liberalism*[1] and the neoliberal project in the 1970s, 1980s and the 1990s (which aim was, according to Harvey, paraphrasing, to disembed[2] capital from these constrains), and if interpretation of Westphallian principles were so conveniently conformed into the (post)liberal narratives (on the basis of "necessities" or "realities" as capitalist pundits would put it) in the form of justification for interventions founded on notions of humanitarian interventions, democracy preservation/imposition or war(s) against terror, the post 9/11 period, on which this text mostly focuses, is surely marked by the utilization of the mixture of state, capital and democracy in the search for a post-liberal framework that could secure the most optimal functioning of global capitalism in all of its economic, social, institutional, ideological, and epistemological dimensions.

Hence, if some rigid element could be devised or pinpointed within these procedures, that rigidness would belong to the rigidly flexible ideological structures of capitalism, or to capitalism as an ideological structure.

So, the text that follows interprets the progressions and coherencies in sustainment and/or perpetuation of the order as an ongoing process in which the rigidity of a certain form of production relations and a certain form of justification of the effect of capital are only parts of a wider epistemological, institutional and ideological agenda of capitalism as a power discourse.

In this sense, whether we are talking about the principles of the Washington Consensus or Bretton Woods in an economic sense; about iterations of the Westphalian principle (or more precisely its specific interpretations) in a political sense or about progressions in normalization of post-Fordist and Fordist modes of production, we are talking about the principles of surpassing certain modes of operations under which the inextricability of economic, institutional, social, and ideological aspects, contained in the notion of capitalism, demonstrated that *capitalism* and/or *global capitalism*, as analyzed in this text, functions primarily as a power (or imperial) discourse of the First World. So, aside from the fluctuations contained in geopolitical turmoil's, that are shifting the locations of economic and political power bases (such is the economic rise of non-Western parts of the globe), the epistemological monopoly on the definition of the (universalization of) principles of global political, social and economic trajectories lies firmly in the hands of Western capitalist epistemologies and institutions.

Hence, capitalism as the power structure in this text does not refer to capitalism as some anthropomorphic (or meta systemic) super structure that surpasses the existence of living oppressors, it refers to capitalism as the specific structure of rule and set of patterns under which the oppressor utilizes either a rationalization or an excess, not only in the name of maximization of profit, but in the name of sustainment of specific ways in which profit is extracted. The ongoing processes in which most prominent profit maximization oriented capitalists are being turned into scapegoats, as happened after the 2008 debt crisis, bears witness to capitalism as an ideological power discourse that is able to exclude most exemplary oppressors and mark them as perpetrators as well as to include the oppressed into the register of the oppressors.

Speaking of power, if power, any power, is seen on the line of Michel Foucault's take (in the context of his analysis of the relation between the power and the subject) on the concept as a form or a technique that

"Makes individuals subjects," (Foucault 1982, 212) then it is the answer to the question to what the individuals are *subjects to* that helps in defining the oppressor. While the subjects can be subjected to a particular version of capitalism or even to a specific neo or proto-capitalist blend of socialism and capitalism, they are still co-opted and de-antagonized in relation to epistemological norms that posit humanist projects, such is *democracy*, as separate from capitalism or from those power structures that defined its (democracies) meaning as allegedly and inherently conflicted with capitalism.

Foucault noticed in relation to the nature of exercise of power that, "Power relations are rooted deep in the social nexus, not reconstituted 'above' society as a supplementary structure whose radical effacement one could perhaps dream of" (Foucault 1982, 222). Hence, the rooting of power deep into the social nexus of power does not negate the exercise of power that, as Foucault noted:

> Can produce as much acceptance as may be wished for; it can pile up the dead and shelter itself behind whatever threats it can imagine. In itself the exercise of power is not violence; nor is it a consent, which implicitly is renewable. It is a total structure of actions brought to bear upon possible actions; it incites, it induces, it seduces, it makes easier or more difficult; in the extreme it constrains or forbids absolutely. (Foucault 1982, 220)[3]

The differentiation between dominant power discourses and society should be made exactly there where capitalist power discourse did not make that differentiation. This is not about the capitalist elites that mask their particular agenda's in the environment of sustaining of a false democracy, nor it is about tyranny of majority that has allegedly (nominally or not) managed to banish the elites in the processes of democratization of society, it is about the minimum of explicit or maximum of implicit consent and / or cooperation among those poles that have been epistemologically and institutionally integrated into what is called *capitalist structures of power*.

Of course, while the majority of contemporary forms of (reactionary, social-democratic, neoliberal, corporate, financial) bourgeoisies or proto-bourgeosies, as well as remnants or modern iterations of monarchic aristocracies could be seen as belonging to capitalist (in case of the West) or proto-capitalist power structures (in case of non-Western entities complicit to First World's capitalism's ideologies), such a simplified explication of a power structure is too wide to be acknowledged as pinpoint explication of the position that the opressor occupies.

Consent to the processes of maximization of implicit traits in the formation of the hegemony that is based on explicit neglect of the inherent link between the capital, its effect and the meaning of humanist projects capitalism has already hijacked (or integrated), proves a much better point of departure toward the defining of what capitalist power structures are, who the oppressor is and who the political subject might be.

With regard to the question of the political subject and in regard to contemporary attempts at subjectivization of the political, it is obvious that the contemporary search for iterations of proletariat, labor and/or class based struggle on the basis of a presumption that the immediate reality (the race and class difference) would or should be positioned outside of production and ideological processes tends only to neutralize the master/slave dialectic. This is happening at the expense of the analysis of the master/slave relation that would or could approach the reinvention of class struggle on the basis that would contain politically ideological and/ or authoritarian aspects that could ideologically fulfill the politicization of social conflicts.

As Fredric Jameson, within the context of analysis of contemporary (let's say postmodern) forms of organization of capitalist production, notices, "Where everything has been subsumed under capitalism, there is no longer anything outside it; and the unemployed—or here the destitute, the paupers—are as it were employed by capital to be unemployed; they fulfill an economic function by way of their very non-functioning (even if they are not paid to do so)" (Jameson 2011, 71).

So, if the search for political subjectivity is based on the contemplation of degrees and meanings of being inside/outside, it implies that the format of the struggle was contextualized either with escapist or inclusivist traits, either, which is more important, by a presumption that political subjectivization or subjective-ness—conceived in accordance to humanist capacities of the (democratic) projects capitalism has already co-opted— would, as mere counterpoint to objective-ness (seen as an ultimate result of commodification) could tackle the normalizaton of the constantly widening gap between the opressor and the opressed in a material sense, and the constantly narrowing gap among these poles in an ideological sense.

The position from which it is being approached to the interpretation of the nature of the differentiation (in regard to the possibility of formation of political subjectivity) should therefore acknowledge that no prefixes of differention were left intact in relation to capitalist based ideologies and the contradictions they normalized.

As Marxist Riff-Raff magazine author, Roland Simone noted in the context of analysis of paradigmatic forms of labor in conditions of globalization of capital:

> Proletariat and capital form the terms of a contradiction, and as such, they cannot be defined as they are in themselves outside of this contradiction. This contradiction is their unity and their reciprocal reproduction. As a reciprocal re-production , the contradiction produces its own temporality, which is the historical process of the capitalist mode of production. Time is internal to the contradiction, it is a durée , and not an a priori which envelops the contradiction and within which it has to

unfold or to play itself out. As reproduction, the contradiction does not bring its terms face to face on equal terms—it is an asymmetrical relation: capital subsumes labor. (Simone 2011)

So, if the extraction of degrees of political subjectiveness is based on a premise of an a priori existence of political subjective potential in some differentiation, then such a demand (that is usually articulated as a demand for radical egalitarianism for all), actually tends to erase the prefix of the enemy out of oppressive classes and contributes to making relative, to obfuscation of the question of the nature of differentiation current power produced, and of the nature of differentiation political subjectivities power would or could produce.

This text therefore sees political subjectivity as a kind of subjectivization that would not reject an asymmetrical dimension of the antagonism between the capital and its political struggles, and that would not exclusively attempt to resolve every contradiction in relation to the lack of radical egalitarianism, but as the one that would format the political process as the struggle for a radically different nature of differentiation on which power discourses and their contradictions and asymmetrical intricacies would be organized.

If the kind of inequalities capitalism organized were represented as both the only form surpassing the utopian notion of "total equality," and the only and/or "the best kind" of inequality, the stumbling of the left could be seen as caused by a tendency that pursues equality on the basis that neglects the politically ideological potentials of other kinds of inequalities.

Rejection of any homogeneous, fixed, ideological aspects of rule that would not be a subject to democratic, apolitical diversification and that would serve as an axis from which possible contradictions would be derived seems to present one of the most essential causes in the post-Cold War's disappearance of the ideological left in the First and what was known as the Second World.

So, since it is always a question of *what* do certain power structure protects/imposes (in a political, ideological, and epistemological capacity), this text finds the possibility for formation of political subjectivity in tendencies that acknowledge political power as the function for production of differentiations, distances, and antagonisms, but not on the basis of prioritization of the results of certain contradictions, but on the basis of construction of other contradictions and asymmetries.

In this sense, this text sees the relation between the position of power and the political subject as happening at that place in which the capitalist shattering of the rigid dimensions of political rule—that actually represent only a shattering of the prerogatives of the political to intervene against unlimited disempowerment of the rigid dimensions that could have been utilized against capitalism and its forms of reinvention—were met by paradigmatic forms of resentment that saw *any* rigid, ideological or authoritarian trait of political rule as a mark of strictly capitalist oppression.

While proponents of immediate recognition of existence of political subjectivity are prone to find potential in contemporary forms of anti-establishment, whether in the form of the commons; the *Multitude*[4]; the "99 percent vs. 1 percent" aspects of the Occupy movement, or in the variety of forms of resentments congregated around the notion of "direct democracy," this text, although acknowleding the importance of sensibilization of class prefixed conflict, rejects the majority of these propositions as viable in the creation of political subjectivity. It does this in order to measure which of these tendencies operate on the basis of presumption that the political subject could be formatted on a basis that rejected ideological and authoritarian dimensions of political struggle and that saw capitalism as the superstructure that operates on the basis of exploitation of everybody on the same basis and in the same measure.

If capitalism as a power discourse relies on the imposition of unipolar hegemony in the formation of the context under which multipolar diversities would, as positive tropisms, be kept in a state of constant oscilation around or toward that unipolarity, we are clearly witnessing global capitalism as a form of globalization (modernization) of hierarchies of exploitation perpetuated by the logic of colonialism and/or colonial style in organization and rationalization of global distribution of wealth.

CONTEMPORARY COLONIALISM, DEMOCRACY, AND RACIALISM

Whether colonialism is seen as a method of expansion of the influence of the First World; as a trait of the nature of control over the distribution of global wealth by the First World or over epistemological rationalization that support such disparities in distribution, it is a form of power that constitutes a subtext of the relations among the First World and other parts of the world as synchrononic to that measure to which the First World is being perceived as being in an anachronic position in relation to synchronizations of all diversities under the umbrella of capitalist democratism.

Aníbal Quijano, one of the classics of decolonial thought and a theoretician who has never neglected the structural relation between the universalized colonial epistemology and power principles invested in reorganization of capitalism on a global scale, has also questioned the ideological nature of linearity of progress contained within universalized notions of progress. As he claimed:

> Not surprisingly then, history was conceived as an evolutionary continuum from the primitive to the civilized; from the traditional to the modern; from the savage to the rational; from pro-capitalism to capital-

ism, etc. And Europe thought of itself as the mirror of the future of all the other societies and cultures; as the advanced form of the history of the entire species. What does not cease to surprise, however, is that Europe succeeded in imposing that "mirage" upon the practical totality of the cultures that it colonized; and, much more, that this chimera is still so attractive to so many. (Quijano 2007, 176)

Hence, while analyzing colonialism as a form, technique, and nature of rule as employed by the Eurocentric (Euro-Atlantic) institutions and ideologies, this text spatially and temporarily places its focus on colonialism, rather than post-colonialism. This does mean that the interpretative width postcolonial discourses contained in interpretation of the nature of polarization of the world are rejected by this text, it simply means that those interpretative dimensions of postcolonial discourse that tend to interpret contemporary colonialism as principally different from classical colonial procedures or structurally separated from overall operation of capitalist democracies are seen as inadequate in approach to the analysis of the role of colonialism in formation and imposition of the universalized modernist discourses under the terms of global capital.

The notion of coloniality, that addresses this modernist colonial entanglement, was explicated by Walter Mignolo, decolonial theoretician whose work on disentanglement of the notion of modernity from universal prefixes has shown that reorganized forms of colonial epistemology have been underlining and/or profoundly influencing the reorganization of dominant forms of capitalist, First World's hierarchies of exploitation. Mignolo wrote:

The basic thesis is the following: "modernity" is a European narrative that hides its darker side, "coloniality." Coloniality, in other words, is constitutive of modernity—there is no modernity without coloniality. Hence, today the common expression "global modernities" imply "global colonialities" in the precise sense that the colonial matrix of power (coloniality, for short) is being disputed by many contenders: if there cannot be modernity without coloniality, there also cannot be global modernities without global colonialities. That is the logic of the polycentric capitalist world of today." (Mignolo 2009a, 39)

Or, as Aníbal Quijano noted: "Coloniality, then, is still the most general form of domination in the world today, once colonialism as an explicit political order was destroyed. It doesn't exhaust, obviously, the conditions nor the modes of exploitation and domination between peoples" (Quijano 2007, 170).

Since it is important to notice the parallels between the processes of reorganization of rigid elements within the processes of liberalization of capitalism and the reorganization of colonialism as a "less" explicit (yet more hegemonic) form of order, the use of the term "colonialism" in this text should be understood as a term that regards coloniality as the form of rule which structurally connects processes of global liberalization/in-stitutionalization of capitalism and processes of universalization of Euro-centric modernity which is being produced into the only, or at least "the best" version of modernity in general.

Santiago Castro-Gómez, another decolonial theoretician who had been articulating the genealogy and current principles in reproduction of colonial divide of the world, has noticed in reference to Mignolo's ap-proach to relation of the modern and the colonial that:

> Mignolo affirms that Enlightenment (Aufklärung) thinking generates what the Argentinean philosopher Enrique Dussel calls "the eurocen-tric myth of modernity." This myth consists of the *elimination of the structural heterogeneity of modernity*, in the name of a lineal process in which Europe appears as a privileged place of enunciation and genera-tion of knowledge. The traditional and the modern stop coexisting and now appear as successive phenomena in time. (Castro-Gómez 2007, 433)

Coloniality as a constitutive of modernity made colonialism a modernist project and it made modernism (at least its Eurocentric definition) a colo-nial project; the nature of the division of the World could actually be seen in a formula First World minus other worlds.

This *minus* does not represent only a reductionist tendency that was poised against the universalizing and/or subjective potency of others, it describes a nature of the macro-dynamism of a relation occidental episte-mology imposed onto the other parts of the world where it positioned itself as a pinnacle of the modernist progressions, of course, but it also positioned itself as an aim toward or around which other diversities/ polarities should congregate. As Castro-Gómez continued in relation to modernity:

> This would be an *exclusively European* phenomenon originating in the Middle Ages, and that later spread around the world through Intra-European experiences like the Italian Renaissance, the Reformation, the Enlightenment and the French Revolution. In this way, the myth of eurocentrism identifies European particularity with universality *tout-court*, and identifies coloniality with the European *past*. (Castro-Gómez 2007, 433)

In other words, while colonialism as an explicit form of control is being *squeezed* out of contemporary occidental imagery as a token of rejection of any responsibility, repercussions, and/or questions regarding the redistri-bution of global wealth, coloniality, as a less politically explicit (but hege-monic all the same) matrix of rule takes a universalizing grasp over the particularity of Eurocentrism on a global scale.

As Quijano has noted, in the context of analysis of First World's cos-mopolitan rationality, paraphrasing, nothing is less rational, finally, than the pretension that the specific cosmic vision of a particular ethnie should be taken as universal rationality, even if such an ethnie is called Western Europe because this is actually pretending to impose a provincialism as universalism.

Since the provincial sensibility of the occidental imaginary was always subverted by the unwanted effect of colonial exploits (such as migration), the traits of rationality, however, were not ascribed to the processes of subversion of provinciality, but were ascribed to the processes that led to these unwanted effects—colonialism and (the primacy of the role of the West) in defining of the notion and preconditions for cosmopolitanism. As Quijano has observed:

> The emergence of the idea of the "West" or of "Europe," is an admission of identity—that is, of relations with other cultural experiences, of differences with other cultures. But, to that "European" or "Western" perception in full formation, those differences were admitted primarily above all as inequalities in the hierarchical sense. And such inequalities are perceived as being of nature: only European culture is rational, it can contain "subjects"—the rest are not rational, they cannot be or harbor "subjects." (Quijano 2007, 173–174)

Quijano was right when he positioned *the one* and *the rest* as the fundamental cornerstones of global polarities; such differentiation has proved being itself the most potent tool for reorganization of racism into an essential tool for the depoliticization of social conflict. It was simultaneously represented as the token of alleged existence of exactly opposite, the "post-racial" trademark of the First World.

Since this text differentiates between forms of racism that are structural and those that are ad hoc/unrelated to structural characteristics of hegemonic tendencies, it specifically tackles structural forms of racism (or racial forms of structures) which serve as core ideologies that are inextricabilly entangled with specific imperial agenda, that of the First World of capital, hence paradigmatic Western (Eurocentric and/or Euro - Atlantic) axis of power from 1492 until today. Hence, Mignolo notes that:

> There is a common argument that goes something like this: Oh, well, after all Blacks (or Latinos/as, Native Americans, Moslems, etc.) are also very racist. Yes, it is often the case, and it has to be analyzed. The starting point would be to distinguish between imperial and subaltern forms of racism, and go from there: if there are forms of Black and Latinas racism, be assured that they are not imperial!!! Imperial racism goes beyond (although it embraces) the particular nation state (of Christian Monarchy of the sixteenth to eighteenth centuries). There is a double dimension in imperial racism, which starts in the colonies and reverts toward the national imperial territory. We are witnessing this phenomenon today with the immigration in the European Union and the U.S. And certainly, the Holocaust was part of it. (Mignolo 2009b, 82)

So, while we witness the existence of a variety of forms of racism outside the paradigmatic West (among Japanese and Chinese/Koreans, among North and sub-Saharan Africans, among variety of inter-European racisms, etc.), the imperial, Eurocentric racism, while continuing to perpetuate its racism on the basis of skin color, continues to most prominently base its racism on religious grounds. The same principles on which anti-Semitic racism was based, have now been invested in epistemological normalization of Islamophobia which was, as racism, normalized both as the reflection of *freedom of speech*, hence *the opinion*, and as a reflection of a ratio employed in contemporary colonial exploits.

This has allowed Eurocentric racism to equate its contemporary fascism with the modernist legacy (as it was case in African, South/North American genocides, and European holocaust), and, more importantly, to represent the shift from one form of racism (anti-Semitism) to another (Islamophobia) as a trademark of transcendence of any racism — where all these forms of racism are in fact being derived from one racist register.[5]

We are therefore talking about the same racism that changes the form of its representation and that represents this shift as a trademark of the grandiose inclusivity of modernist structures that envelope it. Since Guantanamo concentration camp continues to operate under the premise of the preservation of "liberal" values, it is clear not only that the values which concentration camp(s) have to protect are deeply rooted in racial hierarchies, but also that the amount of freedoms (one could attain) contained in such a modernist narrative are determined by racial hierarchies, which were instituted into the core of allegedly neutral processes of *universalization of predicament* created by globalization of capitalism.

This premise, that implies that the processes of universalization and the sustainment of particular forms of (racial) differentiation were inconsistent, was noticed by Imanuel Wallerstein who stated that:

> We start with a seeming paradox. The major challenge to racism and sexism has been universalist beliefs; and the major challenge to universalism has been racist ans sexist beliefs. We assume that the proponents of each set of beliefs are persons in opposite camps. Only occasionally do we allow ourselves to notice that the enemy, as Pogo put it, is us; that most of us (perhaps all of us) find it perfectly possible to pursue both doctrines simultaneously. (Balibar and Wallerstein 1991, 29)

Aside from the ambiguity concerning the implications of who "us" might be, the solution to this paradox was found by pursuing both doctrines simultaneously, demonstrating that the structure of power that has managed to pacify and connect both the racial style of differentiation and various processes of liberalization/modernization was the First World capitalist structure of power. Not only has this power structure managed to organize the depoliticization of the subaltern's resentment as a diversion from the forms of antagonism that would have tackled First World's interests, it has managed to organize the products of depoliticization (non-imperial racism) to congregate around its, imperial, "civilized" racism and to position itself as the position that would determine which racism should be regarded as more or less "prominent" and/or "civilized," hence, perversely enough, as *post-racial*.

Éttiene Balibar's work on analysis of contemporary shifts in institutionalization/formalization and/or general reorganization of racism, provided a description of a socio-ideological framework in which racism reorganized itself. Balibar hence wrote:

> Racism—a true "total social phenomenon" inscribes itself in practices (forms of violence, contempt, intolerance, humiliation and exploitation), in discourses and representations which are so many intellectual elaborations of the phantasm of prophylaxis or segregation (the need to purify the social body, to preserve "one's own" or "our" identity from all forms of mixing, interbreeding or invasion) and which are articulated around stigmata of otherness (name, skin color, religious practices). (Balibar and Wallerstein 1991, 17–18)

Adding to the Balibar's understanding of the meaning of contemporary racism, this text tackles the issue of racism as an ideology of capitalism (that does not hesitate to utilize capitalism as an ideology of rationalization of First World's primacy in distribution of wealth) that exercises control through racialization of diversities in which the delegation or denial of (social) privileges constitutes only a part of the racializing mechanism which main activity is the imposition of classifications among biological, ethnic, religious, social, linguistic, cultural, and above all racial differences that are being produced into twisted traits of political distinctiveness. In that sense, the subject of racial differentiation in modern occidental thinking is an object that is poised to gain traits of subjectivity to that measure to which it conforms its epistemological norms to the universalized epistemological hegemonies. Balibar noted that:

> Ideologically, current racism, which in France centres upon the immigration complex, fits into a framework of "racism without races" which is already widely developed in other countries, particularly the Anglo-Saxon ones. It is a racism whose dominant theme is not biological heredity but the insurmountability of cultural differences, a racism which, at first sight, does not postulate the superiority of certain groups or peoples in relation to others but "only" the harmfulness of abolishing frontiers, the incompatibility of life-styles and traditions; in short, it is what P. A. Taguieff has rightly called a *differentialist racism*. (Balibar and Wallerstein 1991, 21)

While the most tangible racial traits such as skin color could and do ultimately form the mainstay of the processes of racial differentiation or racialization, a concept that was in great measure introduced into a decolonial theoretical vocabulary by Marina Gržinić (Gržinić 2009a)[6] in the context of her analysis of paradigmatic principles invested in depoliticization of social conflict in terms of globalization of capitalism in post 9/11 era.

Although more precise articulation of this concept will follow later, racializaton underlines a situation, especially the normalcy of the situation in which the first Black president of the United States can sustain concentration camps and drone campaigns that are killing thousands of civilians surely bears witness to the existence of a structural, ideological racist (and/or merely fascist) criteria in the normalization of a global hegemony.

The perfidiousness of the motives that stood behind the abundance of attention western mainstream media gave to the case of Pakistani girl Malala Yousafzai (who was shot and wounded by insurgents in Pakistan in 2012, in relation to her pro-women education activism) bears witness to a racial epistemology that was, amidst the hundreds of other children that were killed by the Western forces (some perpetrators have even been awarded in Europe[7]), able to singularize one victim (it did not directly produce) as the token representation of its own racism as the universal form of defense of allegedly universal rights in relation to human prerogatives (on life, education, etc.). This is an epistemological operation that equates the motives of any antagonist of either the First World's exploits (from Afghani insurgents to the radical leftists) and/or the alliance of capital and democracy as belonging to the same register of barbaric totalitarianism. Consequentially, and because of this, this allows the First World to rationalize its own racist epistemologies by connecting them to a register of "universal" civilized values, which allows it to represent the (direct or indirect) mass infliction of death it perpetuates as a token of preservation and/or struggle for some global reconciliation.

In the similar fashion, the inauguration of (one of) the paradigmatic victim(s) of Eurocentric racism, the African descended non-white (Obama), into a perpetrator of modernized racial policy bears witness to the diabolical ability of essentially Eurocentric racism (although in Europe *no* non-whites are allowed to carry the function of premiere or president) to perpetuate its core agenda on the basis of representative or institutional inclusion of, what it considers a paradigmatic subaltern, into the matrix of representation of its racism as *post-racial*. This takes place however only to that measure to which the paradigmatic subaltern accepted to attain privileges through acceptance of this epistemological logic and perpetuation of the monopoly of the First World in defining the meaning of diversification in the condition of global capitalism.

Hence, racism today, as an ideology of subjugation is determined by its effect, not by some truth that is being derived from endless taxonomies based on noticing a variety of proto-racial demenors. Since its contemporary effect contributed mostly to the sustainment of the alliance between First World's capitalism and democracy, it is clear that the structural racism, perpetuated by proponents of this alliance, should be considered as another name for an amount of normalization invested into the effect of differentiation on who could/should be killed and who should/could be commodified.

Although the term *racism* is being used in this text, it should be comprehended as the framework of application for processes of racialization—a paradigm of rule, a paradigm of production of differentiations that utilizes differentiations among various cultural, biological, and linguistical distinctions as an exchange for political forms of antagonism—that imposes particular imperial (white, Eurocentric) racism as institutional, epistemological and imperial ideology that allegedly surpasses all the ramifications of historical progressions and positions itself as an *supra-ideological* ideology of divine origins which is supposed to be interpreted as the ultimate ratification of, not only capitalism's imperviousness to political processes, but of Eurocentric and/or white Western Christian primacy within capitalism as the most "truthful," or more precisely, the most modernist incarnation of capitalism.

As Marina Gržinić noted, "Structural racism is the core logic of global capitalism. Racialization is its internal administrative, judicial, and economic procedure, which regulates the space of financial capitalism as well as the system of representation, theory, and discursivity. Racism is not just an identity politics but something internal to the whole agenda of the transformation of the nation-State under global capitalism" (Gržinić 2013b).

Since the discrepancies in discrepancies of global wealth distribution, such as non-western and/or non-Western Christian proliferation of maximization of profit (such as the success of Chinese, Russian, Indian, or Arab capitalism) tends to be slandered in the paradigmatic populistic western imaginary as being "meaningless," "false," "cheap," or even "soulless" capitalism, the interpretation of the inherent connection of *"true"* capitalism and its Eurocentric racial epistemologies cannot be neglected in its connection with the hegemonic (colonial) framework that secures that organization of discrepancies is equated to progressivism only if discrepanacies work in favor of First World's interests and its particular racial epistemologies.

While racism will remain the most prominent ideology of production of differentiation, there still remains a question as to what or to *whom differential racism* most prominently serves. The function of *differential racism* or contemporary, imperial racism, hence, racialization could be seen, as Marina Gržinić noted, in the following context. According to Gržinić:

> The list of capitalism's victims is divided from within. Some victims have a higher status, while others are unimportant. Through this process, the capitalist Christian project of dispossession does not allow any "identity" to acquire a position from which to denote capitalism as

such. These identities are pitted against each other, without understanding that they are a product of the processes of racialization, presented in the capitalist system as a kind of identity politics. The promise of liberation by capital is therefore a paradoxical and cynical measure in which liberation is presented as an infinity of fragmentations. At work here is the process of capitalism's racialization, a control axis on which endlessly differential forms of capitalist expansion are being conceived. (Gržinić 2013b)

So, while contemporary racism is constituted of racism with and without races (it contains both tangible and non-tangible references), racism and/ or mechanisms of racializations continue to play an essential role in sustaining differentiation within hierarchies of exploitation under which the erasure of politically ideological prefixes to social conflicts is being compensated by the fixation of positioning of one hegemonic matrix of differentiation as the only matrix that could produce the meaning and political limitations of any differentiation. In other words, contemporary global capitalism's racism functions as that kind of ideology that monopolizes the rights to define the meaning of differentiation, which ultimately leads to destruction of class prefixed social conflicts (class based political antagonisms) in favor of (dramatization of) social conflicts found in non-class prefixed register.

Hence, although the primary function of racism and/or racialization (which will be more precisely tackled further in the text) is depoliticization of social conflicts, it here serves as a point of departure toward an analysis of structural connections between capitalism and democracy; democracy and ideology and modernity and colonialism. Since racism (racialization) in this text will be deemed as the ideology of capitalism, it is required that we take a look at the connection between liberalization of capitalism and devaluation of the function of political power that occurred as a consequence of the gap neoliberalism (within the processes of contemporary reorganizations of capitalism) created between politics and ideology.

NOTES

1. Paraphrasing Harvey, this entails market processes and entrepreneurial and corporate activities that were surrounded by a web of social and political constraints and a regulatory environment that sometimes restrained but in other instances led the way in economic and industrial strategy.

2. Although Harvey did not make this connection, Anthony Giddens's notion of disembedding (that Giddens saw as positive in processes of liberalization of capitalism) could be seen in relation to the effects of liberalization in post-modern conditions. As Giddens noted, "The primacy of place in pre-modern settings has been largely destroyed by disembedding and time-space distancing. Place has become phantasmagoric because the structures by means of which it is constituted are no longer locally organised. The local and the global, in other words, have become inextricably intertwined." (Giddens 1990)

3. The notion of immersion of power with or within the whole social nexus should not be seen as an argument that would singularize either society or elites as exclusive carriers of power, it should contribute to the comprehension of power as both the particular and mutual element in the formation of society.

4. "A multitude is an irreducible multiplicity; the singular social differences that constitute the multitude must always be expressed and can never be flattened into sameness, unity, identity or indifference." (Negri and Hardt 2004, 105) As Negri and Hardt added "In a second respect the concept of multitude is meant to repropose Marx's political project of class struggle. The multitude from this perspective is based not so much on the current empirical existence of the class but rather on its conditions of possibility." (Negri and Hardt 2004, 105)

5. As an example, the EU's *active tolerance* (arms embargo, four-year siege of Sarajevo, concentration camps, genocide in Srebrenica) of fascist genocide against Bosnian Muslims (Bosniaks) who, prior to genocide (and, unfortunately, after it), thought that the processes of Euro-Atlantic integrations was genuinely neutral and/or religiously unbiased, demonstrated the primacy of religious-based imperial racism where emerging Christian fundamentalism, capitalism and democracy combined in a process of sophisticated nazification of post-Cold War Europe.

6. Cf. Marina Gržinić. 2009a. "No War but Class War." Available at http://grzinic-smid.si/?p=1095

7. Sebastian Brügge and Sybille Fuchs. 2012. "German officer responsible for Kunduz massacre promoted to rank of general." *World Socialist Web Site.* August 21, 2012. Accessed December 5, 2013. http://wsws.org/en/articles/2012/08/klei-a21.html

NINE

The Hegemonic Capacity of a Gap between Politics and Ideology

The coherence of capitalism in sustaining its modes of exploitation is obviously coupled with its ability to construct a notion of political power complicit with the super-narrative under which exploitation is perpetuated.

Democracy has, as a method of legitimizing political power, been installed in exchange for political ideology and the sustainment of circulation of capital has been prioritized as the primal idelogical consideration of (neo or post-liberal) democratic society. However, there still remains a question of what kind of ideological, institutional and epistemological mechanism manages to pacify not only antagonistic stances in the formation of the critique of dominant power discourses, but also redefine political power as an incubator of pacifying stances toward those discourses. However, as the material control over the disposition of global wealth shows a tendency to shift away from the First World, Eurocentric ideologies have still shown themselves able to retain the First World's monopoly over definitions of the purpose of modernity and the function of political power.

The concept of *political rule*, as a mechanism for the production of society, has therefore been epistemologically redefined as a mechanism for the constant subversion of any coercive dimension *political power* might have deployed against the expansion of capital or against those forms of antagonism that serve that expansion.

So, since iterations of democratic and liberal agendas became (or/are becoming) institutionalized as ideologically viable substitutions for politically ideological rule, the main impetus for the reorganization of capital is not found in the disqualification of the hegemonic dimension that might have been found in the political authority of sovereign power, but in the disqualification of the hegemonic prerogatives of the sovereign that would have tackled the normalization of hegemony by the liberal society itself.

THE EFFECT OF DE-IDEOLOGIZATION OF POLITICAL POWER IN FORMATION OF LIBERAL-DEMOCRATIC NORM

If some common denominator marks the relation between current modes of exploitation and the institutional discourses that sustain them, it consists of an epistemological logic that neutralizes the prerogatives of political power to intervene against the way social wealth is being distributed or to intervene against the ideological basis on which hierarchies of exploitation have been organized.

The representation of the global circulation of capital as some sort of neutral, suprahistorical process that allegedly exploits everyone on a non-discriminative basis is just one part of the formula which privileges the approach to control over circulation still dominated by the First World's colonial, Eurocentric epistemologies.

Within this context, current dominant models of exploitation (neoliberalism or its post-liberal iterations), do not only provide a liberal dimension to contemporary modes of exploitation, but they also define the legitimizing power of the *demos* as the power to legitimize only that kind of political power that rationalizes exploitation as part of the wider, universal progressive and/or modernist agenda.

However, since the universalization of particular interests is an epistemological operation that institutes the effect of capital as attached to the advancement of particular interests (within the context of redefining the function of political power), this universalization reflected itself as an instrument that reformatted the (liberal) norm on the basis of a mixture of expansionist/imperialist/colonialist agendas of capitalism and liberal-democratic institutionalism.

So, the production of some norm that would transcend the conditions in which it was defined was not just left in some beraucratic stasis, its prohibitive potential has been refocused and redefined in order to prohibit the limits of proliferation of politics and/or of political power as the concept that would intervene against the normative defined in such a manner. In simple terms, the democratic potential of liberal capitalist societies was put in positive, progressive relation to the normalization of capitalist transgressions. In other words, the potential of liberal democratic society to subjectivise itself as a protagonist in the mechanism of rule was put in direct proportion to the same societies willingness to equate the limits of liberty with the limits of capital.

This does not mean that the coercive dimension of *order* based on some sort of norm was erased, on the contrary, the coercive dimension of the order was produced as that dimension that would destroy only limitations to the circulation of capital. The political substance and the origin of the motives for employment of some prohibition was transcribed from a politically ideological basis (that would transcend the logic of profit) to those positions which are in harmony with the norm defined as the matrix of rationalization of prohibition used only in favor of the capitalist hegemonic machine.

Carl Schmitt, whose work was (generally speaking) based on the analysis of the principles of transformations of the forms of political ruling in the context of wider introduction of liberalization of authoritarian systems of political rule and democratization of (political) power, in the context of his research in the field of theory of sovereignty suggested that:

> The norm requires a homogeneous medium. This effective normal situation is not a mere "superficial presupposition" that a jurist can ignore; that situation belongs precisely to its immanent validity. There exists no norm that is applicable to chaos. For a legal order to make sense, a normal situation must exist, and he is sovereign who definitely decides whether this normal situation actually exists. (Schmitt 2005, 13)

This kind of order, in which the preservation or the efficacy of the norm was defined in relation to the definition of the situation belonging to its immanent validity, clearly formatted the perception of the norm as the kind of ideological element that would normalize the validity of the regime to define one particular norm as *the* norm.

With regard to the state of exception as the form of rule—whether we see it as suspension of the constitutional dimension of the law, as nondecidability between the law and the norm or as the sovereign's decision on the exception (as Schmitt would have noted)—it was never a primal problem that the state circumvented certain applications of the norm, the primal problem was always the question of which norm was circumvented. To paraphrase Schmitt, the exception is that which cannot be subsumed, it defies general codification, but it simultaneously reveals a specifically juristic element—the decision in absolute purity.

Simply put, if general codification of the norm in contemporary society meant that capitalist transgressions were integrated into the normative (as they have been), the exception to such a normative, the decision in *absolute purity*, could describe the politically ideological momentum in the formation of the social antagonism that would transcend the ideological boundaries of the regime. However, the problem is that capitalism has already absorbed this approach in relation to the surpassing of some norm, only politically ideological prefixes were left out of this formula, which formatted the utilization and employment of exception in favor of capital; in support of its ideological agenda.

If the notion of *absolute purity* implied the existence of a zero level of contamination of the decisionist prerogatives with general codifications (immanent considerations), the way in which political power's preroga- tive to transcend normative boundaries or limitations is being exercised, is the way in which it is utilized in service of absolute ideological goals. Hence, it is used for the epistemological and institutional normalization of the effect of capital. As Schmitt noticed: "The existence of the state is undoubted proof of its superiority over the validity of the legal norm. The decision frees itself from all normative ties and becomes in the true sense absolute" (Schmitt 2005, 12).

Hence, if the preservation of the state is interconnected with the pres- ervation of the circulation of capital that sustains such a substance of the democratic *nomos*, rather than being an exception to it, this is its defining contingency. This puts the prerogatives of the sovereign in motion and is not primarily treated as *extremus necessitates casus* in relation to the pres- ervation of the state, but as essential to the preservation of circulation of capital, its hierarchies and ideologies.

Thus, as it stands in the contemporary liberal paradigm, there is no need for an exception to defy the general codification, what it defies is the installation of an ideological agenda that would mobilize the political (coercive) mechanism of political rule in order to intervene against the utilization of exception in favor of capital, not against the general prerog- atives political power might have had in relation to the exception.

Since the closing of the distance between the subjugator and the subju- gated in liberal democracy was represented as the "post-ideological" era- sure of *all* totalitarian dimensions in democratic ideological structures, any kind of prohibition or politics which might have been employed against the capital, was represented as an ultimate form of totalitarianism which liberal society could not cope with.

However, since we operate on the premise that capitalism's hegemon- ic epistemologies operate by the removal of the adversarial aspect from the perception of the political as an instrument of differentiation, it is clear that the removal of ideological adversity among the subjugated and the subjugator (that after all constitutes liberal epistemological norms), instituted a register of *apolitical* thought into ultimately *political* considera- tions. The resulting universalized ideological totality consequentially converted the left wing into a vague spectrum of liberal, libertarian and/ or neoliberal positions extremely accommodating to the post-ideological super-narrative.[1]

Thus, contemporary liberal inclinations (at least those that represent- ed themselves as socialist or with left wing leanings) utterly failed to utilize their own presupposed (left) political agenda; they succeeded re- markably in adopting an apolitical agenda framed only by the calculus based on logic of the capital. In doing so, the left converted itself into a prominent conductor of creation of an environment in which reactionary movements (in forms of conservatism, neoconservatism, right-wing populism, etc.) could offer themselves as a solution to the globalized, multicultural effect of capital. As political aspects of political rule were discarded, the paradigmatic meaning of *leadership* or *rule* (leadership dimension within the rule) that would contain radical politically ideological substance was discarded as an obsolete element in the formation of the pretense to political rule.

This is not to imply, of course, that all liberally prefixed politics are to be considered as compliant to capitalism and its co-opting of humanist and liberal narratives. Those forms of liberal agendas that were deprived of politically ideological substances and that accepted First World's *post - ideological* universalization (under the aegis of democracy) are to be considered as compliant to disqualification of political dimensions of political power. At this junction, a "momentum of understanding" between liberal and reactionary inclinations formatted both those inclinations as being part of the same, universalized ideological register.

Additionally, the process of legitimization of political power that got delegated to the *demos*, reorganized the mechanism of rule as de-attached from the political agenda in general, all in favor of responding to the demands of the *demos* dominantly motivated by the removal of barriers to consumption.

Consequently, in parallel to the historical imposition of neoliberalism in the 1980s and in parallel to the restructuring of nation-States on free market based colonial exploits, such a mechanism of rule was now (in the post 9/11 era) freed of its focus on ideological diversity (still present in the Cold War). Now, under the umbrella of *ideological universality* and post-ideological agenda's the primacy of ethnic/racial determinations in the formation of western liberal democratic society was instituted into the processes of formation of society as the measure to which society was deemed democratic and as the measure to which it was deemed political or not. State's sovereignty was consequentially squeezed exclusively within supra-historical epistemological logic and became a mark of distinction for agendas that derived their ideological purposes only out of utilitarian dimensions that circulation perpetuates.

Although he spoke of sovereignty in general terms and in terms of sovereign man, Georges Bataille, in the context of his research of the domain of sovereignty, saw the domain of sovereignty as that kind of domain in which "The enjoyment of possibilities that utility does not justify (utility being that whose end is productive activity). Life beyond utility is the domain of sovereignty" (Bataille 1993, 198).

Hence, life *beyond utility* as the domain of sovereignty did not mean that this *beyond* in liberal democracy was found by the surpassing of arbitrary interpretations of the origins of the effect of capital, it meant that it was found by surpassing those rigid elements that presented an obstacle to the globalization of capital. For instance, the effect of capital that the paradigmatic democratic subjectivity experiences on daily basis in, let's say the United States and Western Europe, is being interpreted as the result of the actions of greedy, profit making capitalist who are out-sourcing American/European jobs, who betrayed family values, etc. This is an epistemological and ideological stunt that splits the origin of the predicament into two paradigmatic positions; represented by figures that could be seen as criminally singularized or *phony* capitalists and the *real* capitalists.

Of course, while both these figures belong to the same register and while the criminally singularized capitalist is simply the flat mainstream capitalist that does not differ one jot from the ideological formation of the *real* capitalist, mainstream resentment tends to imagine the substitute for the phony one, imagined as the one which would less elegantly syn-chronize Eurocentric Christian morality and racial institutionalization of the state with the global nature of circulation of capital.[2]

Clearly, since we can postualte that capitalism is trying to represent itself as non-existent as a power discourse and historical power conglom-eration, the domain of utility and the domain of the effect of capital, perceived as a totality, now had to be made most purposefully tangible within such a regime that had, after all, produced this false dichotomy in its interpretation of the origin of the predicament.

Still, the triviality, calculability and political impotence that saturates or simply constitutes the transfer of values between the petty calculus of the liberal democratic *demos* and the position of political power should not be taken as a simple trademark of the interpretative superficiality in a state of evolution toward some less frivolous agenda. These characteris-tics should be comprehended as parts of a wider epistemological context in which notions of *political possibilities* are being formatted as inherently belonging to the domain of utilitarian, not political register of possibil-ities to which the status of utmost purpose is being delegated. As Schmitt noted: "Because of its evenness and calculability, regularity passes over to the third form, the "rationalistic," that is, technical refinement, which, emerging from either the needs of specialized knowledge or the interests of a juristically oriented bureaucracy, is oriented toward calculability and governed by the ideal of frictionless functioning" (Schmitt 2005, 28).

The ascription of rationalistic traits to one kind of regularity surely bears witness to the existence of an ideological agenda behind this strate-gy, however, there is another side to this. It is not the rationalistic traits that are being assigned to the effect of the political process, but it is the destruction of the political process that is being, as a process, made into an incubator of rationalist traits.

This approach to operations of rationalization in contemporary liberal normatives demonstrated that the amount of distortion of political power prerogatives (developed to tackle political and ideological meanings of utilitarian dimensions) were discarded in favor of the endorsement of that power that would represent the politically and ideological emptying of political power as *the* precondition of rationality. In relation to the most prominent protagonists in the formation of the political context, as political theorist Tracy B. Strong noted "The state corresponds to normativism, political movements (*Bewegung*) to decisionism, and the people (*Volk*) to institutionalism" (Strong 2005, vii-xxxv).

Nevertheless, if the current historical stage of reorganization of capital is determined by the institutional delegation of power to the depoliticized dimension of society, namely the people, that power was made actual only in relation to the measure to which it supported various capitalist interests. Schmitt's disposition in this context might be rephrased in the following way.

Liberal-democratic, capitalist states institutionalized the terrain from which normative traits were being extracted as the terrain on which the amount of distortion of politically ideological substance of political power was put in synchronous relation with the amount of non-limitations society in these conditions might have attained. Consequential equalization of non-limitations to freedoms and non-limitations of capital fixated the possibilities of production of rationality only within the boundaries of epistemological logic in which capital's non-limitations equalled the existence of rationality within that logic.

The decisionist prerogatives were fixated to a level by which a variety of diversities among political subjects would not bear witness to the existence of diversities in an attempt to surpass the epistemological and institutional boundaries of the order. What was witnessed instead was an agenda that considered or included assertive tendencies only in order to take a position within the hierarchies of exploitation. Political protagonists complicit to democratic capitalism hence empowered the dichotomy based on inclusion/exclusion within the wider epistemological narrative that represents diversity in exploitation as diversity *eo ipso*, as that kind of diversity liberal society represents as its core value.

The *demos* (as a form of *subjectivisation* of the people), as the result of plutocratic institutional, epistemological and representational conditioning, institutionalized/legitimized only that kind of political authority that failed/fails to integrate coercive, politically ideological aspects into the interpretation of rule that would tackle the origin of the predicament in which the *demos* is being produced as such a legitimizing power.

In other words, on one hand the adversarial distance between the subjugator and the subjugated was minimized under the neoliberal promise of liberation and *detotalitarization* within the boundaries of the "neutral," "post-ideological" market. On the other hand, oppressive mechanisms were deprived of their political contextualization and deployed as pure ideological instruments for the subjugation of those still lacking this kind of *liberation*.

Hence, the notion of *frictionless functioning* between the oppressor and the oppressed, (that was idealized by mainstream democratic discourses) epitomized the ideological logic in which capitalism (and its racial ideologies), were perceived as the untouchable, consensual, universal destiny of all protagonists in the struggle for power. Furthermore, the function of political power was redefined as the tool for production and administration of apolitical diversities and ideological antagonisms whose frictions would be only inter-systemic and whose ends would be determined only by the interests of capital and its accompaning racial ideologies.

DISCHARGE/COMPULSION

The liberal democratic institutionalization of the ideal of *frictionless functioning* did not mean that friction, as a dynamic, was removed from the relation between the oppressor and the oppressed; it was dislocated instead into the axiomatic, apolitical register.

Additionally, this dislocation lead to the erasure of political antagonism between these poles, which meant that the society was included into that relation both as a biopolitical conglomeration (in which amounts of privilege are determined through differentiation between forms of life) and as an entity whose political potency was ontologically grounded in positive relation only to the progressions/reinventions of capitalism. If the whole spectrum of political struggle was conformed within the boundaries of universalized rationality, the preconditions for the invention of the authority (that stood behind the norm) were found within the scope that did not transcend the immediate relation between life and power.

Giorgio Agamben has, in the context of his research of the relation between the state of exception and biopolitical paradigms invested into the production of the dominant forms of bipolarities in cosmology of power, noted that:

> The dialectic of *auctoritas* and *potestas* expressed precisely this implication (and in that sense, one can speak of an originary biopolitical character of the paradigm of *auctoritas*). The norm can be applied to the normal situation and can be suspended without totally annulling the juridical order because in the form of *auctoritas*, or sovereign decision, it refers immediately to life, it springs from life.[3] (Agamben 2005, 85)

The notion of *juridical order that in the form of sovereign decision refers to life*, implies that the authoritarian prerogatives of the sovereign (power) were not obtained on the basis of articulation of life as political category, but that (political) authority was proscribed in direct proportion to which it deemed life as biopolitical contingency. The continuation of existence of juridical order, after the norm was suspended, should not, however, be deemed as a transgression or a hegemonic trait in itself, the hegemonic traits can be found in the kind of norm (and consequentially in the order built upon that norm) that was imposed during or after suspension.

The kind of norm(s) the First World's liberal democratic states perpetuate are obviously based on racial (Eurocentric) ideologies in which authoritarian traits have been derived from the imposition of racial differentiations. The purpose of (or within) such a norm that has been defined as the struggle for differentiation (but only with already defined biological axiomatic of that norm) has been the creation of ideologically viable material on which hegemonic traits can be founded.

Carl Schmitt's view that, paraphrasing, the state is the original power of rule, but it is so as the power of order, as the *form* of national life and not an arbitrary force applied by just any authority. To further paraphrase Schmitt, what is demanded of this power is that it intervene only when the free individual or associational act proves to be insufficient; it should remain in the background as the *ultima ratio*. It seems that Schmitt did not anticipate that the derogation of political origins of power would not lead to the demise of the nation-State (and reorganization of the form of national life into a form of racial-State), but the *power of rule* as the *power of the order* was surely derived from the authority located outside of the political calculus in approach to the definition of (political) power.

Yet, it would be easy to denote the logic of capital as the ratio that was imposed as primal in determination of what kind of authority would format the function of the rule. Even more, it seems that the ratio of contemporary epistemological hegemonies was found in the way in which differentiation was defined in absolute relation to already determined meanings of the effect of capital.

This means that the antagonistic contingency, the interventionist power of the *order* was defined as that kind of power that intervenes in favor of shattering the limits of capital, while it assigns arbitrary traits to those kinds of antagonisms that tackle the nature of the (interventions) power of the order. The discomfort the left wing feels in relation to interpretation and/or adoption of the power discourses is plainly not a symptom of universalization of depoliticized discourse, it is more likely a token of lack of differentiation among the kinds of authority that could stand behind the empowerment of antagonism. If this is a symptom of something, it is a symptom of the left's non-differentiation in approach to the formation of an ideology, hence, the (mainstream liberal) left wing's tendency to disapprove of *any* ideology, only helped capitalism to universalize its racial ideologies as those which have allegedly surpassed the status of legitimate targets which social antagonism could have tackled.

The *ultima ratio* of the power of the order that therefore was reformatted along the processes of liberalization of capitalism received a form, a "rational quality" on the basis of its transcendence of the utilitarian dimension of the effect of capital, but only on the basis that would format the antagonism as the struggle poised to tackle already defined particu-larities within capitalism's ideological structure.

For instance, if the rational traits are being derived from clashes of antagonisms whose ends were already determined as limited (derived from the designed failures of struggles to organize radical social transfor-mation), the amount of ideological substance of such a ratio was clearly made dependent on the amount of antagonism that filled the politically ideological nothingness which stood behind the power of the order.

This *pure nothingness* (in the sense of an utter lack of politically ideo-logical substance) is not the same as the *unknown* (as metaphorical space where political is being structured), it is instead the kind of epistemolog-ical experience in which the lack of political articulation of the purpose of diversification under capital was (is being) compensated by the adoption of the stance that saw the increase in the amount of diversifications as equal to the increase in amount of purpose. In simple terms, the amount of the form was made to equal the amount of the substance. This allowed the order to represent most basic motives in imposition of hierarchies of exploitation as symbols of the existence of a profoundly articulated pur-pose that allegedly filled the grandiose vulgarity of ideological structures that stood behind the forms of that imposition. Since we are talking about the nature of the power of the order of the First World, the more extreme and transparent mass murder, colonial genocide and maximization of profit this world employed became, the more substantiality this order derived for its authority, based solely on its power to intervene in such a way into the social reality.

Furthermore, the zeal for protection of political potency of liberal democratic formalism became insufficient to formalize all the effects of capital. The most extreme dimension of informality in capitalist democra-cy was most potent in destruction of the remnants of state barriers to capital and became instituted as the substitute for the impotency of dem-ocratic formality.

The meaning of *actual, nominal* and *diversity* got completely garbled in the epistemological *nomos* of the order, which completely interrupted the dichotomies between the formal/informal, actual/nominal, etc. This al-lowed the power discourses to determine the amount of legality and legitimacy of their actions by relying exclusively to the advancement of their particular interests. Agamben noted that: "From Schmitt's perspec-tive, the functioning of the juridical order ultimately rests on an appara-tus—the state of exception—whose purpose is to make the norm appli-cable by temporarily suspending its efficacy. When the exception be-comes the rule, the machine can no longer function" (Agamben 2005, 58).

However, since the capitalist exception became the rule (or more pre-cisely, is *constantly becoming* the rule),[4] the only component that cannot function any longer is the dimension of rigidness in juridical order that would transcend the logic of immanent validity: the primacy of this "situation" is defined as *a-historical* or *supra-historical*. What was made rigid in this situation was only the flexibility of capitalism to separate itself as a power structure from its effect and the flexibility of the political power to format itself as an insufficient concept that allegedly has nothing to do with the formation of ideological realities.

Since capitalism's compulsive traits are focused on sustaining hierarchical verticality (which is also racially differentiated) in control over the flow of capital, its ideological horizontality, that does not allow for the tackling of homogeneousness of the First World, could have been freed of its compulsory rigidness, but only to that measure to which it organized inclusion into the hierarchies of exploitation, not the rule. Thus, the regime retained control over the flow of capital and the subjugates found themselves denied the power that would be capable of addressing the compulsory, hegemonic procedures as systemic ones—while they were allowed to legitimatize only those aspects of power that would impose non-limitation to the flow of capital as the non-limitation in subjugates liberty to enter the exploitation.

Old emancipationist mottos, such was *people's power* actually realized themselves in capitalist democracies, but only in that sense and to that measure to which *the people* rejected their struggle for political power and accepted the notion that this same power was separated from the sustainment of exploitative hierarchies.

In this sense, one of the key paradigms within the epistemological hegemony could be seen as being based on the binary between *discharge* and *compulsion*, that imposes the interpretation of the realities of exploitation as differential, inclusive, and less rigid; while the rigid traits of the regime that sustains those hierarchies are represented as the necessary preconditions for shattering of one form of rigidness of exploitation that would only be exchanged for another. The momentum of discharge within this formula comprises the de-totalizing momentum (de-accumulation, flexibilization, "refreshment" of hierarchies of control) in an institutional and representational sense, while compulsory momentum contains the imposition of interpretation of the mere process of reorganization of capitalism as a step toward further inclusiveness.

In this way, *discompulsion* realized itself not just as reproduction of the system of hierarchies (and of sustainment of the hegemonic role of the First World in global circulation of capital), but also as a token of *flexibilization* of hierarchies open to include those antagonist interpretations with tendencies to treat the effect of capital as separate, incidental or non-inherent to the logic of capital and capitalism as a system of obligatory transgression. In Schmitt's terms, *discompulsion* might be seen as codification of the disturbance that subverts the hegemonic capitalist machine and as simultaneous decodification of the homogeneous nature of capitalism as the power discourse.

The effect of this *discompulsion* should be understood in relation to Schmitt's claim that, paraphrasing, the sovereign, who in the deistic view of the world, even if conceived as residing outside the world, had remained the engineer of the great machine, had been radically pushed aside. To further paraphrase Schmitt, the machine now runs by itself.

If the concept of *discharge/compulsion (discompulsion)* allowed the capitalist machine (capitalist exploitation hierarchies and structures of power) to run (to be perpetuated) as the operationalization of political sovereignty without metaphysical or ultimately political elements of rule, the machine that now runs *by itself* is the capitalist machine that, metaphorically, does not need an excuse to overcome the friction between the formal and informal dimensions of the order. The ability of the order to assign positive traits to either dimension of its power was by itself made into an institutional pillar of its ideological structure.

In other words, the gesture characteristic for this concept of *discompulsion*, represents an epistemological procedure whose de-totalizing momentum empties political rule of its prerogatives to produce social reality and transfers those prerogatives to actions that compells the subjugates to compensate politically ideological emptiness with glorification of the effect of capital as the token of struggle against that effect.

The cultural obsession of the democratic masses with outlaws, gangsters, catastrophes etc, which Baudrillard saw as "Black Market in alterity" (Baudrillard 2001, 104) in this context, could be seen as elusive admiration, an obsession of the democratic masses with any kind of "disturbance" that could be codified as an embellishment of an aesthesis of living in capitalism—which is never empty *eo ipso*, but is being constantly and gradually fulfilled only with a transgressive zeal that is epistemologically represented as a form of transendence of politically ideological emptiness.

IDEOLOGIZATION OF DEPOLITICIZATION

The hegemonic potential any rule might entail that is devoid of politically ideological foundations in most general terms is marked by a specific dysfunction in the exercise of ruling. Generally speaking, this kind of dysfunction did not originate from the elevation of the prerogatives of the power of the sovereign (to transcend immediate logic), on the contrary, it originated from flexibility or in an *opening* of some firm structural aspects of the structures of power.

Michel Foucault's take on the analysis of the paradigmatic shifts in production of power in the *post-ancien* regime allowed him to notice that, "The dysfunction of power was related to a central excess; what might be called the monarchical *super-power*, which identified the right to punish with the personal power of the sovereign. This theoretical identification made the king the *fons justitiae*; but the practical consequences of this were to be found even in that which appeared to oppose him and limit his absolutism. It was because the king, in order to raise money, had appropriated the right to sell legal offices, which *belonged* to him, that he was confronted by magistrates who owned their offices and who were not only intractable, but ignorant, self-interested and frequently compromised" (Foucault 1995, 80).

Foucault was referring to the paradigmatic model of social transformations in the post-*Ancien Régime* and post-Enlightenment eras that allowed disparate elements of the citizen bourgeoisie to integrate themselves into the mechanism of ruling. Later (historical) paradigmatic changes in the organization of production, industrial Fordism and post-industrial virtualization, immateriality of post-Fordist labor was also coupled with a paradigmatic shift in the field of social that was, most bluntly said, marked by processes of a high degree of integration of the population (later subjectivized as the *demos*) into the hierarchies of rule.

Of course, while the pre-Fordist, Fordist, or the materially prefixed economy in general stands reserved for colonial peripheries (and/or the over exploited world and its "more dispensable," non-white, non-Christian populations), virtualization of production in the First World of capital demonstrates that the differentiation in organization of exploitation was reorganized according to (or along with, these paradigmatic changes) the relationship the subjugate had toward the function of the political rule.

The more that life in all its aspects was commodified, the more this commodification tended to be interpreted as a particular token of individual liberation. In other words, the more that political subjectivization was deprived of adversarial aspects in interpretation of the hierarchies of exploitation, the more the amount of individual freedom, or liberty in general, was equated to the amount of auto-managment and/or self-government subjectivity was expected to exercise over itself.

To paraphrase Schmitt, what is subject to order must not be coupled with economic, social, or cultural interests; these must be left to self-government. *Self-government* as a concept represents a symptom of a bio-political order in the aspect in which it is expected from subjects to govern their own subjugation. But, in the context of the emptying of political power of its politically ideological aspects, *self-governmentality* should be seen as a reflection of the order's depoliticization of the concept of the social, in which economic and cultural aspects were defined as related to the power and ideological structures of the order. Furthermore, the concept of *self-governmentality* did not just show that capitalism's definition of life was reduced to the interpretation of life as an ultimate commodity, but it epitomized the interpretation of life as specific spatial singularization, with the subtraction of social conflict from social space to a terrain of biological singularity.

As the exercise of rule in capitalist democracy is not based on politically ideological discourse, but on ideological and material control over the totality of social relations seen as biological properties within the social totality, life and death by themselves, are interpreted as both mere oscillations within this relation and are, perversely being perceived, that is, epistemologically instituted as the most *politically* tangible elements around which the definition of *social conflict* is congregated. This means that what is being politicized is not a social agenda or politically ideological discourse, but specific variations of life in a biological, cultural and economic sense. Furthermore, the capitalist hegemonic machine that utilized life as a dispensable commodity, had consequentially created a precondition in which the politicization of life became possible only in relation to either the subjugation of life, the commodification of the *other* (in the First World), or death (in the overexploited world). Here, the most extreme form of subjugation of life—its subjugation to death—was epistemologically internalized in ideological structures of the First World as just another form of commodification, hence, as just another diversity in the sustainment of exploitation.

In this sense, capitalism's search for hegemony uncovered its *political* paradigms as *necropolitical* (Mbembe 2003), a paradigm that entails the exposition of life to the power of death as the regular instrument in perpetuation of global control over the circulation of capital.

Marina Gržinić introduced the concept of the necropolitical into the theoretical vocabulary of the Southeast European region and in great measure into the European decolonial theory (Gržinić 2008b),[5] but also, she did not only interpret Mbembe's articulation of the necropolitical, but upgraded this articulation by defining the necropolitical paradigm as succesive to the biopolitical one (in the context of contemporary reorganizations of capitalism). Marina Gržinić noted that:

> Necropolitics is connected to the concept of necrocapitalism, i.e., contemporary capitalism, which organizes its forms of capital accumulation that involve dispossession and the subjugation of life according to the power of death. The necrocapitalist capturing of the social space implied new modes of governmentality that are informed by the norms of corporate-intensified rationality and deployed in managing violence, social conflicts, fear and the Multitude. (Gržinić 2009b, 3-4)

Necropolitics functions as an institutional, enforcing and epistemological tool of discrimination within hierarchies of exploitation. Since infliction of death was always an integral part of the modes of expropriation employed by the First World and its Eurocentric racist ideologies, paradigmatic democratic man (white Christian male) was designated as eligible for less exploitation, while others (depending on the particular racial privileges assigned to them by the First World) were designated as eligible for more exploitation and/or subjugation to death at a slower or a faster pace.

Additionaly, since the processes of liberalization of capitalism entailed the process of the synchronization of colonial epistemologies with liberal democratic narratives, necropolitical rule showed itself as an instrument under which the, metaphorically speaking, *engraving* of the motives of the subjugator onto the ideological imaginary of the subjugated (maximization of profit, mass murder, etc.) could be utilized as another token in the equalization of victims and perpetrators and in making of the historical predicament mutual.

So, in the sense of the dysfunction of political power, the necropolitical paradigm (or *necropower*) should not be deemed as a politically ideological construct that reserves the right to inflict death in the protection of sovereignty, it is rather a proto-political construct that inflicts death in the imperial global imposition of the one particular, First World's agenda, it deems to be the only possible version of modernist progress. Furthermore, it is not only the process of the infliction of death that necesarilly accompanies colonial exploits, but it saturates the epistemological pillars on which rationality is constructed, allowing the racism that precedes colonial killing to be reintegrated into dominant epistemological narratives as a normalized tool of diversification that makes capitalism rational as something ideologically tangible, something more than mere, centuries long, murder spree. In other words, it is not the epistemological hegemony and capitalism's ideology that politicizes necropolitics, but *vice versa*.

Since these patterns and kinds of proto-politicization reflect a lack of capitalism's need to excuse itself; it seems that the rupture between power and its effect was by itself institutionalized as an ideological viability on the basis of which intensification of globally hegemonic traits of capitalism would be normalized as the search for just another iteration of capital.

This does not mean however that the compulsory and hegemonic dimensions of political power should be discarded in contemplaton of the political form of resistance, on the contrary, they should be situated on politically and ideological bases of differentiation. In other words, the compulsive potential of the anti-capitalist, anti-racist, decolonial struggle should not simply be pacified in the name of ultimate equality—since this would only protect those responsible for the most blatant cannibalization of any kind of right but their own—but formatted as a struggle for different kind of equality and/or equality defined in political way.

THE DYNAMISM OF A STATUS QUO

Since the contemporary status quo operates under the humanistic umbrella of liberal democracy, the social context it has organized obviously
entails forms of social realization that are connected to the erratic nature
of the circulation of capital. This denotes that the neoliberal status quo iss
diversified exactly as the circulation is, in all of its homology.

The status quo therefore is not of a static nature, it is a *heterotopic
homology* that organizes consent on the basis of absorption and/or production of infinite possibilities of differentiations, but only in the apolitical contexts and in positive connection to the power narratives that organized these *possibilities*. The infinity (of possibilities) should not be seen
here as a mere numerological indulgence added to a description of the
trademarks of social dynamics and its extremes, but as a vector, a procedure that constitutes ideological meaning around the amounts of diversity organized in these conditions.

The epistemological basis on which these vectors of differentiation
(which are also very much supported by democratic dogma's related to
both the concepts of *quantitative determination* and the amount of political
options in democratic environments) are organized, should not be conceived as a gap that, metaphorically speaking, drowns tangibilities of
social realities created by the effect of capital. It should instead be regarded as a structural, institutional and ideological strategy that constructs and singularizes diversities of interpretation of social reality as
possible only if that reality was singulared itself.

Consequently, the distortion of the fundamental meaning of the concepts in relation to quantification became turned upside down — *non-limitation* became equated to limitless oppression, while *limitation* was redefined and reassigned only to the political potential to tackle the singularized ideological boundaries. As Marina Gržinić noted: "The logic of the
organization of life in global capitalism and the division of labor that is
attached to this organization is not to achieve a maximum for life, but in
reality is to pledge only the bare minimum for living and sometimes
(today, too often) not even this" (Gržinić 2010c, 1).

The temporal coordinates of today's regime of exploitation are therefore paradoxical. The result (the effect of capital) was organized, made
rational and epistemologically emancipated as the cause for future employment of some other procedures of commodification; murder and exploitation, that would again be contextualized as a reason for further
non-limitation of capital.

The additional problem is that the dynamism of the capitalist status
quo is structured exactly around the *conversion* that allows subjects to
equate the transcendance from one form of commodification to another
as the actual transendance of commodification.

What is being transcended, in the context of the emptying of power, is the meaning of the political power of rule. This was redefined as the power to intervene in order to rearrange this transcendence; but only within the hegemonic epistemic frame formatted by the circulation of capital. As Marina Gržinić noted: "By making reference to Santiago López Petit, we can state that the repetitive performative mechanism functions as indetermination, indecision, irresolution, or what he calls gelatinization. What was before a solid ground, a materiality of intervention is today a process of multiplication that removes, empties the ground from its materiality" (Gržinić 2009b, 3-4).

In other words, the multiplication of interventions, the multiplication of limits and/or non-limitations only represent the intervention of spreading of capital/shattering of the limits of capital, hence resource appropriation and commodification. It was not just the social antagonism that was emptied of its political role in the organization of adversarial stances in the pretension for power, but it was also the definition of power (and the position of power) that was emptied of political ideologies and reformatted as an administrator of pure ideology to a social space in a mixture of variations. Gržinić noted that, "Gelatinization corresponds, as argued by Santiago López Petit, today to global capitalism as reification corresponded to modernity. If reification was in relation to the distinction between the living and the dead, gelatinization requires a triadic model, according to López Petit, the living, the dead and the inert" (Gržinić 2009b, 3-4).

The living might be seen as privileged subjectivities exposed to less commodification, the dead could be seen as the (racially differentiated) others subjected to extreme commodification and death, while the inert could be seen as the property of "those in the middle," as the property of the social space in which the extreme differentiation among the living and the dead was made into the only possible format of normalcy of that space. As Gržinić wrote:

> Therefore, in a difference from Marx's analysis of commodity fetishism, today we do not have something normal on the level of society from which the analysis of the form of its presentation in art, for example, or in theory, will show us that actually what is a normal content situation is in reality the opposite, something strange and different from what is said, etc. Today, in a difference from Marx, that was the point of reference for Althusser, we live in a time in which the social reality is abnormal and the form of its articulation is here not to normalize this abnormality but to intensify it through voiding this abnormality of any content, meaning, etc. This emptying is going on as obviousness. (Gržinić 2009b, 3-4)

In this sense, the intensification in the normalization of abnormality equated to a lack of content, meaning, etc., in relation to the existence of a surplus of content and meaning formatted in global capitalism's ideological structure; as one that receives amounts of substantiality in direct proportion to which social reality was depoliticized. So, in contemplation of the epistemologies of resistance, one of the essential components within such epistemologies should be, as Gržinić stated via López Petit, "What it is necessary to do today is to call for the repoliticization of reality, and to de-link ourselves from its political neutrality" (Gržinić 2009b, 3-4).

Moreover, it is necessary to format the repoliticization as specific counter-point for the coercive aspects of politically ideological rule and/or political compulsory mechanisms that would impose different foundations upon which antagonisms and conflicts would be based.

LIBERALIZATION OF POLITICAL POWER AND ITS CONSEQUENCES

The reorganization of capitalism on various liberal bases (and its post-liberal iterations) in the post-Cold War era, specifically in the post 9/11 era, and the liberalization of the prerogatives of political power entailed the eradication of compulsive and/or coercive aspects of power in relation to the production of society (that were mobilized in favor of employment of coercive mechanism) for the protection of interests of capital and imposition of its ideologies.

Consequentially, the notion of power itself became separated from its political articulation and produced a structure that combines coercive, institutional, administrative, epistemological and ideological elements only in relation to the perpetuation of the complete immersion of capital and society.

As Agamben, by referring to Benjamin, noted: "What the law can never tolerate—what it feels as a threat with which it is impossible to come to terms—is the existence of a violence outside the law; and this is not because the ends of such a violence are incompatible with law, but because of its 'mere existence outside the law'" (Agamben 2005, 53).

However, since the global capitalist regime employs violence both inside and outside the law, what it actually does is it puts the violence employed inside the law under scrutiny that would justify more of violence outside the law. It is not the violence in the name of protection of capital that is put under scrutiny as such, it is the inadequacy of the amount of violence employed inside the law that is represented as the regime's predicament; an institutional, formalist bottleneck that does not allow the regime to function in its full capacity in order to employ violence indefinitely and without justification.

For instance, Hollywood's obsession with heroes that circumvent the law/the system and "get things done" in the name of "justice" reflects an ideological tendency and/or an ongoing process that constructs aureole of legitimacy around the violence located outside the law. The presumption this process creates in paradigmatic epistemological imaginary is one that sees the system as bad (corrupted, dysfunctional, etc.) because it is not violent enough and/or antagonistic enough—but not toward capitalism as a system of obligatory transgression and its racial ideologies—but toward ideologically defined culprits, enemies, and other antagonists; usually those that expose capitalism as the system of obligatory transgression. In a wider sense, this presumption codifies the interpretation of the dominant format of power in capitalism as dysfunctional because the law or its application, obstruct it.

What the system deems as threatening is actually the exercise of *other* politically ideological, revolutionary, anti-imperial violence that exists outside its grasp on the inside/outside binary; the kind of violence that would present this capitalist binary as a mere false dichotomy.

As Agamben continued: "The task of Benjamin's critique is to prove the reality (*Bestand*) of such a violence: 'If violence is also assured a reality outside a law, as pure immediate violence, this furnishes proof that revolutionary violence—which is the name for the highest manifestation of pure violence by man—is also possible'" (Agamben 2005, 53).

Aside from the contemplations on the proof some possibilities entailed (or not), the effect of considering the possibility of violence is a much more important point of departure in the interpretation of power and/or of political shapes in/through which power could be antagonized.[6] So, aside of the domain of imminent *possibilities* one of the major obstacles against politically ideological (left) revolutionary violence can be found in an implication that some allegedly neutral, truthful or positive contingency should not be tackled and continued to be regarded as unrelated to the power and its ideological structures.

In this sense, the interpretation of the revolutionary struggle in the frame of reference that disconnected the inter-twining relationship between the consistencies of capital and capitalism's co/opting of humanistic narratives (democracy, human rights, humanity, civilization, etc.) proved themelves as explicitly belonging to capitalist institutional hierarchies and its ideologies. As Agamben noticed in reference to Benjamin, "The proper characteristic of this violence is that it neither makes nor preserves law, but deposes it (*Entsetzung des Rechtes*) and thus inaugurates a new historical epoch" (Agamben 2005, 53).

An historical epoch and its subsidiary forms of rule that the alliance of capital and democracy have already inaugurated—the era of capitalism's search for hegemony on the basis of normalization of racial states under the aegis of discovery of post-liberal paradigms on the basis of multiplications of iterations of already colonized humanist (as defined by the First World) epistemologies—has already deposed the law as the epitome of a firm, *non-transcendable* element in the application of (political) power.

In other words, while retaining its power discourses within the frames of law-abiding norms and institutional discourses, capitalism has already formatted itself (or its most expansionist aspects) as a twisted, purely ideological and hence, apolitical revolution, and/or it has hijacked revolutionary traits in relation to the deposition of the law, for the destruction of formal dimensions of institutional discourses and for the organization of ideological structures that evade the constitutional dimension of the law.

What made the substance of this revolutionary thrive, as a most extreme opposite to revolutionary struggle was, of course, the lack of political dimensions in the process of its formation in favor of purely ideological ones. So, what does this mean for the left-wing, for anti-imperial struggles, decolonial struggles? It means that the politically ideological dimension of revolutionary struggles should not discard the option of integration of the interplay between the notions of formality/informality, humanity/inhumanity, democratic/non-democratic into their own ideological structures, but with the difference that such an ideological formation stays essentially based on politically ideological approaches to differentiation among friends and foes.

If some kind of centrality and/or homogeneous ideological structure should be built around the processes of the employment of divisive aspects in ideologization of politics (by anti-imperial, left struggle) they should be posited on the (epistemological) basis of the search for higher amounts of political *and* ideological purpose of the model of social differentiation such a stuggle would strive to create.

However, contemporary capitalism already has its own homogeneous, central ideological structure and/or ideological super narrative that allows to various social differentiations and (political) divisions to exist, even tackle inconsistencies of an order, but only as they stay placid in relation to capitalism and its logics. We are talking about democracy, more precisely we are talking about the function of the eternal moving toward the, always lacking, democracy in full capacity.

NOTES

1. Schmitt reffered to Donoso Cortés who, paraphrasing, considered continuous discussion a method of circumventing responsibility and of ascribing to freedom of speech and of the press an excessive importance that in the final analysis permits the decision to be evaded.

2. The European Union's utter institutional negligence and/or support of a number of reactionary tendencies in the post-Cold War era, radically erasing the division between the state and the church, exemplifies this twisted, yet utterly ideological, split in interpretation of the social predicament.

3. These are the concepts that, paraphrasing Giorgio Agamben, expressed the originary sense through which the Roman people conceived their communal life. *Auctoritas* should be seen as that private, informal power, that according to Agamben, paraphrasing, referred to the power that suspends or reactivates law, but is not formally in force as law. Further paraphrasing Agamben, the notion of *potestas* we can see in

reference to public power (power derived from the people) the commons and/or public dimensions in cosmology of power. As Agamben pointed out, paraphrasing, *auctoritas* and *potestas* are clearly distinct, and yet together they form a binary system.

4. This continuation entailed in the notion of *constant becoming* should be comprehended as that kind of methodological trait of imposition of capitalist conditions that also has an ideological and institutional function. We emphasize this because the same continuation makes sure that capitalism (its expansion) never gets too totalizing. In other words, this momentum makes sure that capitalist institutions does not *devour* the state (and its institutions) completely; keeps the state (and the power prerogatives encompased in its institutions) at disposal for interests of capital and ideologicaly perpetuates the notion of the state as if it is "above" the capitalist interests.

5. Cf. Marina Gržinić. 2008b. "Rearticulation of the State of Things or Euro-Slovenian Necrocapitalism." *Reartikulacija* no. 3. Ljubljana (Slovenia), pp. 3-5.

6. Of course, it is one thing to base revolutionary violence on the basis of separation from reality and/or on the basis of the construction of another reality, but it is another thing to base the contemplation of revolutionary violence within the already situated super-narratives of the political realities which revolutionary violence would antagonize.

TEN

The Function of Democracy in Normalization of the Hegemony

Contractions of capital, such as the so-called debt crisis, have always been *occasions* through which capital, as an economic, epistemological, and social relation, has managed to reorganize itself.

Whether we are talking about the way in which social wealth is being distributed (more precisely, how radical disparity in that distribution is being made rational), or about how wealth is being expropriated from the overexploited world by the First World, we are talking about how capital manages to organize differentiation in exploitation, in synchronous relation with the humanist narratives that make the effect of capital relative and the function of political power ambiguous.

Since the prerogative on the definition of the function of political power in democracy (as the grand contemporary humanist narrative) has been delegated to the *general will* of the *demos* and since the political power in democracy has been epistemologically and institutionally normalized as an agency of capital (that limits the reaches of political antagonism), the current relation between *the demos*, political power and capital has consequently been constituted in order to legitimize the exploitations of the of capitalist system.

In other words, the status of legitimacy the *general will* has, in democracy, has become equal to the legitimacy of capital in monopolizing the definition of legitimacy (and/or the *norm* in general) and equating the non-limitation of social struggles only to non-limitations of capitalist exploitation. Of course, to say that the democratic system of power legitimization has allowed political proliferation only to the ruling classes, to the elite, would be too simplistic. On the other hand, the implication (that various anti-establishment agenda's tend to emphasize), that democracy is flawed because it allows the elite to distance their own interests from

the wider social interest, implies that a more proper version of democracy would be *desirable* because it would be able to reduce the distance
between the public interests and representatives of the same interests.

In more precise terms, this implication operates with the presumption
that the political contingency of the *demos* was inherently inhibited by
flaws in the perpetration of democracy; the grand humanist narrative
that stands alongside capitalism. Contrary to the popular opinion (especially on the left) that tends to see capitalism and democracy in an antagonistic relationship, the basic premise is that the capitalism operates as an
addition to the perpetration of democracy (in a utilitarian, ideological,
and epistemological sense) as a system whose sustainment, institutionalization and ideologization of an empty (democratic) formalistic frame
was (or is being) converted into the very purpose of power that is being
legitimized through it.

THE WILL TO (LACK OF) POWER

The concept of "the people as the sovereign" that is subsumed within
democratic discourses, implied that the prerogatives of the sovereign
power (seen as the embodied form of political power with prerogatives
for intervention into social reality), had been given to the people, but it
also implied that the form of political antagonism that could tackle dominant power structures should not surpass the presumption that the
amount of legitimacy of those power structures was equal to the amount
of the people's capacity to reflect the origin of their predicament. Carl
Schmitt stated that: "The general will of Rousseau became identical with
the will of the sovereign; but simultaneously the concept of the general
also contained a quantitative determination with regard to its subject,
which means that the people became the sovereign" (Schmitt 2005, 48).

Since in the current historical stadium of democracy (a regime of circulation of capital) neither politics nor political ideology was instituted as
the power that shapes social reality, Schmitt's thesis applies to that measure to which nominal and actual effects of power interlace with the circulation of capital.

Disqualification of prerogatives of the political power to produce the
society was therefore (by capitalist-democratic institutions) coupled with
the presumption that the people's democratic prerogatives were in antagonist relation only toward the limitations of capital. The ambiguity, or the
pacification, of the relation between the ruler and the ruled, the lack of
distance among those positions that should have been situated to tackle
each other, was (amidst the general processes of liberalization of capitalism from the 1970s to the 2000 s) therefore pacified in favor of capitalism
that was perceived and epistemologically institutionalized as the only
tangible limit within which social antagonisms should reside.

Schmitt's *quantitative determination* or the democratic, apolitical glorification of some transcendentally positive value of quantitative determination (*the majority of votes*) could therefore be seen as a component of a form of rule. The ambiguity between the function of a political power and capitalism was kept in a state where any social struggle was limited (prohibited) by the logic of capital, while the non-limited prerogatives were epistemologically ascribed only to the people's potential for diversification of the ways in which to achieve inclusion into the hierarchies of exploitation.

To paraphrase Schmitt, the necessity by which the people always will what is right is not identical with the rightness that emanated from the commands of the personal sovereign. Schmitt continued: "The unity that a people represents does not possess this decisionist character; it is an organic unity, and with national consciousness the ideas of the state originated as an organic whole. The theistic as well as the deistic concepts of God become thus unintelligible for political metaphysics" (Schmitt 2005, 49).[1]

Aside from his treatises on the wider implications on the role of the sovereign, Schmitt's perspective allowed the relation between the sovereign (as the position of political power that could transcend social reality) and the people (to whom the power was delegated in contemporary power cosmology) to be seen as an actual derogatory process which the interventionist, or widely antagonistic, nature of political power should contain.

The democratic concepts such as "collectivization of power," "dispersal of power," etc., thus reflected themselves in the contemporary context as those concepts that actually reduced/dispersed the potential of politically ideological interventionism in favor of an apolitical process in which the mere method of legitimization of power (the democratic electoral dynamism) was constitued as sufficient and/or as the ultimate goal of politics. In other words, it was not the politically ideological possibility that *people* might have produced that was made legitimate by democracy, but the *people's* rejection of politically ideological possibilities that was converted, or epistemologically constituted, into people's political potential—which has consequently legitimized capital, or the reality of its effect, as the only ideological context in which political potential should have been sought. Aside the fact that different democratic models derive sovereignty from different contingencies (the people, the crown, the divine, etc.) this claim denotes *the people* as the protagonist that is being called upon, prominently included into the power cosmology.

In this sense, it could not exactly be said that the intelligibility of political metaphysics was completely banished from the paradigmatic democratic imagination, it is more likely that the limits of metaphysical intelligibility were produced either as inherently *limited*, in the sense that would allow capitalism (and its First World center) to retain in its hegemonic position, or as *unlimited* but only to that measure that allowed capital (and its First World center) to reorganize/reinvent itself through unlimited intensification of commodification of every aspect of existence. In simple terms, people's potential for "freedom" was equated with its potential for the legitimization of the nonlimitation(s) of capital.

Such an interpretation of the political contingency of the *demos* (as the form of subjectivization of the people in general democratic narratives) allowed the regime to destroy the political prefixes of this contingency, hence redefining the terrain on which "freedoms" should be won.

As the interpretation of people as an organic unity, biological axiom and/or ethnic/racial/religious conglomeration was/is being institutionalized in the First World (or, in general: in capitalist democracy) such a terrain on which the freedoms are being won actually diverts social struggle(s) from being based on political, ideological or class issues to being based on race/identity/culture issues. The most legitimate form of search for *political* freedom or positioning was produced through the inclusion of ideological dimensions within the very method through which these issues were, or are, being deprived of politically ideological dimensions of social and/or political antagonism.

That being said, the success of ascending the hierarchies of rule in democracy was not conditioned only by the amount of financial power ruling classes might have invested in sustaining their position, or by the amount of populism integrated in an oppositional political program, it was primarily conditioned by the measure to which the power pretenders equated the shattering of the limits of freedom with the shattering of the limitations to capital.

The contemporary tendency of various anti-establishment movements in the First World to base their resentment on the critical axis that addresses the discrepancy between the 1 percent privileged and 99 percent less privileged, does have a merit in the sense in which it evoked class prefix to a social conflict. However, the lack of a politically ideological dimension (the lack of an ideologal base to these political and class struggles) that has not (or not yet) been installed into these agendas, was met on the other side (the establishment) by intensification of First World capitalism's search for hegemony, on the basis of the ascription of ideological traits to, either its expansion (that includes colonial exploits) or to itself as a "social instrument" that would secure the protection and creation of work places. In Europe, the spectrum of meanings of capital as a *social instrument* has received a national prefix with respect to the preservation of the social aspect of the state. In reality this has meant that the racist immigration politics of the European Union, the employment of racial and religious criteria in differentiation among the labor force, etc., represent tokens of preservation of the social state.

In general, any social struggle that fails in its political ideologization, fails to address the institutional, epistemological, political and material basis on which the terrain for differentiation is being produced. Any hypothetical "victory" of the currently popular anti-establishment movements would maybe tip the scales from 10 percent/90 percent to 20 percent/80 percent, but in doing so, it would only "refresh" the current hierarchical structure and reinvent capitalism along with its *inclusive and humanist* democratic narrative, (as a matter of fact this has already happened after the 1968 rebellion when the new, liberal face of a capitalist master was able to liberalize capital and stem the 1980s and 1990s era of neoliberal "prosperity"), while the concept of social resentment would become synonymous with integration into the circulation of capital. In the meantime, capitalism as an inherently racist (white, Eurocentric) system would continue to present itself as a system that included all, equally into its circulation, *ergo*: exploitation.

So, since the relation between democratic formalism and capitalism as a social relation has been most prominently structured in the First World and since it was specifically the First World that equalized its modernity and the accumulation of wealth based on colonial plunder, it was not hard for the Euro-Atlantic axis of power to universalize particular paradigmatic western notions of the purpose of people's "freedom potential." Consequently, this has allowed the capitalist regime (in particular the First World) to monopolize the definition of democracy and to put it in complete synchronization with the needs of capital; reorganizing the spread of capital as the spread of democratic and generally humanist agendas.

Simultaneously, this has allowed First World capitalism to liberalize/ modernize its Eurocentric racist/colonial epistemologies and various (still institutionalized) forms of Eurocentric fundamentalism under the aureole of *democratic consensus*. Of course, in familiar colonialist fashion, these processes subsumed the exploitation, murder and genocide that were put in synchronous relation with the spread of "civilized" values to the overexploited world, helping, as Eurocentric agents would say, the overexploited to "rediscover their freedom," hence democratic potential.

Anyhow, since the antagonistic potential of the people (in the most prominent First World's democracies) in relation to the regime was deprived of its politically ideological dimension (which has influenced the popular definition of the establishment as the specific conjunction of interests of the capitalist elites and the government) this has allowed for the formation of the anti-establishment mainstream in the form of a resistance movement(s) against capitalism that regards capitalism not as an inherently criminal system, but as an "undemocratic" system whose totalizing nature allegedly originated in a mere metastasis of its inconsistencies.

This is important in the interpretation of the relationship between capital and democracy because it allowed the system to create a distance between those dichotomies whose political potential have already been deprived and to depoliticize, or to narrow, the distance betwen those dichotomies that retained political potency. For instance, *political potential* ascribed to the concepts of inclusion/exclusion; representation/misrepresentation; integration/non-integration; free market liberalism/religious fundamentalism; liberty/lack of liberty; transparency/lack of tranparency; gay/hetero; and so on, puts these false dichotomies in a relation where they are pitted against one another, but only within the boundaries of the limits strictly imposed by the regime.

As Marina Gržinić, in the context of her analysis of the genealogy of transformation of power and of principles of relation between the power structures and the subordinates in the contemporary momentum of globalization of capital, has noted:

> In the post-Cold War era, sacredness is transferred from the State to the victims. According to my elaborations in the past on the topic, this shift very much follows the way of functioning of global capitalism that is grounded in hegemony on one side and fragmentation, multireality and multidispersity on the other. It follows as well the change from Fordism to post-Fordist capitalism, that happened in the 1970s, this shift presents itself today in a different relation between capital and power." (Gržinić 2010d, 15)

On the other hand, the political potential, the distance that originates among the dichotomies between the oppressor/oppressed, ruler/ruled, privileged classes/non-privileged classes, colonial violence/decolonial violence, killer/victim was deprived, distorted and, in general, narrowed, made relative and/or distorted. This *erasure* of the essential political antagonism and distortion of the distance that should have existed between these poles, allowed the capitalist-democratic regime to represent any social conflict between these poles either as totalitarian forms of political antagonism (the regime allegedly has nothing to do with), or as an "uncivilized" consequence of a lack of democratic demeanor. Thus, all those issues, whose political scope contained politically ideological potency for radical intervention against institutional and epistemological basis, upon which the alliance between capital and democracy rested, were excluded from the proper democratic discourse and were assigned to either the "totalitarian" or "extremist" register.

However, it was not enough for the regime only to organize a number of false dichotomies and to depoliticize a number of political dichotomies, it had to reorganize the whole epistemological terrain on which differentiation was being produced.

The *solution* was found in the form in which the political and apolitical thrive; they would be kept in a *dynamic stasis*, that would ensure that the fundamental politically (and/or ideological) prefixed meanings of these concepts would be distorted/shattered; the oppressed were convinced that they actually found freedom, the enslaved were convinced that their enslavement was a necessary precondition for emancipation and the descendents of victims of colonial genocides (as well as victims of today's colonial exploits) are being convinced that those killings were actually a "good thing" which those victims had (or have) to bear on the "hard road" to modernity, etc.

So, since it obviously does not stand (or since it does not stand structurally) that the will of the people or the will of the moral majority was excluded from taking part in the creation of the political agenda, and since the people's exclusion from the possibility for political intervention into social reality became celebrated in democracy as its (*the people's*) utmost "political" accomplishment, it was obvious that the concept of the people was included into the cosmology of power as an organic/apologetic mass, open for commodification (in the First World) or exploitation (in the overexploited world), untouchable by political processes or history (as a compensation for this previous role) but only to that extent to which they legitimized capitalism as the pinnacle of modernity. According to Schmitt: "Tocqueville in his account of American democracy observed that in democratic thought the people hover above the entire political life of the state, just as God does above the world, as the cause and the end of all things, as the point from which everything emanates and to which everything returns" (Schmitt 2005, 48).

If we put aside particular democratic models, the implication that the democratic subjects were included into a more intimate relationship with the ruler/s through the exclusion of their politically antagonist contingencies, presents a presumption which resides at the ideological core of democracy's relation with the capital. This ideological structure does not only epistemologically constitute the temporal mark of democratic capitalism as the *post-ideological* or *final* system in history (in reference to Francis Fukuyama's interpretation of post-ideological at the end of history), but also extracts capitalism from history in general by placing its expansive ability at the point of departure of history and by placing its absorbing ability at the end of an historical processes as the linchpin of the civilization which that process produced.

In relation to the function of democracy, the implication that the will of the *demos* was ultimately *right* and/or *objectively positive* demonstrated that the dominant epistemological matrices were congregated around the delegation of primacy to the pure ideological axiomatic and/or around the emptied performance of the political, hence, around purely ideological processes at the expense of the politically ideological process.

As the *demos* was extracted, elevated above the political life of the state, it simultaneously meant that it had been neutralized as an politically antagonistic contingency, only to be pushed or descended into the spectrum of everyday considerations to which the status of utmost political priority had been ascribed. On one hand, frivolity, banality, performativity, deification of the form with primacy given to method above substance, and on the other hand, the reinvention of the substance on the basis of the reproduction of organistic, reactionary, fascist ideologies constituted the main epistemological pillars of the experience that saturates paradigmatic democratic subjectivity.

Therefore, since democratic capitalism operates with purely ideological rationalizations of the operations of capital, the performance as a concept was deprived of its connection with the politically ideological *a prioris*. All of this consequentially resulted in the institutionalization of politics as performance, as a process whose iterations did not serve or lead toward some politically ideological goal, but were kept in a constant repetitive state where the iterations of performativity themselves were represented as tokens of existence of a purpose; but only within the logic of the capital and its racially ideological matrices.

The epistemological institutionalization of the idea that the ideological environment in which the mere existence of a performative antagonism was seen as ultimately positive and political, represents, of course, a substitute for a politically ideological struggle, but it also represents the inauguration of a method through which the extraction of politically ideological connotations is being made—the performance itself—as ideologically viable social niche. For instance, it was not the political implication behind the motives[2] of the performance which the Pussy Riot group pulled off in Moscow, and was embraced by the First World's mainstream (or parts of its anti-establishment), its utter minimal, almost circus like form of dissent that was represented as the maximum of the political struggle.

Of course, the over-emphasized significance delegated to this event, was used as a diversion[3] from the exact same issues Western democracies have with the authoritarian and/or dictatorial role of the free market logic; lack of politically articulated freedom of speech (see WikiLeaks case); clero-fascist influence in European Union; institutional racism; fascist infiltration into the political mainstream of the West; concentration camps (Guantanamo, Bagram, secret prisons, drone campaigns in Pakistan, Afghanistan, Yemen, etc); racist immigration politics, etc. But, what is more important in this context is how the representation of this case in the First World's mainstream was *over-performatized* into proof of existence of a political sensibility par exellance.

Whether we are talking about the performativity of the alleged existence of political and ideological substance behind the capitalist democratic regime or whether we are talking about the utterly hypocritical, double-standards in approach to various transgressions, this case is therefore far more important as a reflection of the way through which the paradigmatic First World's epistemological imaginary differentiates the interpretation of the political. It interprets it as an act whose politically ideological dimensions are tied up with performativity of the interventionist prerogatives of politics, hence as an *act* whose politically ideological dimensions were designed as performative. The same interventionist prerogatives were, on the other hand, tied up with the potency of democratic formalism in order to normalize all non-performative, *informal* aspects of the effect of capital.

The complacent and complicit aspects of democratic public discourse in the First World therefore tend to format an ideological interpretative mechanism that sees itself as a contingent corrective of capitalism's inconsistencies, but, that being said, it actually functions as a mechanism that converts (*corrects*) capitalist consistencies into inconsistencies, putting along the way the degree of its own democratization in direct proportion only to the degree to which these inconsistencies were, or can be formalized into consistencies. For instance, the movie industry and popular culture in general is already showing a tendency to interpret the 2008. stock market crash through singularization of particular actors of this crisis[4] as if their particular transgressions, not capitalism as the system in which transgression is obligatory, were ultimately responsible for *the crisis*. Mainstream perception of capitalism was therefore, by the paradigmatic democratic moral majority in the First World, instituted on an axis that separated capital from its effect or on the axis that separates capitalism from history in general, which meant nothing else but playing into the hands of capital, allowing it to represent itself as a mutual, human project that equally exploits all humanity.

However, since the distance between the oppressors and the oppressed was narrowed along the processes of liberalization of capitalism by the capitalist co-optation of humanist projects (whether it resulted in depoliticization of the left in the West or in increased amount of colonial invasions in the overexploited world under the aegis of spreading democracy), democratic formalism based on rationalist interpretation of capitalist transgressions (particulary of those committed by the First World/Eurocentric agents) seems to have become unfit to contain the intensification of radical class division, disparity in wealth distribution, reinvention of fascism on a liberal basis and so on, hence the effects of capital in their full capacity.

This does not mean that the performativity of the political ceased in the epistemological reinvention of the capitalist regime, the performance of existence of mutual approaches to exploitation was compensated by the intensified *humanization* of the non-performative strategies of capital.

So, in its search for hegemony, the capitalist colonial regime had to hijack more of the universal, humanist, liberal, and civilized traits and ascribe them as inherent, directly into its own hegemonic register, hence tying them directly to its non-performative dimension of exploitation, commodification, and mass murder. As Marina Gržinić has noted:

> If there was a unity between capital and power in Fordism, today they stay in a relation of a co-propriety. Unity meant silence instead of (or

as) justice; today it has changed into truth instead of (or as) justice, where truth is the proliferation of the stories by the victims, measured by a co-propriety of capital and power. This transition from silence to speech, from forgetting to recounting, is translated into the resurgence of morality of international relations that seeks to expel violence from history. Practically, this means to depoliticize justice while not taking it out from the daily politics and power relations. (Gržinić 2010d, 15)

Therefore, the mutualization of the predicament, the allegedly equal exploitation of all and alleged consensual acceptance that capitalism has surpassed the boundaries of history as a political process, became a wild card for capital and its *humanist* dimension which it started to use in the reorganization of its hegemony into a global project in which any transgression would be seen as a consequence of anything else, except capitalism itself and its racial ideologies.

THE FUNCTION OF DEMOCRATIC FORMALISM

As Santiago López Petit, theoretician and analyst of the paradigmatic patterns in ideological, representational, institutional, and epistemological reorganizations of capitalism, has suggested:

Democracy . . . is no longer a form of government in the traditional sense, but the formalism that makes global mobilization possible. Global mobilization is the project inscribed in neoliberal globalization. As such it consists in the mobilization of our lives in order to (re)produce—by just living—this full capitalist reality that is imposed on us as plural and unique, as both open and closed, and, above all, as irrefutably obvious. (López Petit 2011, 2)

Of course, López Petit's view in regard to total neoliberal mobilization could be approached by looking at it without the presumption of the existence of "us" in democracy.

This remark should be read as an addition to that part of analysis of democracy that sees it as a formalism sustaining class division; it should be read as a contribution to the analysis that sees democracy as a part of capitalism's reorganizations. More precisely, as part of the analysis that sees democracy as an instrument for the *mutualization* of (ultimately making relative) predicaments (created by the capitalist democratic regime) in all of its aspects—especially those aspects in relation to the origins of the predicament and in relation to the ways this predicament was interpreted or tackled.

If we say that democracy (as a humanist project or its contingent framework) has been appropriated or co-opted by capitalism in a form that has allowed its formalist aspect to organize only limited intervention into the social reality, democracy—as a framework that does not surpass its role as an instrument for legitimization of integration into the ruling

hierarchies, with all of its "successes" and failures—has always been reserved for those made *eligible* for ascendance to positions of power or
positions that would "guarantee" a lesser amount of exploitation, it has
been reserved for those in (financial, racial) positions to utilize democratic leniency toward the transgressions of capital and for those racially
deemed as fitting to experience the legacy of a western democratic program.

For instance, the revolutionary legacy and liberal dimensions of the
French Revolution were never applied to the victims of (French or any
other European) colonial rule. In the case of French apartheid established
in colonial Algiers (1830–1962), the Algerians were never *eligible* to become subjects in the democratic project or seen as equal subjects within
the *"Liberté, égalité, fraternité"* formula. After the defeat of colonial apartheid forces, during the colonialist's retreat, those Algerians who served
with the French (The Harkis)[5] were (in overwhelming majority) disposed
of by the European colonialist.

The contemporary actuality of the collusion of democratic and colonial exploits is not only visible through the utter lack of Euro-Atlantic (especially the EU's) acknowledgement, or even slightest recognition of, its
own colonial history,[6] but is visible through open utilization of democratic values in the transparent imposition of colonial conditions to Libya,
Afghanistan, Iraq and/or to the European colonial peripheries that entail
a majority of ex-socialist/Eastern Bloc states.[7]

In reference to López Petit's claim, democratic mobilization does not
only organize full capitalist reality by reproducing ways of living (differentiating within forms of life), but also through the active infliction of
death (differentiating within the forms and amounts of death). The epistemological frame of reference in which definitions of living and dying
were put in proportional relation to a particular definition of the meaning
of the humanist legacy, allowed therefore for the erasure of differences
between the perpetrators and the victims, which consequentially con-
verted/twisted the acts of killing (committed by the owners of monopoly
on definition of humanity) into an inherent part of the process of the
imposition of "civilization" on its victims.

This racial logic that allowed capitalism to divert the political prefix
and class context of the social struggle into the field of race and religion
simultaneously allowed for defamation of any politically-ideological
and/or decolonization struggle as "anti-humanist," and/or ultimately
"non-civilized"—all under the utterly hypocritical aegis of protection of
freedoms (i.e. free speech, self-determination, apolitical empowerment,
etc.).

The institutionalization of racial differentiations between forms of living and dying actually normalized the racially motivated killing as a
mere part of the process of sustaining the First's world role as definer and
imposer of global capitalism. In the same way, it also allowed epistemo-

logical hegemonies to assign pure ideological purpose to living and dying—merely living was symbolically and epistemologically inaugurated into being the pinnacle of political participation in liberal democracy, while murder, organized under the same democratic aegis, was represented as (some) dying amidst the struggles for the universal causes found in particularly defined meanings of freedom, democracy, etc., rather than as a crimes inherently tied to capitalist colonial expansions, First World's racism, and ultimately, profit.

If the relation between democracy and global neoliberal mobilization rested on the organization of ambiguity in relation to definitions of the universal, plurality, openness, uniqueness, etc., the homogenization of the momentum of *us* turns out to be one of the main motives the hegemonic epistemological regime uses in construction of its ratio.

This has allowed the erasure of responsibility for mass racist murders committed in the First World, as well as allowing the formalization of a variety of transgressions which represented the death of a victim as a death allegedly *needed* in an alleged struggle of the same victim for integration into the First World's liberal narrative, hence the western, imperial version of the freedom.

So, since humanist projects with democratic and liberal prefixes were co-opted by capital and since democratic formalism seems to have become unsuited to normalizing the intensified disparities in global distribution of social wealth, the search for hegemony (or the search for new levels of normalization of the hegemony) had to be located exactly within institutional and epistemological frames that would present new levels of hegemonization as new levels of possibilities which humanist projects co-opted by capitalism allegedly entailed.

THE HEGEMONIC ROLE OF THE DEMOCRATIC

Santiago López Petit differentiates between *democracy* and *the democratic*. As he stated, "If the defenders of 'true' democracy have themselves to add adjectives in order to characterize it (participative, inclusive, absolute, etc.), it is because the situation is ripe to criticize the term" (López Petit 2011, 2). As López Petit further claimed:

> The function of "the democratic" is to guarantee that global mobilization successfully merges with our own life. Successfully means that 'the democratic' helps to effectively manage conflicts generated by runaway capitalism, channeling expressions of social unease, because the democratic severs the political dimension of our own reality and neutralizes any attempt at social transformation. (López Petit 2011, 2)

In approach to this differentiation, López Petit consulted Carl Schmitt's distinction between *politics* and *the political*. This is an approach that carries importance, but, the differentiation between politics/political and democracy/democratic should be based on an acknowledgment that the political substance these bipolar concepts had, or should have had, is not the same. As Schmitt claimed:

> The general definitions of the political which contain nothing more than additional references to the state are understandable and to that extent also intellectually justifiable for as long as the state is truly a clear and unequivocal eminent entity confronting nonpolitical groups and affairs—in other words, for as long as the state possesses the monopoly on politics. . . . The equation state = politics becomes erroneous and deceptive at exactly the moment when state and society penetrate each other. (Schmitt 2007, 22)

Thus, if the dichotomy between *politics* and *the political* considered the liberalization or *dispersion* of the interventionist dimension of *politics* (as the institutionalized form of the political) in favor of that aspect of *the political* that does not incubate dichotomies, but acts upon already defined/produced dichotomies by the *politics*, democracy and its own iterations (that have always been instituted as organizers of the erosions between the state and politics or more precisely as organizers of the erosion between the political and its ideological dimension) cannot be considered, not even as contingent spaces that could have produced politically ideological substance out of the entanglement of the state and capital based upon the interpretation of politics as both political (production of dichotomies) and politics (acting upon already produced dichotomies).

If democracy was always a token of institutionalization of this relation—the dispersal of firm political decisionism in favor of populist, nonpolitical dimensions—it never had any political substantiality *eo ipso* that could have transcended dominant epistemic and power narratives that operated alongside it.

Yes, of course, López Petit may be right to the extent that he saw *the democratic* as the next (or as such the current) phase in global capitalism's search for hegemony, but the question remains, was it only *the democratic* that severed the political dimension within the social struggles, or was it the relation the *democratic* had with *democracy* that derogated the political dimension in its attempts at social transformation? If we resort to Schmitt's own take on these concept López Petit referred to, Schmitt notices that, paraphrasing, the political is the most intense and extreme antagonism, and every concrete antagonism becomes that much more political the closer it approaches the most extreme point, that of the friend-enemy grouping.

Since *democracy* organized the general narrowing of the distance between the institutional emanation of political power (the state) and *the people* in direct proportion to the reducing of the political prerogatives of the state, the nature of the antagonism it created proved itself unable to confront the exact framework within which such antagonisms were jux-taposed.

Attempts at social transformation, within which the epistemological frames are subjugated to the super-narrative of democracy, were there-fore always a kind of inter-systemic *cul de sac*, never transcending the firm boundaries within which various kinds of attempts at social trans-formation were realized. But, since we operate on the premise that capi-talism needs further narrowing/erasure of the antagonist distance be-tween the epistemological frames of political imaginary and the institu-tional materiality of the hegemony it organized, then the definition of the concept of social transformation itself has to be seen as already con-formed to the dominant narrative that equated the non-limitation of so-cial change only to the non-limitation of capital. The democratic as a reflection of apoliticized politics therefore imposed it self as an instru-ment of antagonization of hegemonic aspects of (institutionalized) poli-tics which in effect does not antagonize the institutional discourses, but allows them exactly to become less visible as an object of antagonization. As Petit continued:

> "The democratic" is not easy to define. The central nucleus of formal-ism is constituted by the articulation between the *war-state* and *post-modern fascism*: between heteronomy and autonomy, between control and self-control. . . . The democratic is built upon a double premise: 1) Dialogue and tolerance refer to a purported horizontality, because they channel all differences to a question of mere personal opinion and cul-tural options; 2) The conception of politics as war presupposes declar-ing an internal or external enemy, invoking a vertical dimension. "The democratic" would produce the—apparent—miracle of bringing oppo-sites side by side in a continuum: war and peace, pluralism and repres-sion, freedom and prison. (López Petit 2011, 3)

However, if *the democracy* organized a framework under which the oppo-sites that came into a collision did not tackle the epistemological framing of the same terrain on which these collisions (social struggles) happened, and if we see the number of predicaments paradigmatic democratic man experiences in relation to the inherent impossibility of intervention against the hegemonic regime, this man's political vision actually does not see democracy as a fitting framework in which his efforts could be realized. Such a vision, in the same way as capitalism did, sees the combi-nation of the *humanist* dimension of democracy and *the democratic* (as its informal, *Realpolitik* nature) as the proper framework within which effort, prominence, freedom, emancipation, and profit could be attained and/or maximized.

To be clear, López Petit's analysis in regard to the nature of *the demo-cratic* and its double premise stands, but *the democratic* can hardly be seen as standing in conflicting relation to *democracy* or as solely being a totalitarian tendency astray from *democracy*. The interplay between both however, in relation to capital, could be seen as a pool from which capital can derive its humanist, mutualizing spectrum of rationalizations of the effects of capital.

Additionally, if *the democracy* (and its institutions—parliamentary, representative, or liberal democracy in capitalism, etc.) had secured a formalized context under which the opposites would be kept tangible/conflicting (only in regard to the questions that in affirmative fashion regard the nature of capitalist hierarchies of exploitation), the democracy (and its iterations) could now be seen in a role that (as a response to aseptic formalism) institutionally formalizes and epistemologically normalizes tangible aspects of the democratic First World's rule—exploitation, racism, utter class disparity, murder, colonialism, and so on.

This informal, but actual dimension of the regime is therefore the dimension paradigmatic democratic man finds as the one he/she can be in cognitive consonance with, because this dimension has been found to be the only one that can guarantee both the possibility of ascendance in social hierarchies and the ideological tangibility/purpose of living (or dying) in such an order. However, since this informal dimension of democracy has been built upon the constant oscillation between the formalism of *democracy* and actuality of *the democratic* (as López Petit saw it) the only gestures, actions, strategies and effects of power that have proved themselves as ideologically tangible are the effects of capital themselves. Processes of expansion of capital, commodification, institutionalization of various forms of the regime's criminality, ideologization of identity, cultural and racial differentiation (at the expense of class and political ideological differences) presented themselves as the only tangible *actualities* or *realities* usable in democratic efforts. Of course the actuality/tangibility/reality of the effect of capital itself proved to be the only potent incubator of the ideological content for construction of the purpose of capital.

The organization of the interplay between the empty formalism of *democracy* and the macabre, hegemonic function of *the democratic* (as López Petit saw it) proved itself as a central part of capitalism's hijacking of the humanist legacy and the reorganization of capital on a humane basis. As such, this consequently produced not just the liberal-democratic norm, but it fixated and limited the scope of social conflict firmly within the frames that reproduce any kind of diversity as additions (multiples) on the terrain on which capitalism can reorganize, legitimize and normalize First World's colonial transgressions and racist ideologies.

Of course, the erasure of political differences, or more precisely, the complete distortion of the meaning of war and peace, oppression and freedom, commodification and labor was the aim of these operations. This institutional and epistemological strategy could be seen as being based on the production of ideology directly outside of the process of keeping the opposites in their niches within the grand democratic narrative, with their potential for social transformation kept elusive to the extent to which it was political, and utilized to the extent to which it could function as the potential for the next reorganization of capitalism.

So, the double premise on which *the democratic*, in terms in which López Petit interpreted it, resides could be seen, perhaps in a paradoxical manner, as based on both *the democracy* and the *democratic*. More precisely, by having:

1. the democracy that is making sure that the dichotomies between plurality-oppression, war-peace, diversity-homogeneity are erased or kept in horizontal apolitical stasis under the formal institutional umbrella which guarantees that political inhibition stands in indirect proportion to the possibilities for multiplication of diversifications, and by having
2. the democratic that organizes transgressive, totalitarian and ideological aspects as a compensation for politically ideological struggles and that functions as the only social-political tangibility within the aseptic frames of democracy.

We could say that the organization of a war-State, as well as postmodern fascism are parts of the operations of *the democratic*, but in relation to *the democracy* they represent tokens of verticality, that is, ideological verticality in organization of the ideological purpose of the relation between capital and its humanist dimensions.

In other words, the war-State makes sure that life is being put in a dispensable relation with the hierarchies of exploitation, while postmodern fascism, (which was in the First World produced as a modernized extension of colonial epistemologies), produces and oppresses the *others* as the only tangible diversity and/or differentiation within the hierarchies of exploitation—the racial differentiation. The war-State and postmodern fascism ultimately converge into the racial-State with the monopoly on the definition of humanity, which is perversely enough, *informally* conceived as a response to the contraction of capital, but actually functions as a token of the capitalist search for hegemony. As López Petit notices:

> The efficacy of "the democratic" lies in the way it shapes public space—and in the end our relation to reality—as a space of possibilities, that is, of personal elections. More freedom means the multiplication of choices, but the refusing of all other options is never possible. . . . "[T]he democratic" acts, above all, as the mode of subjection—of subjection to our reality—which establishes the partition between the thinkable and the unthinkable. (López Petit 2011, 3)

This is true, but since the basic design of the relation between the democracy and capital was meant to serve as a framework that would normalize radical disparities in distribution of social wealth between the First and overexploited world and since these disparities have started to show themselves more intensively within the First World itself, the boundaries of the dominant political imaginary of the First World began to experience the limitations framed by this relationship as unfitting.

If the partition between the *thinkable and unthinkable* (i.e., the experience of the limits imposed by the logic of capital) began to crumble in the First World, it happened only in favor of the search for the unthinkable within the epistemological frames that would address the predicaments created by capital as problematic. This is because capitalism either did not have enough of ideologically hegemonic dimensions or because democracy did not prove itself as capable enough of normalizing an astounding amount of wealth distribution disparities or atrocities committed in the name of either profit or democracy.

This means that the effect of capital is being perceived by the paradigmatic moral majority in the First World as the effect of those aspects of democracy (diversity, rule of law, freedom of movement, etc.), which have never existed as institutional/political/judicial practices, and that *the democracy* did not prove itself as fitting to formalize all of the informal dimensions through which prominence/emancipation/wealth could be secured.

Furthermore, that which never existed in democratic capitalist rule (such is the politically ideological purpose that would have transcended the logic of the profit and the dominance of Eurocentric racial ideologies) is now used/perceived by a paradigmatic western democratic man as the problem and cause of the failure of the neoliberal promise. In other words, the capital and its epistemological regime tend to be interpreted by First World moral majority as problematic because they are not hegemonic enough.

Of course, these are the epistemological frames that entail clear reiterations of a fascist image now underway in the First World of capital, where the dominant format of the response to capitalist exploitation received a form/request that sought for more hegemony/racial differentiation to be employed by the regime as a token of protection of privileges that were assigned on a racial basis. Of course, this perverse differentiation created between capitalism as dominant social relation, and its effect is a pure capitalist reorganization strategy on the grounds that would, on the basis of false dichotomies, create only greater amounts of homogenization of capital and society.

Since capitalism was never a homogeneous matrix of that kind that exploited all in the same way or to the same degree, the basis on which differentiation within these hierarchies of exploitation is being produced (racism, class division, etc.) is now being perceived (by the paradigmatic western moral majority and apologetic pundits of the *capitalo-democratic* regime) as an escape route from the formalist nature of the relation between capitalism and democracy. In other words, those minimal amounts of critique, that is, politically antagonist positions that were organized under democracy are now being produced into the most totalitarian aspects of democracy.

All of this consequently has led to the actual craving for the ideological prohibition, political limitation and hegemony that is increasingly being perceived by the apolitical democratic masses as the *solution* for aseptic democratic formalism. Additionally, this craving has realized itself in a shape that seeks a constitution of *true* democracy and *true* humanism in a form of a consensual normalization of the fascist hegemony under the formalist umbrella of protection of various human rights and freedoms.

Therefore, hegemony is being democratized or, more precisely, democracy is being made hegemonic as a tool of coping with those aspects of formalism in relation between the democracy (and its iterations) and the capitalism that proved themselves to be not adequate enough to formalize the increase of capitalism's global hegemonic traits. In other words, the conglomeration of values based on the equalization of non-limitations of liberties and non-limitations of capital formatted the search for purpose of those liberties in the form of an ideological structure of hegemony in which infliction of death for the sake of profit represents just a way of shattering the limits of liberty.

THE IDEOLOGICAL ROLE OF DEMOCRATIC INFORMALITY

Thus, since democracy and its iterations constitute parts of capitalism's utilization of the role that concepts of *formality* and *informality* have in formation of the function of political power, the politically ideological prefixes to basic dichotomies of oppression/freedom, diversity/homogeneity were epistemologically eradicated in favor of the installation of capital as the system that evades the ramifications of the social conflict.

As such, the co-opted humanist project distorted the political picture in positive relation to the unthinkable and created the conditions in which ideological viability was extracted from the register of possibilities, resulting in strategies, actions and gestures in positive relation to the reinventions and reorganizations of capitalism. In other words, the ideological purpose is being derived from the effect of capital, not from the field of rationalizations of that same effect.

Mass-murders committed in colonial invasions and/or in protection of First World's values were therefore converted into tokens of the existence of ideological purpose behind the capital; commodification became a token of the productivity/economic viability of the regime; war-States became the only possible tangibility of the state that had been completely immersed as the extension of the market; while (Euro Atlantic) racism became the measure of the ideological prowess of the capitalist democracy as the "consensual," "universal," humanist project. In colloquial terms, colonial, racist murder, exploitation, and commodification brought "action" into impotent formalism of democratic politically ideological emptiness.

The transition from *democracy* to *the democratic* therefore never ends, it realizes its hegemonic potential through constant conversion, spilling over from one (formal) pole to the other (informal) pole, making a context where the formalist emptiness of democracy and its humanist contingency serves only as a tool for the formalization of openly totalitarian operations of capitalism and reorganizations of the modernist project on a transparently racist, colonial, exploitatory, and hegemonic basis. To paraphrase Lopez Petit, the project of modernity implied, above all, conceptualizing the self-institution of a society for which transcendental instances that can legitimate order are no longer available.

However, since the self-institution of society was put in direct relation to the re-institution of capitalism as social relation, it seems that these instances were found in a context in which legitmization of the order was procured through self-institution of an order as that transcedental instance that would determine the best format in which society would be *self-instituted*.

Capitalism's mutualization of the historical aprioris (as a process by which the First World's is evading it's responsibility for past and current racial, genocidal policies through mutualization of responsibilities within the narratives of alleged universal, post-ideological consensus humanity has on globalization of capitalism), surpassing of the politically ideological context and the rejection of the logic of cause and effect allowed capitalism to transcend the distance between itself and the humanist legacies it absorbed (absorbs). So, while the relation between the capital and humanist projects oscilate at some, constantly narrowing distance for a certain amount of historical time, it seems that the method through which that distance is being reduced was produced into ideological raw material which capitalism could use to legitimize its order and the subjugated could use as compensation for the lack of any politically ideological substance within such an order.

The substance of the order, its *arche* (as ultimate underlying substance), was therefore conceived in a paradigmatic democratic image, as possible without the essential politically ideological dimension, suitable for the organization of society that would transcend given social reality. Hence, the same *arche* was organized to function as a fixed point between the arbitrary myriad of apolitical diversities and purposes found in the apotheosizing of the most extremely non-arbitrary strategies and actions, resulting in the effect of capital in its full capacity—racism, fascism, wealth distribution disparity, exploitation, apolitical profanity, commodification, etc.

That being said, a neologism such as *archeicism* could be used as a form of description for a specific method of institutional and epistemological construction of the *arche*, a higher purpose constructed from the pure, given, profit driven, politically and ideological non-articulated effect of the relation between capital and its humanist "back up" in the form of democracy and/or its iterations. In this sense, the epistemological, institutional and representational operations entailed within this process represents a shift from biopolitical to necropolitical governance—institutionalization of the form of rule and of a hegemonic epistemology that bases its ideological nucleus on the ideologization of processes which inflict death and integrate acts of murder and extreme commodification into its ethical and humanist register.

This *archeic* or *necro-archeic* operation not only eradicated the political function of power that called for production of the people or for institutionalization of society through the political process, it normalized the perception of social reality as separated from capital, which ultimately turned the act of frivolous interpretation of the same reality into a pinnacle of political prominence. Additionally, this has made the most serious effect of capital (colonial, racist) murder for profit look like a jovial semifact that allegedly happened with no connection to capitalism or the epistemological regimes of the First World.

Consequently, or *a priori* for that matter, this meant that the erasure of all political and ideological criteria—either in the exercise of power or in the process of making power legitimate—created another terrain on which criteria or prominence had been created in direct proportion to the transgressions created under the democratic aegis. Additionally, the same operation showed that the institutional and epistemological normalization of the effect of capital is simultaneously being instituted into the final limitation of the social struggle—producing the ultimate limitation as the pinnacle of the non-limitation of social antagonism.

The rejection of the politically ideological dimension in construction of the *arche* does not mean that the method of ascription of meaning as fundamental ideological operation has been erased. *Archeicism*, as a context that organized that ambiguity between *democracy* and *the democratic;* oppression and plurality; diversity and homogeneity; lack of political articulation as its surplus, has been/or is being inaugurated into an ideological eligibility, tangibility and viability, and by that logic, into a purposeful context in its own right.

This temporal, continuous process of mixing, twisting, and perverting of contingencies of humanism, freedom, etc., evolved from being fixed on a specific set of meanings into an *arche* that derives its substantial ideological material out of such a dynamism itself.

In the end, the subsequent institutionalization and normalization of the mere dynamics through which mere effect is being produced into ideological *arche*, has been represented as historical progression, a modernist, *universal* super narrative which was, in an openly hegemonic manner, found to be the only way to provide a substantial foundation for the future of the capitalist order.

NOTES

1. Although Schmitt's elaborations on the nature of sovereignty were influenced by his personal theism (which, we speculate, affected his comparison of the symbolical figure of God and the personalized figure of a sovereign) and despite his flirting with reactionary concepts, the idea that a link existed between the processes of derogation of the personal dimension of sovereignty and the diminishing of the interventionist dimensions of political power, surely implied that the antagonist aspect of the relation between the ruler and the ruled was deprived of its politically ideological aspects.

2. Lack of freedom of speech, critique of authoritarianism, critique of lack of democracy, freedom of speech, etc.

3. In the same way in which dissidents from *splinter* states such as Iran, Cuba, etc. are produced into almost instant prominence in the West.

4. Documentary movie *Chasing Madoff* (Jeff Proserrman 2011, Cohen Media Group) might serve as an paradigmatic example of this tendencies.

5. Harki (adjective from the Arabic harka, standard Arabic haraka حركة, "war party" or "movement," i.e., a group of volunteers, especially soldiers) is the generic term for Muslim Algerians loyalists who served as auxiliaries in the French Army during the Algerian War from 1954 to 1962. The phrase sometimes extends to cover all Algerian Muslims who supported the French presence in Algeria during this war. In France, the term is used to designate the Franco-musulmans rapatriés ("repatriated French Muslims") community living in the country since 1962, and its metropolitan born descendants. In this sense, the term Harki now refers to a distinct ethnocultural group, that is, French Muslims, distinct from other French of Algerian origin or Algerians living in France (Wikipedia 2013). In regard to the contemporary status of Harki relates issues, check an article "France forced to confront betrayal" (Jeffries 2001).

6. Slovenian journalist Sebastjan Leban has in this context noticed "If by any chance the reader stops at chapter 11 with the title *European union on the world stage* and the subtopic on Africa one will immediately notice that there is a basic discrepancy between the written general concern for the developing nation and the diction used to describe it. By referring to the period of colonization and stating that the relations between Europe and sub-Saharan Africa dated a long way back, and that decolonization, which began in the early 1960s turned this link into a different kind of association between sovereign countries, means to proclaim that the master-slave dialectics ceases to exist within the limits of (de)colonization. Nowhere in the text either the colonizers or the guilty are mentioned or a clear condemnation of colonization can be found together with the atrocities it brought about. No, the EU condemned Communism and Socialism putting them side by side with Fascism and Nazism, but it is incapable of condemning its own genealogy of horror" (Leban 2012).

7. We acknowledge a vast amount of geopolitical, historical, and political differences that might have led to turmoil these countries in specific time period went through. Libya's inner anti-Gaddafi uprising in 2011, and interior stability Saddam's regime managed to sustain prior to invasion of Iraq in 2003 are obviously different preconditions that preceded the regime changes and consequent *instabilities* in those countries. In the same way, wars in ex-Yugoslavia could not be seen as directly imported from the outside as well as anti-Soviet sentiment in Eastern Europe was not completely imposed from the West. But, we are here basing our premise on those common denominators that, as ideological subtexts, influenced (the motives and/or the results) of an open outside aggression (in case of Iraq), a mixture of outside aggres-

sion and internal revolution (in case of Libya) and in case of Eastern Europe where virtually all post–Wall revolutions led to adoption of free market economy and capitalist democracy which are those common denominators we've mentioned.

ELEVEN

The Revival of Ideological Firmness: Racial-State and the Formalization of Necropolitics

Given that political, economic and military power that resides in the European Union (or in the First World in general) is the power of particular states, it is hard to see the Union as a collective institutionalization of some political agenda that has surpassed either the logic of capital, or the dominance of epistemologies grounded in Eurocentric ideologies.

Since the logic of capital constitutes the main logical matrix upon which contemporary rule of global capitalism is being based upon, the role Eurocentric racial epistemologies play within this dimension contributed greatly to the sustainment of racial hierarchies within the hierarchies of exploitation and to the representation of capitalism as the system that exploits all in the same way. The *post-ideological* or *post-racial* prefixes First World ideologies like to assign to themselves showed that the racial hierarchies were reorganized accordingly, and to that measure to which First World's capitalism has succeeded to universalize its own particular agenda and to normalize racism as an institutional discourse within modern democratized narratives.

The expansion of the EU in the last twenty years was clearly marked with the simultaneous expansion of a single model of political and economic rule: capitalist free market democracy. The same model did not mark the end of the nation-state, although it profoundly influenced relations between the state with supranational capital that is beginning to assume its dominant form; under the umbrella of democratic formalism. As Subhabrata Bobby Banerjee noticed in his analysis of the paradigmatic changes in relation between the state and capital in contemporary globalization:

225

Rather than marking the death of the nation-state as some theorists of globalization like to argue, the global economy is premised precisely on a system of nation-states. Neoliberal globalization can be seen as a marker for the final hegemonic triumph of the state mode of production. The nation-state then is a fundamental building block of globalization, in the working of transnational corporations, in the setting-up of a global financial system, in the institution of policies that determine the mobility of labor, and in the creation of the multi-state institutions such as the UN, IMF, World Bank, NAFTA and WTO. (Banerjee 2009, 10-11)

It seems that the dichotomy, or alleged dichotomy among supranational and national states was produced on the basis of the formula that had allowed nation-States (on the Euro-Atlantic axis) to both represent their own particular interests as being subjugated to the allegedly neutral international circulation of capital and to present the contemporary colonial procedures as an "innocent," yet most "propulsive," dimension in the global spread of capitalism. As Banerjee noticed:

Old patterns of imperialism can be seen in the dominance of neoliberal policies in today's global political economy. Transnational corporations often wield power over Third World countries through their enticements of foreign investment and their threats to withhold or relocate these investments. In return for foreign investments and jobs, corporations are able to extract from impoverished and often corrupt Third World governments tax concessions, energy and water subsidies, minimal environmental legislation, minerals and natural resources, a compliant labor force and the creation of Special Economic Zones (SEZ) which are essentially states of exception where the law is suspended in order for the business of economic extraction to continue. (Banerjee 2009, 10-11)

These states of exception entail not only the evasion of the constitutional dimension of the law of mainstream institutional discourse, they themselves are embroiled in procedures of the expansion/reorganization of capital, with this reorganization being something that surpasses the mere process of maximization of the profit.

For instance, in case of post-socialist Eastern Europe, the most ideologically prominent buzz word in the last twenty years or so, *Euro-Atlantic integration*, carried a cluster of positive meanings that equated the amount of infiltration of capital and the level of attained democratic freedom. In other words, democracy was institutionalized as an epistemological and institutional aureole of legitimacy for those sorts of freedoms that allowed, firstly, local ethno-nationalist reactionary policies to ravage, both materially and epistemologically, the state as a political organization and secondly, that allowed the bourgeoisie, neoliberal elites to legitimize the processes that normalized infiltration of foreign capital and their own accumulation of profit at the expense of every social dimension of the state. As Banerjee stated:

Imperial formations in the contemporary political economy are more "efficient" in the sense that formal colonies no longer need to be governed. Imperialism has learned to manage things better by using the elites of the former colonies to do the governing, and the structural power of supranational institutions like the World Trade Organization, World Bank and International Monetary Fund and markets to do much of the imperial work. (Banerjee 2009, 10-11)

Clearly, the lack of need for explicit political governance from outside instituted auto-colonialism, and became the cornerstone of epistemologies based on equalization of democracy and capitalism in which complicity to one's own subjugation meant that the political vision and interpretation of the function of the state was also subjected to this servile sensibility. As Achille Mbembe, post-colonial theoretician and the author of the concept of the necropolitical has noticed:

Unlike certain Western experiences, the extension of the role of the state and the market was thus not automatically achieved through the disruption of old social ties. In a number of cases, state domination—or the *étatisation* of society—was achieved through the old hierarchies and old patronage networks. Two consequences of this process merit mention. On the one hand, it paved the way, more then occured in other parts of the world, to an *unprecedented privatization of public prerogatives*. On the other, it not only allowed a degree of socialization of state power generally poorly understood by analysts, but also the *correlative socialization of arbitrariness*. (Mbembe 2001, 32)

Although Mbembe is referring to post-colonial Africa, the principles behind these procedures might be clearly seen in the context of their specific application in the post-colonial era globally, within the processes of globalization of capitalism in general. As an example, we can take a look at the principles on which the expansion of the EU is based in the context of Mbembe's remarks. Hence, the auto-colonial paradigm in a number of Eastern and Southeastern European states (whether public institutions were nominally privatized or not), was marked by the infiltration of state institutions. In most cases reactionary patronage networks (functioning as ethnic, nepotist, or merely criminal agents) progressively degraded the social prerogatives of the state to the level on which privatization by capital was represented as the salvation and as a token of the fight against the "old, corrupted, socialist patronage networks"; a token of inscription of inherent criminal nature to the overall political program of the left wing.

Mbembe's *socialization of arbitrariness*, in this context, was an institutional and ideological operation that stripped politically ideological prerogatives from the interpretation of the role of the social dimension of society. Processes of socialization in an apolitical society, were, therefore, devised as processes that only socialize *arbitrariness* in relation to the epistemological, institutional and power discourses that have, in the first place, produced the *social* as a mere framework in which experiences of either complacency or resentment could oscillate; with no connection to these discourses. This arbitrariness consequentially received the form of various populist sentiments that interpreted the effect of capital as the symptom of an insufficient amount of privatization and/or as the symptom of *insufficient* arbitrariness in formation of political institutional discourses.

That being said, the socialization of arbitrariness is actually a process in which political prerogatives of the state (that could have acted as a barrier to capital) were ideologically stigmatized, while the prerogatives for determination of the meaning of the effect of capital were delegated to society as an apolitical reactionary conglomeration.

The populist or moral majority in Europe, now (in the fallout of the 2008 debt crisis) tends to find resolution to its own class predicament (created by capital) by ethnic/racial cleansing of the labor market and reactionary interpretations of the function of the political. This point is demonstrated by how capital was interpreted in a racial context where the European populist masses saw it as problematic because it increased the level of exploitation of them.[1]

At the same time, dominant sentiment in various eastern EU members or aspirants for joining the EU, especially in the former Yugoslavia, began to perceive Europe or the West in general *only* as the institutional embodiment of dogmatic reactionary values, completely neglecting, slandering and denying the history of western revolutionary struggles. In Croatia, for example, the EU had been seen by the moral majority as the procurer of modernity to that measure to which the EU (as a whole and/ or some of its more prominent members) tolerated the Croatian fascist project (formation of the post-socialist state on basis of institutional and ideological enunciation of radical ethnocentric, right-wing nationalism), while in Serbia, the EU was (is) being slandered because the moral majority saw it as too multicultural and as a betrayal of the idea of a national-socialist Europe that would allegedly have embraced the Serbian fascist, genocidal project (Greater Serbia). It should be noted that the apologetics of the Serbian fascist project have, for some time now, been trying to infiltrate, or "sell" their project as if they have been a part of some anti-globalist or anti-imperialist struggle. However, this is nothing but an attempt to make relative a genuine fascist project (which was tackled by the First World not because it was a fascist project, but because it threatened the First World's regional dominions).

The processes of *socialization of the state* (as symptoms of the demise of the political state) legitimized the arbitrariness in the interpretation of the function of politics and utilized the state as a mere pacifier of patronage networks and as a tool for privatization of public prerogatives. At the same time, such a socializing impetus redefined the hierarchies of rule as being those that would formalize the effects of capital by further destroying the barriers to capitalist infiltration of the whole field of the social.

Socialization of the state for that matter, should be seen as a procedure that deprives the political rule of its political dimension, and hence a procedure that, under the pretense of social sensibility, formats the notion of the social within a racial/organicist image in collusion with either capitalist or racist ideologies that organize their differential nature of exploitation. Thus, the *socialization of the state* (as an epistemological mechanism that *socializes* the banishment of the role that political ideologies should play in the production of society) contributed to the false perception of capitalism as the system whose transgressions are incidental, not inherent and systemic.

In regard to the perpetration of this perception, the institutions of civil society in both the First World and its colonial peripheries (or semi-peripheries) could be seen as institutional reflections of those ideological narratives that tend to dislocate the origin of various social predicaments into the field of mere dysfunctions of capitalism. This *dislocating* tendency should not be seen in the guise of an ideology, but as a depoliticizing procedure that deprives the political and ideological aspects of their origins as well as their social predicament. These procedures contribute to the perception of commodification as separate from the main, democratic institutional discourses under which the same commodification has been organized.

In general, the notion of the *civil society*, as defined by Eurocentric institutions, presents a part of the context in which class and political prefixes to social struggles were replaced by social, sexual, religious, and identity prefixes, which generally implied that these struggles should be poised only to fight for a higher degree of emancipation within the capitalist hierarchies of exploitation.

It is noticeable that within European public discourse, the EU is increasingly being referred to as the community of its *people*, rather than *political subjects* (states and political societies), which implies that citizen subjectivities are increasingly being perceived by institutions as cultural, biological, religious and racial rather than political contingencies. In the context of the demise of the political dimensions of the state this is important because the imposition of the biological pretext to the interpretation of the function of the political, institutionalized the presumption that society was (is) primarily a biological, ethno-centric community, not a political community.

The Eurocentric focus on the issues of integration is therefore nothing more than rationalization of the racial criteria in approach to the definitions of citizen's rights. In a hypothetical scenario in which integration (as defined by mainstream discourses), would be achieved, those racially segregated would still be considered as subversive elements that undermine the society (now from inside) which, after all, was the exact thing that happened to *completely integrated* Jews (before the Holocaust) who were, among other things, found guilty of too much integration (or "stealthy subversions" as historical Nazis would have put it).

The fact that the oppressive apparatus (of the capitalist state) in internal affairs tends to single out racially or religiously non-European (non-white, non-Christian) subjectivities while at the same time the apparatus of foreign affairs is being used for colonial resource extraction under the guise of help to those who are already discriminated against in Europe, only demonstrates the Eurocentric racial style of differentiation in approach to the definition of the society constitutes European institutional discourse as biopolitical, or more precisely *necropolitical.*

In the wider context, if biopolitics as a ruling paradigm was, aside from other implications, based on the differentiation of forms of life, necropolitics, as Achille Mbembe has defined it presents: "The notion of necropolitics and necropower to account for the various ways in which, in our contemporary world, weapons are deployed in the interest of maximum destruction of persons and the creation of *death-worlds,* new and unique forms of social existence in which vast populations are subjected to conditions of life conferring upon them the status of *living dead*" (Mbembe 2003, 40).

If we take a look at necropolitics as *historicization of biopolitics* (Gržinić 2009c, 22-24) it could now be seen as the paradigm of rule that differentiates among the amounts of death that could be inflicted for the sake of either capitalist maximization of profit or the sustainment of the monopoly on the definition of civilization. This means that systematic infliction of death, as both the strategy and the effect of capital, now constitutes the dominant ideological paradigm in the establishment of global hierarchies of exploitation within which capitalist racist/racialist ideologies are being imposed as the ultimate forms of differentiation in an allegedly *consensual* global modernist project. As Banerjee noticed:

> Thus, rather than marking the "death of the nation state," globalization as capitalist imperialism is dependent on a system of multiple states which required a new doctrine of "extra-economic, and especially military, coercion." The ability to deploy extra-economic coercive power is analogous to "Operation Infinite War," a Hobbesian "state of war" which to quote Hobbes "consisteth not in actual fighting, but in the known disposition thereto during all the time there is no assurance to the contrary.'" (Banerjee 2006)

The deployment of extra legal measures, which are in harmony with the normalization of the state of exception (in short, the discarding of the constitutional dimension of the law), are actually completely in tune with the institutional and epistemological rationalization of the extra economic, colonial measures in force for the maximization of profit for the First World. In other words, the "infinite war" (the infinite First World's ravaging of the overexploited world) did not represent a symptom of the demise of the nation-State, it represented a symptom of the reorganization of the nation-State on the level at which the imposition of Eurocentric racist ideologies were entangled with First World imperialism—and represented just another protagonist in the allegedly post-ideological neutral process of the global circulation of capital.

This does not mean that the European democratic discourse (in general) has failed, it means that the same European democratic discourse (to a large degree) was utilized as the formalistic context under which the capitalist calculus and Eurocentric racism could situate their own particular agendas at the core of the allegedly universal modernist project.

DEMOCRATIZATION OF COLONIAL EPISTEMOLOGIES

Walter Mignolo, prominent decolonial theoretician whose profound analysis (in great measure) focuses on a structural relation between colonial epistemology and modernity suggested that:

> There is no modernity without coloniality; coloniality is constitutive of modernity. Modernity is not a historical period, but it is a rhetoric grounded on the idea of salvation by the agents telling the story and placing themselves at the last moment of a global historical development and carrying the flag and the torch toward the bright future of humanity. The rhetoric of modernity has been, since its inception, the rhetoric of salvation: by conversion (Spanish and Portuguese mendicant orders), by civilizing missions (British and French agents); by development and modernization (U.S. experts in economy and politics guiding the Third World towards the same standards as the First); and salvation through market democracy and consumerism. (Mignolo 2008, 20-22)

In accordance with this, the concept of *salvation* implies that contemporary colonial institutional and epistemological discourses have not just ascribed the license for interpretation of modernity to Eurocentric agents, (i.e., to itself), but have also imposed a monopoly over the definition of civilization to those who were (are) delivering *salvation* through the currently dominant model of capitalist exploitation, neoliberalism in a democratic package.

While the basis of sovereignty in the First World states still resides in material and military power, the sovereignties of the peripheral states were put in direct proportion to compliance with the dictate of capital and consequently, to the First World's interests.

This fractioned sovereignty referred to, as Mbembe stated, paraphrasing, the tutelary government exercised by the World Bank, International Monetary Fund, and private and public lenders was no longer limited to imposing respect for broad principles and macro-economic balances. In practice, as Mbembe notices, paraphrasing, the tutelage of international creditors was considerably strenghtened and now involves a range of direct interventions in domestic economic management.

So, since it is obvious that the supranational/national state dichotomy in capitalism is fake, the democracies that fostered *fractioned sovereignty* formatted and/or downscaled their own sovereign prerogatives to a level where they function as an impotent set of institutions whose function becomes potent only in the organization of conditions for legitimization of the interest of capital and following racial ideologies that determine the levels of exposure to either commodification or death.

The role of democratic formalism in its relation to the apparatus of the state, in this sense, became the role of disruption of those politically coercive aspects that would have tackled social inconsistencies without relying exclusively on the logic of the market.

Thus, the notion of rights in neoliberal democratic discourses, the market driven economy or in capitalism in general for that matter, was not contextualized in relation to the political forms of dissent that would have tackled the economical and ideological super-narratives, but were institutionalized in relation to demobilization of the politically ideological aspects of the state in favor of sustaining a range of organizations and/ or agencies that would substitute the state in the protection of the rights of those deemed, not as political subjects or citizens, but commodities.[2] As Achille Mbembe noticed:

> By doing everything possible to dismantle state intervention in the economy (such as controls, subsidies, protection), without making the state more efficient and without giving it new, positive functions, the result has been that the state's (already very fragile) material base has been undermined, the logics underlying the building of coalitions and clienteles have been upset (without being positively restructured), its capacities for reproduction have been reduced, and the way has been opened for it to wither away. (Mbembe 2001, 75)

This is not only a question of the extent to which the democratic state organized its demise as a political entity in favor of the circulation of capital, but this is also a question of how the interchange between the prerogatives of capital and the democratic state have been organized. Hence, while the dominant epistemological logic in capitalist democracy treats the effect of capital as the non-systemic, incidental property assigned to the erraticism in circulation of capital, systematic formalization of the effect of capital (wealth disparity, class differences, institutional racism) is being regarded as incidental only if it fails to completely institutionalize the same effect.

Since the aseptic political impotency of democratic formalism, by design, functions as a context in which attempts at social transformation are kept within the institutional and ideological frames dictated by capital, the informal dimension that secures unlimited approach to all spheres of life has consequently been delegated to the capitalist power structure and equated to the non-limitation of social and individual freedoms (as long as they secured the destruction of barriers to capital and the destruction of barriers to institutional normalization of racialization as the dominant paradigm in formation of the differentiations within the context of social struggles).

THE *TELOS* OF A RACIST DEMOCRACY

So, since racism as the constitutive element of Eurocentric epistemologies and its institutions continues to be an instrument that contaminates and diverts social conflict into a field of race, culture, and identity, it also continues to obfuscate capitalism if seen as Christian project of dispossession. According to Walter Mignolo:

> Since the sixteenth century and the modern/colonial foundation of racism, certain regions of the world, and people dwelling within it, were classified as "lesser." Who was in the position to classify? Not Black Africans, American-Indians or Arabic Muslims. No, they were classified, but had no say in the classification. The classification, and success, was invented and implemented by Western Christian theologians, and later on, by secular philosophers and scientists. Thus, knowledge was cast as *universal*, although it was created and enacted in one region (Western Christianity) and by a particular community of bodies (White Males publicly assuming the rightfulness of heterosexuality). (Mignolo 2008, 20-22)

From the perspective of his analysis of how capitalist exploitation hierarchies and colonial, racial epistemologies complement each other, Walter Mignolo noticed that:

> It so happened that human agents who controlled knowledge and money had the authority (not necessarily the power) to classify and manage sectors of the human population. Their authority was an invisible structure that was nevertheless imprinted on their bodies and minds. That invisible structure has been described as "the colonial matrix of power" in its synchronic as well as diachronic dimensions. (Mignolo 2009b, 75)

The concept of racialization that Marina Gržinić introduced into the decolonial theory of the Southeast European region (Gržinić 2009) in 2009, in the context of her articulation of paradigmatic shifts from biopolitical to necropolitical paradigms in organization of rule (of global capitalism), represents the ultimate form of racism. Racialization is a racist super narrative or an internal clock of capitalist hierarchies of exploitation which, by differentiating among the privileges delegated to racialized subjects, keeps them pitted against each other which ultimately blocks the formation of politically ideological antagonisms that would be pitted against capitalist and colonial epistemologies and First World's imperial racism.

The aspect of racist mechanism of differentiation (racialization), which is important in the context of the meaning of the erasure of the distance between the oppressors and the oppressed is that aspect of racialization that functions as a device for the dislocation of the basis of antagonism into a field of body-politics or those necropolitical[3] procedures that imprint both the designated racial role and the motives of the subjugator on the subjugated.

The designation of a racial role is clearly a process in which "qualities" are determined on a biological basis, more precisely, on an axiomatic, already determined basis (skin color, religion, place of origin), in which some inherent trait of life is being perceived as the carrier of either rational qualities or irrational criminal traits. Of course, inherent rational qualities are assigned to those of white European/Christian descent whose transgressions are interpreted as belonging to the register of an incident, while the transgressions of the others, depending on the level of "racial prominence" delegated to them, are interpreted within the register of systematic inherency. However, the aspect of racialization in regard to imprinting of the motives of the subjugators to the (racially) subjugated, presents a token of inclusion of the subjugated into the project of globalization of capitalism in which the eradication of political antagonism between the rulers and the ruler was produced into a precondition of that inclusion.

The aim of these institutional and epistemological processes of depoliticization was to shift the focal point from where the authoritarian dimension of political power was being derived onto the terrain on which political power was interpreted as the mechanism of rule among already determined meanings that were added to diversities. Since the extremes of the subsequent social struggles among these diversities were defined as potent only to change positions within the racial matrix, the political purpose of these struggles was defined as the struggle that only strives to get close to the master, which determines "democratic qualities" in accordance to racial criteria—while the lack of the distance between the master and the slave, created amidst these processes, served as a subversion of struggles based on political sorts of antagonism. Additionally, the flexibility of the First World's racial epistemologies to include diversities as racially determined conglomerations was represented as a pillar of liberalization within the rigidness of the First World. Therefore, colonial epistemology had formatted the process of globalization of capitalism as the context in which a higher degree of depoliticization of the subjugate's predicament guaranteed an increase in the levels of intimacy with the First World's master. This does not mean that the racially profiled subjugater/subaltern was allowed to penetrate into those aspects of hierarchies

of rule that would allow control over the meaning of such a differentiation, they were allowed only to struggle for lesser amounts of commodification.

The equalization of Eurocentric ideologies and the project of modernity meant that the sustainment of Western Christian based theology or,
more precisely, epistemic logocentrism focused on perpetration of the
central role of European man at the core of Eurocentric racial epistemology was put in progressive positive relation with those parts of modernist
legacy, emancipation, secularization, etc., which were defined not as politically antagonist tools that would have tackled racial ideologies and the
primacy of Eurocentrism within the same ideologies, but as methods of
further representing of capitalism as the (only) modernist project.

Of course, since the First World's motives in imposition of its version
of modernity or democracy are influenced primarily by the geopolitical
calculus and the logic of capital, it was not surprising the complete set of
contradictions were entailed in the rationalization of its colonial exploits.[4] However, the entanglement of First World's, especially European
Union's institutional and epistemological discourses with the church was
much more systematic and less contradictory.

While these discourses systematically wipe out the fundamental political dimension of modernity as well as the distance between the church
and the state, they also function as an epistemological instrument that
posited Christian ethics and versions of morality into an allegedly antagonist position toward those effects of capital that actually never existed
(freedom of movement for *all* people). This serves as the instrument that
institutionally formats the proper European states or EU in general as the
"natural" organization that is primarily based on biologistic/organistic/
religious criteria in determination of the amount of its citizens rights: race
and religion, that according to Eurocentric ideology, were deemed as
carriers of abilities, rationality, and democratic potentials.

Additionally, epistemological utilization of those aspects of Christian
theology in regard to the concepts of forgiveness, mercy, love, etc., that
were installed into the perception of justice as transcendental category
(which allowed *forgiveness* to be exercised only toward Eurocentric fascist
transgressions), are now also used as a rationale that justifies the historical revisionism that in Europe equates the fascist and communist ideological projects, which is an ongoing operation that consequently rehabili-
tates colonial and fascist genocides, legalizes racial criteria in employment of oppressive power and institutes racial crimes into the democratic
normative as if they were some universal, mutual human legacy.

In Eastern Europe something similar is happening, where for instance,
democratic changes were allowed to the Catholic church in Croatia to
openly apotheosize a number of Nazi collaborators from the World War
II, as in Serbia, where as a result of intense nationalistic and/or openly
fascist politics in the last twenty years, a number of WWII Nazi collabora-

tors were or are being institutionally and epistemologically rehabilitated as, perversely enough, "anti-fascists."

However, there is another dimension to all of this. Democratization, liberalization and secularization of a colonized country was put in terms in which the First World's version of modernity was accepted as the only one possible. This process actually entailed the banishment of all transcendental elements from the political visions of those subjected that could have or would have tackled the universality of the First World's rationality.

This means that all those elements, especially those non-secular elements that could have been utilized as the dimensions of decolonial struggle (that would transcend capitalism as the apotheosized universal project) were (are) being banished and ascribed into the pre-modern register. On the other hand, all those non-secular elements that tended to collude with capital and colonial epistemologies were ascribed to a modernist register, but only to that measure to which the Eurocentric First World's monopoly on definition of the purpose of civilization and modernist progress has been allowed to pose as the position that determined the amount of *modernist prominence*, ergo racial "prominence" of that non-secular tendency.

Hence, secularization in the context of contemporary colonialism does not serve as a political instrument that politicizes the state or elevates the interpretations of social predicaments into the class context, but it functions as typical colonial instrument that discards politically ideological angles of social predicaments in favor of particular materials and ideological interests of the First World and its hypocrisy in the institutionalization of secularity.[5]

For instance, there was a recent decision brought by the European Court of Human Rights that legitimized the crucifix in Italian public schools, stating (in the court's decision) that: "The Court found that, while the crucifix was above all a religious symbol, there was no evidence before the Court that the display of such a symbol on classroom walls might have an influence on pupils" (European Court of Human Rights 2011).

So, how can one have *proof* that some symbolical contingency had made *tangible* influence? Of course that crucifix as an object of wood and metal does not make any influence, but the Human Rights Court bluntly neglected or even denied the existence of its symbolical order whatsoever. The symbolical disposition of a Christian crucifix in the public school (in an allegedly secular country) therefore clearly implies that Christianity in Europe should be seen as that conglomeration that can *tolerate* other religions, but itself cannot be an object of critique.

Hence, it was stated by the Court that "There was nothing to suggest that the authorities were intolerant of pupils who believed in other religions, were non-believers or who held non-religious philosophical convictions" (European Court of Human Rights 2011). But, it was *only* the Christian crucifix that hung in the classroom, as there should be no religious symbols in a secular country at all or there should be all of them. So, according to this insane logic, pictures of Hitler, pictures of Nazis or a picture of Columbus could as well be placed in the classrooms Europewide because there is no *evidence* that those *pictures*, as such, killed anyone, because there is no evidence that the *pictures* of Nazis committed genocide and because it was not the *picture* of Columbus that initiated the colonial holocausts in the Americas.

Of course, primacy given to Christian versions of morality and ethics by hegemonic European institutional and epistemological discourses added to the perception of the state and the society as *rooted* into some supra-historical biopolitical container that defined the society and/or the state as natural, not political conglomeration. If the "natural traits" are being perceived as a reflection of some divine right that surpasses political processes, then the largest amount of natural traits were ascribed by Europe as based on Christian roots to itself. Consequently, only the carriers of such natural traits were converted into carriers of natural rights to devise the ways through which such *naturality* would be embedded into the modernizing processes. The natural traits of the others, on the other hand, were (are) being perceived as inherent and as such deemed as *transcendable* or *civilizable* only with the help of Europeans.

This is actually a clear case of the reinstating of ethno-centrism (*Volksgemeinschaft*) into the core of modernity as defined by contemporary Eurocentric ideologies (within the EU), that, now after multiculturalism has so conveniently "failed" (as German chancellor Angela Merkel put it on one occasion in 2011), continues to be a constitutive basis on which the same ideologies organize epistemological interpretations and institutional policies in regard to processes of emancipation and pluralism.

So, the distinctive ways in which identities are multiplied, transformed and put into circulation, implies that the function of a political power has already been defined by the contemporary Eurocentric imaginings as the kind of power that should only function as an organizer of diversities, identities, etc. within the already determined limits of political possibilities.

Hence, the notion of political power was, along with the processes of liberalization of capitalism, imagined as that type of antagonistic agency that should organize only the ways in which subjectivities are trying to improve their distinctiveness within the hierarchies of exploitation. Of course, proper Eurocentric subjectivity does not have a problem with exploitation when *the other* is exploited, *or even* when he/her is commodified, but only as long as the racial hierarchies of exploitation situate the European on a racial scales "higher" then Arabs, Africans, Mexicans, etc.

Consequently, political power was, by proper European democratic discourses, imagined as the power that allowed the concept of *rights* to be

contextualized as non-separable from an axiomatic set of values determined by biological and ultimately provincial and tribal perceptions of
society that should only legitimize power that would depoliticize general
struggles for power in favor of struggles for positioning within the hierarchies of exploitation.

Mbembe noticed how, in post-colonialism, paraphrasing, state power
creates, through administrative and bureaucratic practices, its own world
of meanings—a master code that, while becoming the society's central
code, ends by governing, perhaps paradoxically the logics that underlie
all other meanings within that society. Since the state power and/or the
power of the state in the First World does not create any particular political agenda that would tackle already set limits of a social conflict, any
master code it created could be seen as a congregation of meanings that
separated such power from its effect and from it as being part of a political process in general.

Hence, what posits the European Union in its role of racist colonial
agent is its own epistemological monopoly on the definition of itself as
the one that cannot be judged. Santiago Castro-Gómez saw the position
the First World assigned to itself as "'The hubris of the zero-point': the
knowledge of the observer who cannot be observed" (Castro-Gómez
quoted in Mignolo, 2008).

Aside the other implications of this remark, what was officially forbid-
den to challenge or depart from in the First World was its specific notion
of *dissent* that was, along with the processes of liberalization of capitalism, converted into a sub-narrative of complicity, not into a form of political antagonism. As such, this dissent primarily tends to function as a *fail
safe* heuristic device that, through its repetitive singularization of the perpetrators, tackles only the specific executioners of (political, financial,
military) power, not the epistemological, material and ideological basis
and origins of that power.

In that sense, the problem with the European left (in general), or more
generally the "resentment" in Europe does not lie in its failure to recognize the social and political effects of the capital, the problem lies in its
interpretation of that effect as separate from, both the monopoly on the
definition of the humanist projects such as democracy and as separate
from the inherent, systemic, non-incidental cannibalistic, and racist nature of capitalism and its ideologies.

Consequently, if the logic of such a democratic resentment resides in
compliance with the perception of capital as universal project that exploits everyone the same or with the perception of the function of political power as limited by the ideologies of Eurocentric epistemological
hegemonies, then the politically antagonist *forte* of such a resentment can
only contribute to the further ideologization of the non-limitations of
capital and of its separation from history as a political process. So, the
consequent banishment of political ideology resulted in a kind of demo-

cratic *telos* that was based on distortion of the adversarial link between the basic dichotomies in the cosmology of power—the dominator and the dominated.

BETWEEN ZERO AND INFINITY

The iterations of various kinds of systemic or subjective non-limitations in diversification of the experience of living or dying under capitalist hegemony are also functioning as ideological/epistemological elements that provide ideological substance to the purpose of those diversifications.

Hence, it seems that the mere quantitative property of possibilites for such iterations—that could be seen either as a form of inclusion into the hierarchies of exploitation, or as a form in which exploitation was organized—have been, in direct proportion, put in equal relation to the alleged existence of political and ideological substances behind which those procedures allegedly should have lead to.

The concept of the *new limit* or a concept of a *new frontier* that so intensively saturates the paradigmatic vision of proper western democratic man, although in an imprecise and metaphorical manner, does reflect the evading nature of elusiveness of the politically ideological substantiality within capitalism as a social order.

Although Alain Badiou's work does not exactly qualify as decolonial theory, we rely to author's articulation of the, so to say, epistemological principles invested in dominant patterns of discernability of the *order* in relation to differentiation and interpretation of that *order*. Badiou noted that:

> The qualitative "something" is, itself, discernible insofar as it has its other in itself. The quantitative "something" is, on the other hand, without other, and consequently *its determinateness is indifferent*. Let's understand this as stating that the quantitative One is the being of the pure One, which does not differ from anything. *It is not that it is indiscernible: it is discernible amidst everything, by being the indiscernible of the One.* What founds quantity, what discerns it, is literally the indifference of difference, the anonymous One. (Badiou 2005, 167)

The *Anonymous One* is seen, not as an ever-eluding aim or an ever-eluding political possibility, but simply as a politically non-substantial, purely ideological dimension located at the core of the democratic-capitalist normative. Such a normative not only depoliticizes the interpretation of origins of social predicaments, but also pacifies the scope, the far-ends of *resolutions* of that predicament(s).

These epistemological and institutional strategies demonstrated that it was not just the political prerogatives of the State that were derogated, but the same prerogatives were erased from the notion of political power

in general. In other words, some of the key prerogatives of political power—the production of society and the production of political ideologies
that surpass normative boundaries—were exchanged for policies that are
designed to merely reinvent society within already conformed narratives.

Thus, disqualification of the prerogatives of political power does not
function as a reduction, prohibition or as a dictate, but as an instrument
that actually frees the democratic subjugates to resent, but only as long as
their resentment reflects their desires for transgression of the limits to
consumption, not the transgression of the *values* sustained by dominant
capitalist epistemological narratives.

Mbembe has stated that, paraphrasing, state sovereignty as a colony
combined the weakness of, and inflation of, the notion of right: *weakness
of right* in that, in relation to power and authority, the colonial model was,
in both theory and practice, the exact opposite of the liberal model of
debate and discussion; *inflation of right* in that, except when deployed in
the form of arbitrariness and the right of conquest, the very concept of
right often stood revealed as a void.

For instance, a great deal of discussions (in the European public discourse) that accompanied the occupation of Iraq, Afghanistan, or the colonial nature of the intervention in Libya, in the majority of cases (critically) regarded only small aspects of the methodology of the conduct of
those wars, not their colonial nature. Hence, in such a way, this *inflation*
of the notion of right meant that the dislocation of the political calculus
into the context of non-specific reasoning was related only to the phan-
tom-like significance of procurement of democracy and the free market.
As an exchange for rejection of the politically ideological contextualization of rights, a void (as a break in connection of power and its effect) was
produced and *filled* with a myriad of human right protections (freedom of
speech, etc.), that were utilized only as means through which interplay of
capitalism and democracy would subject some society to practically colonial conditions.[6]

Despite the fact that the *filling* of the void with humanist agendas did
not protect any rights but those of the First World's interest in the maximization of profit, the ultimate positive trait given to such a hypocritical
approach to these issues served as an obfuscation of highly differential
and diversified criteria in employment of human rights issues.

For instance, as it was reported by *The Huffington Post* (Barzak 2011),
former French foreign minister Michèle Alliot-Marie paid a visit to Gaza
in 2011 to ask for the release of a single Israeli soldier held by Hamas in
spite of thousands of Palestinians being held in Israeli prisons. This did
not only reflect the utter ideological bias in approach to the definition of
totality in which rights should be protected, but this and similar cases
also reflect the ability of Eurocentric and/or capitalist racial ideologies to
differentiate within the racial containers it sustains.

The First World's support of Israel (more precisely of its right-wing), while at the same time the same First World (specifically Europe), simultaneously tolerates increasing number of anti-Semitic regimes and sentiments,[7] is not paradoxical, but exactly reflects the ability of First World epistemological hegemonies to sustain heterogenic property of a racist scale.

In this context, the support of Israel comes from the institutional discourses that derive their ideological coherence exactly from Eurocentric racial epistemologies that have been responsible for millennium long prosecution of Jews in Europe. Critique of Israel in the West tends to automatically be equated to anti-Semitism, while anti-Semitism has been identified as the only possible form of racism, which has allowed the Eurocentric First World's epistemology to pose not only as an post-racial agent, but as an openly racist institutional discourse. In regard to the fact that Eurocentric ideologies still inscribe inherent criminal traits on a racial basis, it is clear that the support of Israel comes from the same epistemological pool in which the Jews have been "promoted" to a higher position in direct proportion to which Israel's policies were actually the policies of the First World.[8]

The management of the interplay between the racial prefixes of protagonists and antagonists within global social struggles has removed politically ideological prefixes from the terrain on which differentiations are being produced and has produced the differentiation as utterly racially contextualized. The effect of such an epistemological and institutional normalization of depoliticized criteria, in approach to the meaning of differentiation, has contributed to the definition of what should be considered the proper result of social struggles.

Since the "proper" (white, heterosexual, Christian consumer) subjectivity is being regarded by Eurocentric racial ideology as the subject that inherently harbors rationality, the proper form of social realization of that rationality was seen in the form of apolitical, although less dispensable, commodity. On the other hand, those racially classified as carriers of irrationality (non-whites, non-Christians, and/or non-Western Christians for that matter) were (are) expected to either try to become commodifiable objects (never subjects), or be killed amidst Eurocentric racist colonial exploits and/or oppression.

This logic comprised a subtext of an empty experience of life in market democracy (in the First World) that realized itself as a repetitive pattern of a subjective search for either diversification in the commodification (in the case of lower classes) or a maximization of profit (in case of ruling classes). The extra-economic, ideological significance that was assigned to such a purpose was derived directly out of the amount of ideological traits inscribed to the way in which racial subjugation of the others and destruction of the overexploited world was being done.

The ascription of purpose to an experience of being a commodity through racist ideologies is an epistemological and institutional operation. An operation which, by constant reinvention of forms of subjugation and repetition of ascribing of such values, emulates the existence of social antagonism in general, or more precisely, imposes the racial prefix to the notion of social antagonism at the expense of political and class prefixes.

The repetition of this operation in the First World (that is been colloquially experienced as the lack of radical political changes and as the lack of politically ideological substantiality within attempts at social transformation) on one hand negates the ideological dimension (the systemic quality of a link between the regime that organizes and the exploitation), and on the other provides a variety of *possibilities* for various postmodern diversifications/dislocations of this unarticulated experience into a variety of imaginary and epistemological containers that, by their apolitical and/or purely ideological nature confirms only the utter homogenization of the world under capitalism and its racial ideologies.

As Marina Gržinić, in her analysis of paradigmatic principles invested in epistemological reproduction of the (global capitalist) order has noted, in reference to López Petit, "Postmodernism abolishes the distance and situates man inside the world that is made of signs and ahistorical languages. The global era oscillates this distance between zero and infinity. That is why there is the feeling of the absence of the world and at the same time we witness its over abundance" (Gržinić 2009b, 3-4).

If the abolishment of the distance is interpreted as the normalization of the abolishment of politically antagonistic dimensions of ideological discourses, the oscillation (seen here as the political process) was conformed and conditioned to function only between one or another iterations of the effect of capital. This means that the political process as the form in which political ideology is being derived was completely discarded in favor of the extraction of ideologies out of already determined roles in the global order.

Regarding the notion of infinity, it would be productive to recall what Badiou noted on that notion when he noted that, "The contraction in virtuality of repetition in the presence of that which repeats itself; a contraction named 'infinity' on the basis of the void in which the repetition exhausts itself" (Badiou 2005, 166).[9]

So, if the *void where the repetition exhausts itself* is the effect of capital that constantly needs more ideological purpose, the exhaustion of the repetition seems to have been coupled with the installation of more hegemonic traits to the infinite property of diversification. Simply stated, the, predicament created by the regime is being resolved with more of the same.

However, since the ideological substantiality that was derived from the infinity of repetitive diversifications remained elusive and kept getting exhausted, the nature of capitalism's search for hegemony had to be located on an axis that fixed both the point of departure and the point of arrival of any diversification at the place where any established coherence between the effect of capital and power would serve only in favor of increasing the hegemonic dimensions and purely ideological nature of the same power.

Consequently, non-limitations in diversifications of commodification in the First World, equated to the same notion of the non-limitations of the regime as the ideological viability of hierarchies of exploitation. Epistemological normalization of any non-limitation in making of profit, such are the exploitations imposed on the overexploited world, actually presents a surplus of the ideological purpose capitalism can derive.

As the notion of social conflict in capitalism was defined as a conflict without politically ideological dimensions (which of course does not exclude purely ideological conflicts), placing of the same conflict into a context in which it would infinitely repeat itself allowed capital to limit the far ends of that conflict and to make it potent only as a contribution to diversification of the same hierarchies of exploitation. Consequentially, the lack of substantiality of political purpose of such a conflict was simultaneously converted into a surplus of substantiality of power that a social conflict allegedly could not antagonize. In this way First World institutional and epistemological hegemonies tend to separate themselves from history and/or erase themselves as a politically tangible form of power.

Additionally, since the notion of infinity implies transcendence of the political prefix of historical time, the prerogative of infinite reorganization was assigned to institutional and power discourses that are based on this Eurocentric/Euro-Atlantic racial matrix that allegedly transcends the ramifications of the friction between power and its effect. In regard to Gržinić's premise, what was made infinite was the non-limitation of the ways in which capital and its racial ideologies would reorganize itself, while the value of a zero was assigned to the teleological dimension of capital and its own agents who pose as the base from which every diversity departs or should depart from.

Hence, the process of liberalization, which is at the nucleus of contemporary iterations of capital, actually functions as a method through which capital liberalizes its indefinite spread and through which capital equates its racial ideologies to modernity.

NORMALIZATION OF NECROPOLITICS

Therefore, contemporary Eurocentric colonial epistemologies, now reorganized under the democratic formalist umbrella, play an essential role in the First World's search for hegemony on the basis of institutional and epistemological construction of pure ideological discourse that is being situated as the distortion of the link between the effect of capital and the power discourses that are sustaining capitalism. In this context, the imposition of the prefixes of identity, culture and race as dominant prefixes of social conflict consequently situated *race* as that kind of position around which social antagonisms have congregated. As Achille Mbembe noticed:

> That *race* (or for that matter *racism*) figures so prominently in the calculus of biopower is entirely justifiable. After all, more so than class-thinking (the ideology that defines history as an economic struggle of classes), race has been the ever present shadow in Western political thought and practice, especially when it comes to imagining the inhumanity of, or rule over, foreign peoples. Referring to both this ever-presence and the phantom-like world of race in general, Arendt locates their roots in the shattering experience of otherness and suggests that the politics of race is ultimately linked to the politics of death. (Mbembe 2003, 17)

By *shattering experience of otherness*, the contemporary European experience represents therefore a shattering experience of the non-existence of any kind of political ideology that would have surpassed the utter provinciality of Eurocentrism, whose cosmopolitan dimension is being derived from infinite consumption of the surpluses of global wealth. Eurocentric ideologies are actually in fear of a political process. Eradication of politically ideological prerogatives in favor of prerogative given to racial prefixes of social conflict (that essentially accompany the ratio behind global colonial plunder), also served as a further mark of progression of the Eurocentric-Atlantic democratic state toward the racial-State—a necropolitical form of sovereignty that equates the amount of infliction of death and segregation to the amounts of achieved modernity.

From another perspective, the function of political power in the First World of capital in general ruptured along the lines where particular democratic dissent (with no regard to struggles for rule on politically ideological basis), became epistemologically and institutionally utilized as an instrument that equated the furthering of freedom with the shattering of limitations to capital.

The only coherent ideological experience this logic provided for paradigmatic democratic man was therefore the possibility of attaining a degree of distinctiveness in commodification (in simple terms said, for being *higher* on a consumption chain and/or being less exploited). This possibility was consequentially produced into an ideological corner stone on which such a notion of possibility was, in direct proportion, equaled with the notion of liberty, hence, with the possibility of attaining (more) liberty. The imposition of capitalist hierarchies of exploitation was therefore equaled with the creation of possibilities for attaining of more freedom and this is an ideological equation that inscribes other forms of differentiation among subjects, such is racism, into an ideological register that deems or tends to regard racism (as well as racially motivated institutional policies) as a "less elegant," yet allegedly non-ideologically motivated form of social differentiation. The multiplication of the possibilities for differentiation was therefore equaled with the multiplication of possibilities of differentiation but it was also the multiplication of the possibilities for exploitation (and rationalization of exploitation) that was equaled to the possibilities of attaining freedom which always comes tomorrow. This notion requires an additional angle of approach. Alain Badiou noted that: "The quantitative One, the indifferent One, which is number, is also multiple-ones, because its in-difference is also that of proliferating the same-as-self outside of self: the One, whose limit is immediately non-limit, realizes it self 'in the multiplicity external to self, which has as its principle or unity the indifferent One" (Badiou 2005, 168).

What non-limitation paradigmatic democratic man experiences as liberty is actually a form of non-limitation in consumption and a form of non-limitation in the normalization of racially motivated inflictions of death for the sake of profit within the necropolitical paradigm of rule. The sensibility of proper democratic subjectivity in Europe (and/or in First World of capital in general) was, metaphorically speaking, located in the ambiguity between possibilities and impossibilities. The impossible traits were inherently ascribed to the antagonisms on politically ideological and class bases, while the unlimited traits that were ascribed to the possibilities for infinite diversifications of exploitation were simultaneously instituted as the ideological purpose of such an order.

The processes of racialization (as the processes of reorganization of capital on a racial basis) are therefore processes of colonial infliction of death and subjugation as determined by racial ideologies of the First World, which are in turn processes of ideologization and institutionalization of race (as apolitical differentiation) into the normative core of epistemologies on the basis on which increase in hegemonization of global capitalist rule is equated to the increase of mutual, universal and modernist traits of that rule. The necropolitical normalization of the infliction of death for the sake of profit therefore received yet another status mark of distinction within the processes of the maximization of profit; it had developed into the only exercise of politics ideological capitalist racial system could have deployed.

Consequentially, it seems that the next phase of the reorganization of capital will take shape in the form of the further entanglement of capitalist institutions and humanist projects, in those forms of democracy that could formalize the intensification of the necropolitical effect of capital. In other words, it seems that the First World's search for hegemony will widen the scope of the processes of Eurocentric epistemological contamination of the conglomeration of meanings humanity represents which could lead only to the complete equalization of ideological project of humanism and the necropolitical form of capitalist rule (which is simply capitalism), hence to the complete normalization of the lack of distance between the rulers and the ruled.

NOTES

1. For instance, post-socialist democratization of Poland had entailed both the in-stitutionalization of the free-market agenda and the clero-fascist prohibition of abortion and segregation of sexual minorities. Sarkozy's neoliberal government in France in similar fashion engaged itself to liberalize the state's prerogatives while it deported Roma communities and segregated religious (mostly Muslim) minorities of Algerian origin as a means of sustaining populist diversion from political issues, Berlusconi's rule in Italy installed patronage as the precondition of assendence within the hierarchies of rule, Hungary's right-turn almost institutionalized anti-semitic and anti-Roma stances as the political normative, not to mention various racist immigration policies proprietary to the EU as a whole.

2. Militarization of various private security contracts in the West (or globally for that matter) obviously speaks in support of this claim.

3. Achille Mbembe saw that necropolitics as "Contemporary forms of subjugation of life to the power of death (necropolitics) profoundly reconfigures the relations among resistance, sacrifice and terror" (Mbembe 2003).

4. The invasion of secular Iraq as a token of a war against religious fundamentalism, not to mention the infamous Iraqi WMDs.

5. The fact that the Vatican felt as called upon to determine who was and who was not eligible for joining the Union and/or to determine what kind of "roots" (allegedly) the secular EU had, obviously demonstrates that the First World interprets *secularity* in very ambiguous, extremely biased fashion.

6. The glorification of various pro-democratic icons in the West seems to occur in that amount of measure in which these *icons* foster the notion of freedoms as freedoms that would only lead to affirmation of the equation between capitalist free market and democracy. As it recently (2012) was a case with glorification (in the western mainstream media discourse) of a Burmese opposition politician and the head of National League for Democracy (NLD) Aung San Suu Kyi.

7. Which, we can presume, are in a dormant, or at least in semi-formal state as long as dominant political discourses in Israel are complacent with the current geopolitical/epistemological layout.

8. Strategic shift of Israel's politics in some hypothetical scenario (left-wing takeover and/or making peace with/recognition of the Palestinian state without foreign interference) would probably, we can speculate, be reflected by the transparent re-instatement of open anti-Semitic stances and zeals within the First World's institutional, popular and power discourses.

9. Badiou distinguishes two kinds of infinities, good and bad. Paraphrasing, the *bad infinity* relates to the objective process, transcendence (having-to-be) representation while the *good infinity* relates to subjective virtuality, immancence, unpresentable.

TWELVE

The Unending Transition

To say that the current state of democracy is strictly connected to the neoliberal model of capitalism would not be untrue, but this broad premise still demands interpretation of the regime of capital in a context that transcends its specific modalities; such as neoliberalism. Hence, as today's regime of circulation of capital is not a homological structure and/or a hierarchy, neoliberalism as an ideological model or a methodological characteristic of capitalism does prove itself to be part of the wider capitalist agenda; colonialism.

In the same way in which expropriation, radical class division, privatization, commodification, fascism, and other effects of capitalism were, (by mainstream political imaginary of Southeast Europe), seen as incidents, rather than systemic traits (or from reactionary perspective, necessary functions in the process of modernization) of capitalist democracy, in the same way capitalism was seen as unrelated, separate from colonialism.The colonialism we are talking about does not represent only a reflection of the direct imposition of the will of First World's power structures (in economic, political and ideological aspects), it represents institutional-epistemological structuralization of colonial relations between the center and the periphery which has become the dominant political and existential experience of the *late* transition in Southeast Europe.

As Walter Mignolo, from the perspective of his analysis of imperial forms in the time of intensified globalization of capitalism under the neoliberal super narrative, has noticed: "Although it is true that colonialism ended with twentieth century decolonization, coloniality was again re-framed by the leadership of the United States" (Mignolo 2008, 20-22).

In this context, today's formation of coloniality or the *colonial matrix of power* as Mignolo called it, was created, according to author: "During the European colonial conquers in the sixteenth century, and this matrix

247

could be described through four interrelated domains in which the struggle for control, accommodation, resistance, re-existence, etc. takes place"
(Mignolo 2008, 20-22).

As Mignolo continues these domains are: "The control of economy
(labor, land, natural resources); the control of authority (government,
army); the control of gender and sexuality (control of family life and
reproduction of the species based on the Christian/bourgeois family) and
the control of knowledge and subjectivity (epistemology, aiesthesis)"
(Mignolo 2008, 20-22).

THE ECONOMY WITHIN CONTEMPORARY COLONIAL RELATIONS

In the context of control over economy, procedures of expropriation of
societies' resources, depoliticization of the field of the social, privatization, (auto)subversion of political sovereignty in favor of the particular
market agenda's of the First World and pacification of class divisions etc.,
could be seen as reflections of a strategy with which specific internal
(such as auto-colonial) and external (direct colonial) control over the
economy is being established. Additionally, all of these procedures could
also be seen as reflections of a specific disposition of zones of interest in
an economic and geopolitical sense.

Southeastern Europe, that was recently reinvented as the *Western Balkans* region, fitted into this context to that measure to which the ruling
classes (neoliberal and ethno-national bourgeoisies), have, protected by
colonial masters, secured typical, yet modernized, colonial conditions for
institutionalization of a debt-based economic model within the wider
procedures of institutionalization of capitalism.

Fragmentations of Yugoslavia on ethnic and religious bases (during
the nineties wars) that were tolerated by the First World, were tolerated
as a precondition for the positioning of a region within a specific colonial
niche. This phase did not precede the following processes of transition
toward the Euro-Atlantic axis of power, it was a primal phase in structuring of the relation of the region with the colonial center. All the ravaging
of the social dimensions of the state and the political society in favor of an
identity-based society was instituted as an institutional and epistemological process by which, extreme disadvantage for such a periphery and
extreme benefit for the colonial center, was represented as a necessary
part of the inclusion of the region into the First World.

The utter destruction of local economy, society and political sovereignty, which nationalistic and neoliberal bourgeoisies created during
these processes were represented, either by their descedents, or by the
First World as predicaments of destitution that were just a phase in redis-
covering the true potential of capitalism. According to Slovenian journalist Sebastjan Leban: "Neoliberalism thus modernises its capitalist matrix

adding to it the social moment, which is first completely voided and then placed at the service of capital. Therefore the ideology of neoliberalism not only replaced the ideology of socialism but wrapped it like a degenerated concept in a new image now propagated as a neoliberalistic invention" (Leban 2008, 24).

In the case of Southeast Europe in general, no matter whether we are talking about reactionary populism or about neoliberal social-democratic options (that tends to be based on badly aethetisized reactionarism) — auto-colonialism was scrutinized only in a partial fashion, as a daily political instrument for defamation of some other reactionary and/or neoliberal option; it was not scrutinized for being in systemic connection with capitalism, not to mention its *lack of* connection of colonialism and democracy. The positioning of the region within the colonial niche was therefore acknowledged and celebrated as an example of protagonist integration into the First World's civilizational register which was, of course, perceived as universal.

So, a duality between the nationalistic reactionary bourgeoisie (that is ideologically based on concepts of ethno-centric, racial state and populism) and allegedly *post-ideological* or allegedly *non-ideological* social-democratic options (pure neoliberal options that saw the free market model as the only form of upgrade possible from ethnocentric options), was instituted as a dominant political binary, able to antagonize only each others methods in perpetuation of capitalist hierarchies of exploitation and in formulating politics as the form of ideological consensus and capitalism as the only form of modernity.

As Achille Mbembe, in the context of his articulation of the contemporary forms of colonialism and genealogies that led to these forms (alhough talking in the context of post-colonial Africa) has noted, paraphrasing, that unlike certain Western experiences, the extension of the role of the state and the market was thus not automatically achieved through the disruption of old social ties. In a number of cases, still paraphrasing, state domination—or the *étatisation* of society—was achieved through the old hierarchies and old patronage networks.

According to Mbembe, on the one hand, it paved the way, more than occurred in other parts of the world, to an *unprecedented privatization of public prerogatives* (Mbembe 2001, 32). On the other, further paraphrasing Mbembe, it not only allowed a degree of socialization of state power generally poorly understood by analysts, but also the correlative socialization of arbitrariness.

In Southeastern Europe, where all social dimensions of the state had not yet been completely privatized, this colonial model reflected itself through contamination of social institutions of the state by a patronage network of influence and through the institutionalization of the state as an arbitrary agent. This ultimately resulted, not only in the *socialization of arbitrariness*, but also in arbitrary socialization of the state—of course, not in the sense in which the state would have protected the public sector, but in the sense in which processes of privatization and utter banishment of class/social struggles were conducted under the aegis of elevated social sensibility.

Social-democratic political options of neoliberal provenience in this way imposed themselves as those options that would convert the state into an instrument for the sustainment of the neoliberal concept within which the model of *cooperation*, (i.e., *partnership* between the public and private sectors); this state was represented as alleged compromise that would allegedly work for the interests of both public and the private sectors. Of course, this did not mean that the division of these sectors was protected by the state, this was a way in which a grey zone, a zone of indifferentiation among these sectors, was institutionalized in favor of a private sector that was reframed as a model of salvation for a social sector which was, in the first place, destroyed and/or deprived of any protection by the state.

Socialization of the state in colonial terms does not present a *social state* that would create a (political and oppressive) barrier against capital, but the state as a machine, potent only for pacification of unlimited circulation of capital at the expense of the political interpretation of the social predicament and in favor of populist interpretations of the needs of the people—to whom the political and financial strenghtening of public prerogatives was presented as the socialist inhibition of *rediscovered* democratic freedoms. The alleged conflict between the public and the private in the Southeastern European periphery is therefore being reproduced in a following way.

Nationalistic (in sense of anti-imperial, not in sense of chauvinist nationalism) prefixes in the formation of politics were being deprived of left wing (anti-imperialist) aspects and produced as chauvinist, right-wing agendas whose perception of the *strong* state did not entail the notion of the state as a barrier to colonialism, but exactly the opposite, as a conductor of colonial conditions—hence, the state was perceived (and structured) as an agent that exercises oppression only in favor of capital and functions as an agent that diverts social conflict and struggles into the fields of ethnicity, identity, religion, and race. This does not mean that the *democratic agenda* has been discarded, on the contrary, democracy has been embraced and utilized as an (ideological and institutional) instrument that legitimizes (formalizes) the prevention of the production of a political society out of the people—keeping the people's prerogative for legitimization of power in its default state, hence glorifying the people as political and democratic accomplishment *eo ipso*.

In this sense, the typically reactionary conversion of the populus (defined exclusively in relation to ethnos and ideologies of blood and soil) into a carrier of sovereignty, not only legitimized arbitrariness and reactionary proto-politicization as the main motives with regards to the legitimization of power (in an election process), it also made the carrier of power into a procurer of historically predestined aims the people allegedly always sought. Of course, that predestined aim was found in capitalism, while the colonial niche *people* were situated in, was, metaphorically speaking, structured as a living ethnographic museum in which the struggles for the placing of an identity into western narratives substituted the struggles for political formation of society.

On the "other" side, social-democratic options structured their position within the colonial condition on the basis of emphasizing the role of the state that was seen as *social* only to that measure to which it could institutionalize political power as the concept that would dislocate the prefixes of oppression from populist, ethnic and biological into those of the free market.

In such a way, exploitation based on the free market model has been represented as the one that allegedly transcended archaic modes of oppression because it now allegedly oppresses indiscriminately. But, since forms of social democracy in colonial conditions ideologically located themselves as *post-ideological*, it eventually, and in cooperation together with the right wing, contributed to the formation of the *demos* as an apolitical basis for relativization of the effects of capital.

Consequentially, the resentment against capitalism produced in the West tends to receive a shape of populist "resistance" against racially defined interests ("Jewish capital," "Arab capital," "Chinese capital," etc.), which is a sentiment that adds to broader formation of obscene "critique" that is actually a racially prefixed attack on those aspects of capitalism that have never functioned and/or existed, such as racially unbiased social mobility, etc.

Social-democratic forms of resentment with the effect of capital were developed into a form that either saw capitalism as a system of equal exploitation of all, or in a form that perceived the political potential of the *demos* as the potential only for the equalization of democratic freedom to the freedoms not to be engaged in ideological articulation of capitalism as the hegemonic power system. As Mbembe noticed, paraphrasing, progression of the state in the name of efficiency gains is connected with the denial of the legitimacy of its (the states) intervention in economic matters. According to Mbembe, paraphrasing, these policies have created the conditions for a privatization of the sovereignty. Still paraphrasing Mbembe, the struggle to privatize state sovereignty largely overlaps the struggle to concentrate and then privatize the means of coercion, because control of the means of coercion makes it possible to secure an advantage in the other conflicts under way for the appropriation of resources and other utilities formerly concentrated in the state.

In wider sense, working class resentment in Southeast Europe, is not being articulated as a class struggle for rearticulation of the meaning of labor or for political articulation of the ideological basis on which the labor was organized, but it was organized as a pathetic plea to the regime for delegation of more resources that would after all be *eaten* by debt.

If some kind of pattern could be found in the conduct of laborers struggles, in the specific case of Croatia, it comes down to a couple of mutual marks—laborers subsume their predicament through an apolitical epistemological filter that does not make any connection between capitalism and non-existence of political society and tends to accuse eclatant capitalist structures for being *communists* which allowed the church to pose as some obscene social agent; the unions, instead of producing class based antagonism in the context of the social struggle encourage laborers to pacify their demands in favor of their democratic rights, while the media outlets, otherwise conditioned by corporate interests, reflect the social predicaments either through phenomenological/anecdotal "analysis" of corruption they see as incidental in capitalism, either through systematization of pathetic patterns of empathy derived from religiously based versions of morality.

Amidst all this, oppressive and juridicial apparatus (in Croatia, but also in all of ex-Yugoslavia), that function almost exclusively as a system for protection of interests of capitalist (neoliberal and/or neoconservative) bourgeoisie and as a system that actively neglects the utter lack of distance between the church and the state, functions as a phantom representation of the existence of the political State or of the political sovereignty.[1] This situation was seen by prominent theoretician of decolonialization and activist Frantz Fanon[2] in the following way: "The national bourgeoisie in the underdeveloped countries is not geared to production, invention, creation, or work. All its energy is channeled into intermediary activities. Networking and scheming seem to be its underlying vocation" (Fanon 2005, 98). Further, according to Fanon:

> At the core of national bourgeoisie of the colonial countries a hedonistic mentality prevails—because on a psychological level it identifies with the Western bourgeoisie from which it has slurped every lesson. It mimics the Western bourgeoisie in its negative and decadent aspects without having accomplished the initial phases of exploration and invention that are the assets of this Western bourgeoisie whatever the circumstances. . . . In its decadent aspect the national bourgeoisie gets considerable help from the Western bourgeoisie who happen to be tourists enamored of exoticism, hunting and casinos. The national bourgeoisie establishes holiday resorts and playgrounds for entertaining the Western bourgeoisie. (Fanon 2005, 101)

In accordance with such foundations for economic development, that are based on the concept of intermediacy in expropriation, the concepts of *self-sustainability* and *competitiveness* were adopted in the public imagination as those concepts that reflect the alleged possibility of the colonial economy to compete with the colonial center.

Since the premise on which neoliberal and populist (neoconservative) positions base their *visions of progress* entails a preconception that it is possible for them to create a *dynamic* local economy. The same dynamism is being exercised as a brutal destruction of strategic industries in favor of structuring the economy as a service for attraction of foreign investments, as an administrative service that organizes resource extraction and services debt based economy and as a tourist service that is designed as a tiny, more or less exotic niche, that answers to the needs of Western bourgeoisie. In the context of capital's need for cheaper input (labor, raw materials, cheap land), David Harvey noted that: "The general thrust of any capitalistic logic of power is not that territories should be held back from capitalist development, but that they should be continuously opened up" (Harvey 2003, 139).

So, since this opening up was not designed to allow to colonial peripheries to proliferate themselves as major protagonists in colonial power structures, the only forms of *competitiveness* and *self-sustainable development* possible under these conditions are the forms of competitiveness in struggles for integration into the local ruling classes and/or hierarchies of exploitation while the amounts of *self-sustainabilty* are in direct proportion to the success in avoiding of the precarious working relations.

THE CONTROL OF AUTHORITY

Whether within the context of multilateral relations or within the context of the formation of the subjective experience of the colonial conditions, the notion of authority in this context is related to the concept of master and the servant. The meaning of *authority* in colonial conditions, Achille Mbembe contextualized through a notion of the *commandement* that he saw in the following way. According to Mbembe:

> Commandement, in a colony, rested on a very specific *imaginary* of state sovereignty. On the one hand, it combined weakness of, and inflation of, the notion of right: weakness of right in that, in the relations of power and authority, the colonial model was, in both theory and practice, the exact opposite of the liberal model of debate and discussion; inflation of right in that, except when deployed in the form of arbitrariness and the right of conquest, the very concept of right often stood revealed as a void. (Mbembe 2001, 25)

The notion of the void in this context could be seen as a trait of the structure that determines the ideological validity of some political and/or ideological differentiation. While the democratic will of the people in Venezuela, Bolivia or Iran is being stigmatized by the First World and represented as the mask of dictatorships, the hegemonic traits of the First World's democracy are being represented as necessary components in the imposition of proper versions of ideology. The notion of right that stood revealed as a void means that the notion of right was firmly tied up to its ideological explication or justification, but it also means that the particular ideological justification and/or notion of the right was produced into a universal transcendental authority.

The right revealed as a void actually reflected how the monopoly on the definition of the meaning of some transgression is being applied. This allowed to both the carriers of definition of *proper* ideological conduct and to its colonial periphery to legitimize their exploits (invasions, colonial occupations, etc.), as well as it allowed the First World to present its hegemony as an essential component in the preservation of the appearance of that hegemony in the form of liberty. One aspect of colonial violence, as Mbembe noticed: "Regarded itself as the sole power to judge its laws—whence its one-sidedness, especially as, to adopt Hegel's formulation, its supreme right was (by its capacity to assume the act of destroying) simultaneously the supreme denial of right" (Mbembe 2001, 25).

The supreme denial of right was (is), of course, an essential institutional, epistemological and ideological instrument that puts the amount of infringement of those rights in direct proportion to the sustainment of ideology; into direct proportion to the amounts of rights which are preserved by these systematic infringements. The transparent existence of concentration camps, as it was in Abu Ghraib and Bagram, and as it is in Guantanamo is possible because these camps are not seen by the paradigmatic mainstream as symptoms of consistency in perpetuation of hegemonic traits of the order that sustains these camps, but as symptoms of the protection of the rights of those privileged by First World's ideological structures. It is clear that what was once seen as an inconsistency, is actually an eclatant example of one of the most systemic characteristics of the system.

The fact that the military and, especially, the economic power base recently moved away from the West, only meant that the western power structures reorganized the authoritarian *tissue* of their epistemologies on a liberal basis under aegis of which the amount of imposition of democracy can be completely equated to the First World's strategies for preservation of its own central position in ideologization of the globalization of capital. Another aspect of colonial violence, according to Mbembe, paraphrasing, was produced before and after, or a part and parcel of, the conquest, and had to do with legitimation. As Mbembe stated:

> Its function was, as Derrida speaks of a somewhat different issue to provide self-interpreting language and models for the colonial order, to give this order meaning, to justify its necessity and universalizing mission—in short, to help produce an imaginary capacity converting the founding violence into authorizing authority. (Mbembe 2001, 25)

In the context of the colonial periphery, colonial authority was congregated onto a transversal that made the effects of capital rational by locating them into a positive relationship with the erratic nature of *democracy building*. Hence, the increase in the amount of exploitation was perceived as an inherent part of the perpetuation of the alliance of capitalism and democracy.

Consequently, the concept of the *political* in general was deprived of its politically ideological dimensions of the social struggle and transcribed into a register potent only to generate antagonism in the fields of an axiomatic spectrum where the notion of diversity was strictly connected to matters of identity/race/religion/ethnicity which were then produced as the only prefixes of a (proper) struggle for political power.

In the context of Southeast Europe, the public imagination's fixation on questions of identity has evolved into a fixation with the idea that political agenda should be perceived as aiming to integrate certain identities and/or cultures into the First World's colonial epistemology. The amount of legitimization specific policy received was equated to the amount of authority which that policy delegated to the First World, or more precisely, to the amount of significance it delegated to its own miserable colonial niche within the colonial hierarchies of prominence.

For instance, as the Croatian newspaper *Jutarnji List* reported, the head of Croatian social-democratic party Zoran Milanović prior to Croatia's entrance in European Union (that happened in 2013) noted that "by entering into the EU, Croatia becomes a part of the community to which, by its culture, Croatia has always belonged to" (Šajn 2012).

The concept of *belonging*, if integrated into a political vocabulary, directly implies that those who utilize this concept perceive politics as an instrument of struggle for positioning into already determined niches; as an instrument for the organization of devotion to already defined authorities and as an instrument for placing ideological discrepancies into a context in which, allegedly, some universal consensus on the adequacy of capitalist democracy was already achieved. The aforementioned statement therefore contains all the primitive, provincial, servile, ethnocentric, racial and reactionary trademarks that constitute an *authentic* auto-colonial vision of the notion of politics and political authority.

At the same time, under the aegis of an alleged post-ideological consensus, these trademarks constitute an authentic (purely ideological) epistemological container that aims to eradicate any possibility of having any form of politically ideological decolonial struggle.

THE CONTROL OF SEX AND/OR PACIFICATION OF THE CIVIL
SECTOR WITHIN COLONIAL RELATIONS

In the most general terms, the issues of sexuality, family, gender, etc., are, in colonialist terms, utilized as instruments for the diversion of antagonism from political issues to a spectrum of issues which a surplus of ideological, not political, meaning was delegated. In this context, as Mignolo claims:

> De-linking from the imperial/colonial control of gender and sexuality (e.g., through the invention of the concept of "woman" and the Christian, and then of the liberal heterosexual normativity) implies envisioning a world in which gender distinction and sexual preferences are not determined by a moral code dictated by the truth of a transcendental behavior or by the needs of the market, but basically, by dignity and love not regulated by economic needs of capitalism and the concurrent collaboration of state institutions. (Mignolo 2008, 20-22)

On the contrary, Southeast European public discourses are articulating issues of gender distinction and sexual preference through an epistemological apparatus that addresses this question of representation in favor of a moral code and the needs of the market; trademarks of the only system under which these issues could have been articulated at all. The lack of any de-linking from colonial epistemologies was represented an an ultimate form of the surplus of that de-linking.

For instance, the right wing fosters the "concept of woman" as a particular part of a male dominated family which is not only able (or allowed to be able) to struggle politically, but also able to struggle for the domination of the patriarchal family or for the family which is seen as the foundation of society.

On the other hand, the social-democractic part of the political spectrum integrates or emancipates women or gender minorities either; by copying western style emancipation in which levels of inclusion are determined by a statistical number of women or gender minorities in positions of power; by perceiving these subjectivities as apolitical singularities able to materially integrate themselves into a capitalist production relation, and/or to epistemologically adopt such a narrative into struggles for the organization of equality. Amidst all this, gender minorities tend to play into the hands of capital by formatting their struggles on this apolitical basis, which could be seen as a form of ultimatum by a regime that offers them an increase in degrees of emancipation if they discarded politically ideological dimensions of the struggle that could be connected with wider class struggles. As Mignolo noted: "Distinctions between male and female or sun and moon, were made and were basic for the organization of society, but 'women' in Western Christianity and its secularization in the bourgeois family, was one dimension of the colonial matrix of power (e.g., a package of economic, political and ethical control and domination)" (Mignolo 2008, 20-22).

Colonial control over reproduction and (the interpretation of) sex should therefore be understood as the kind of control that is realized through the interchange of dogmatic and liberal perspectives. In other words, conservative and liberal aspects of capitalism are exercising this kind control by imposition of the notion that only the free market and supporting ideologies allow for an articulation of these issues.

According to Mignolo, who articulates neoliberalism as just one model in the processes of reorganization of global capitalism and/or perpetuation of global colonial divide, wrote "Neo-liberalism is the latest version we know of the history of imperial modernity/coloniality and capitalism as lifestyle, in which growth and accumulation takes precedence over humans and life in general" (Mignolo 2008, 20-22). In relation to this matter, Mignolo stated:

> Notice that slavery never stopped. The human being continues to be a commodity, like any other commodity (e.g., dispensable life), but are no longer Black Africans, but women from the ex-Second and Third World. The global trafficking of women, is not a trafficking of women from Norway, France, the U.S. or Germany. Enslaved women are from Moldavia, the Ukraine, East and South Asia, Argentina, Russia and several other non-European locales. (Mignolo 2008, 20-22)

In this context, the dimensions of control in regard to sex and reproduction showed themselves as models of pacification of the social conflict through perpetuation of rigorously stereotypical conflict with regards to questions of sexual orientation, birth control, control of the body, the nature of integration of the queer population etc. What is stereotypical in this kind of conflict is the situation in which these questions were produced into issues around which the dominant poles of the political spectrum in Southeast Europe like to disagree.

While the right-wing advocates reactionary patriarchal-clerofascist types of control over reproduction and imposes feudal social constructs (*family as the cornerstone of society*), social democracy plays a more elegant game in the making of these issues sensible, but not because it wants to politically articulate strategic, structural and ideological foundations of a role of sexual rights in the condition of capitalism, but because it has based its political program on—either the aseptic allegedly post-ideological "rejection of every ideology," or on a subtler adoption of the market logic that produced the aforementioned problems. Of course, in regard to the positioning of a major part of the so-called civil scene, the question of control of sex and reproduction, metaphorically speaking, represents a *Trojan horse* within which protagonists infiltrate themselves into the anti-establishment—reflecting along the way their relation to these matters as a relation that sees these issues as if deprived of an ideological background, hence as they were mere inconsistencies in an otherwise *fine* systemic blue print.

The civil sector's treatment of this predicament as if the individuals concerned were mere dysfunctions of the regime did not deny ideological control of sex, sexuality, and reproduction, but this same predicament, through this *incidental* approach, was deprived of its ideological foundations in relation to its connections with capitalism, which ultimately resulted in the interpretation of questions of gender minorities, sexuality, and reproduction as if they actually were commodities, whose rights should allegedly be protected by a civil, NGO sector, as a service to which the state outsourced the care about these issues.

Consequentially, the majority of protagonists in the struggle for the rights of sexual minorities in Southeast Europe, especially in Croatia, tend to frame their agenda as devoid of politically ideological dimensions to that extent that liberal democracy is perceived as if it has no connection with capitalism, as if liberal democracy in some mythical "full capacity" would actually reduce or end social exclusion.

It is not that this kind of activity represents a spin for, let's say the European Union, but this way of formulating social struggles was(is) endorsed by the EU (as Eurocentric agent) as *the* role model for the struggle for human rights. In other words, as if human rights violations were mere incidents based on, not yet adequate, proliferation of the liberal democratic regime. For instance, at the same time prominent EU human rights agents were satisfied because of Paris having a gay mayor, Sarkozy's regime was conducting racist deportations of parts of the Roma community out of France.

Generally, the civil sector that treats social reality as either separate from the institutional and ideological effect of capital, or from the colonial dimension of the organization of the social order (both in the West or its periphery) exactly in a way that deprives the struggles for same rights of their ideological dimensions, thereby realizing itself as a distinct apologetic stance that belonged to the regime. To paraphrase Mbembe, it immediately becomes apparent that there can be no civil society without places and spaces where ideas of autonomy, representation, and pluralism can publicly crystallize, and where juridical subjects enjoying rights and capable of freeing themselves from the arbitrariness of both state and primary group (kin, tribe, etc.) can come into being.

In the context of southeast European colonial frames it seems that the moral majority was derived from a pool of inferiority complexes toward the Western metropolis that defined the freedom struggle as a struggle for a western version of democracy, hence as a struggle for (re)inscription into a registry of (reactionary aspects of) the western version of civilization. Consequently this has formulated freedom struggles (including their gender related aspects) only as struggles for more prominence in hierarchies of exploitation. An obsession with the overemphasis of democratic prefixes in some social struggles in this sense has not politicized these struggles, but has equated the (democratic) will of the majority and the moral majority. This has resulted in the creation of a dominant episte-mological narrative in which the amount of political legitimacy has been put in direct proportion to the amount of consent it receives from the moral majority.

Additionaly, an implication that the moral majority, or the majority in general, fostered some predestined freedom potential that was allegedly inhibited by flaws in the imposition of democracy, in this context, formu-lated the paradigmatic mainstream anti-establishment in Southeast Eu-rope not as a political agent that would de-link itself from colonial episte-mologies through the production of an inherent link between capital and its effects, but as that kind of position that actually helps capitalism by de-linking its effects from its methods of rationalizaton in relation to morality and otherwise humanist issues.

THE CONTROL OF KNOWLEDGE IN THE CONTEXT OF THE FORMATION OF ANTI-ESTABLISHMENT

Generally speaking, the spectrum of the motives invested into the forma-tion of, broadly understood, *anti-establishment* struggles in Southeast Eu-rope have shown themselves as extremely pervious to dominant, colonial epistemic frames.

For instance, the agenda (or great parts of the agenda) that stood behind the recent (2010) student protests in Croatia was not only contam-inated by a reactionary style of making relative of ideological projects by some of the students. As Croatian newspaper *Jutarnji List* reported on April 23, 2009, some of the students involved into these protests stated that they were not "against Jesus because they liked Jesus and Marx alike." Although this was not a predominant position among the protest-ers, it was notable, and did reflect a wider rejection of almost any politi-cally ideological positioning in formation of the struggle. The student's utter rejection of any kind of leadership authority and the rejection of any ideological dimension that could (should) have been integrated into the resistance against the subjection of university to the free market logic resulted in the formation of resentment on the basis of complete adoption of the notion that political potency could be attained only through de-mocratization of the struggle. As if rejection of a leadership structure was proof to the moral majority that the resistance was not actually planning to become politically *and* ideologically subversive.

The organizational "cramp" such a protest found itself in was not only marked by a complete dispersion of any ideological and authoritarian dimensions (hierarchical and leadership dimensions within the resis-tance), but also by the search for justification of the resentment to reac-

tionary moral majority; such was the state in which all subversive potential was actually deployed against the agenda of the protests.

The concept of *direct democracy* that was adopted as the subtext of the
resistance and was regarded as a desired form of rule (seen as subversive
to capitalism) implied that the majority contained some politically antag-
onizing potential that was allegedly inhibited by the representational aspect of democracy; as if direct inclusion of the commoners into the ruling
hierarchies would be adequate to undermine capitalism as the power
structure. The consequent perception of a notion of public interest as
separate from ideological aspects of capitalism contributed to the overall
interpretation of capitalism as separate from democracy and as a system
that is perpetuated only by elusive elites which have allegedly obtained
positions of power completely outside of the processes of democratic
legitimization of power. It is not a problem of course if current modes of
struggle did not offer a *concrete* alternative to the current regime, the
problem is that contemplation about forms of resistance is fixated either
in interpretation of capitalism as the system in which the elites exploit
everyone in the same way, or in the interpretation of capitalism as a
system that could be antagonized without the ideological dimension in
formation of the political. The *floating* of direct democracy over the actual
modes of protest pushed the resentment closer to mere reinvention of the
method through which democratic principles based on quantification-
legitimization are being sustained. But more dangerously, endorsement
of a concept of direct democracy actually contributes to depoliticization
of the social struggles because it tends to silence the essential need of
existence of a politically ideological distance between the ruler and the
ruled.

Also, the concept of direct democracy which is nominally directed
against the neoliberal model of capitalism, through its rejection of representational aspects in democratic organizations of power in favor of some
leaderless structure based on non-articulated interest of the protesters,
actually reinstates exactly the liberal dimension to the processes of reorganization of capital within which people's desires (that were already
conditioned by capitalism's ideologies) are offered as an ultimate solution to the predicaments created by capital.

Generally, the majority of spectra of meanings that congregate around
the civil society and/or anti-establishment mainstream realized themselves mostly as expert knowledge about the localized functions of the
regime—where the effect of the regime was (in a generalized manner)
ascribed to its inadequacy to put its inconsistencies in order.

This tendency addresses only specific parts of the regime, such is
neoliberalism, and abolishes or evades the addressing of general structural characteristics of the colonial capitalist regime as a heterogeneous,
highly discriminative and differential exploitation matrix. Hence, the tendency to base the construction of knowledge about the order on a basis

that deems capitalism as transgressive *only because* it is, allegedly, inconsistent contributes to an interpretation of capitalism as separate from dominant epistemological matrices that surpass the exclusive domain of material power. As Walter Mignolo has noted:

> The accumulation of money went hand in hand with the accumulation of meaning (e.g., knowledge): major banks, major stock markets, major museums and universities are in France, England, Germany, Spain, Italy, Portugal and the U.S. It is only recently that history has been moving toward a polycentric accumulation of money, although the control of meaning (e.g., knowledge) is still in the hands of Western (countries mentioned above) institutions. (Mignolo 2008, 20-22)

So, one of the key ideological trademarks of dominance of colonial epistemology in a colonial periphery is the formation of the meaning of knowledge as particular and applicable only in the colonial periphery and in relation to the periphery.

It would be easy to say only that the knowledge in peripheral and semi-peripheral colonies is being treated (by the First World center) as traditional and/or anecdotal. As such it is being validated by the First World only to that extent to which anecdotal knowledge acknowledges the right of the First World to define it and to the extent to which the institutional framework in which that knowledge was organized accepted the utter superiority of western institutions in determination of the political meaning of knowledge in general.

The First World's hubris in regard to these matters does not just geo-racially condition knowledge (prohibits the peripherial knowledge from tackling the First World's epistemologies), but it represents a part of the mechanism of control in which the First World's monopoly on the definition of knowledge is represented as the pinnacle of evolution of any epistemological logic.

COLONIAL MODERNITY AND DIFFERENTIATION WITHIN HIERARCHIES OF OPPRESSION

Although it is important to notice that modernity is, paraphrasing Mignolo, not a historical period, but a rhetoric grounded on the idea of salvation by the agents telling the story and placing themselves at the last moment of a global historical development, in this context it is also important to state that such a definition of modernity was, (by major political protagonists at the time of the southeastern European post-socialist transition) installed into the very core of envisioning of the form of the political. In the case of Southeastern Europe, it was not only that the broad spectrum of meanings modernity contains (or might have contained) that was universalized but it was the effects of capital that was inextricably connected to the presence of modernist grounds in the formation of society.

Dominant epistemological ideas in Southeastern Europe did not therefore try to make exploitation, commodification, racism, etc., rational, it embraced these processes as modernist processes *eo ipso*. It did not matter to which measure these processes enslaved or destitute Southeastern European demographics because the (auto) colonial, servile sentiment was reinvented as the only progressivist "political" standpoint and proper ideological stance that could tackle destitution. Consequently, the transition of Southeastern Europe (toward the Euro-Atlantic type of free market based democracy) was succesful to the point to to which it was an auto-colonial project. Needless to say, the grounding of such an interpretation of modernity influenced both reactionary and social-democratic poles of the political spectrum in a way that tied the interpretation of political sovereignty directly to such a modernist narrative, and visions of the purpose of sovereignty strictly within the epistemic colonial boundaries. From a historical perspective, Mignolo has noted that:

> The rhetoric of modernity has been, since its inception, the rhetoric of salvation: by conversion (Spanish and Portuguese mendicant orders), by civilizing missions (British and French agents); by development and modernization (U.S. experts in economy and politics guiding the Third World towards the same standards as the First); and salvation through market democracy and consumerism. (Mignolo 2008, 20-22)

Within the context in which these paradigmatic progressions took place, the periphery, however, cannot be seen as exclusively being on the "receiving end" within the colonial relation, that is, the periphery has proven itself as capable of contributing to its own subjection, as well as to reproduction of the epistemic matrix that sustains capitalist hierarchies of exploitaton in a global context. Of course, this all has to do with the way racist matrixes were or are being utilized into sustaining of exploitative hierarchies.

The aesthesis of coloniality in Southeastern Europe has therefore reflected itself as a subjective experience within which rudimentary sensations of colonization (ethno-national based disputes, commodification, debt slavery, etc.) have been taken as the raw material on which (levels of) colonial domestication were/are performed as tokens of emancipation into the western modernist narrative.

It seems that the auto-colonized subjectivity ascribes itself into a western historical register through the reinvention of the alleged role it had in historical colonizations (deeming along the way colonial holocausts in an apologetic manner as if those were "necessery, neutral processes"). Secondly, the auto-colonized subjectivity reinvents itself as being positioned higher on the racial scales than the others colonized in the region. It was domesticated *before* the others, which allegedly should be a *fact* that would guarantee more affection from the master in contemporary processes of domestication. Consequently, these forms of historical revisionism, in the specific case of Croatia, produced both a reactionary, fascist moral majority and neoliberal social-democratic option that do not perceive the West, in most banal terms, as a heterogeneous geography that has produced various revolutionary responses and variety of class based struggles, but only as a ethnocentric institution whose ethnocentrism (*Volksgemeinschaft*) allegedly presents a precondition of modernity. This consequently equates auto-domestication, auto-colonialism and utter servility (to such perceptions of the West) as a context in which sustainment of racist, chauvinist, populist dogmas is seen in direct proportion to the attained amount of degrees of modernity. In general terms, racial and discriminatory consistencies of capitalism's racial ideologies are, according to the colonized imaginings of Southeastern Europe, seen as traits that guarantee marks of distinction in differentiation within the hierarchies of exploitation, in the same way as they were designed by the Eurocentric ideologies of the First World. The political differentiation was therefore pushed into a domain of obscurity in favor of adoption of racial criteria as the most important criteria of a auto-colonized society on its way toward total ascription into *civilization*—hence First World's definition of modernity.

In this way, not only the degree of integration into a colonial relationship was equated to a degree of attained modernity (or democracy), but, in accordance to the segregational matrix of racial hierarchies, privileges for elevation within these hierarchies were assigned in accordance to racial *compatibility* of those who are being classified. Less unknown subjects within Southeastern Europe (with western Christian prefixes) are therefore rewarded with a surplus of privileges in domestication, while the less known subjects (with non-Christian or non-western Christian background) were found as less privileged in a the process of domestication.

The rationalization of capitalism's process of differentiation that is based on race in such a way defines the terrain on which the struggle for distinction is being organized as a terrain on which only racial idiosyncracies have been ratified as the only valid distinctions that could attain higher levels of modernist development. While the colonial center (the First World) positioned itself outside the historical and political reference frame to which Santiago Castro-Gómez referred to as the hubris of the zero point that, paraphrasing, represents (or points toward) the knowledge of the observer who cannot be observed, it organized the knowledge about exploitation on specific homogeneous/heterogeneous epistemological foundations.

On one hand, the process of racialization defined the terrain on which differentiation is being attained as racial, biological and as the terrain of identity politics. On the other hand, it utilized all the positions attained on this basis as tokens of representation of its own particular hegemonic agenda as universal and mutual under which any differentiation in exploitation was represented in a distinctive fashion of integration into the globalized capitalism presented as the pinnacle of modernist progression.

This homogenous/heterogeneous momentum should not by any means be comprehended in a dichotomic context, it should be understood as an interchangeable structural discourse that erases political prefixes to differentiation (social, class, and anti-imperial struggles) and produces the colonial condition and adoption of a particular colonial epistemology as a precondition for organization of any social struggle. Of course, in relation to paradigmatic components of colonial epistemology, the heterogeneity of exploitation (racist classifications, differentiation in choosing whether some demography would be exposed to death, genocide or just to commodification, etc.) was made rational by conversions of exploitation/infliction of death into instruments of salvation for those still deprived of capitalist democratic rule. As Gržinić noted in regard to the role Eastern Europe has in contemporary European imaginary:

> Former Eastern Europe is not an adjective, but a placeholder in time that is accelerated to such a degree that the politics of memory presents itself as a memory of what was once political. What was once political is transformed through the perfomative repetition into pure ideological knowledge, but with a proviso saying that therefore we should not be preoccupied with it, as it's all just a pure process of performativity anyway. (Gržinić 2010d, 15)

In this sense, at the core of institutional and epistemological oppressive mechanisms in Southeastern Europe lays the rhetoric that shapes the notion of antagonism into a framework that puts the (auto)colonial *nomos* of exploitation into a positive relation with the consent to define the ideological as an empty container for the twisted reinvention of the political as a performance that only embellishes and converts the colonial project into a *necessary* modernist project.

In such a way, necropolitcs (as extreme intensification of exploitation and commodification or, paraphrasing Gržinić, as historicization of biopolitics) was installed into a major paradigm of rule that is able to normalize existence as a process of enslavement or dying and that is also able to (re)invent social conflict as a struggle for ascendance on the hierarchies of privilege defined by agents of Eurocentric apartheid that continue to present its provinciality as pinnacle of civilization.

NOTES

1. Furthermore, institutional iterations of the colonial center, such is the EU, relate to Southeast European states as successful to that measure to which they were not political or politically sovereign states.

2. Whose work through an analysis of French colonial oppression in Algiers from 1830–1962 managed to expose some of the main concept invested in perpetuation of colonial epistemology and modernist narratives.

THIRTEEN

The Effect of the Depoliticization of the Distance between the Oppressor and the Oppressed

Since capitalism has always been capable of intertwining its ideological agenda with specific humanistic projects, it should not be so hard to recognize liberal democracy (and other varieties of its post-liberal shape) as being the current form of the reorganization of capitalism. The institutional and epistemological procedures of depoliticization of social conflict, (that constitute an integral part of the perpetuation and/or sustainment of capitalist hierarchies of exploitation), could therefore be seen as procedures that neutralize specific dimensions of antagonism between the subjugator and subjugated.

While the First World's paradigmatic forms of both compliancy and resentment in relation to capitalism were constituted on the basis of disengagement from class and/or revolutionary-based political struggles, the overexploited world's population that is now, (under the aegis of the *post-ideological* reconfiguration of the world) encouraged to politically reinvent itself in the form of apolitical *demos*, was also integrated into the processes of pacification of radical disparities in distribution of global wealth. The overexploited were integrated to the extent to which their resentment was deprived of its political dimension in structuring of dominant forms of resentment.[1]

So, after apolitical antagonism was idealized as the *core value* in the First World's structuring of power relations, the *affection* among these positions (as a reflection of both First World's control over the major parts of global wealth and as a reflection of strategies of depoliticization that constituted processes of liberalization of capitalism) was now offered to those at the receiving end of exploitation hierarchies (the overexploited world and First World's peripheries) as the only political ideal that could create preconditions for modernization, ergo, inclusion of that world into the global circulation of capital.

THE ERASURE OF POLITICAL DICHOTOMIES

Since contemporary reinventions of capitalism (i.e., its liberalization) are being conducted in relation to the dominant humanistic super narratives, the procedures for sustainment of hierarchies of exploitation themselves have also been reorganized as neutral, global projects able to pacify disparities in the global distribution of wealth in the so called *postcolonial* world.

Generally speaking, the postcolonial prefix that tends to frame the general discussion about the nature of polarity of the world in this context should not be seen as a paradigmatic explication or a confirmation of some given geopolitical reality, but as a token of the flexibility of capital to reorganize (or represent) its agenda as non-authoritarian and/or non-hegemonic. Achille Mbembe has, in the context of his research on the modes of authoritarianism in the postcolonial world, noticed that "For the present, it is enough to observe that, at any given moment in the postcolonial historical trajectory, the authoritarian mode can no longer be interpreted strictly in terms of surveillance, or the politics of coercion" (Mbembe 2001, 128).

Mbembe's remarks provide a point of departure toward the analysis of contemporary modes of exploitation that do not disregard the existence of the authoritarian nature and imposition of colonialism, but locate authoritarian dimensions in the register of the apolitical. We could say, in this sense, that the authoritarian dimension of rule is no longer organized and interpreted in terms of politics and/or political at all. Mbembe wrote, "Precisely because the postcolonial mode of domination is a regime that involves not just control but conviviality, even connivance—as shown by the constant compromises, the small tokens of fealty, the inherent cautiousness—the analyst must watch for the myriad ways ordinary people guide, deceive, and toy with power instead of confronting it directly" (Mbembe 2001, 128).

Since the order represents the process of destruction of (politically) ideological dimensions as traits of it being less tyrannical, the apolitical context we are talking about should be understood as the process in which intensification of depoliticized procedures reflect exactly the intensification of tyrannical traits of that order. The processes of ideological neutralization of the dominance of global circulation of capital and of maximization of profit serve as aspects of rationalization of selective nature of imposition of capitalism, but these processes also serve as instruments for reduction or fixation of subjugates and/or subalterns political horizon strictly within the First World's ideological reference frames. The same ideological dimension was not utilized only to provide a ratio for coercive imposition of these conditions, but it has been utilized as an instrument for neutralization of any politically ideological dimensions in formation of subjugates resentment.

Consequentially, a context was produced in which the basic dichotomy of rule (the relation between the subjugator and the subjugated) was converted into an obscene relation in which the political realization of the subjugate was made directly proportional to the degree of acceptance of the dominator's notion of politics as apolitical instrument for integration into the circulation of capital. As an example, Libyan rebels' usage of notion of *freedom* during the country's 2011 uprising could have been seen as an example in which the political sovereignty of Libya (aside from the eccentricity of its authoritarian dimension) was actually seen (by the rebels) as an obstacle to the country's integraton into the market economy, ergo, its recolonization by Euro-Atlantic powers.

Nevertheless, the political meaning of the concept of *intimacy* installed between the subjugator and the subjugated requires further examination, particularly the interplay between (the hegemonic redefining of) political power and sustainment of capitalism as a non-limitable system of expropriation. The transaction of values between the subjugator and the subjugated in contemporary forms of globalization of capital is inextricably entangled with the First World's imposition of particular explications of humanistic, post-ideological or liberal democratic contingencies as universal. The lack of an explicitly political dimension in the process of coercion of colonial conditions did not require from the subjugates only to format their position as auto-colonial, but the amount of auto-colonial stances was equated to the amount of existence of humanist, liberal democratic dimensions among the subjugates.

Hence, ideological utilization of allegedly neutral contingencies of humanity such as; modernism, progress or civilization had to be coupled with the neutralization of political distance between the (colonial or auto-colonial) masters and the subjugates.

On one hand, most simply stated, paradigmatic subjectivities in the First World were (are) privileged to realize themselves, either as less commodified, or as *prominent* within the hierarchies of exploitation. On the other hand, privileges assigned to, most generally speaking, non-white, non-European subjectivities in the over-exploited world, were of that kind that put the prospect of biological survival in direct proportion with the amount of adoption of extreme forms of commodification, coupled with utter vulgarity in the processes of formation of political agendas within these conditions. To paraphrase Mbembe, in the post-colony, an intimate tyranny links the rules and the ruled—just as obscenity is only another aspect of munificence, and vulgarity a normal condition of state power.

This vulgarity Mbembe speaks of so effectively depicts the demise of the political in the context in which pacification of the politically ideological dichotomy between the ruler and the ruled did not normalize the oppressive link between them, it actually reorganized and normalized the notion of oppression by situating/representing it as a fundamental precondition for acquiring privilege. Of course, any privilege assigned to the subaltern does not contain the possibility of ascendance to power within the hierarchies of rule, it offers only the prospect of gaining of a lesser degree of exploitation.

Hence, if the politics in most general, administrative sense, was reformed into some sort of *mutual* project, sympathetic of both subjugates and the subjugators (*partners* as neoliberal democratic mantra's suggested) the very concept of *takeover* of the political power seems to have been deprived of any political or materialistic relevance.

If the notion of political rule was epistemologically deprived of its politically ideological function to produce society and organize separation from dominant narratives and epistemologies, the fundamental prerogative of rule—to radically intervene in society—would be exchanged for the rule redefined as an instrument for radical formalization of either utilitarian indulgencies, or dissent, but only within the framework that implied that the dissent should represent only the thriving repositioning in a matrix of exploitaton. According to Mbembe:

> If subjection appears more intense than it might be, this is because the subjects of the *commandement* have internalized authoritarian epistemology to the point where they reproduce it themselves in all the minor circumstances of daily life—social networks, cults and secret societies, culinary practices, leisure activities, modes of consumption, styles of dress, rhetorical devices, and the whole political economy of the body. (Mbembe 2001, 128)

The *commandement* in the postcolony, according to Mbembe:

> Seeks to institutionalize itself, to achieve legitimation and hegemony (*recherche hégémonique*), in the form of a *fetish*. The signs, vocabulary, and narratives that the *commandement* produces are meant not merely to be symbols; they are officially invested with a surplus of meanings that are not negotiable and that one is officially forbidden to depart from or challenge. (Mbembe 2001, 103)

The imposition, or the reproduction of the dictate demanded by this *commandement*, was related to the convivial aspect of power in the sense in which authoritarian aspects of hegemony were legitimized/pacified through (or as) the actual normalization of the process of degradation of antagonism among the rulers and ruled.

Consequentially, it seems that the fetishist element in capitalism's search for hegemony was found within the procedures that increase the scale of hegemony on the basis of the eradication of its explicit political forms and on the basis of production of pure ideology into a twisted political form. In the eyes of the auto-colonial subject, the fetishist element was located within, or as, the unattainable striving for position within colonial hierarchies that were, by the same subject, actually seen as genuinely neutral, and according to this twisted logic, as genuinely political. As Mbembe put it, in relation to the subjection of authoritarian epistemology:

> The subjection is also more intense because, were they to detach themselves from these ludic resources, the subjects would, *as subjects*, lose the possibility of multiplying their identities. Yet it is precisely this possibility of assuming multiple identities that accounts for the fact that the body that dances, dressed in the party uniform, fills the roads, "assembles *en masse*" to applaud the passing presidential procession in a ritual of confirmation, is willing to dramatize its subordination through such small tokens of fealty, and at the same time, instead of keeping silent in the face of obvious official lies and the effrontery of elites, this body breaks into laughter. And, by laughing, it drains officialdom of meaning and sometimes obliges it to function while empty and powerless. (Mbembe 2001, 128-129)

Furthermore, according to Mbembe:

> It is here that the official "sign" or "sense" is most easily "unpacked," "disenchanted" and gently repacked, and pretense (*le simulacre*) becomes the dominant modality of transactions between the state and society, or between rulers and those who are supposed to obey. This is what makes postcolonial relations not only relations of conviviality and covering over, but also of powerlessness par excellence—from the viewpoint both of the masters of power and of those they crush. However, since these processes are essentially magical, they in no way erase the dominated from the epistemological field of power. (Mbembe 2001, 129)

· Of course, this does not mean that the contemporary colonial (ultimately capitalist) hegemony was "softened," it was just reorganized on the basis of *mutually benefitting cooperation, joint social enterprise,* or a *compromise* between the subjugator and the subjugates in the global capitalist project. Consequentially, *disenchanted* taboos, empty gestures of cultural self-realization and empty diversification were made to pose as a *diversity,* but only within the framework in which the degrees of proliferation of political stances were equated to the degrees of adoption of politics as a reflection of the consensus on the function of politics. As Mbembe stated:

> What defines the postcolonized subject is the ability to engage in baroque practices fundamentally ambiguous, fluid, and modifiable even where there are clear, written and precise rules. These simultaneous yet apparently contradictory practices ratify, de facto, the status of fetish that state power so forcefully claims as its right. And by the same token they maintain, even while drawing upon officialese (its vocabulary,

signs, and symbols), the possibility of altering the place and time of this ratification. (Mbembe 2001, 129)

While the postcolonized subject (or a subjugate) was engaged in *baroque* practices, the colonialist First World's structures, while *keeping silent in the face of vulgarity and effrontery of the demos*, restructured the notion of power into a concept that utilized modes of sustainment and expansion of capital (including state power) as tools for maximizing the profit and profit based ideology.

Therefore, what was officially invested into a surplus of meanings was the effect of capital, colonial atrocities, and radical class division etc., which have been ideologically dramatized and turned into tokens of the alleged existence of a politically ideological design that allegedly surpasses the logic of the profit that stands behind the effect of capital. Paraphrasing Mbembe, this means that the recognition of state power as a fetish is significant only at the very heart of the ludic relationship.

Hence, if identities, styles, habits, and cultures, have been produced as primal ideological categories that have served as proper substitutes for political prefixes in differentiation, the perpetuation of intimacy as an ideal for relationships among the protagonists in power struggles influenced the adoption of the presumption that neutralization of the politically ideological prefixes of dichotomies (within the cosmology of power) was the only way through which political prominence might be achieved. That being said, the political power was consequentially converted into a tool for the mere administration of degradation of politics into the domain of cultural, apolitical, and racial conflicts. So, the dominant forms of subjectivization of society into a post-ideological *demos* (amidst the processes of global imposition of capitalist democracy) ensured that structuring of the proto-political agenda of the subjugates never resulted in the restructuring of the politically antagonist agenda in relation to capitalism, but only in restructuring of the ideological apologetic stances toward capitalism.

Consequentially, the experience of resentment that was caused by the effect of capital had been de-accumulated (or *unpacked*) and gently repacked into a sense of ideology that allowed the sensation of purpose of power to be tangible (to the subjugate) only as a feeling of exploitation, while the perpetuation of exploitation (as an ever elusive possibility for assendence within the exploitation hierarchies) was equated to the sense of purpose that was lacking within the apolitical interpretation of the origin of the predicament.

FLEXIBILITY OF RACIAL HIERARCHIES

So, in the context in which sense of purpose is being sought on the basis of various apolitically prefixed diversities, the most *prominent* mode of control over diversification was found in those ideologies that simultaneously allowed one homogeneous center of power to both diversfy within that context and to keep its control over the levels of "prominence" that were being delegated amidst these differentiation processes. These ideologies are of course racial ideologies, which make the process of administration among racial differentiation a process of racialization.

Since the First World's colonial epistemology, based on Eurocentric ideologies, regards itself as being above the historical process and all of its ramifications (which reflects itself in perpetuation of the grasp of the definition of civilization and humanity with no regard to shifts in disposition of global power), the racial hegemony it organized[2] proved itself as being strictly homogenous in a structural sense, yet subtly heterogenous in an expansionist, global sense—inclusive only to the degree that would guarantee the sustaining of firm control over the formations of epistemological matrices and definitions of meaning of various progressivist and/or inclusive tendencies—even if control over material power started to wane.

Hence, European or Euro-Atlantic structural racism does not only represent the fixed hierarchical institutional racism, but represents a specific conflation able to integrate, secularize, that amount of diversity that would formally serve as a token of its own diversity but actually serves as a rationalization for segregation of others designated as incapable for ascendance in the political, but capable enough for ascendance on scales of commodification.

Aimé Césaire, decolonial thinker and one of the founders of négritude movement in Francophone literature has, in relation to paradigmatic representatives of European peoples, noted that: "[T]hey tolerated that Nazism before it was inflicted on them, that they absolved it, shut their eyes to it, legitimized it, because until then, it had been applied only to non-European peoples" (Césaire 2000, 36), is important because it subsumed the Eurocentric logic of the judging of racism that does not seem capable of applying any racism to itself, which is an unwillingness probably compensated by, on the one side, over-emphasizing the rhetorical judgment of certain racism, anti-Semitism, etc., and on the other, under-emphasizing through institutional cynicism either that same anti-Semitism or any other racism for that same matter.

David Cameron, the British prime minister, in a speech on the end of multiculturalism (2010) noticed that "[W]hen a white person holds objectionable views—racism, for example—we rightly condemn them. But when equally unacceptable views or practices have come from someone who isn't white, we've been too cautious, frankly even fearful, to stand up to them" (New Statesman 2010). So, it is easy to notice the typical rhetorical hijacking of the monopoly on judgment that actually says only a white man can condemn a white man, every other judgment is racist or "extremist."[3]

Therefore, if the locus of enunciation of societies subjugated to the regime of capital circulation is distinctiveness in forms of subjugation, the only diversities that hierarchies of exploitation can make ideological are cultural, biological, etc.; this means by situating them as the content of allegedly political discourses and consequently making politically ideo-logical discourses empty of their agenda, history and of their socially organizing potential.[4]

Thus, processes of globalization of capital on the basis of entangle-ment of Eurocentric racial ideologies and liberal democratic agendas have managed to equate the demise of antagonistic politics with the gran-diose rediscovery of politics within the strict coordinates of colonial mod-ernism. This resembles a situation Mbembe called the *time of entanglement* where: "All sharp breaks, sudden and abrupt outbursts of volatility, it cannot be forced into any simplistic model and calls into question the hypothesis of stability and *rupture* underpinning social theory, notably where the sole concern is to account for either Western modernity or the failures of non-European worlds to perfectly replicate it" (Mbembe 2001, 16).

Internal logic of colonial epistemology progressively reflected itself in the following way—the colonial racist epistemic reference frame was equated to a universal modernist project while the process of assendance on the hierarchical scale was contextualized as nothing more than the assendence toward the positions that would ensure higher amounts of affection from those who defined such a modernity. This defined the neoliberal capitalist promise of liberation as nothing more than a striving only for less commodification, less destitution and maybe less death. As Gržinić and Tatlić have, in their analysis of wider functions of racializa-tion, observed:

> It means that the procedure of racialization in wider sense implies that the social conflict is (or should be) congregated around the struggle for positions within the hierarchies, which were axiomatically determined. The whole dynamism of a social conflict was therefore singularized onto one point from which departure (not separation) is allowed—but only if that departure ended on a mere other location within the same hegemonic social space. (Gržinić and Tatlić 2012, 13)

Overzealous tendencies of (the majority of) eastern European states to delegate their sovereignties (in the post-Cold War era) to the iterations of First World's domination, such as the European Union, and/or to engage themselves into overseas colonial invasions, is just one (geopolitical) re-flection of this tendency. The other reflection, however, can be found in a tendency of the First World, especially its European part, to differentiate among the origins of totalitarian projects. While the ongoing process of relativization of communism and facism in Europe based on ascription of inherently totalitarian and murderous traits to communism, fascism on the other hand is being interpreted as a project separate from its origins that lay firmly in Eurocentric racism and judged only by that aspect that considered it the surplus of Nazi imperial tendencies. As Aimé Césaire has noted:

> It would be worthwhile to study clinically, in detail, the steps taken by Hitler and Hitlerism and to reveal to the very distinguished, very humanistic, very Christian bourgeois of the twentieth century that without his being aware of it, he has a Hitler inside him, that Hitler *inhabit* him, that Hitler is his *demon*, that if he rails against him, he is being inconsistent and that, at bottom, what he cannot forgive Hitler for is not *the crime* in itself, *the crime against man*, it is not *the humiliation of man as such*, it is the crime against the white man, the humiliation of the white man, and the fact that he applied to Europe colonialist procedures which until then had been reserved exclusively for the Arabs of Algeria, the "coolies" of India, and the "niggers" of Africa. (Césaire 2000, 36)

These processes of differentiation within the racial core of paradigmatic First World's epistemologies are not, however, the symptoms of depoliticization, these processes are constitutive to the institutionalization of the boundaries within which depoliticization is being produced as an inherent, inextricable part of the reorganization of capitalism on the basis of the co-opting of various humanist prefixed contingencies which are then defined as inherently apolitical. Furthermore, the concepts of democratization and liberalization that were consequently utilized as super narratives for the reinvention of capital on liberal or post-liberal bases, created a context in which the fundamental meaning of the concepts in relation to formation of political states were entwined.

The concept of secularization that was made devoid of its political connotations (i.e., separation of the church and state, etc.) was consequently put in place as an epistemological instrument which allowed white, Christian bourgeoisie and reactionary structures on the Euro-Atlantic axis to reinvent (*gently repack*) themselves as neoliberal, non-dogmatic, *post-ideological* structures. The flourishing of fascism in East European parts of the EU and/or its peripheries in this sense is not the symptom of straying off the road of capitalist democracy, it is the symptom of pretty much correct recognition of the ideological basis on which more "prominent" western democracies reside.

The intensity and transparency of various forms of fascism in Eastern Europe is just a symptom of a lack of elegance in the entanglement of fascist and capitalist democratic agenda's and it is this lack of elegance, not the fundamental ideological incompatibility, that is being made the focus of the impotent, formal critique of fascism by western parts of the EU. In this sense, the paradigmatic contemporary fascist does not see him/herself as a fascist and/or as a proponent of an explicitly political fascist agenda, they see themselves as post-ideological (neoliberal or neoconservative) subjects who "just wanted the things to be as they were meant to be and everybody should know its place," meaning that Euro-Atlantic powers should not be held responsible for century-long plunders and genocides and be allowed to continue to ravage the overexploited world, while their victims should either die, or stand in lines waiting for an opportunity to get to the West and receive a tiny amount of wealth which was taken from them in the first place.

The secular traits of majority of EU's states are therefore just performative and/or in no antagonist relation with the role of the reactionary/ populist/racist policies, the role of the church and otherwise ethnocentric racial policies of major European powers. Walter Mignolo has suggested that:

> "Secularization" was able to detach God from Nature (which was unthinkable among Indigenous and Sub-Saharan Africans, for example; and unknown among Jews and Muslims). The next step was to detach, consequently, Nature from Man (e.g., Frances Bacon' *Novum Organum*, 1620). "Nature" became the sphere of living organisms to be conquered and vanquished by Man. (Mignolo 2009b, 86)

The colonial ideologies that saw indeginous populations as mere parts of nature the white man should have tamed, are still actual of course, but the very dynamism of reorganization of the colonial capitalist matrix is more important in relation to these procedures. So, if the paradigmatic shift in reorganization of capital was illustrated by liberalization (financialization, labor immaterialization, precarization, post-Fordist virtualization) of capital, and by democratic and humanitarian rationalizations of the contemporary colonial procedures in the over-exploited world, the dominant poles the colonial epistemic machine operated with, had also to be reorganized.

Instead of having a duality between Nature and Man, the basis of differentiation was changed into a duality between the body of a subjugate in a state of latent death and the body of a man as a commodity. The parallel between secularization and modernity in this sense is primarily important not because of the role it had in the reinvention of colonial power, but because it emphasized the flexible possibility of the regime to, spatially or temporally, reintegrate its own transgression as a token of its function, formatted as: (a) the pacification of all the diversities into a bizarre collusion based on a struggle for the rights to become commodified (or less dispensable); or (b) to kill, hence producing necropolitics as the First World's capitalist politics par excellence.

When the neoliberal promise of de-ideologization of the social conflict managed to conduct systemic depoliticization of the class struggles, destroying in the process the antagonist potential of politics, it actually produced completely (politically) ideologically empty basis for murder—

rationalizing mere profit and mere fascist barbarism as an apex of a contemporary modernist, ultimately *civilizing* mission of the First World.

If (politically) empty ideology as basis of differentiation was *filled* with racism as compensation for political ideology, and if the super-narrative of this process was found in dogma reproduced under the liberal democratic aegis, then the protagonist in cosmology of power whose social contingencies were ultimately cannibalized was the *demos* itself—not as some non-specific notion of the people, but as a form of consent to the idea that political authority and purpose of the order could be attained through shut down of the politically ideological (ultimately class) dimension of the social conflict.

CAPITALISM'S OCCAM'S RAZOR

If some common denominator could be found within the preconception most widely comprehended as the resentment the West fosters in regard to its interpretation of capitalism as an ideological discourse, that denominator is found in the notion that the people being inherently inhibited, was prevented from taking a more prominent role in the mechanism of rule.

So, bearing this in mind, the problem with capitalism's *inclusive* hierarchies does not lay in the fact that they are not inclusive, but that they in fact *are*. In the same way the problem with the reduction of the distance between the ruling and ruled does not lie in the fact that such a reduction destroyed politically authoritarian dimensions of the rule, but in the fact that it did not.

This does not mean that the hegemonic oppression of capital ceased (nor are we talking about capitalist destruction of the state), on the contrary, it only means that its authoritarian dimension was completely discarded on a political level and reinvented on the level that ascribed authoritarian dimensions to the perpetuation of commodification/exploitation/infliction of death as the terrain on which social conflict should be realized.

The principle known as the Occam's Razor (or *Lex Parsimoniae*)[5] which states that among competing hypotheses, the one that makes the fewest assumptions should be selected, is very applicable in the context of the meaning of capitalism's erasure of political distance. Since the notion of competing hypotheses in the political context implies the existence of competing ideological prefixes in the formation of such hypotheses it is clear that the one ideology that made fewest assumptions (about the possibilities of other ideological approaches to politics) was the ideology that can be immanently verified; capitalism's racialist ideology.

More precisely, the utilization of the principle of *Lex Parsimoniae* as a tool for the depoliticization of a social conflict has instituted an epistemological principle that dictates that the act of reducing the possibilities for the existence of competing hypotheses should be regarded as the overriding principle in the formation of social conflict.

In the so-called *postmodern* condition—in which the complexities of diversification of exploitation were "turned outward" and mobilized as tools for making relative the basic divides in the mechanism of rule—the origin of a predicament, created by the effect of capital, was found in the intricate nature of the relationship between the rulers and the ruled. A solution to the exploitation was, or is being, found, not in the politicization of the relationship between subjugator and the subjugated, but in the reduction of the distance between these positions, which allows capitalism to represent the intensification of its hegemony as the liberation of the subjugates from the complexities in subjugation.

Postmodern traits of an era (in sense in which diversifications would be politicized) were therefore designed to fail, but to fail in a way in which the potency for social transformation would be found either in higher degrees of transparency assigned to the register of subjugation, or in higher degrees of homogenization of the capitalist institutional and epistemological center; the First World.

The search for authoritarian dimensions of order was therefore imagined as non-related to the possibilities of construction of authoritarian dimensions in some other (politically prefixed) ideology. On the other hand though, the same search was reinvented as the search for other ways in which authority, based on capitalism's ideologies, could reorganize its hierarchies. In other words, those contingencies that had already received a degree of authority within the processes of liberalization of capitalism, found themselves as its central carriers.

It was not therefore *the people* that were reduced to a meta-function or to some apolitical niche within the political mechanism, it was the notions of *ideological diversity* and *politically ideological antagonism*, to which the meta status or the status of the redundant assumption was ascribed. The *Lex Parsimoniae*, as one of the key methods of perpetuating the depoliticization of social conflict, actually formed the immediate *nomos* of the order and its institutions into the ultimate ends, the *telos* social struggle might achieve.

As a result, the profane nature of capitalism and its racial ideologies could not be made rational on the basis of any complexity in articulation of the order, it was made rational as the result of the destruction of the possibility of differentiation between the authorities that could reside within some ideological structure. In simple terms, the most immediate and the most tangible kind of authority was selected as the most appropriate.

To paraphrase Mbembe; the subjugated have internalized authoritarian epistemology to the point where they reproduce it themselves in all the minor circumstances of daily life. In this context, this means the reduction of the possibilities for other assumptions in formation of the hypothesis actually lead to the notion that the only source from which authority could be derived belonged to the immediate, most tangible situation. The application of *Lex Parimoniae* in this context meant that the increase in the level of affection between the ruler and the ruled was perceived/epistemologically instituted as a reflection of a search for ideological authority only in the domain in which authority was already decided. Consequentially, social conflicts were formatted not as searches for paradigmatically different ideological hypotheses, but as searches for different versions/angles of the same authority within the same hypothesis.

So, being liminally aware of the empty authoritarianism behind capitalism's ideologies, paradigmatic contours of social conflict in the First World formatted themselves as struggles that could construct more purpose around those contingencies to which the authoritarian dimension was already ascribed. The reactionary/conservative aspect of resentment formatted its paradigmatic stance on a demand that the distance between the power and the people be destroyed in favor of the people as the only power contingency that could organize authentic hierarchies of exploitation on a populist (racial) basis, hence, that could organize "authentic" hegemony.

The liberal, social-democratic aspect of resentment, on the other hand, formatted its agenda on the basis of a demand that the distance between the power and the people (hence the meaningless fixation on the issues of lack of representation) should be destroyed in favor of full representation of people's interests, and hence in favor of installation of a myriad of non-articulated agenda's of otherwise non-articulated notions of the people as a substitute for an authoritarian dimension of politically ideological rule.

The political ideology that does and/or should have a radical authoritarian dimension based on the politicization of the contingency of the ideological was therefore completely left out of the calculus of the social struggles, which were contaminated by liberal/democratic notions that the relationship between any ruler and the ruled should not be marked by a distance.

In the global context of a colonial divide, it seems that the deduction of subjugates/subaltern's experiences of political powerlessness resulted in acknowledgment of the inherent political emptiness of the ideology that stood behind the regime of capitalist exploitation. But, since such emptiness was represented as the pinnacle of any political proliferation, it also seems that efforts to resolve such a predicament were based on an apologetic vector that represented the intensification of levels of commodification as the solution to the experience of powerlessness. This means that the possibilities for attaining any distinction and/or mere survival were strictly tied to the immanent realities of the existence of hierarchies of exploitation. In other words, the domain of possibilities was tied to the non-existence of political articulation of the complex totalities of the order.

On the other hand, the dominant experience of the regime, as experienced by paradigmatic First World's liberal democratic man, was cornered into a context in which the point of departure for interpreting the order was focused around the possibility of constructing ideological purposes, but only around those diversities within the processes of commodification and subjugation.

This means that the differentiation employed in sustaining hierarchies of exploitation was perceived as a precondition for the sustainment of higher disparities in the distribution of wealth (lesser amounts of commodification of the First World) and as a form of differentiation that could derive amounts of distinction and ideological purpose without relying on the domain of the political articulation of the purpose of unlimited maximization of profit. As Ludwig Wittgenstein noted in relation to the (political) meaning of Occam's Razor, "If a sign is not necessary then it is meaningless. That is the meaning of the Occam's Razor" (Wittgenstein 2010, 36).

Hence, if something within symbolical order functions as if it had meaning, then it has meaning. So, the structure of the meaning that was derived out of the neutralization of the politically ideological dimensions of antagonism acquired meaning on the basis of the sustainment of that process of neutralization by itself. A model of acknowledgment of the purpose of that meaning was epistemologically instituted as the model from which the amount of purpose be derived, from eradication of possibilities of installing ideological dimensions into the hypothesis that would be able to politically tackle and resolve the meaning of intricacies invested in diversification of the hegemony.

The *pure ideology* capitalism operates with, therefore exercises meaning on the basis of destruction of any political articulation that could have found an authority in different ideological containers. The *lex parsimoniae* of capitalism's hegemonic epistemologies therefore uncovers the processes of normalization. This narrowing of the antagonist distance is actually a *rigorously flexible* process of normalization of certain kinds of ideologies, authority and purpose; elements which are firmly grounded in capitalism and its racial ideologies.

Nevertheless, while the reduction of the distance between the subjugator and the subjugated still continues to be an instrument of normalization for the discriminative capitalist/colonialist hegemonies, the politics of the left (in politicizing the demand for global redistribution of wealth), should not neglect the necessity of constructing authoritarian dimensions to the ideologies formed on a politically anti-capitalist, anti-imperialist basis, as well as this it should base its decolonial discourses on a rigorous foundation that should singularize the myriad of diversities in perpetuation of exploitation into one firmly politically ideological discourse.

NOTES

1. In other words, the democratic progress of the over-exploited was defined (and validated) in direct proportion to the degree by which the neoliberal promise of the allegedly *non-discriminative* free-market economy was adopted by the subjugates as the neutral terrain on which social conflict is being exercised.

2. Since the colonial plunders of the New World that started in 1492.

3. Hence, neglecting the historical fact that the white colonialist already "stood up" against the non-whites.

4. David Cameron, by stating "[you] yourselves in Germany were long-scarred by terrorism from the Red Army Faction" (New Statesman 2011), implied that any ideological struggle should be criminalized per se, hence, reinventing the regime (that the Red Army Faction tackled) as an innocent order, absolved of any historical responsibility.

5. "A rule in science and philosophy stating that entities should not be multiplied needlessly. This rule is interpreted to mean that the simplest of two or more competing theories is preferable and that an explanation for unknown phenomena should first be attempted in terms of what is already known. Occam's razor is named after the deviser of the rule, English philosopher and theologian William of Ockham (1285?-1349?)" (The Free Dictionary 2013).

FOURTEEN

Substantialization of Depoliticized Ideology

The potential of capitalism to produce a variety of cultural and allegedly *political* diversities under its institutional and epistemological rule and, to simultaneously sustain a homogenous dimension in its organization of hierarchies of exploitation, has, for some time, been a valid subject of critical discourse.

The continuous end of capitalism; capitalism's internalization of its inconsistencies into its own affirmation; the non-limitation of capital in its expansion into all spheres of material and cognitive existence etc., are the concepts, or approach vectors, that have established themselves as critical in the depiction of structural characteristics in the reproduction or rein-vention of capitalism.

Some of the most important approaches in the analysis of capitalism as the diversified, yet highly homogenous form of global rule, could, in an intentionally simplistic manner, be subsumed into a couple of interre-lated aspects of capitalism. The first aspect is capitalism's expansion into all spheres of life by progressive internalization of the consistency of its effect into an inconsistency separated from capital as form of power. The second is, that in compensation for differentiation in the organization of exploitation, capitalist ideologically produced notions of diversity, multi-plicity and difference as unrelated to politically ideological aspects of social antagonism. However, what is most important here is how these constitutive impetuses of capital correlate to one another.

HOMOLOGOUS HETEROGENEITY

According to Santiago López Petit, as interpreted by Marina Gržinić:

> Capitalism . . . is not an irreversible process but a reversible and conflic-
> tual event. The core of this reversibility is presented by Petit in the
> following way. He states that in the world today all is brought back to
> one single event, and this is not the crisis, nor even Obama, but what he
> calls the *unrestrainment* of capital (in Spanish *des[z]boc[k]miento*), that
> can be more colloquially grasped as *"unrestraining"* or *"unleashing"* of
> *capital*. Neoliberal globalization, as stated by Petit, is nothing more than
> the repetition of this single event, that is, the unrestrainment of capital.
> (Gržinić 2009b, 3-4)

In broad terms (and in order to develop this thesis) the *unrestrainment* of
capital (as one single event) subsumes the limits which capital encounters
and at the same time marks the point at which capitalism starts to reproduce itself again toward the next contraction point; toward the new limit
it will shatter. These contraction points do not represent the end of capitalism, of course, they represent the points at which new organizational
modes (under which the same hierarchies and ideologies can be and) are
being reconfigured in order to be able to conform old narratives into
newly created conditions.

So, López Petit's thesis could be seen as a depiction of capital as a
system that cannot be something else after it has reinvented itself into
another form, or after it has appropriated some humanistic super-narrative, such, for instance, as it has done with democracy.

On the other hand, and since capitalism functions in a fashion that
allows it to be extremely discriminative in both the sense of class (which
forms the basis of the exploitation hierarchies in the First World), and
race (that justifies exploitation and colonial genocides in favor of the First
World), capitalism can be seen as reinventing itself, in the most general
terms, based on a juxtaposition that operates within extreme poles: in the
imposition of degrees of limitation or non-limitation within the greater
scope of capitalism's hijacking of the objective aspects of historical progression.

In this sense, the implication is that the operations congregated
around the processes of (repetition of) limitation and non-limitation of
capitalism (infiltration of capital into all spheres of life) are simultaneous
and connected in the sense in which the impossibility of the regime to
separate its effect from its structural reproduction was coupled with its
ultimate possibility to epistemologically represent its hegemonic structure as detached from its effect, or from the historical process in general.

Simultaneously to these operations, the forms of diversities that dwell
under this regime (extremely formalized and emptied of any possibility

of intervention in social reality) were produced as ultimate possibilities of interventionism, but only within already defined boundaries.

These boundaries, additionally, are usually the boundaries that were epistemologically defined and institutionally limited through capitalism's hijacking and/or integration of the emancipationist and/or humanist narratives or projects. The grand narrative of democratic freedom, that today stands behind this apolitical (or obscenely political) contingency of diversity, serves therefore only as an instrument for diversification of capitalism as one single event, and as the narrative that represents the level of its collusion with capitalism as a precondition of the existence of a plethora of choices.

López Petit, as mentioned before in this text, differentiated the notions of *democracy* and *the democratic*,[1] where he noted that, to briefly paraphrase him, the function of the democratic is to guarantee that global mobilization successfully merges with our own life, channel expression of social unease, because the democratic severs the political dimension of our own reality and neutralizes any attempt as social transformation.[2]

As decolonial critical discourse has shown, the notion of capitalism as a homogeneous configuration of exploitation hierarchies that exploit all the same, was simply a model of reorganization of capitalism that has managed to infiltrate various anti-establishment agendas and made them antagonize capitalism only under the aegis of capitalism being a mutual threat to all. In wider sense, this has allowed to the aseptic, impotent social conflicts that tend to correct democracy, to be represented as pinnacles of political antagonism in democracy, while the most prominent effects of capital, that is, capitalism itself has been normalized as the "true" and most potent antagonism whose next iteration would be able to "make a difference," hence tackle (current shape of) capitalism.

Petit does have a point on the wider function of the democratic which—in relation between Schmitt's politics and the political and Petit's democracy and the democractic—helps us see the democracy as a concept of rule in which politics sustains such political antagonisms that operate with already determined possibilities of that same political antagonisms.

The ideological incubation of *possibilities* (or the diversification of impossibilities) in capitalism reflects not only how capitalism has managed very well to connect its agenda with institutional discourses that belonged to humanist projects (such as democracy), but how it has also managed to base its ideological foundations on epistemological grounds that have implied a separation between the effects of capital and the humanist projects it appropriated.

This has allowed capitalist expansion modes, like colonialism, to function under the aegis of a humanist project *and* to be deemed as separate from the allegedly undeterminable political contingencies humanist projects might have entailed in relation to the production of society. Such a depoliticization of some contingency, epistemologically constituted capitalism as an ideology able to act as both the inhibitor of political potentials of humanist agency and as the master procurer of "true" human potentials; but only to the extent to which "true" potentials were defined as *apolitical* and put in complicit relation with capitalism.

Hence, it could not be said that capitalism's ideologies neglect the socio-political dynamics historical processes entail, they recognize those processes, but only as a set of conflicts in which the primacy of capitalism and its ideologies are situated at the far ends of every social conflict.

It could be said that the impossibilities produced or performed as *limitless possibilities* (freedoms) present limitless possibilities only for capital, the impossibilities continue to be performed as possibilities for the subjugated. This relationship, or false antagonization of these two poles, represents a general (or at least most tangible), subtext of the epistemological on the basis of which capitalism organizes its reproduction. How then could the wider framework of capitalist reproduction be seen? According to Lopez Petit, as interpreted by Marina Gržinić:

> The unrestrainment of capital, creates a paradoxical spatialization that requires two repetitions: on the one hand, according to Petit, a founding repetition with which a system of hierarchy is reestablished, leading to the constant reconstruction of a center and a periphery; on the other hand, a so-called de-foundational repetition that presents itself as the erosion of hierarchies, producing dispersion, multiplicity and multi-reality. The unrestrainment of capital, as argued by Petit, implicates both repetitions at once. (Gržinić 2009b, 3-4)

The founding repetition that reinstates or reorganizes hierarchies of rule and control, operates within fields such as technological breakthroughs; material organization of expansion, that is, colonization; development of the means of expansion; organization of commodification and circulation of capital; processes of integration of the state into the agency of capital and of course the sustainment of a tight grip over the means of production (in today's terms, the circulation of capital). Constant reconstruction of the center and periphery does not mean however that the center loses its grip or that it delegates amounts of control to the outside of the hegemonic core,[3] it means that the peripheries are being produced both in a state of constant opening to capital and as complicit to particular agendas that are represented as universal global projects.

So, since the growing non-Western economies still seem to be nothing more but production plants for the First World—not political sovereignties capable of political intervention into (or against) global production paradigms or of separating their production and political configurations from the global mainstream—the epistemological power base and hegemonic control over the ideological meaning of capitalist organization of production still resides firmly in the First World.

The processes of financialization of capital, virtualization of production and circulation, and the virtualization of labor in the First World are, in this sense, parts of the founding repetition. This process keeps the First World in control of the regime of circulation, and allows the reorganization of capital only on the basis that keeps rising economies' raw production prowess in a depoliticized state of flux and does not allow a paradigmatic shift in the organization of those countries politics (in most general and in anti-imperial sense) toward systems which could tackle western imperialism. As Gržinić noted, "Marxism, says Petit, has traditionally connected the critique of capitalism with the defense of the idea of a limit that is accessed by capitalist development and proper to it. To access the limit means to reach the point of its imminent collapse" (Gržinić 2009b, 3-4).

Gržinić added, "What is happening today is the logic that stands at the core of capital: production solely for the benefit of capital in order to generate profit, surplus value, and not for the benefit of social life. Such a situation, that is an antinomy at the core of capital, does produce a living contradiction, but it is not bringing capitalism to an end" (Gržinić 2009b, 3-4).

So just as reaching *a limit* facilitates a collapse of one specific dimension of rigidness in the configuration of capitalism's hierarchies of exploitation, so the next iteration of capitalism becomes marked by a lesser level of explicitness and a higher level of oppression. This also means that the rigidness, intensity or the scope of exploitation has by itself been intensified. The exploitation was, apparently paradoxically, *rigidly made flexible*, hence, the exploitation becomes explicitly intensified while the levels of explicitness that were erased become equated only to the political aspects of explicitness in organization of exploitation, which allows capitalism to become more elusive as a conglomeration of power in direct proportion to which it has become hegemonic and infiltrated every aspect of life.

These are operations that could be seen as connected to the de-foundational aspect of repetition, which is a process that organizes the heterogenic, differential dimension and ideological structure of capitalism's hegemony. Simply put, this repetition takes care to ensure that the reaching of the limit merely presents a non-paradigmatic shift in the configuration of exploitation.

The multiplication of realities and diversification of apolitical stances in subjective interpretations of the hierarchies of oppression therefore organize the epistemological and institutional impetus that diversifies, but does not tackle the homogeneous (founding) aspect of control. Whether it is by being in a form that represents capitalism's differentiations (on the basis of its racial ideologies) as the system of equal exploitation of all, or it is by being a form that pacifies and represents the inherent impossibility of apolitical (or obscenely political) resistance as possibilities for intervention against the processes of reorganization of capitalism, these interpretations operate within the diversifications that were already conformed within the boundaries of epistemological hegemony.

However, since we can see founding repetition as something that entails vertical momentum (the re-establishment of hierarchies) and de-foundational repetition as something that entails horizontal momentum (that organizes ideological structuring along the horizontal vector and allows for the erasure of hierarchies of rule from being targets of political antagonism) a question still stands, where do these trajectories go in an epistemological spatial and temporal framework, and what will their geo-temporal coordinates and speed of repetition mean in the production of social-political realities?

CONTEMPORARY IDEOLOGICAL TEMPORALITY AND *MUTUALIZATION*

So, if we see founding repetition as moving forward in time, we see it as moving at a pace that is being experienced as material-tangible time, or as time that is produced by the tempo dicated by capitalist conquest of material territories and utilitarian aspects of existence. Hence, this trajectory's repetition, produces a format under which utilitarian properties of capital (with regards to the reorganization of production) are being configured. Since this trajectory clearly corresponds to the reestablishment of hierarchies, the constitutive characteristic of this trajectory is the hierarchical vectorality that intersects the spatial/temporal plain at a position located at the initial starting point of the future; in the present or at the last conceivable point in the present.

Since multiplication of realities, various strategies of virtualization, production of cultural matrices and identity based policies, depoliticization of culture, art, and politicization of performativity, are those strategies de-foundational repetition operates with, its vector can be seen as horizontal and/or as the one that ensures that ideological structures are produced as if they had no connection to hierarchical verticality.

This repetition could be seen as one that produces a dichotomic relation between the (horizontal) repetition of the effects of capital and (vertical, hierarchical) reconfigurations of capitalism as a system of power. More importantly, this relation has allowed capitalism to extract ideological viability from horizontal, de-foundational repetition of capital and keep its (ideological and epistemological) hegemony out of the range of those social and political antagonisms that produce its agenda in strict relation to the operations of founding repetition; those agenda's that tend to see capitalism as *post-ideological* system. Although the qualitative characteristic of this kind of repetition is abundance, its form is minimalistic and it was deprived of any kind of redundancy or totalizing dimensions that would have exposed this minimalistic form as a mask of the totalitarian nature of diversifications within the hierarchies of exploitation.

Thus, although de-foundational repetition happens simultaneously with founding repetition and saturates the founding vector with ideological abundance, its trajectory in geo-temporal coordinates seems to move back and forth in time in longer leaps then the temporal mark proprietary to the founding repetion of capital does.

This means that its trajectory reconverts historical events, spectrums of meaning and symbolical conglomerations and reinterprets them in a fashion which affirms/synchronizes the epistemologial normative within which contemporary capitalist/imperial regimes reside. In simple terms, it goes back and forth in historical time, reinteprets/reconverts it, and situates it in the present and the future of exploitation as the apologetic stance of contemporary forms of capitalism and as an instrument that situates (more of capitalism) in the future as the response to the effect of capital in the present.[4]

As a result, the dominant predicaments contemporary world finds itself in which have its historical origin are being *mutualized* which means that those parts of the world responsible for the radical discrepancies in distribution of world's wealth are now reinventing themselves as victims of themselves. As Marina Gržinić noted in reference to implications the "Former West" project,[5] but in regard to wider epistemological strategies capitalism employs:

> This speculative character of the *former Western Europe* resembles with perfect accuracy the speculative character of financial capitalism at the present, as well as its crisis. Be sure that in the future we can expect projects, symposia and statements in which the imperial colonizing forces, Britain, France, Netherlands, etc., will try to prove how they were also colonized in the past, and that what is happening to them in the present is the result of some strange forces having nothing to do with the internal logic of capitalism itself that has two drives only, making profit at any cost and privatization. (Gržinić 2010d, 15)

If we make a historical parallel, in the period from the 1950s to 1990s, western mainstream imagination was concerned with the embellishment of one ideological pole in a bipolar world with liberal traits. In the period from the 1990s to the 2000s the same imaginations were focused on the erasure of political prefixes to social conflicts (in favor of cultural, ethnic, identity based politics). The period after 2001, (after 9/11) brought a new paradigm in organization of paradigmatic political vision of the western imaginary mainstream. Not only was the erasure of the antagonist distance between the rulers and the ruled (as part of the process of liberalization of capitalism) integrated into an ideological norm, but the same norm was produced in a shape that implied that all ideologies were (or should be) extracted from the apolitical view that saw history as a predestined, ideologically frictionless set of events. Dominant rhetorical pattern in contemporary mainstream public discourse that reduces the antagonistic distance between the instances of power and the subjects (the state/company/oppression apparatus does not any more work *for you*, but *with you*), could also be seen as the *mutualizing* impetus on a micro social scale.

On a macro scale, *mutualization* represents the operation of erasure or distortion of the roles in the cosmology of power, not only in the present, but along all temporal linearity that allows capitalism to pose as the supra-historical power that have allowed capitalism's racialist ideologies to pose as unrelated to the power base that creates and sustains them as institutional discourses. As Gržinić notices:

> While the East is excluded more and more from the materiality of its history, knowledge, memory, etc., the West is just performing it. It plays with a speculative format of itself; it wants us to think that its roots of power and capital are fictional! But this is not a strange move today, as it comes in a time when we talk about financialization; the word *former* in front of West presents a speculative matrix that gives the West the possibility to not be conscious of its own historical and present hegemonic power—and therefore not responsible for it. (Gržinić 2010d, 15)

Of course, this aspect of repetition ultimately erases capitalism and its power structures from historical time, reinstating today's exploitation hierarchies as reflections of a mutual agenda in the formation of homogenous reality in which it was (is) allegedly impossible to distinguish the perpetrator from the victim. This depicts de-foundational repetition as a genuine spatio-temporal instrument of erasure of political causality of cause and the effect—as well as presenting the instrument for the erasure of a basic political dichotomy somewhere between the oppressor and the oppressed.

To paraphrase López Petit, if crisis, or better, this global crisis is important it is because it launches a new social deal. This new social deal gives people the right to participate in the global mobilization that produces the world; more precisely, in this fully capitalist reality without an outside that is our world. As López Petit added, "The social contract becomes a personal contract. It is also clearly formulated: 'life in exchange for the most absolute employability'" (López Petit 2011, 5).

In the context of the back and forth trajectory of the de-foundational dimension, it means that the possibility of the privileged subject is being reproduced simultaneously as a phantom possibility for a non-privileged, racially segregated subjectivity to whom the existence of a phantom possibility by it self is offered as an already attained form of *success*.

Hence, this is the process of depoliticization and de-antagonization of the present of exploitation where this present becomes part of a *neutral*

historical trajectory that was dependant and existent only in positive relation to the progress produced by the founding aspects of capitalism and
those power structures that rule over it. In the context of López Petit's
remark, we could add that what we get is life in exchange for the ever-
eluding prospect of political life in the First World and life in exchange
for the prospect of not losing one's life in the over-exploited world.

The operations of this repetition are therefore normalizing the way in
which differentiation is being organized in globalized capitalism. Extreme forms of commodification and murder (including racial and colonial genocides) were integrated into the normative while the epistemological format in which the political is being perceived as fixating on the
interpretation for politics as congregated only around the most tangible
dimension of the effect of capital—the infliction of death. Consequentially, the dominant paradigm under which the rule is being organized became a necropolitical paradigm, institutional and epistemological discourse that both erases death as a political category and formats infliction
of death as proper ideological discourse.

CONFORMING OF DIFFERENTIATION

Marina Gržinić, in the context of articulation of López Petit's thesis,
notes, "The unrestrainment of capital is, as argued by López Petit, the
only event that—being repeated in any moment and any place—unifies
the world and connects everything that is going on within it. Repetition is
also de-foundational to the degree with which, according to López Petit,
capital repeats indifference for equality" (Gržinić 2009b, 3-4).

At the same time, capital differentiates between inequalities and extracts dimensions of equality out of the wider contexts in which inequality is normalized. In other words, capitalism extracts ideological prowess
for itself in which the lack of politically ideological prefixes of differentiations were compensated with differentiations and diversifications only
within hierarchies of oppression. Thus in such a world, it puts the lack of
political purpose of existence in indirect proportion to the amount of
possibilities for differentiating within hierarchies of exploitation.

In wider terms, through differentiation of inequality, capital differentiates between positions determining which amounts of equality should
be delegated to whom. These are actually pure racialist hierarchies in
which the highest amount of equality was delegated to those subjects that
were defined as subjects (white male European heterosexual Christians)
while the amount of equality delegated to those subjects defined as objects was conditioned—the more the object acknowledges the centrality
of the Eurocentric epistemologies in universal narratives, the more *equality* it allegedly receives. In general, this kind of inequality, based on profit
and racial ideologies, is being produced as *the* diversity *ipso facto*, that is,

as the precondition for transcendence of the formalized notion of equality in exploitation.

Equality and *inequality* have therefore been extracted out of strictly dichotomist or antagonist relations. They have been put in cooperative relation to capital (or in relation to capitalism as the form of power) in order to deprive the notion of *inequality* of politically ideological potency (that would antagonize the capitalist transgressor) and to produce *equality* as the impotent sterile plain on which highly discriminative configurations of exploitation can receive an aureole of mutual respectability both subjugators and subjugates. For instance, and as Marina Gržinić notices:

> The European Union continuously speaks of how everything is now becoming increasingly democratic as well as more liberal and open to democratic possibilities and potentialities, while in reality we witness fascist tendencies, racist public speeches, and a torrent of attitudes of hate that have become normalized and cohabit easily with the neoliberal capitalist machine, which is disgustingly tolerant of the social and political processes of discrimination. (Gržinić 2010c, 4)

The criteria employed in determination of a criteria for exploitation and oppression is still determined by white, Euro-Atlantic imperialist racist ideologies, that under an aureole of alleged anti-racial (post-racial) policies positions the question of differentiation as non-separable from repetitions of capitalism.

POLITICAL FUNCTION OF PURE IDEOLOGY

So, while we can conclude that the founding repetition organizes expansions of capital, reconfigures its hierarchies by moving forward in a temporal sense and the de-foundational repetition organizes its ideological structure along its action of movement back and forth along the temporal linearity, a question of the meaning of their pace still remains.

It seems that de-foundational repetiton, despite its trajectory that goes back and forth in historical time at a steady pace, *accelerates* in the present, perhaps only one moment ahead of founding repetition. It seems that it accelarates only to that measure to which it manages to provide and/or precede the founding repetition, in order to create an epistemological container that is able to instananeously conform the effect of founding repetition into the ideological structure of the capitalist regime.

It could be said that this accelerating momentum allows for instantaneousness repetition of both repetitions, plus one moment. Hence, instantaneousness or simulatenousness of both repetitions means that the founding impetus is instantly being reproduced as de-foundational, ideological impetus. This momentum of acceleration allows the regime to represent the ideological properties of de-foundational repetition as subversive to the founding repetition, but actually this momentum was designed to be subversive only to those aspects of founding repetition that keep it away from shattering more limits to the spread of capitalism or that keep it from becoming more hegemonic.

In the most banal terms, the acceleration of de-foundational repetition prevents the establishment of a coherent political link between these two repetitions and prevents us from seeing the structural connection both repetitions have in sustainment of dominant ideological narratives contemporary capitalism perpetuates.

Of course, this repetition erases the connection between *power* and *social reality* in temporal linearity, but it also operates as the epistemological filter that converts the methodology that founding repetition uses (in its shattering of the limits to capital) for the purpose of tackling any antagonism that normative demarcations could foster. Simply put, only those antagonisms that shatter the limits of capital were epistemologically instituted as capable of tackling any limitations. In other words, while this momentum mutualizes or narrows the degrees of separation between the rulers and the ruled, it structures antagonism as socially potent only if it is referential to the particularities with which differentiation in inequality is organized. Gržinić saw three major fields with which López Petit tackles global capitalism as reality, capital/power, and democracy. As she noted:

> These segments are linked together through two almost old fashioned mechanisms that are evidently still operative today: circularity in the way of self-referentiality and empty formalism, on the one side, and tautology that produces obviousness, on the other. Tautology means obviousness. This tautology, as argued by Petit, presents itself today as the complete and total coincidence of capitalism and reality. (Gržinić 2009b, 3-4)

This coincidence does not reflect, of course, some static state of things that transcends the effect of capital and its power discourse, it reflects a dynamic process that keeps repetitions in a constant state of "catch up" with each other and congregates them around one other; which is a process that ultimately produces dominant social reality. This is a dynamic in which the founding aspects of capitalism are catching up with de-foundational repetition, but it does so at a pace that does not allow either repetition to coincide totally. Gržinić claims: "The date of the event that made that reality and capitalism coincide totally is, as argued by Petit, September 11th, 2001. Petit states that the outcome of September 11th, 2001 was the excess of reality, it was the moment when reality exploded" (Gržinić 2009b, 3-4).

In this context, this explosion has, metaphorically speaking, *paused* the accelerating momentum of de-foundational repetition of capitalism, which uncovered the effect of founding repetition without its ideological mantle. De-foundational repetition was, metaphorically speaking, slowed to the degree where it unmasked the founding repetition as being a purely mechanistic operation of reproduction of capitalism as separated from its de-foundational, rationalizing rhetorics.

Death and/or transparent exposition of (possibility) of dying therefore could be seen as the main element that the collision of reality and capital produced on 9/11, because it was briefly exposed death as a political and ideological category (that does happen as a result of political and ideological struggles), not as a category that belonged to "post-ideological" social reality that happens in a post-historical era.[6] Consequentially, in the aftermath of the event, when the de-foundational repetition, metaphorically speaking, separated itself from this collision, it conformed, or more precisely, detached death from the register of political causality and attached it to a register of post-ideological linearity of experience of history—it was normalized, deprived of politically ideological dimensions and ascribed to an epistemological register that perceives historical progression only as a progression that leads toward a universal, global consensus on capitalism (and its democracy) as the pinnacle of human civilization.

In other words, the representational and epistemological dramatization of the 9/11 deaths in the First World was coupled with the ideological *de-dramatization* of those deaths that were (are being) inflicted by the First World. But, since processes of the infliction of death were integrated into the epistemological normative as the ideological agenda (without explicit political dimensions), these processes demonstrated that the dominant paradigms in capitalism's search for hegemony are *necropolitical* and/or as processes for the extraction of ideology directly out of the effect of capital; but not from the rationalizations of that effect.

In other words, the transparent infliction of death—that is inherently contained within the First World's strategies of imposition of particular interpretations of the modernist agenda as universal—was integrated into the processes of reorganization of colonialism (capitalism) on the basis that now epistemologically institutes mass murder, plunder, occupation, and perpetuation of concentration camps as forms of something more which capitalism allegedly entails, aside it being simply a murderous racist system focused on the maximization of profit.

The predicament of the victims of the First World's imperialism in Iraq, Afghanistan or those being tortured in neoliberal democratic concentration camps (Abu Ghraib, Bagram, Guantanamo) are not seen as originating from the operations of capitalism as (First World's) profit-making racist machinery, rather, their predicament was integrated into the First World's hegemonic epistemology as proof of the existence of some substantial agenda that allegedly stood behind the plunder and murder organized by that capitalist machinery. In this way, the imperialist power structure based completely on the maximization of the profit and sustainment of racial ideologies, proscribes to itself those elements of *statehood* that allegedly transcend primal motives of the imperial machinery.

So, this *statehood* should not be comprehended as a reflection of existence or some sovereign (politically ideological) entity that surpasses the logic of profit, it should be comprehended as part of the process of capitalism's search for hegemony, whose ideologies (while being based on Eurocentric racism) are, either by sustaining or surpassing univerzalized notion of modernity, formatting the modern and its iterations as having no connection to the political or ideological dimensions of dominant power discourses. Gržinić notes that:

> Petit states that the classical concept of modernity is about modernization. It is presented as an endogenous process that is caused by factors within the system. Modernity is presented as the work of reason itself. Likewise, modernity constructs a rationalist image of the world that implicates the duality subject/object, and the distance is, says Petit, that of man and the world. Postmodernism abolishes the distance and situates man inside the world that is made of signs and a-historical languages. The global era oscillates this distance between zero and infinity. That is why there is the feeling of the absence of the world and at the same time we witness it's over abundance. (Gržinić 2009b, 3-4)

We could see the relation between *zero* and *infinity* as the relation in which *zero* represents the non-limitations of founding repetiton in the expansion and (re)territorialization of capital, while *infinity* could be seen in connection with the de-foundational aspect; infinite in its ability to produce *ratio* to capitalism. Consequentially, such a dynamism between these extreme values has shown that *infinity* became a propulsory dimension of *zero*, hence, the possibilities of institutional and epistemological structures to renew their hegemonic positions through infinite diversifications of the forms of exploitation it organized. But, what does this mean as regards to the functions of repetitions of unrestrainment of capital?

The acceleration of de-foundational repetition in relation to the founding repetiton could be seen as the function that does not allow the diversities (it organized) to tackle the hierarchical structures supported by founding repetition. More precisely, if the space between *zero* and *infinity* is the only space in which political processes in capitalism might take place, the function of acceleration of the de-foundational repetition might be seen as that which does not allow the political process (or to the effect of capital for that matter) to surpass the space between the extreme poles posited as the origin and the far ends of the antagonisms these social processes might have entailed.

But, more importantly, it seems that the acceleration of the de-foundational paradigm that organizes the narrowing of the space betwen the zero and infinity is part of the process of formation of an epistemological normative in which constant narrowing of the antagonist distance between the oppressor and the oppressed (constant depoliticization), has been instituted into the purpose of the First World's political and ideological normative. As Marina Gržinić wrote:

> In the past, the social reality was presented as "normal"; that means on the level of content, it was displayed precisely differently from what was occurring in everyday life, therefore on the level of its reflection, on the level of the (art) form, it was necessary to produce something "abnormal"; something as a formal invention or as an excess, as an excessive surplus (in accordance with the social and political system in which they appeared, be it socialism or capitalism), in order to say that what was in reality on the level of content a normality, was in fact a lie. But what we have today is precisely the obverse; on the level of the "content," so to speak, in reality the world is captured as it is, in its full extension of abnormality, monstrosity, exploitation, expropriation, while on the level of the form, this abnormality is normalized, is presented in such a way that the meaning of powerful content becomes empty, obsolete. (Gržinić 2009b, 3-4)

Metaphorically speaking, while the ideological structure of capitalism is making sure that capital is always something more then it is, that structure itself does not believe that it is anything more than what it is. In other words, the inability of capitalism's ideological structure to produce politically ideological substance has itself been converted into the repetition that fulfills its promise to attain political purpose by never actually attaining it.

The distance between *zero* and *infinity* is therefore shrinking at the pace at which politically ideological prefixed spaces of social and ideological conflict are being erased, while the acceleratory property of defoundational repetition makes sure that purely ideological residue can be utilized through its transcribtion to the founding, unarticulated propulsory property of capital. The oscillation of this shrinking (maximum oppression presented as minimum oppression) has been converted into ideological material, and since it has been rendered as not being in need of any kind of political articulation, it has, as a self-collapsing movement, been promoted into the purpose of the highest value in capitalism's ideological structure.

If their speed, vector, trajectory (emptied, formalized apolitical diversity going one step in front of material reality), or the fricition among them are the only tangible configurations of reality, then the simplest solution for making capital a single rational event, was to reproduce these frictions into ideological substances *incurvatus in se*, by themselves for themselves.

The mutualization of the predicaments; the erasure of the political out of the ideological; the conversion of death into the proof of existence of an alleged purpose that stands behind the logic of profit are all the results of these operations. In other words, the mere method through which something is being made ideological or depoliticized has been made ideological, while the political meaning of the ideological substance has been made ultimately irrelevant. Gržinić has noted: "If we follow Althusser's definition of ideology as an imaginary deformed representation of the imaginary relationship of individuals to their real conditions of existence (by which he meant the relations of production), we should say that what ideology misrepresents today is not the reality, but itself" (Gržinić 2009b, 3-4).

In colloquial terms, the *solution* to the contemporary predicament entails the relationship between the method and the substance that was found in the erasure of the substance that reflected reality as the product of dominant power discourses and/or historical materialism. More precisely, this means that ideology (without political aspects) represented itself as a substitution for the political dimension in the ideological. This has, consequentially, institutionally and epistemologically situated those ideologies that had political substance as impotent, while those ideologies that were based on supra-historical, racial, biological foundations were rendered as politically propulsive.

So, the ideologization of the political (antagonism), that should be produced on the basis of the primacy given to the constitutive relation between historical processes and dominant power discourses, should base the production of its ideological substantiality within (and in regard to) the constant politicization of this relation.

Anti-capitalist and anti-imperialist struggles should therefore ideologize politics as a tool of widening the distance between the ruler and the ruled, as a tool of destruction of the current obscene affection between these poles which would be an ultimate precondition in creation of political antagonism(s) able to tackle radical (class, racial, wealth distribution, etc.) discrepancies that the affection between oppressors and the oppressors makes rational. Hence, politically ideological struggle should not bother itself with correcting the effect of capital within already colonized humanist narratives, it should construct a coherent link between the self-collapsing nature of founding and de-foundational repetitions of capitalism in order to make them collide, but only within their own particular de-universalized niche. Thus, in the same fashion in which capitalism perpetuates its control through depoliticization of its effect and its ideologies, politically ideological, left-wing agenda should extract its ideological coherence out of the constant, yet only apparently paradoxical, politicization of politics.

NOTES

1. See chapter 10, "The Function of Democracy in Normalization of Hegemony."

2. Of course, one of the major effects which democracy (alongside capital as a single event) created, was the representation of, obviously differential exploitation, as a homogeneous matrix of exploitation of all on allegedly equal basis.

3. Especially in regard to the production of dominant ideological narratives and epistemological hegemonies.

4. For instance, the most prominent effect of this repetition lies in operations of historical revisionism that subsume the processes of making relative the roles which perpetrators of colonial genocides, colonization, racism, fascism, the African, South American, and European holocausts, global plunder, etc., had in history.

5. That was organized in The Netherlands as part of International Research, Publishing and Exhibition Project, in the period 2009–2012, curated by Charles Esche, Maria Hlavajova and Kathrin Rhomberg (http://www.formerwest.org)

6. We are referring to Francis Fukuyama's coneptualization of the end of history.

Conclusion

In the time of general depoliticization, the epistemology/sex/politics/art/
capital matrix is *an institution* of power and ideology as well as it is a
privatization process that has to be seen in its historical, economic, and
(a)political dimensions working together with historical formats of capitalism.

The point of this book was to contest regimes of esthetics, knowledge,
and histories, their complicity with power, money, and universalized
projects of knowledge and to insist on multiple histories that condition
our understanding of such regimes. These histories are material and have
to be always rewritten anew. The process of subjectivization has to be
constantly re-articulated.

We exposed clearly that *de-subjectivation* is just a contemporary form
of the historical process of subjectivation and that this *subject* is nothing
more than a name for the possible agency established by western epistemology.

Therefore the questions we posed are: what kind of processes of subjectivization is produced? And what is the role of art, politics, culture,
knowledge, and capital in the present moment? The answers are disturb-
ing: the *subject* in contemporary global capitalism is just a brand or a
style, it is far away from the political subject that is capable to reflect and
integrate, in its form and in its content, those radical antagonist forces
that would be capable to dismantle systematic discrimination, subjugation, etc., on the basis of a pertinent political theory and politicization of
its function.

Racialization was in this context seen as the framework and ideological logic that organizes this interplay between misdirected antagonism,
as well as the contemporary form of a First World's colonial epistemologies and colonial power structure—which are now using new civilizing
narratives (democracy, globalization) as forms of obfuscation (univerzal-
ization) of particular interests. As a result, we determined, that this racialization had led to the erasure of historical responsibilities and even to
performative self-victimization of the most prominent perpetrators that
put forward radical discrepancies in the distribution of wealth and privileges.

Racialization is the rationale behind the counting of bodies (that is a
colonial mathematical operation), it determines which bodies matter,
which have the status of undiscussed brand(s) and which are sorted in

relation to systematic *identitarian* classifications that are, in the end, re-producing a system of racial and class division. Therefore, this book ana-lyzes the dynamics of a reproduction of a system that perpetuates the situation in which politics is being designed and defined to succumb to the logic of capital, which results in re-redirection away from race- and class-based conflicts and toward conflicts confined to the boundaries of race, identity, culture, religion, etc.

Racialization in this sense is not just a contemporary form of imperial racism, it is the principle ideology of capitalism. As such it functions as the principle form of subversion of class-prefixed social conflicts and diverts these conflicts into the fields of race, religion, ethnicity, and cul-ture. Racialization however is not merely a method of production of dif-ferentiation, it is a contemporary form of Eurocentric epistemological logic that secures the centrality of the role of the First World in definition of progress, modernity and civilization in general.

In this sense, necropolitics was defined as the paradigmatic principle of ruling, a principle of shaping political power, not only as the power that determines who will live and who will not, but as the power that structures the process of continuous differentiation between form and quantity in the imposition of death as political process *par excellence*. Al-though it could be said that the primal role of any form of rule comes down to the differentiation between friend and foe, necropolitics func-tions as the kind of power that does not determine the confines of this binary on the basis of political consideration, but on the basis of other logics employed in the structuring of the political imaginary—the logics of capital and race.

Necropolitics, Racialization, and Global Capitalism means to determine that necropolitics and racialization (as ideological, epistemological, and institutional strategies) synthesize a plethora of strategies, concepts, and rationales capitalism uses in its institutional and ideological reproduc-tion. In this sense, necropolitics and racialization are postulated as the key principles on the basis of which power discourses and dominant matrices of reproduction of society function. The aftermath of the crum-bling of principle ideological divide of the twentieth century, between capitalism and socialism, is now depicted by the domination of capitalim that, within itself, organized a divide which it uses for the reproduction of itself as a grand (allegedly ahistorical) narrative of progress. While necropolitics functions as a tool of maximization of profit and conquest, racialized ideologies make those actions rational, but also tend to posit themselves as antagonistic toward relentless expansion of capitalism in all spheres of living, only to make the progressions of that expansion rational. In the aftermath of the financial crisis of 2008, it was racialization that diverted class conflict into the field of race, while necropolitics si-multaneously started to use racial hate and fearmongering as tools that justified austerity politics, hence, further devastating the social dimensions (if any) of the state.

This book has tried to depict, criticize and reflect on all the complexities and effects this internal "division" of capitalism, and the interrelation of necropolitics and racialization have produced.

In this sense, when chapter 1 postulated contemporary Europe as "European apartheid," chapter 8 postulated that Eurocentric liberalism is a mode of making apartheid rational. When chapter 2 established a structural connection between capitalist deregulation and the transformation of biopolitics into necropolitics, chapter 9 established that de-ideologization in politics was that kind of "deregulation" of political power that deprived it of its prerogatives to surpass the logics of capital.

When chapter 3 determined that a racial-State entailed both the nation-State and the war-State, chapter 10 determined that democracy is the humanist narrative that conceals the racial-State under the aureole of overcoming of the nation-State. When chapter 4 determined that epistemology of global capitalist power is a colonial epistemology, chapter 11 established that the ideological firmness of the colonial First World is being restructured on the basis of the inauguration of necropolitics into a primal token of existence of *Statehood*: of a profit driven capitalist State that allegedly surpasses the logic of capital.

When chapter 5 dealt with the status and predicaments refugees are experiencing in the First World, chapter 12 articulated the situation that produced these same refugees in the first place. When chapter 6 tackled the questions of transfeminism, dehumanization, and dissident feminisms in a wider analysis of the depoliticization of subcultures (and their political potentials), chapter 13 tackled the wider context of the depoliticization of the distance between oppressed groups and oppressors.

Finally, when chapter 7 found that the concept of repetitive reproduction of capitalism empties (political) content of social struggles, chapter 14 added to this by articulating that the same *emptying* is simultaneously coupled with substantializaton of that emptied space with purely ideological agenda, which represents depoliticized social reality as the peak of its politicization.

The most important outcome that comes from the book is the political act of historicizing every, *naturalized* (by capitalism) mode of production, of life, of State, of politics and art. In this respect we exposed and reworked migration, nation-State and citizenship, but at the same time we did not leave out the politics of counter-acting and intervening. Democracy, emancipation, humanization and insurgency were also deeply inspected, dissected and put under detailed forensic procedures in all listed forms of upheaval and revolution. We as well historicize them. We claimed that citizenship is today at least divided within itself, we have *biopolitical* and *necropolitical* citizenship. We identified three forms of State, the nation-State, war-State, and the racial-State.

We understand that the modes of racialization are in the foundations of the processes we tackle, from historical colonialism to present-day coloniality, where anti-Semitism in the process of racialization takes its central role. We did not leave aside the processes of subjugation, dispossession, exploitation, extortion, and finally (and simply): death, a system of afflicting pain and killing through direct and indirect regimes of murder; working hand in hand with war, deprivation, isolation, and dehumanization.

To summarize, we engaged in and with contemporary transfeminist and dissident positions in order to propose a transmigrant movement, working with theories of transfeminism and decolonial perspectives. In this way, a space is opened up: for reflecting on the fundamental premises of transformation in the understanding of art, theory, and history, but without the rejection of a critical stance and an acknowledgement of the need for intervention against capitalism and its methodologies of dispossession and devaluation of life.

Marina Gržinić and Šefik Tatlić

Bibliography

Adalat, Khan. 2013. Interview by Marina Gržinić and Tjaša Kancler, recorded on December 5, 2013 in Vienna, Austria. Available at http://africa-europe.net/?p=158.

Agamben, Giorgio. 1998. *Homo Sacer: sovereign power and bare life.* Translated by Daniel Heller-Roazen. Stanford: Stanford University Press.

———. 2005. *State of Exception.* Translated by Kevin Attell. Chicago and London: The University of Chicago Press.

Ahmed, Sara. 2004. *The Cultural Politics of Emotion.* Edinburgh: Edinburgh University Press.

———. 2006. "The Non-Performativity of Anti-Racism." *borderlands e-journal* . vol. 5, no.3. Available at http://www.borderlands.net.au/vol5no3_2006/ahmed_nonperform.htm

———. 2008. "Liberal Multiculturalism is the Hegemony—It's an Empirical Fact—A response to Slavoj Žižek." Darkmatter: In the Ruins of Imperial Culture (19 February 2008). Available at http://www.darkmatter101.org/site/2008/02/19/

———. 2012. *On Being Included: Racism and Diversity in Institutional Life.* Durham and London: Duke University Press.

Aigul, Hakimova. 2013. Interview by Marina Gržinić and Tjaša Kancler, recorded on August 4, 2013, in Ljubljana, Slovenia. Available at http://africa-europe.net/?p=30

Appadurai, Arjun. 1993. "Number in the Colonial Imagination." In Breckenridge, C. A., and P. V. D. Veer. eds. *Orientalism and the Postcolonial Predicament.* Philadelphia: University of Pennsylvania Press.

Badiou, Alain. 2005. *Being and Event.* Translated by Oliver Feltham. London and New York: Continuum Books.

Balibar, Étienne. 1988. "Y a-t-il un 'neo-racisme'?." [Is there a 'néo-racism'?]. In Balibar, Étienne, and Immanuel Wallerstein, eds. *Race, nation, classes: Les identités ambiguës.* [Race, Nation, Classes: Ambiguous Identities]. Paris: La Découverte.

———. 1997. *La crainte des masses: Politique et philosophie avant et apres Marx.* [The Fear of the Masses: Politics and Philosophy Before and After Marx] . (Collection La Philosophie en effet). Paris: Galilée .

Balibar, Étienne and Immanuel Wallerstein. 1991. *Race, Nation, Class: Ambiguous Identities.* Translation of Étienne Balibar by Chris Turner. London: Verso.

Banerjee, Subhabrata Bobby. 2006. "Live and Let Die: Colonial Sovereignties and the Death Worlds of Necrocapitalism." *borderlands e-journal.* vol. 5, no. 1. Available at http://www.borderlands.net.au/vol5no1_2006/banerjee_live.htm.

———. 2009. "Histories of Oppression and Voices of Resistance: Towards a Theory of the Translocal." *Reartikulacija.* #9. Ljubljana (Slovenia). pp. 10-11.

Barzak, Ibrahim. 2011. "Michèle Alliot-Marie, French Foreign Minister, Palestine Trip: Pelted with Eggs and Shoes." *Huffington Post.* January 21, 2011. Accessed March 5th, 2013. http://www.huffingtonpost.com/2011/01/21/michele-alliotmarie-frenc_n_812156.html

Bataille, George. 1993. *The Accursed Share—Volumes 2 and 3.* Translated by Robert Hurley. New York: Zone Books.

Baudrillard, Jean. 2001. *Impossible Exchange.* Translated by Chris Turner. London: Verso.

Beller, Jonathan. 2009a. "The Martial Art of 'Cinema': Modes of Virtuosity *a la* Hong Kong and the Philippines." Lecture held in Ljubljana, 2009, at the graduate module "Intercultural study. Comparative study of ideas and cultures," within the seminar conducted by Marina Gržinić, University of Nova Gorica, Slovenia and The Scientific Research Center of the Slovenian Academy of Sciences and Arts (ZRC SAZU), Ljubljana. Manuscript.

Beller, Jonathan, and Marina Gržinić. 2009b. "Discussing Contemporary Capitalism and the Cinematic Mode of Production." Interview by Marina Gržinić. *Reartikulacija*. #9. Ljubljana (Slovenia). Available at http://grzinic-smid.si/?p=913

Bhabha, Homi. 1994. *The Location of Culture*. New York: Routledge.

Bourcier, Marie-Hélène. 2005. *Queer Zones 2, Sexpolitiques*. Paris: La Fabrique.

———. 2011. "Politique et théorie queer: la seconde vague."[Politics and Queer Theory: the Second Wave]. I nterview by Sylvie Duverger. *Nonfiction.fr*. Available at http://www.nonfiction.fr/article-4344-politique_et_theorie_queer__la_seconde_vague.htm

———. 2013. "Notre féminisme de l'égalité est triste et peu affirmative." [Our Feminism of Equality is Sad and Just a Bit Affirmative]. Interview by Anne-Claire Genthialon. March 18, 2013. Available at http://next.liberation.fr/sexe/2013/03/18/notre-feminisme-de-l-egalite-est-triste-et-peu-affirmatif_889497

Brown, Stephen, 2010. "German Muslims must obey law, not sharia: Merkel." *Reuters*. October 6, 2010. Accessed December 5, 2013. http://www.reuters.com/article/2010/10/06/us-germany-muslims-idUSTRE69552W20101006

Brügge, Sebastian and Sybille Fuchs. 2012. "German officer responsible for Kunduz massacre promoted to rank of general." *World Socialist Web Site*. August 21, 2012. Accessed December 5, 2013. http://wsws.org/en/articles/2012/08/klei-a21.html

Burke, Anthony. 2002. "Borderphobias: the politics of insecurity post-9/11." *borderlands e-journal*. vol. 1, no. 1. Available at http://www.borderlands.net.au/vol1no1_2002/burke_phobias.html

Butler, Judith. 1990. *Gender Trouble: Feminism and the Subversion of Identity*, London and New York: Routledge.

Caixeta, Luzenir. 2013. "Minoritized Women Effect a Transformation in Feminism." Translated by Aileen Derieg. In The Editorial Group for Writing Insurgent Genealogies, eds. *Utopia of Alliances, Conditions of Impossibilities and the Vocabulary of Decoloniality*. Vienna: Löcker. pp. 145–148.

Carr, Brian. 1998. "At the Thresholds of the 'Human': Race, Psychoanalysis, and the Replication of Imperial Memory." *Cultural Critique*. no. 39 (Spring). pp. 119–150.

———. 2004. "Paranoid Interpretation, Desire's Nonobject, and Nella Larsen's *Passing*." *PMLA* 119.2. pp. 282–295.

Castro-Gómez, Santiago. 2007. "The Missing Chapter of Empire—Postmodern Reorganization of Coloniality and Post-Fordist Capitalism." *Cultural Studies* 21:2, 428-448. Available at http://www.tandfonline.com/doi/abs/10.1080/09502380601162639

Césaire, Aimé. 2000. *Discourse on Colonialism*. Translated by Joan Pinkham. New York: Monthly Review Press.

Coronil, Fernandó. 1996. "Beyond Occidentalism. Toward Non-Imperial Geo-historical Categories." *Cultural Anthropology*. vol. 11, no. 1. pp. 51–87.

Crary, Jonathan. 2013. *24/7 Late Capitalism and the Ends of Sleep*, London: Verso.

Crenshaw, Kimberlé. 1995. "The Intersections of Race and Gender." In Crenshaw, Kimberlé, Neil Gotanda, Gary Peller, and Kendall Thomas, eds. *Critical Race Theory: The Key Writings That Formed the Movement*. New York: New Press.

Dietze, Gabriele. 2010. "Occidentalism, European Identity, and Sexual Politics." In Brunkhorst, Hauke, and Gerd Groezinger, eds. *The study of Europe*. Baden Baden: Nomos.

Escobar, Arturo. 2004. "Beyond the Third World: Imperial Globality, Global Coloniality and Anti-globalization Social Movements." *Third World Quarterly*. vol. 25, no. 1. pp. 207–230.

European Court of Human Rights. 2011. "Crucifixes in Italian State-school classrooms: the Court finds no violation." March 18, 2011. Accessed December 14, 2012. http://www.echr.coe.int/echr/resources/hudoc/Lautsi_pr_enG.pdf

Fanon, Frantz. 2005. *The Wretched of the Earth*. Translated by Richard Philcox. New York: Grove Press.

Foucault, Michel. 1982. "The Subject of Power." In Dreyfus, Hubert, L. and Paul Rabinow. eds. *Michel Foucault: Beyond Structuralism and Hermeneutics, 2nd edition with an afterword by and an interview with Michel Foucault*. Chicago: Chicago University Press.

———. 1991. "Governmentality." In Burchell, Graham, Colin Gordon, and Peter Miller. eds. *The Foucault Effect: Studies in Governmentality*. Chicago: University of Chicago Press. pp. 87–104.

———. 1995. *Discipline and Punish – The Birth of the Prison*. Translated by Alan Sheridan. New York: Vintage Books.

———. 2004. In Bertani, Mauro, Alessandro Fontana, eds. *Society Must be Defended: Lectures at the Collège de France, 1975—76*. London: Penguin.

Garcés, Marina. 2002. *En las prisiones de lo possible* [In the Prisons of the Possible]. Barcelona: Edicions Bellaterra.

Giddens, Anthony. 1990. *The Consequences of Modernity*. Cambridge: Polity Press.

Gilly Adolfo, and Rhina Roux. 2008. "Capitales tecnologías y mundos de la vida. El despojo de los cuatro elementos" [Technological capital and worlds of life. Dispossession of the four elements]. *Revista Herramienta*. Available at http://www.herramienta.com.ar/foro-capitalismo-en-trance/capitales-tecnologias-y-mundos-de-la-vida-el-despojo-de-los-cuatro-elemen.

Gomes Pereira, Pedro Paulo. 2008. "Body, Sex and Subversion: Reflections on Two Queer Theoreticians." *Interface*. (Botucatu) vol. 4 no.se. Available at http://www.scielo.br/pdf/icse/v12n26/en_a04.pdf

Gratton, Peter. 2010. "Change We Can't Believe In: Adrian Johnston on Badiou, Žižek, and Political Transformation: The Cadence of Change." *IJŽS*. vol. 4, no. 3.

Greif, Tatjana. 2008. "Schengen in Practice." *Reartikulacija*. # 3. Ljubljana (Slovenia). Available at http://grzinic-smid.si/?p=870

Grosfoguel, Ramón. 2008. "Transmodernity, Border Thinking, and Global Coloniality: Decolonizing Political Economy and Postcolonial Studies." *Eurozine*. Available at http://www.eurozine.com/articles/2008-07-04-grosfoguel-en.html

———. 2011a. "A Decolonial Perspective." Lecture series and workshop with and by Ramón Grosfoguel at the Institute for European Ethnology. Berlin: Humboldt University.

———. 2011b. "Decolonizing Post-Colonial Studies and Paradigms of Political Economy: Transmodernity, Decolonial Thinking, and Global Coloniality." *TRANSMODERNITY: Journal of Peripheral Cultural Production of the Luso-Hispanic World*, School of Social Sciences, Humanities, and Arts, UC Merced. Available at http://www.dialogoglobal.com/granada/documents/Grosfoguel-Decolonizing-Pol-Econ-and-Postcolonial.pdf

Gržinić, Marina. 2008a. *Re-politicizing Art, Theory, Representation and New Media Technology*. Cooperation with the Academy of Fine Arts in Vienna. Vienna: SCHLEBRÜGGE.EDITOR.

———. 2008b. "Rearticulation of the State of Things or Euro – Slovenian Necrocapitalism." *Reartikulacija*. #3. Ljubljana (Slovenia). pp. 3–5.

———. 2009a. "No War but Class War." Available at http://grzinic-smid.si/?p=1095

———. 2009b. "Capital, Repetition." *Reartikulacija*. #8. Ljubljana (Slovenia). pp. 3–4.

———. 2009c. "Subjectivization, Biopolitics and Necropolitics: Where Do We Stand?" *Reartikulacija*. #6. Ljubljana (Slovenia). pp. 22–24.

———. 2010a. "From Biopolitics to Necropolitics and the Institution of Contemporary Art." Pavilion. no. 14. Special Issue: *Biopolitics, necropolitics and de-coloniality*, Marina Gržinić, ed. Bucharest: Artphoto Asc.

———. 2010b. "Justice and Global Capitalism." *Reartikulacija*. #10–13. Ljubljana (Slovenia). pp. 20–21.

———, ed. 2010c. "Necrocapitalist Education, Market Freedom, Desustainability." *Center for Global Studies and the Humanities, Duke University—The World and Knowl-*

edge's Otherwise Project. vol. 3., Dossier 2, (September). pp. 1–4. Available at https://globalstudies.trinity.duke.edu/wp-content/uploads/2010/08/GrzinicIntroW-KO3.2.pdf
———. 2010d. "De-Coloniality of Time and Space." *Reartikulacija.* # 10-13. Ljubljana (Slovenia). p. 15.
———. 2011. "Southeastern Europe and the Question of Knowledge, Capital and Power." *The Global South—Special Issue: The Global South and World Dis/Order* vol. 5, no. 1. Levander, Caroline and Walter Mignolo, eds. Bloomington: Indiana University Press, pp. 51–64.
———. 2012 "Europe: Gender, Class, Race." *S and F online—Special Issue: Feminist Media Theory: Iterations of Social Difference..* no. 10.3 (Summer). Beller, Jonathan, ed. Available at http://sfonline.barnard.edu/feminist-media-theory/europe-gender-class-race/3/.
———. 2013a. "Entanglement." *Identities.* vol. 10, no. 1–2. Available at http://www.identitiesjournal.edu.mk/documents/IDENTITETI-VOL10-NO.-1---2.pdf.
———. 2013b. "A Refugee Protest Camp in Vienna and the European Union's Processes of Racialization, Seclusion, and Discrimination." *E-flux journal* #43, 03. Available at http://www.e-flux.com/journal/a-refugee-protest-camp-in-vienna-and-the-european-union%E2%80%99s-processes-of-racialization-seclusion-and-discrimination/
———. 2013c. "Decoloniality As/In/At the Frontier." In The Editorial Group for Writing Insurgent Genealogies, eds. *Utopia of Alliances, Conditions of Impossibilities and the Vocabulary of Decoloniality.* Vienna: Löcker. pp. 207–214.
Gržinić, Marina and Sebastjan Leban. 2008. "De-grading Capital(ism) and its production of fear." Manuscript.
Gržinić, Marina and Rosa Reitsamer, eds. 2008. *New Feminism: Worlds of Feminism, Queer and Networking Conditions.* Vienna: Löcker Verlag.
Gržinić, Marina and Šefik Tatlić. 2012. "Global Capitalism's Racializations." *De-Artikulacija—Platform for Theory, Arts, Protests and Politics* #0. pp. 11–15.
Hamza, Agon. 2009. "The Specter of Ideological Apparatuses." *Reartikulacija* # 8. Ljubljana (Slovenia). Available at http://grzinic-smid.si/?p=879
Harvey, David. 2003. *The New Imperialism.* New York: Oxford University Press.
———. 2005. *Brief History of Neoliberalism.* New York: Oxford University Press.
Hazan, Pierre. 2010. *Judging War, Judging History: Behind Truth and Reconciliation.* Stanford, California: Stanford University Press.
Höller, Christian. 2002. "An Interview with the Post-Colonialism Theoretician Achille Mbembe." *Springerin.* no. 3.2. Available at http://www.springerin.at/dyn/heft.php?id=32&pos=0&textid=0&lang=en.
hooks, bell. 1990. *Yearning: Race, Gender, and Cultural Politics,* Boston: South End Press.
Hudson, Michael, 1972. Super-Imperialism: The Economic Strategy of American Empire, New York: Holt, Rinehart, and Winston.
Iveković, Rada. 2008. "French Suburbia 2005." In Gržinić, Marina and Rosa Reitsamer, eds. *New Feminism: Worlds of Feminism, Queer and Networking Conditions.* Vienna: Löcker Verlag.
Jameson, Fredric. 2011. *Representing Capital—A Reading of Volume One.* London: Verso.
Johnston, Adrian. 2009. *Badiou, Žižek, and Political Transformation: The Cadence of Change* Evanston, IL: Northwestern University Press.
Johnston-Arthur, Araba Evelyn. 2004. "Weiß-heit" [Whiteness]. In BUM – Büro für ungewöhnliche Maßnahmen, eds. *Historisierung als Strategie. Positionen. Macht. Kritik* [Historicization as a strategy. Positions. Power. Critique]. Vienna: Eigenverlag. pp. 10–11.
Johnston-Arthur, Araba Evelyn and Andreas Görg. 2005. "Campaigning against Racism." In Birk, Daniela, Erika Doucette, Nicole Hauber, Gabriele Gerbasits, Markus Griesser, eds. *Dossier on Political Anti-Racism.* Innsbruck, Austria: TirolerKulturInitiativen / IG Kultur Tirol. pp. 8–16. Available at http://igkultur.at/bibliothek/dateien-wolfie/reader_polanra

Johnston-Arthur, Araba Evelyn and Belinda Kazeem. 2007. "CAFE DEKOLONIAL. 'SAG ZUR MEHLSPEIS'LEISE SERVUS...'" [Decolonial café. "Say silently Good Bye to the pastry..."]. *Reartikulacija*. # 1. Ljubljana (Slovenia). Available at http://grzinic-smid.si/?cat=383&paged=3

Journal for Critique of Science, Imagination and New Anthropology (Časopis za kritiko znanosti, domišljijo in novo antropologijo—ČKZ). 2008. Special issue entitled "The Story of an Erasure. " Ljubljana: Študentska založba.

Jutarnji List. 2009. "New Generation Rebels: They Don't Smoke, Don't Drink, Don't Have a Leader." *Jutarnji List*, April 23, 2009. Accessed June 12, 2013. http://www.jutarnji.hr/buntovnici-nove-generacije--ne-piju--ne-puse--nemaju-vodu/203032/

Jeffries, Stuart. 2001. "France forced to confront betrayal." *The Guardian*, August 9, 2001. Accessed December 12, 2013. http://www.theguardian.com/world/2001/aug/19/warcrimes

Kašić, Biljana. 2008. "Where is the Feminist Critical Subject?." In Gržinić, Marina, and Rosa Reitsamer, eds. *New Feminism: Worlds of Feminism, Queer and Networking Conditions*. Vienna: Löcker Verlag.

Kilomba, Grada. 2008. *Plantation Memories: Episodes of Everyday Racism*. Münster, Germany: Unrast Verlag.

Leban, Sebastjan. 2008. "The Strategy of the Modernisation of the Ideological and Structural Matrix of Neoliberalism." *Reartikulacija*. #5. Ljubljana (Slovenia).

———. 2010. "Eu – Visione." (manuscript)

Lôbo, Marissa. 2010. "What is Anastácia keeping silent? Or what does Anastácia see?," *Reartikulacija*, #10-13. Ljubljana (Slovenia). Available at http://grzinic-smid.si/?p=920

———. 2013. "Iron Mask, White Torture: What is Anastácia Keeping Silent? What Does Anastácia See?." Translated by Njideka Stephanie Iroh. In The Editorial Group for Writing Insurgent Genealogies, eds. *Utopia of Alliances, Conditions of Impossibilities and the Vocabulary of Decoloniality*. Vienna: Löcker Verlag. pp. 269–275.

Lockward, Alanna. 2010. "IngridMwangiRobertHutter: Masks and Skin Politics as a German DeColonial Knowledge Production." *Reartikulacija*. # 10–13. Ljubljana (Slovenia). Available at http://grzinic-smid.si/?p=920

López Petit, Santiago. 2009. *La movilización global. Breve tratado para atacar la realidad* [Global Mobilization: A Brief Treatise for Attacking Reality]. Madrid: Traficantes de Sueños.

———. 2011. "What if we refuse to be citizens?—A Manifesto for Vacating Civic Order." *borderlands e-journal*. vol. 10. no. 3. Available at http://www.borderlands.net.au/vol10no3_2011/lopez-petit_refuse.pdf.

Lorde, Audre. 1984. *Sister Outsider: Essays and Speeches*. Berkeley, CA: Crossing Press.

Losurdo, Domenico. 2005. "The American Colonial Roots of the Third Reich." Lecture in Milan on May 15, 2005.

Lugones, María. 2007. "Heterosexualism and the Colonial/Modern Gender System." *Hypatia* 22, # 1. pp. 186 –209.

Maldonado-Torres, Nelson. 2011. "Thinking through the Decolonial Turn: Post-continental Interventions in Theory, Philosophy, and Critique—An Introduction." *Transmodernity* (Fall). Available at http://escholarship.org/uc/item/59w8j02x

MacCarroll, Margaret Catherine. 2005. *May Ayim: A Woman in the Margin of German Society*. MA Thesis. Florida State University. Available at http://etd.lib.fsu.edu/theses_1/available/etd-04102005-231408/unrestricted/MaggieC.MacCarrollThesis2Sp05.pdf

Magun, Artiom, Alexander Skidan and Dmitry Vilensky. 2007. "Potentialities." *What is to be Done?*. no. 16. Moscow (March). Available at http://www.chtodelat.org/index.php?option=com_content&task=view&id=327&Itemid=167

Mbembe, Achille, 2001. *On the Postcolony*. Berkeley, CA: University of California Press.

———. 2003. "Necropolitics." Translated by Libby Meintjes, *Public Culture*. vol. 15. no. 1. pp. 11–40. Available at http://muse.jhu.edu/login?auth=0&type=summary&url=/journals/public_culture/v015/15.1mbembe.html

————. 2006. "Postcolonial Thought Explained to the French." An Interview with Mbembe conducted by Mongin, Olivier, and Nathalie Lempereur and Jean-Louis Schlegel for the French magazine *Esprit* in December. Available at http:// jwtc.org.za/the_salon/volume_1/achille_mbembe.htm

————. 2010. *Sortir de la grande nuit. Essai sur l'Afrique décolonisée* [We Must Get Out of The Great Night: Essay on Decolonized Africa]. Paris: Découverte.

————. 2011. "Provincializing France." Translated by Janet Roitman. *Public Culture.* vol. 23. no. 1.

————. 2012. "Theory from the Antipodes: Notes on Jean and John Comaroffs' TFS." *Theorizing the Contemporary.* Cultural Anthropology Online, February 25. Available at http://culanth.org/fieldsights/272-theory-from-the-antipodes-notes-on-jean-john-comaroffs-tfs

Mignolo, Walter D. 2008. "De-Linking Epistemology from Capital and Pluri-Versality—A conversation with Walter Mignolo by Marina Gržinić, Part 1." *Reartikulacija.* #4. pp. 20–22.

————. 2009a. "Coloniality: The Darker Side of Modernity." In Breitwisser, Sabine, ed. *Modernologies.* Contemporary Artists Researching Modernity and Modernism, Museu d'Art Contemporani de Barcelona (exhibition catalogue, pp. 39-49) Available at http://www.macba.cat/PDFs/walter_mignolo_modernologies_eng.pdf

————. 2009b. "Dispensable and Bare Lives—Coloniality and the Hidden Political Agenda of Modernity." *Human Architecture: Journal of the Sociology of Self-Knowledge* VII, 2 (Spring). pp. 69–88. Available at http://www.okcir.com/Articles VII 2/Mignolo-FM.pdf

MIT Center for International Studies. 2002-2006. "Iraq: The Human Cost, Major Studies of War Mortality." Accessed December 14, 2013. http://web.mit.edu/ humancostiraq/, http://web.mit.edu/humancostiraq/reports/human-cost-war-101106.pdf.

Mitropoulos, Angela. 2009. "Legal, Tender." *Reartikulacija.* # 7. Ljubljana (Slovenia). Available at http://grzinic-smid.si/?p=899

Močnik, Rastko. 2011. "The End of University, the Triumph of Higher Education: Will Theory Remain Without Institutional Support?." Manuscript.

Mohanty, Chandra Talpade. 1984. "Under Western Eyes: Feminist Scholarship and Colonial Discourses." *boundary 2.* vol. 12/13 (Spring-Autumn), pp. 333–358.

————. 2003. *Feminism without Borders: Decolonizing Theory, Practicing Solidarity.* Durham, NC: Duke University Press.

Moi, Toril. 2001. *What Is A Woman? And Other Essays.* Oxford: Oxford University Press.

Moraga, Cherríe and Gloria Anzaldúa. 2002. (Third Edition). *This Bridge Called My Back: Writings by Radical Women of Color.* Berkeley, CA: Third Woman Press.

Müller, Gin/i. 2013. Interview by Marina Gržinić and Tjaša Kancler, recorded on December 4, 2013 in Vienna, Austria. Available at http://africa-europe.net/?p=154

Negri, Antonio and Michael Hardt. 2004. *Multitude.* London: Hamish Hamilton.

New Statesman, 2011. "Full Transcript David Cameron Speech on Radicalisation and Islamic Extremism Munich." *New Statesman.* February 5, 2011. Accessed June 3, 2011. http://www.newstatesman.com/blogs/the-staggers/2011/02/terrorism-islam-ideology

Nimako, Kwame. 2013. "Toward the 6th Summer School on Black Europe: Interview with Kwame Nimako." Online site of The International Institute for Research and Education (IIRE), Amsterdam, The Netherlands. Available at http://www.iire.org/ nl/iire-activiteiten/16-other-activities/483-towards-the-6th-summer-school-on-black-europe-interview-with-kwame-nimako.html

Oliver, Kelly. 2001. *Witnessing: Beyond Recognition.* Minneapolis: University of Minnesota Press.

Omi, Michael and Howard Winant. 1994. (Second Edition). *Racial Formation in the United States: From the 1960s to the 1990s.* New York and London: Routledge.

Ong, Aihwa. 2006. *Neoliberalism as Exception: Mutations in Citizenship and Sovereignty.* Durham, NC: Duke University Press.

Osuri, Goldie. 2009. "Identity and Complicity in Necropolitical Engagements: The Case of Iraq." *Reartikulacija*, # 8. Ljubljana (Slovenia). Available at http://grzinic-smid.si/?p=907

Papić, Žarana. 2002. "Europe after 1989: ethnic wars, the fascisation of social life and body politics in Serbia." *Filozofski vestnik*. Special Issue: The Body. Marina Gržinić Mauhler, ed. Ljubljana (Slovenia): Institute of Philosophy ZRC SAZU. pp. 191–205.

Patterson, Orlando. 1982. *Slavery and Social Death*. Cambridge: Harvard University Press.

Peitz, William. 1988. "The Post-Colonialism of Cold War Discourse." *Social Text*. no. 19/20.

Perera, Suvendrini. 2002. "What is a Camp . . . ?." *borderlands e-journal*. vol. 1, no. 1.

———. 2006. "Race, Terror, Sydney, December 2005." *borderlands e-journal*. vol. 5, no. 1.

Peitz, William. 1988. "The Post-Colonialism of Cold War Discourse." *Social Text*. no. 19/20.

Płonowska Ziarek, Ewa. 2001. *An Ethics of Dissensus: Postmodernity, Feminism, and the Politics of Radical Democracy*. Stanford: Stanford University Press.

Preciado, Beatriz. 2007. "Reportaje después del Feminismo. Mujeres en los márgenes" [Report after Feminism: Women on the Margins] *El País*, January 13. Available at http://webs.uvigo.es/pmayobre/textos/varios/despues_del_feminismo.pdf

Preciado, Beatriz. 2013. "Pharmaco-Pornographic CapitalismPostporn Politics and the Decolonization of Sexual Representations." Translated by Marina Gržinić. In The Editorial Group for Writing Insurgent Genealogies, eds. *Utopia of Alliances, Conditions of Impossibilities and the Vocabulary of Decoloniality*. Vienna: Löcker Verlag, pp. 245–255.

Quijano, Aníbal. 1997. "Colonialidad del poder, cultura y conocimiento en América Latina." [Coloniality of Power, Culture and Knowledge in Latin America]. *Anuario Mariateguiano*. no. 9. Lima (Peru).

———. 2000. "Coloniality of Power, Ethnocentrism, and Latin America." *Nepantla: Views From the South*. vol. 1, no. 3. pp. 533–580.

———. 2007. "Coloniality and Modernity/Rationality." *Cultural Studies*. 21:2. pp.168–178. Available at http://www.tandfonline.com/doi/abs/10.1080/09502380601164353#.UpdLP8RJ51E

Ramonet, Ignacio. 2008. "Vulture Funds: A New Category in Capitalism." Available at https://www.adbusters.org/magazine/76/vulture_funds.html

Rancière, Jacques. 2004. "Who is the Subject of the Rights of Man?" *South Atlantic Quarterly*. 103.2/3. pp. 297–310.

Rolnik, Suely. 2003. "The Twilight of the Victim: Creation Quits Its Pimp, to Rejoin Resistance." *Zehar*. no. 51, San Sebastian (Spain).

Schmitt, Carl. 2005. *Political Theology—Four Chapters on the Concept of Sovereignty*. Translated by George Schwab. Chicago: The University of Chicago Press.

———. 2007. *The Concept of the Political—Expanded Edition*. Translated by George Schwab. Chicago: The University of Chicago Press.

Shalem, Efrat and Yanai Toister. 2006. "The Matrix of Curating." *seconds*. Online publishing project, Leeds Metropolitan University UK (issue 3). The Young Artist Award, The Israel Museum (exhibition catalog, pp. 54–55). Available at http://www.slashseconds.org/issues/001/003/articles/eshalem/index.php

Simone, Roland. 2011. "The Present Moment." *Riff-Raff / Sic # 01*. Available at http://riff-raff.se/texts/en/sic1-the-present-moment

Singh, Nikhil Pal. 2009. "Cold War." *Social Text*. no. 100. Durham, NC: Duke University Press.

Slabodsky, Santiago E. 2009. "But there are no longer any anti-Semites! Vicious Circles, Jewish Destinies, and a Complementary Framework to Read De-colonial Discourses." *Human Architecture: Journal of the Sociology of Self-Knowledge*. vol. 7, no. 2.

Spillers, Hortense J. 1987. "Mama's Baby, Papa's Maybe: An American Grammar Book." *Diacritics*. vol. 17, no. 2 (Summer). pp. 65–81.

————. 1996. "'All the Things You Could Be by Now if Sigmund Freud's Wife Was Your Mother': Psychoanalysis and Race." *boundary 2*, 22.3. pp. 75–141.

————. 1998. Interviewed by Tim Haslett for the *Black Cultural Studies* web site collective in Ithaca, New York, February 4. Available at http://www.blackculturalstudies. org/spillers/spillers_intvw.html.

————. 2006. "The Idea of Black Culture." *CR: The New Centennial Review*. vol. 6, no. 3 (Winter).

Stanley, Eric. 2011. "Near Life, Queer Death. Overkill and Ontological Capture." *Social Text*. vol. 29. no. 2 (Summer). Available at http://www.academia.edu/863819/ Near_Life_Queer_Death_Overkill_and_Ontological_Capture.

Stoler, Ann Laura. 2011. "Colonial Aphasia: Race and Disabled Histories in France." *Public Culture*, no. 23. Durham, NC: Duke University Press.

Strong, Tracy B. 2005. Foreword to *Political Theology—Four Chapters on the Concept of Sovereignty by Carl Schmitt*, vii–xxxiii. Translated by George Schwab. Chicago: The University of Chicago Press.

Šajn, Nikolina. 2012. "EU campaign has officially started! Look at the video clips for the EU. Pusić: We are deciding whether Croatia belonged to Europe politically" *Jutarnji List*, January 3, 2012. Accessed December 12, 2013. http://www.jutarnji.hr/ vesna-pusic--izadite-na-referendum-i-glasujte-za-eu/997295/

Tatlić, Šefik. 2010. "Communication and Mass Intellect." *Pavilion*. no.14. Bucharest.

————. 2011. "Anti-Semitism, Decoloniality and the Performative Forms of Judgment," (manuscript).

Theodore, Nik, Jamie Peck and Neil Brenner. 2008. "The City as Policy Lab." *Area Chicago* (ART/ RESEARCH/ EDUCATION/ ACTIVISM), no. 6 (August).

The Research Group on Black Austrian History and Presence/Pamoja. 2013. "Welcome to Cafe Decolonial. 'Sag zur Mehlspeis' leise Servus . . .'" Translated by Iris Borovčnik. In The Editorial Group for Writing Insurgent Genealogies, eds. *Utopia of Alliances, Conditions of Impossibilities and the Vocabulary of Decoloniality*. Vienna: Löcker Verlag. pp. 53–57.

Tucker, Daniel. 2008. "Inheriting the Grid." *Area Chicago* (ART/ RESEARCH/ EDUCATION/ ACTIVISM), no. 6 (August).

The Editorial Group for Writing Insurgent Genealogies, eds. 2013. *Utopia of Alliances, Conditions of Impossibilities and the Vocabulary of Decoloniality*. Produced by the Post Conceptual Art Practices Class (Prof. Marina Gržinić) at the Academy of Fine Arts in Vienna, Vienna: Löcker Verlag.

Virno, Paolo. 2004. *A Grammar of the Multitude: For an Analysis of Contemporary Forms of Life*. New York: Semiotext[e].

Vlaisavljević, Ugo. 2009. "From Berlin to Sarajevo." *Zarez*. year XI. No. 267. Zagreb (Croatia). October 15.

Wittgenstein, Ludwig. 2010. *Tractatus Logico—Philosophicus*. Translated by C.K. Ogden.Project Gutenberg: ebook edition (EBook #5740.). Available at http:// www.gutenberg.org/files/5740/5740-pdf.pdf.

Index

About the Authors

Marina Gržinić is professor of philosophy that works as researcher advisor at the Institute of Philosophy at the ZRC SAZU (Scientific and Research Centre of the Slovenian Academy of Science and Art) in Ljubljana. She is professor at The Academy of Fine Arts in Vienna. Marina Gržinić has published hundreds of articles and essays and several books.

Šefik Tatlić is a theoretician from Bosnia-Herzegovina. He received his MA in Journalism (Faculty of Political Sciences, Sarajevo) and is currently enrolled at the doctoral program in sociology at the University of Zagreb, Croatia. His theoretical work focuses on political philosophy, decolonial theory, and social studies. His publications include a number of essays in the field, published in Slovenia, Bosnia, Croatia, Serbia, Germany, Austria, Italy, Romania and the United States.